Historical Perspectives on Business Enterprise Series

OIL BARON
OF THE
SOUTHWEST

Edward L. Doheny and the

Development of the Petroleum

Industry in California and Mexico

Martin R. Ansell

OHIO STATE UNIVERSITY PRESS

COLUMBUS

Library of Congress Cataloging-in-Publication Data
Ansell, Martin R., 1957–
    Oil baron of the Southwest : Edward L. Doheny and the development of
the petroleum industry in California and Mexico / Martin R. Ansell.
        p.   cm.—(Historical perspectives on business enterprise series)
    Based on the author's doctoral dissertation, University of Texas at Austin.
    Includes bibliographical references and index.
    ISBN 0-8142-0749-9 (cloth : alk. paper).
    1. Doheny, Edward L. (Edward Laurence), 1856–1935.
2. Industrialists—United States—Biography.   3. Petroleum industry and
trade—California, Southern—History.   4. Petroleum industry and
trade—United States—History.   5. Petroleum industry and trade—
Mexico—History.   I. Title.   II. Series.
HD9570.D64A57   1998
338.7′6223382′092—dc21
    [B]   97-37567
JK   CIP

Text and jacket design by Paula Newcomb.
Type set in Minion by Graphic Composition, Inc.
Printed by Thomson-Shore, Inc.

9   8   7   6   5   4   3   2   1

For my father, Raymond M. Ansell, who I know would have been proud to see this book finished, and to my son, Isaac M. Ansell, who I hope will be equally generous when he's old enough to read it.

CONTENTS

ACKNOWLEDGMENTS

Because the subject of this book was a controversial historical figure who left few trails to follow, tracking him down proved to be a
singularly independent effort. Having said that, however, no one succeeds
without help. Over time, there have been a host of unsung heroes in the
form of researchers and archivists from around the country who had a
hand in digging out bits of information that appeared to have no connection to Doheny upon first discovery but formed crucial links later on. In
particular, I would like to thank Connie Menninger of the Kansas State
Historical Society, who made numerous forays into the records of the Atchison, Topeka, and Santa Fe Railroad to discover new material. Several
members of National Archives staff, especially Fred Klose and Laura Mc-
Carthy of the Pacific Coast Branch, were very helpful in extracting long-
buried legal cases that filled out a significant part of the story. And Monsignor Francis Weber of the Archival Center of the Archdiocese of Los
Angeles rescued the final scraps of Doheny memorabilia from the auction
block and made them and himself available to me on numerous occasions.
The maps in the book were drawn by Joe Sambataro. Having begun this
project as a doctoral student at the University of Texas at Austin, I owe a
debt of gratitude to Lewis Gould, who oversaw the initial work with an
even hand, a long rope, and consistent encouragement. When it was completed, he was also instrumental in persuading Mansel Blackford, the co-
editor of this series, to take a look at an excessively long dissertation mas-
querading as a book.

Above everyone else, however, I owe the success of this work to my
wife, Carol. She not only endured a project that lasted years beyond what

I anticipated, but she read innumerable versions of chapters, argued points, and made essential contributions at every step of the way, all the while pursuing a career of her own. And during her only hiatus, I can vividly recall several weeks when she sat with our newborn son on one side and a stack of my pages on the other helping me edit the final draft of the manuscript. Love is the only thing that accounts for such effort, and I will always be thankful for it.

INTRODUCTION

In 1923 B. C. Forbes, like a latter-day Horace Greeley, proclaimed that the twentieth century belonged to the West. The region's untapped natural resources guaranteed a predominance much like the industrial leadership of the East in the preceding era. Blessed with an abundance of minerals, timber, and oil, the western states, and especially California, called forth a new generation of entrepreneurs. And by that time a number of western pioneers had already made it into the top ranks of the nation's business elite.[1]

One of the most successful of these empire builders was Edward L. Doheny, who was credited with having discovered more oil than any other living person. Doheny opened the Los Angeles oil district to commercial production in 1892 and helped develop every major oilfield in Southern California by the end of the decade. In 1900, he went to Mexico and repeated his success on a vast scale. Thereafter, based on his California and Mexico operations, Doheny built up the largest fuel oil business in the world.

Despite these achievements, very little is known about the development of Doheny's career and the methods by which he succeeded. A major reason for this dearth of information has to do with Doheny's part in the Teapot Dome oil scandal of the 1920s, which came at the end of a long career and fixed his reputation as a scoundrel in the public mind. Then, the continuing ideological battles between the United States and Mexico over the role of foreign oil companies, which led to the nationalization of the industry, cast Doheny into further disrepute.

My interest in him began with a study of Mexican history, in which

Doheny was presented as the consummate capitalist exploiter. In seeking a more balanced appraisal, however, I discovered that no biography of him had yet been written and that only a handful of articles about him had appeared since his death in 1935. Hoping to locate his personal papers for the other side of the story, I turned to the Doheny Memorial Library at St. John's Seminary in Camarillo, California, only to learn that none existed. St. John's housed Mrs. Estelle Doheny's extensive book collection, which consisted of medieval manuscripts on religious topics, American classics, and some valuable art work and furnishings from the Doheny mansion in Los Angeles which had been left in the hands of the Catholic Church. Sadly, because the collection was never made available to scholars in any concerted way and was very expensive to maintain, the Church decided in the late 1980s to sell the contents of the library, relegating the remains of the Doheny estate to the auction block.

Fortunately, a few items remain and now make up the Estelle and Edward L. Doheny Collection at the Archival Center of the Archdiocese of Los Angeles in San Fernando. The collection includes several letters between Edward and his second wife, Estelle, written during the early years of their marriage, a couple dozen pieces of business correspondence, and some photographs of Mexico. Most of this material survived purely by accident, after Estelle incinerated the bulk of her husband's papers in the basement of their Chester Place home. Apparently, she did this just after he died, in accordance with his wishes, succumbing perhaps to a combination of loyalty, shock, and desperation. For someone as devoted to the preservation of books and historical documents as she was, Estelle could not have been comfortable with such an irrevocable act. However regrettable, she saw it as the only way to halt the negative attacks on Doheny's character which had chased him to his grave and to thwart the future efforts of biographers and historians.[2]

Of course, her action only made things worse by giving free rein to everything but the truth. In the end, the lack of documentary evidence polarized the interpretations of Doheny's life. His family, friends, and close associates have been excessively laudatory, while his detractors have found nothing good in anything he did. The most frustrating thing about both of these approaches is that neither one is based on more than a handful of facts. And the material written about him while he was still alive is hardly more informative.[3]

Although the local newspapers in California and Mexico and the financial press in New York followed the development of Doheny's companies in detail, the first articles about Doheny himself did not appear until he was over sixty years old and almost twenty-five years into his oil career. Mostly, they consisted of propaganda pieces touting his Mexican oil business. Clarence Barron's *The Mexican Problem,* for instance, is a compilation of articles written for the *Wall Street Journal* in 1917 which emphasized the strategic value of Mexican oil for America and the Allies during the war in Europe. In the few pages devoted to Doheny's personality, Barron emphasized his experiences as a young man, when he worked on a government survey of Indian Territory, broke and sold government horses, and prospected throughout the Rocky Mountains. Those western roots, Barron contended, accounted for the success of the nation's most powerful independent oil producer.[4]

In California, the first popular article appeared in *Sunset* magazine in 1918. Like Barron's articles, Wilbur Hall's "How Doheny Did It" portrayed the oilman's life as the culmination of the ideal western experience. In particular, Hall contrasted Doheny with his boyhood friends back in Fond du Lac, Wisconsin, who were either too timid or too unimaginative to follow their destiny to the frontier. In making this presentation, Hall intended to use Doheny's life as an inspirational example for others to follow, but he was frustrated by a lack of material. "Doheny says he dislikes publicity," Hall lamented, "and from his actions I believe him. He is a hard man from whom to glean first-hand information of value to the young and striving." To compensate for Doheny's silence, Hall embellished the few facts at hand and presented an attractive image of Doheny as a poor prospector turned millionaire by dint of hard work and sacrifice.[5]

The next effort to capture Doheny in print came from B. C. Forbes in his 1923 book *Men Who Are Making the West.* Like Hall, Forbes followed Doheny around for days trying to dig information out of him, and likewise he came away empty-handed. Doheny put up an impenetrable front, leaving Forbes to elaborate on a paltry number of facts. But knowing his audience, if not his subject, Forbes wrote Doheny up as a sure-fire western hero. In his account, Doheny was a "dare-devil" westerner who rolled through one bonanza after another, always looking for new worlds to conquer. Contrary to Hall, who dwelt on Doheny's early failures, Forbes claimed that Doheny had been a fabulously successful miner who gave away fortunes just for the challenge of winning them back again. According to this account, Doheny single-handedly discovered several mining districts, settled towns, fought wild Indians, and faced down armed desperadoes in the street. Although there was a grain of truth in some of these stories, others were pure fabrication.[6]

Unfortunately, when the public demanded more information about the men involved in the oil scandal in 1924, journalists from the major news-papers and magazines followed Forbes's lead, perpetuating this dime-novel interpretation of his life. By this time, Doheny was encouraging the myths, because he hoped to benefit from the public's attention. This was particu-larly evident in his testimony during the official hearings and trials related to Teapot Dome, in which he and his attorneys relied on these superficial frontier images to establish his character and honesty.[7]

In all of his remembrances, Doheny never elaborated on what his early life was really like. He especially avoided any discussion of his childhood, his siblings, and his parents. The biographer, therefore, is left with barely a hint of the kind of influences and examples that propelled Doheny through his formative years and must, instead, deal with the impact of his environment, his associates, and his experiences as an adult. The rest is simply conjecture.

On a few points, however, I have been able to fill in basic information not covered before. In particular, Doheny's experience in New Mexico dur-ing the 1880s turns out to be a far different story than the one related by Forbes and subsequent writers. Nevertheless, no amount of sleuthing can make up for Doheny's reticence to talk about his past. Doheny's ambition was self-evident in his work, and many aspects of his personality were equally well defined, but his private side remains closed. This leaves us with a sketch rather than a detailed portrait.

In tracing out Doheny's life as I do, I have deliberately chosen not to burden the reader with a lengthy discussion of Teapot Dome. In the first place, the legal issues behind the case have been sufficiently outlined in other works and will not benefit from another treatment. More important, the basic facts of the case were never in dispute. What was at issue was the intent of the individuals involved. And that has remained a matter of polit-ical interpretation, over which debate swirls to this day. A recent biography of Doheny, written from the political left, charges him not just with Teapot Dome but with every crime imaginable from adultery to murder and polit-ical assassination. As the apotheosis of the negative tradition, the book presents Doheny as the personification of evil. Few historical figures out-side of that other oilman John D. Rockefeller can still generate this degree of hatred so many years after their deaths.[8]

My goal is to put the leasing of the naval oil reserves in its proper per-spective from Doheny's point of view—particularly within the context of his business interests. Until now, the tendency has been to assume the worst about Doheny's role in the oil scandal, despite his eventual acquittal on all charges, and to work backward, imputing similar motives to all of his earlier activities. In reality, Doheny's interest in the Elk Hills petroleum reserve resulted from a series of events in the early 1920s that combined personal, political, and financial considerations. From this perspective, the decision to develop the reserve was secondary, and possibly detrimental, to his larger goals. And it was certainly not the culmination of some immutable destiny as others seem to suggest. Obviously, my own conclusions about Doheny's guilt or innocence as related to Elk Hills come out along the way. But more than anything else, I believe that Doheny's long and productive career should not be lost, overshadowed, or deliberately distorted because of an infatuation with political intrigue.

This book opens, then, with an outline of Doheny's early years, before he entered the oil business, along with a discussion of his lengthy stint as a prospector in New Mexico. This is the one place in the narrative where we get a glimpse of Doheny's personal life and some possible insight into why he never discussed it later on. The second chapter covers his domination of the Los Angeles oil industry in the early 1890s and details his partnership with the Santa Fe Railroad as he moved out of the city. Here, we begin to see the entrepreneurial genius of Doheny at work and get a taste of his ultimate ambition. What disappears at this point, however, is all discussion of his family, for reasons that become apparent along the way. Taking momentum from his work in California, chapter 3 examines the growth and development of the Mexican oil industry and explores the full range of Doheny's methods of operation at the time. Thereafter, chapters 4 through 6 alternate between his work in California and in Mexico, as he built up his extensive oil holdings and put together one of the largest petroleum companies in the world.

Once his business has been fully established, chapters 7 and 8 turn to the political side of Doheny's activity as it related to the First World War and, especially, to the Mexican Revolution. Doheny was an active lobbyist for the industry in the United States and worked to blunt the edge of radical reform in Mexico. His efforts on both fronts were impressive, if not wholly successful, and represent the extent of influence open to business leaders of the day. Chapter 9 outlines Doheny's political life after the war: his role as a prominent Democrat, his work on behalf of the civil war in Ireland, and his concerns about protecting the Pacific Coast from a perceived Japanese threat. The final two chapters deal with the peak years of Doheny's career in the early 1920s, as he worked to put his oil companies into full competition with the largest organizations in the United States, only to find himself embroiled in the political scandal that led to a reversal of fortune and brought an extraordinary career to a bitter end.

1 EARLY YEARS IN THE WEST

Although Doheny came to be identified with California and the West, he grew up in Fond du Lac, Wisconsin. His father, Patrick, had been born in Ireland in 1808. His mother, Ellen, was an Irish-Canadian born in St. John's, Newfoundland, in 1818. As a young man, Patrick emigrated to Canada and worked as a seal fisherman before he married Ellen, a schoolteacher, in the mid-1840s. Sometime later, the couple moved to New York State, where Edward's older brothers were born in the early 1850s. Patrick's occupation during these years is unknown, but for lack of better prospects he moved his family to Wisconsin around 1855. Edward was born the next year, on August 10, 1856, followed by a sister and one more brother.

Most of the Irish families who migrated to Wisconsin during this period were searching for cheap farm land. Patrick, on the other hand, chose to settle in Fond du Lac, an industrial city at the southern end of Lake Winnebago and about thirty miles inland from Lake Michigan. Apparently, he did not have any agricultural experience and looked to the sawmills or the railroads for employment. The census records for 1860 and 1870 listed him simply as a laborer, but whatever he did, it provided enough to support a modest home and a growing family.

From what he later remembered, Doheny had a relatively normal childhood, with a few exceptions. Most notable was his education, which started sooner and lasted longer than was usual for the time. With his mother's blessing, no doubt, Doheny begged for permission to start school at the age of four. His father relented, as much to keep him "out of the way at home" as anything else, but Edward proved to be an adept student who

moved easily through his courses. As a teenager, Doheny stayed in school
when most others dropped out to take jobs, although he worked part-time
at one of the local sawmills for a time before he almost lopped off a couple
of his fingers running a knot saw. Such accidents were common, and Doheny bore the scars on his right hand with pride as a permanent reminder
of his working-class roots.[1]

He proved far more skillful in the classroom and finished high school
in 1872 at the age of fifteen. His education, however weak by the standards
of the established eastern schools, was still a rarity in the late nineteenth
century and included instruction in geography, geology, chemistry, and
university-level algebra. As one of only two graduating seniors for the year,
Doheny delivered an honorary speech at the convocation. According to a
local reporter, Doheny's talk on the subject of success impressed the audience with "bold assertions, solid facts and good sense." Mr. Doheny, the
reporter concluded, was "no ordinary thinker; . . . he don't search through
libraries to see if his thoughts—his ideas, conflict with those of great men,
but gives them expression in plain, unmistakable language. Mr. D will be
a leader—not a follower. We need more such. Some of his sentences were
not as smooth as oil, but the meaning was there, and need not be misunderstood . . . that man will make a creditable mark."[2]

Living in Wisconsin's "second city," a place with a business college, a
growing economy, and a population of over thirteen thousand, Doheny
could surely have found a route to success at home. Instead, he left town
the day after his graduation, intending to join a federal surveying party
leaving from Atchison, Kansas. This plan no doubt came out of the pages
of the Fond du Lac newspapers, which at the time featured articles on the
geological surveys, published items on lost Aztec gold mines in Arizona,
and ran advertisements from the Burlington Railroad offering information
on "How to go West."[3]

Overcome by the lure of the frontier, Doheny departed on July 2, 1872,
still a month shy of his sixteenth birthday. An older brother bet him that
he would get so homesick that he would never make it on his own. And
when he got to Kansas and discovered that the survey party had already
been gone for several weeks, he almost turned back. Over fifty years later,
Doheny remembered this incident as one of the greatest disappointments
of his life. But he stuck it out, doing everything from selling books door-
to-door to working in a hotel—just to keep from returning home and
proving his brother right. Ultimately, his perseverance paid off, and he
found new opportunities that took him into the mining regions of the
Rocky Mountains where, by the mid-1870s, he was hunting for silver and
gold.

In 1880, after a long period of wandering throughout the West, Doheny arrived in New Mexico at the age of twenty four. During this time, he truly lived up to B. C. Forbes's romantic claim that "rarely did Prospector Doheny sleep under other ceiling than the wide heavens. Each night he lay down with his faithful rifle at his side, his six-shooter ready for action and a hunter's knife at his belt."[4] Based at the silver camp at Lake Valley, in the southwestern corner of the territory, Doheny continued his search for wealth.

And there were opportunities to make money, especially when Doheny was among the first contingent of miners to head into the Black Range Mountains north of Lake Valley. As early as November 1880, he and four other men located two of the most promising mines in the area: the Mountain Chief and the Miner's Dream. These properties sat alongside the Iron King mine, located about a week earlier by H. W. Elliott, from which the Kingston mining camp got its name. In the beginning, Doheny made a respectable profit, but hardly a fortune, from his efforts, giving his mining claims names that epitomized the dreams of the prospector: the Brilliant, the Old Reliable, and the Phoenix. At this point Doheny was strictly a prospector, not a miner, and his goal was to sell the locations for profit, not work them for ore. But when the average claim sold for about $100, local prospectors rarely covered the cost of their operations and needed to keep churning up properties just to stay alive.[5]

Finally, though, Doheny had two good years, in 1882 and 1883, when he located and sold several mining claims for a substantial sum of money. His run of luck began in May 1882, when he and a partner located the Phoenix and the Old Reliable. Two months later he bought out his partner's share for $150, held the claims for almost a year, perhaps doing a little development work to improve their value, and sold them for $6,000. Doheny also filed claims on the Brilliant and the Maud Muller mines in August 1882 and sold a two-thirds' interest in both mines for $1,000 a few weeks later. The buyer returned shortly and bought out Doheny's remaining interest for another $4,000. In a promotional brochure published by the *Kingston Tribune* in 1883, the editor wrote that the ground around the Brilliant was covered with large chunks of silver-bearing ore and speculated that, if it was "intelligently developed," it would prove equal to its name.[6]

That Doheny would immediately sell out his share of such a potentially profitable investment illustrated the psychology of the prospector who was always searching for the elusive bonanza. In these early years, especially, Doheny repeatedly sold good properties for an initial payoff and rarely settled down to work any of them for a steady income. Just a week after

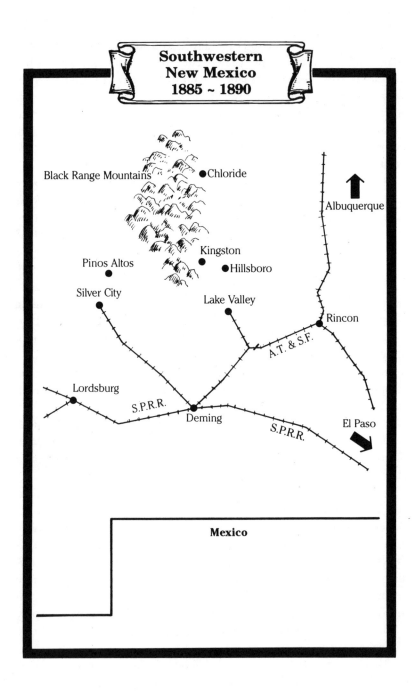

Southwestern
New Mexico
1885 ~ 1890

Black Range Mountains   ●Chloride

Albuquerque

Kingston
Pinos Altos   ●
●   ●Hillsboro

Silver City
●   Lake Valley
●   Rincon

A.T. & S.F.

Lordsburg
●
S.P.R.R.
Deming   El Paso
●
S.P.R.R.

Mexico

selling the Brilliant, Doheny also sold the house and lot he owned in Lake Valley for $600 to the local blacksmith. He made another quick profit by purchasing two more town lots for $125 and selling them four days later for twice what he had paid. Between July 1882 and July 1883, then, Doheny earned a total of $12,575 from the sale of his various properties.[7]

In the fall of 1883, Doheny moved to Kingston, which had become the center of activity for the region. At the time, as one of his friends later recalled, Doheny was a good-looking man with "regular features, ruddy complexion, and blue eyes." He was obviously well educated and supposedly even took a job for a while teaching school in the area. Since the forty-dollar-a-month salary was nothing in comparison to his income from prospecting, taking a regular job must have been an attempt to settle down for a while. Perhaps he needed the stability while he courted Carrie Lou Ella Wilkins, one of the few eligible young women in town.[8]

Doheny and Carrie became acquainted when he stayed at the Occidental Hotel, an informal gathering place for Irish-American miners where her mother, Mariah Brophy, worked. As a well-known leader among that group, Doheny was probably a frequent boarder, if not a permanent resident. Apparently, Mariah and Carrie had been among the first inhabitants of the camp back when, as one observer noted, "the brush on Main street was so thick that no person could ride through it." How, or why, they ended up in Kingston is unknown. Carrie's father, Dr. Wilkins, had been an Army surgeon who was killed during the Civil War. Presumably, Mariah's maiden name was Brophy, or she must have later married a Mr. Brophy, but nothing much is known about her before she came to Kingston. According to the Territorial Census, compiled in 1885, Mariah was forty-three, was originally from Ohio, and had lived for a time in Kansas, where Carrie was born. Carrie was twenty years old and Doheny was just shy of twenty-seven when they were married on August 7, 1883, at the Catholic Church in Silver City.[9]

An interesting side issue to his marriage concerned Doheny's relationship with his family in Wisconsin. Apparently, he had not written to his parents during the eleven years since he left home. Tragically, when he finally did write home to tell them about Carrie, there was no one there to receive the letter. His father, who would have been sixty-four, had died a few months after Doheny left home. His mother and sister passed away several years later. As for his brothers, the oldest one was unaccounted for, and the youngest had died while Doheny was still at home. His one remaining brother was living in Chicago and either did not receive the forwarded letter or chose not to answer it. In any case, when he did not hear

Occidental Hotel, Kingston, ca. 1885. Carrie Doheny, holding her daughter, Eileen, is sitting on the balcony rail. Mariah Brophy, Carrie's mother, is sitting in the chair. Photo by J. C. Burge, courtesy of the Museum of New Mexico.

back from anyone in Fond du Lac, Doheny waited another thirteen years before Carrie persuaded him to go back and see what had happened to his family. Doheny's lack of interest in his Wisconsin roots indicates the possibility that, rather than succumbing to wanderlust in 1872, he may have been running away from a difficult life at home.[10]

When he and Carrie headed back to Kingston to begin their own family, Doheny was forced to reconsider a number of things about his life. In particular, it seemed that his days as a footloose prospector had come to an end. Few prospectors were married, and even fewer brought their families to the mining frontier. Almost by definition, family responsibilities and the demands of a mining career pulled men in opposite directions, and Doheny suffered under the strain during his remaining years in New Mexico. His predicament paralleled that of his future oil partner, Charles Canfield, who arrived in the Black Range in the early 1880s with his family in tow and moved his wife and child into the camp at Chloride, in the northern end of the district. When his plans failed, Canfield sent his wife back to Nebraska to live with her relatives while he returned to prospecting. Although Canfield eventually became a local legend when he made a major strike on the Comstock mine in Kingston, he endured several years of lonely deprivation before his circumstances changed. And he was one of few prospectors who actually succeeded in making a small fortune from his labor. Most just hung on until debt and depression forced them back home or on to the next mining area.[11]

As one of a handful of family men in Kingston, Doheny did not have to endure the extended periods of loneliness and isolation so common to a miner's life, but he still had to deal with the frustration of mining, itself. And during the worst times, with Carrie and baby Eileen (born in 1884) beside him, Doheny faced the immediate consequences that Canfield avoided when he sent his family back home. With such an obvious motivation to succeed, Doheny worked diligently over the years, but he never struck it rich. Most of the time, he barely made any money at all.

During the Dohenys' early years of marriage, Kingston was a classic western boomtown. According to its 1883 promotional pamphlet, Kingston "grew as by magic." But like all the boom towns that preceded it, Kingston rose out of the wilderness on the collective dreams of its new inhabitants. A reporter for the *Mining and Scientific Press* described the camp in its heyday: "The town extends about a mile and a half along the creek; contains about 1,500 people and over 200 houses, principally board houses covered with canvas. The dust is about a foot deep. There are no churches, but about 30 saloons. Restaurants by the dozen. I noticed 2 hardware stores, 3 assay offices, 5 real estate offices, house and sign painter, contractor and builders."[12]

Another writer later asserted that it was from this location that "the prospector sallied forth a poor man in the morning, returning a millionaire in the afternoon for he had 'struck it rich.' Here fortunes grew in a single day to vanish as quickly by games of chance, under the shadow of pines, at night." B. C. Forbes observed that stories claiming that silver could be effortlessly scooped up off the ground "spread like wildfire" and brought thousands of people, "mostly daring gentlemen of fortune," into the camp. Hoping to equate his subject with that adventurous breed, Forbes falsely reported that "riches poured into Doheny's lap by the tens of thousands of dollars."[13]

Despite all the excitement Kingston generated, a reporter for the *Silver City Enterprise* concluded that, in actuality, "there are a few of what can be called good mines around Kingston, although the value of most of them cannot be determined until more work has been done." While this appraisal was probably intended to deflate the hopes of Silver City's latest rival, it proved accurate in portraying the situation in Kingston over its short life as a mining center. There were always good properties to be found in the area; the problems were filtering out the hyperbole and securing the financial backing to make the mines pay.[14]

As the history of western mining has shown, profits came only with intensive capital investment. The individual prospector sometimes worked a mine for himself, hoping for that one-in-a-million chance to strike it rich, but could go only so far without money from outside investors despite years of backbreaking labor. Unfortunately, this meant that someone other than the original locator very likely would be the one to reap any reward. The result for the mining camp as a whole was a constant battle between the local journalists and merchants, who tried to lure in outside capital through extensive advertisement, and the miners, who hesitated to invite in another set of fortune hunters.[15]

Replaying a scene common to the mining regions of the West, the management of Hillsboro's *Sierra County Advocate* stated that its aim was to "bring our resources prominently before the country at large" and to "boom the town and develop the country." But the local mining papers usually descended to the level of shameless huckstering that has made the reality of mining camps so hard to discover. Along these lines, the *Kingston Tribune* stated that papers "crowded to the margin with spicy locals and well-timed editorials" were "equal to two 40-stamp mills in the way of developing the mines around them." Unfortunately, the spice was almost always intended to make up for a lack of other ingredients.[16]

Kingston, then, was a camp where prosperity was always within sight but just out of reach. The local press celebrated each successive boom and lamented the equally frequent depressions, up one month down the next, in a constant search for signs of hope. In reality, Kingston remained a poor man's mining camp, a place where the mines "pay from the grass roots."[17]

After surviving the frenzy of a mining boom in 1882 and 1883, Kingston settled into an existence as a quasi-stable community. Although the initial boom did not thrust the camp into the ranks of the major mining towns, it was clear that the area had the mineral potential to attain some stability. To that end, Kingston pinned its hopes on the arrival of two forces, the Santa Fe Railroad and the eastern capitalist, and on the elimination of a third, the Apache Indians. The Apaches harassed the local population for a time before they were driven out, and a few capitalists, mostly from Britain, eventually found their way to the camp. But the railroad never did arrive, thus depriving the camp of an essential element of success. Early in 1880, the Santa Fe Railroad had moved southward from Colorado into New Mexico, under the energetic direction of A. A. Robinson. Thereafter, it continued south into the Rio Grande Valley and turned west to make a connection with the Southern Pacific at Deming. Investors from Silver City, the only stable mining town in the area, banded together and built their own connection to the line as early as 1883. The next year, in Sierra County, the Santa Fe made a spur to Lake Valley, thirty miles shy of Kingston.[18]

Throughout this period, the miners at Kingston pleaded for a rail connection, either at their camp or at nearby Hillsboro, as their only salvation. Although the initial strikes that put Kingston on the map occurred in rare pockets of high-grade silver, the local mines produced large quantities of refractory ore that had to be transported to smelters as far away as Denver. But that required a long wagon trip to Deming or Silver City, and consequently the ore piled up unprofitably alongside the mines because it cost more to haul out than it returned in silver. Several companies built processing plants in both Kingston and Hillsboro to relieve the burden temporarily, but a lack of funds and local mismanagement kept these smelters from operating steadily enough to eliminate the problem. Over time, the growing piles of low-grade ore sat as visible reminders of a bright future cut short for lack of a railroad. Eventually, the Santa Fe sent an engineer out to investigate the Kingston area in the early 1890s, but by then it was too late; the combination of widespread economic depression and the saturation of the silver market had put the camp out of its misery.[19] As one of Kingston's long-time residents, Doheny saw this process through almost to the end.

When he and Carrie settled into married life in Kingston in 1883, the camp had already evolved from the raucous boom town it had been at its founding. While the population fluctuated with the fortunes of the camp, the Dohenys were among the 300 to 400 residents who lived there year round. In June 1885, according to the Territorial Census, they were living with Carrie's mother at the Occidental Hotel, among the other families and small businesses at the center of town. Along the periphery, only a few blocks away, this core group of a dozen or so families gave way to a less stable population of single miners, and this section quickly faded into the isolated prospector's cabin or rancher's house only a few miles out. Because most of the major mines lay within a mile or two of the camp, the miners were able to commute from town each day, while the prospectors still spent a good deal of time away from home.

Mostly, Edward tried to stay put and develop his existing claims. He also tried to extend himself by working as a manager for several mining outfits, a job that required some degree of administrative skill and organizational ability. He also joined a group, fronted by St. Louis investors, that started a new mining company. By 1886, Edward and Carrie had purchased two lots and a house for themselves on the south side of Main Street, and in March of that year, Doheny also purchased the Occidental Hotel, complete with furnishings, for $650. Two stories, roughly ten to fifteen feet across the front, and probably no more than thirty feet deep, the hotel mirrored the ramshackle appearance of the camp itself. Three months later, Edward sold the hotel back to his mother-in-law for $350, apparently absorbing a $300 loss on the property. If these were the flush times, they were short-lived, since Doheny was soon strapped for cash.

County records reveal that, from the fall of 1886 until December 1889, when they left Kingston, Carrie and Edward's resources continued to dwindle. Several times over this period, circumstances forced them into debt. These were not the strategic business loans of someone with the resources to sustain them, but the recurring small loans of people living on the edge. This process began in September 1886, when Doheny mortgaged a quarter interest in the Mountain Chief claim to the Percha bank for $200 on a ninety-day note. The next month he and Carrie deeded over their house in Kingston to the local banker for $500. In December, Doheny borrowed another $272.50, secured by the quarter interest in the Mountain Chief plus a quarter interest in the Mammoth claim, located the month before. By the next July, Doheny was able to pay back the house loan and cancel the debts on his mining claims. But in late August, he again turned the house and lots over to the bank for $300 in gold coin. This time the bank kept the note for over two years. The day he and Carrie left Kingston in December 1889, they sold their house for $750.[20]

Considering his windfall from Lake Valley, an obvious question is, how did Doheny go through the $12,000 he started with in such a short time?

The answer touches on the major obstacle for prospectors like himself. Mining, even on the smallest scale, took an inordinate amount of money. In 1882, for example, one mining expert, using a New Mexico mine as a hypothetical case, estimated the cost of locating and developing a mine for a one-year period at $10,000. This sum included the time and labor of the prospector, food and supplies for the year, recording fees, and the extraneous expenses necessary to promote the property. Given these development costs, it was no wonder the prospector could not exist for long without financial support. An 1885 article in the Kingston newspaper described the pathetic circumstances that led many a "starved miner" to spend his last cent developing his claim.[21]

The prospectors who were most likely to make money were those who worked their claims when they could afford it and labored for somebody else when they were broke. Under the best circumstances, such a prospector might be able to sustain this process by selling the ore from his diggings, as many Kingston miners tried to do. Unfortunately, except for the rare pockets of rich material, most of the low-grade ore from the Kingston mines was simply too costly to handle. From all indications, Doheny followed this same path. Although he located and sold a number of mines in his early days at Lake Valley, he spent years working on the Miner's Dream and the Mountain Chief to no avail. His was the typical case of hard work and sacrifice meaning nothing without a large measure of good luck. On this score, one Kingston correspondent wrote, in April 1885, that the Miner's Dream was particularly "unfortunate" because, even though the mine had one of the best showings in camp, neither Doheny nor any of his lessees ever seemed to "get on to the pockets." At the time, the mine was being worked on a lease, and the commentator was unintentionally prophetic when he noted that the bond holders had reluctantly "quit work on the Dream."[22]

While it took Doheny a few more years before he gave up on his dream, he had been carrying the seeds of doubt and depression for a long time. He expressed these thoughts clearly in a letter written to a former mining associate in July 1886. His tone of resignation speaks volumes about the prospector's life: "You know I lost on every partner I had, that I could have sold time and again without them. But there is no use of complaining about what we have missed. The Comstock claim which we gave to Johnnie Roach and Dan Ferguson has turned out $400,000 in three months, but it is petered out now and neither the Miner's Dream or Mountain Chief have produced a dollar, such is luck."[23]

The next year started off better when Doheny joined with three other

Kingston men to form the Satisfaction Mining Company. Like many of the mining operations in the district, the company depended on its St. Louis office to promote the property and generate the necessary investment income. The Kingston representatives who filled the administrative positions at the mine were R. C. Troeger, a druggist and mine operator, who put up the largest share of local money; F. A. Urban, the owner of a hardware store in Kingston, who became the president of the company; and Doheny, who served as the mining superintendent.[24]

Initially, the mine produced well, and by early March the local paper reported on a strike in a "magnificent" body of ore three feet wide. Mysteriously, little more than a week later, the Satisfaction shut down operations. No public information was forthcoming to explain what had gone wrong, except for a report that thirteen local miners had lost their jobs and were owed three months' back pay. It was possible that the story about the new strike had been a last-ditch effort to secure funds from local investors and, failing that, the Satisfaction Mining Company collapsed.[25]

Although the Kingston newspaper added nothing more, the mining investors' section of the *St. Louis Globe-Democrat* followed Kingston properties in some detail. While the Satisfaction Mining Company was either too small or too new to receive direct attention, an adjacent mine, the Lochiel, had its story played out for St. Louis investors, and that account sheds some light on Doheny's situation. The Lochiel, the Satisfaction, and two other producing properties sat along an independent vein of high-grade ore. When the Lochiel company collapsed in early April, the stockholders blamed their losses on gross mismanagement by the mine superintendent, but responsibility lay further up the management hierarchy. The properties were being mined for stock investors rather than minerals. In particular, one of the Lochiel's directors, a St. Louis mining investor named Charles Greene, staged a fight among the members of the board, which drove the stock price down from sixty cents to twelve-and-a-half cents per share. Neither Greene nor his principal opponents on the board had any of their own money in the mine, having received their stock free of charge when the company was organized. After they boomed the property and sucked in the unsuspecting stockholders, they either wasted the funds on unproductive development or simply pocketed the cash. Either way, when the company ran out of money, they walked away unharmed, free to reopen the mine once the original investors pulled out. Since Charles Greene was one of the seven directors of the Satisfaction Mining Company, he probably employed the same scheme with that operation. And as superintendent, Doheny was probably blamed for the disaster just like his counterpart was at the Lochiel.[26]

While Doheny had little invested in the business besides a few months of his own labor, the experience took its toll on his outlook. For the next two years, Kingston continued to experience the false booms and harsh depressions that had plagued it from the beginning. The local reporters still saw capitalists getting off every stagecoach, ready to turn fortune around, even though this always seemed to result in the best mining properties ending up in the hands of English investors. None of that made much of a difference to the camp as a whole. The decline in the profitability of silver and the high cost of shipping ore to the smelter kept Kingston at a standstill, while each successive downturn in the local economy let loose another handful of miners who could not hang on any longer.

A few large companies provided jobs for the miners who stuck it out, and Doheny might have traded in a chance to make a big strike for a steady income, since working for wages in between prospecting trips was a common practice. For example, when Albert Fall, the future secretary of the interior and Doheny associate, came to Kingston in 1886, he spent a good deal of time working "on the hammer" for someone else. Doheny was still prospecting on a lease when he and Fall first met, and he later recalled that Fall had the better deal because he was at least getting paid. Still, Doheny could not hold out forever, and his situation continued to deteriorate. Certainly, times were desperate during the summer of 1889, when he was forced to paint the new drug store in Hillsboro just to make ends meet— perhaps the final indignity that led him to pack up and leave in December.[27]

Having made that decision, however, and perhaps to stay close to Carrie's mother, he and Carrie went only as far as Silver City. The Kingston paper reported that "Mr. Doheny will study law under Mr. Pickett, a well known lawyer of this district." Whether Doheny was really serious about this or was looking for any reason to move on is unclear. Silver City had several times Kingston's population, sat at the center of a well-developed mining region, and was a logical place to search for greater opportunity. Following his stated plans, Doheny went to work for H. L. Pickett as a mining consultant and presumably hoped to study law as he worked.[28]

There are few references to Doheny's efforts on behalf of Pickett's clients, which consisted primarily of making diagrams and models of mining claims for evidence at trial. As for his study of the law, there is no other information. What is certain is that Doheny did not stay with Pickett very long, and contrary to one of the cherished myths about his life, he never passed the territorial bar, never became a partner in a Silver City law firm, and never practiced law in the same judicial district as Albert Fall. Neither did he, as one story claimed, undertake his legal studies from a hospital bed after falling down an open mine shaft and breaking both legs.[29]

While Fall became a noted attorney in the region before he went on to Washington as a New Mexico senator, Doheny secured a commission as a notary public and set up an office in May 1890 to file mining claims and patents. He advertised his services and the extent of his legal training in the *Silver City Enterprise* with the following notice: "Edward L. Doheny, Reports on Mines and Mining titles. To Mine Owners: The undersigned is prepared to examine and report on mining propositions and titles to mining claims, and to do the necessary legal and clerical work connected with obtaining United States Patents for mining locations, guaranteeing the greatest possible dispatch, and giving advice in regard to the most economical and expeditious manner of procuring patents to mineral lands. Call on or address, Edward L. Doheny, Silver City, N.M., Office over Crawford's store."[30] Doheny ran this notice for almost a year, even though he never concentrated on the notary business.

Besides the difficulties of earning a living, mounting concern over Carrie's health was also troubling Doheny at this time. Apparently, she had been suffering from some unnamed malady for several years. On at least one occasion in Kingston, Doheny had to borrow money to take her to El Paso for treatment. Described by a longtime resident as "excitable" but deserving of help, Carrie received the reluctant support of Doheny's friends. Several generations later, there are rumors in the family that Carrie might have been an alcoholic.[31]

As reported in the press, however, Carrie suffered from the altitude of the mining camps and had been seriously ill for most of October and November. In March 1891, Edward took her to El Paso for treatment once again, and she was contemplating a convalescent trip to San Diego. In the meantime, Mariah made repeated trips to Silver City see her and to take care of Eileen. Perhaps because of Carrie's weakened condition, Mariah held her marriage to Martin Barber, another Kingston miner, at the Doheny home in Silver City in January 1891. Although Mariah continued to live in Kingston, she was able to relieve Edward of some of the responsibility of caring for his wife and daughter.[32]

Worried about his financial circumstances and the need to provide for his family, Doheny let the notary business fall by the wayside and plunged back into the mining business in November 1890, when he joined up with J. C. Carrera, another part-time consultant for Pickett. Carrera was one of the best-known mineralogists in the Southwest and was a professor at the Agricultural and Mechanics College at Mesilla Park, New Mexico.[33] Carrera had acquired an interest in some lead mines in the Pinos Altos mountains at the end of October and offered Doheny a partnership in the operation.

Initially named Carrera & Co., the outfit was recognized as Carrera & Doheny by December. The exact business relationship between the two men is unclear, but their collaboration brought compliments from one mining reporter who saw new fortunes on the rise:

> The skill employed in the opening up of the Alpha and Omega mine, belonging to Huston & Thomas, west of Pinos Altos is meeting with unprecedented success. The Messrs. Carrera & Doheny since the inception of their management have uncovered lead riches which hitherto have had an existence only in the imagination of the owners. The daily tonnage keeps a dozen or more ox teams employed, and the transportational facilities of the Silver Branch of the A. T. & S. F. railroad are at the moment, inadequate to move the accumulations of a single weeks product from this wonderful property.[34]

The Alpha and Omega Mine was one of the oldest properties in the area and one of the best lead-bearing mines in the district. It had fallen victim to the poorly written tariff provision of 1873, which imperiled the lead mines of the western states by allowing direct competition with similar ore from Mexico. Under pressure from lead miners, Congress eventually included a duty on Mexican lead ore in the McKinley Tariff of 1890. Doheny and Carrera, in taking advantage of the new situation, made the Alpha and Omega an enviable possession once again.[35]

For several months, Carrera controlled the lease on the mine, and Doheny served as manager of the property. This arrangement fell apart in February 1891, when a disagreement between the men forced them to close down and stop production. Speculation about a change in the management of the mine in early March was confirmed when Doheny bought out Carrera's share and became a one-third owner of the lease. At that point, the mine was still productive, and Doheny was shipping out a carload of ore a day. By July, everything seemed to be going so well, a local reporter wrote, that Doheny and the owners of the property were clearly "in bonanza."[36]

For eight months before July 1891, the *Enterprise* printed no fewer than a dozen notices on the mine, beginning with one that claimed that the immense quantities of ore contained in the Alpha and Omega would "soon give New Mexico a good name abroad, and will greatly assist in restoring confidence in this county with the mining world." Suddenly, however, there was no further mention of the mine or Doheny's connection to it. Apparently, Carrera left Pinos Altos in May to become the purchasing

agent for the International Smelter of El Paso, the same processing plant to which Doheny delivered his ore. But in late June, the smelter was "knocked out by floods" and taken over by its creditors. Although Doheny was still shipping out large quantities of ore in July, the lack of smelting capacity forced him to abandon his work on the mine by the end of the summer.[37]

Given this latest predicament, Doheny decided it was time to make a bigger move than the one that had brought him to Silver City. He decided to head to California, where a number of his old friends and partners had already started in again. Despite his repeated failures, or perhaps because of them, Doheny left New Mexico with some invaluable skills that were readily transferrable to the oil business. His knowledge of geology and his understanding of mining claims, leases, and land titles were obvious assets. The hard lessons learned about corporate finance, stock investments, and business relations were more subtle but no less important credentials.[38]

Beyond all that, Doheny's experience as a prospector and miner certainly entitled him to call himself a western pioneer. But the reality of his life was nothing like the fanciful stories written about him in his later years, and the need to substantiate his frontier character did not make it necessary for him to dredge up the painful details of his past. In fact, given what his life had really been like, Doheny told Albert Fall at one point later on that he was glad there was no actual record of their years in New Mexico. Without a doubt, if one had been available, it would have shaken him out of his nostalgia for what he recalled as a time "when all the world seemed bright, and the future held nothing in store that seemed to be unconquerable."[39]

2 OIL AND RAILROADS IN SOUTHERN CALIFORNIA, 1892–1902

Supposedly it was a chance encounter with Charlie Canfield that turned Doheny toward California. Canfield had been one of the lucky few to leave Kingston a wealthy man in the mid-1880s, but he had squandered his fortune on a string of bad investments in real estate and race horses. By the fall of 1891, he was out on the prospector's trail once again when he and Doheny met, accidentally, on a train platform in Victor, California, now known as Victorville. There were many other former New Mexicans working in the Oro Grande Mountains near San Bernardino. T. F. Chapman, one of Doheny's old neighbors and one of the most successful Kingston miners, had a mine and mill set up in Victor, and F. A. Urban, Doheny's former partner in the Satisfaction Mining Company, had gone there as well. So when Doheny's lead mining business at Pinos Altos fell apart, he had a number of friends ready to welcome him to the West Coast.[1]

Before Doheny decided to make a permanent move to California in October 1891, he had already become involved in a legal fight over an abandoned gold mine that sat next to one of Canfield's claims. Apparently, Canfield had been acting as the agent between the landowner and a potential purchaser at the time Doheny came on the scene. After that, the two worked to scuttle the deal by disputing the markers and the deeds of the previous owners so that Doheny could file a new claim. In the end, after threats of gunplay and charges of fraud from both sides, the case fell apart, leaving Doheny and Canfield to try their luck elsewhere.[2] Their next venture involved a group of investors who wanted to set up a company to test a new smelting process to treat low-grade ore. This deal involved two Los

Angeles real estate brokers, M. M. Morrison and Joseph A. Chanslor, along with J. B. Rentchler, Canfield's old partner from Kingston who had obviously done a much better job of handling his money. Together, these three put up $9,997 of a $10,000 investment, leaving Doheny, Canfield, and another miner to throw in a dollar apiece and all of the labor. This too, fell apart for unstated reasons.[3]

By the fall of 1892, Doheny was flat broke and looking for another opportunity. He found it in Los Angeles. Although he would later claim to have stumbled into the oil business by accident, there is ample reason to believe that he was not as ignorant of the industry as he let on. As an educated miner interested in smelting and extraction processes, Doheny would have kept up with the literature and news on the subject through the pages of the *Mining and Scientific Press,* a standard in every camp and mining town in the West. And even a casual review of that journal would have revealed numerous accounts of oil production in Southern California. If Doheny had been paying any attention at all in January 1892, he would have seen the following notice reprinted in several local papers: "The Brea Mine: The *Herald* has alluded to the recent discovery of a large deposit of petroleum products near the city's west limits. . . . A shaft was sunk on the hill which gave a surprise in the shape of a ledge of bituminous rock . . . [then] another fine vein of asphalt was uncovered . . . and a small stream of oil commenced to flow out of the face of the bluff. This week the company will put their cheap fuel on the market. Those who wish to see one of the curiosities of Los Angeles . . . should not fail to take a trip to the brea mine. It is just a quarter of a mile west of Westlake Park."[4]

Thus, despite the apocryphal stories of total ignorance, Doheny probably knew more than he let on. But his role as the founder of the Los Angeles oil district is nonetheless unique. He was not the first person to extract oil in the city, and he was certainly not the first to experiment with the petroleum he found near Westlake Park, but he was the first person who managed successfully to promote its use at the precise moment that the railroads and other industries recognized oil as a viable fuel. In marked contrast to his experiences in New Mexico, Doheny was finally in the right place at the right time.

Oil exploration had been going on in Southern California for at least thirty years before Doheny began digging in the oil seeps of Los Angeles. By the late 1880s, there were almost one hundred producing wells operating in the hills surrounding the city. At its peak this business represented a financial outlay of several million dollars in what was already a capital-intensive industry. Within the city of Los Angeles, itself, there had been numerous attempts to drill for oil going back as early as 1863, when one budding entrepreneur supposedly spent $65,000 trying to prove the value of the city's oil resources. There was also a well-publicized report by the California State Mining Bureau in 1888 listing every known oil well and petroleum exude in the state, including the ones in Los Angeles.[5] Years later, Doheny praised the value of this report, if not its author, W. A. Goodyear: "It can scarcely be credited that he knew the significance of the information which his annual report conveyed to the experienced prospector. That report, made some years before I went into the oil business, was really my best guide in the discovery of the various oil districts which it was my good fortune to open up in that state."[6]

Obviously, Doheny made good use of the information available to him and did not succeed on luck alone. The real challenge was not to find the oil but to overcome the prevailing apathy about it. Still, Doheny's "discovery" of oil in Los Angeles was attributed to a stroke of genius that made him a legend in the California oil industry.

As Doheny most often told the story, he was living in a cheap hotel on the west side of the city when he saw a wagon loaded down with pitch. Curious, Doheny stopped the driver and found out that the material came from a spot near Westlake Park and was being used as fuel by the local ice plant. Hearing that, Doheny supposedly raced off to see the oil exudes for himself. "My heart beat fast," he recalled, as he watched the sticky material ooze out of the ground:

> I had found gold and I had found silver and I had found lead, but this ugly-looking substance I felt was the key to something more valuable than any one of these metals. Without ever having seen an oil district or an oil derrick . . . my natural prospecting instinct told me that these tar exudes bore the same relation to the petroleum below that the resin on the outside of a pine tree bears to the more limpid sap within . . . It was almost incredible that the possibilities of this spot had not been recognized by people connected with the nearby communities. The whole thing seemed too good to be true; yet it was true.[7]

Convinced that he could sell the oil, Doheny persuaded Canfield to become a partner in his latest endeavor. While they could not afford a lease in the Westlake area, they obtained some cheaper property in central Los Angeles which had also been flooded with oil in the past. The saturated ground at the corner of West State and Patton had later been cut up for fuel, leaving a large hollow along one street. Now, utilizing their mining skills, Doheny and Canfield dug a shaft into the depression hoping to locate the source of the oil. Initially, their technique was less a product of ignorance than it was a matter of utility and finances. A 4 foot by 6 foot miner's shaft allowed for more seepage into the hole than a drill bit and cost much less than the $5,000 required for the average well.[8]

As they went to work using the miner's method, a witness recalled watching Doheny handle a shovel while Canfield ran a windlass to take out the debris. They continued on like this for thirty-eight days before they struck oil at a depth of 155 feet. Canfield's account of this first well mentioned only that the shaft slowly filled with oil as they entered the final section. But Doheny recalled that they first hit a pocket of gas at this point that "crackled like pop-corn" as it came up through the shale, which convinced them to get out of the shaft before they were asphyxiated. They found another way to finish the job after Doheny remembered a method used for drilling artesian wells, which he had seen as a boy in Wisconsin. Adopting the same technique, he brought in the well by driving the sharpened tip of a sixty-foot log into the bottom of the shaft. Unfortunately, the gas pressure was not sufficient to produce a flowing well, so the oil had to be hoisted out of the well with the windlass and a bucket.[9]

In the days and weeks that followed, the aspiring oilmen were the only ones interested in their discovery. By now, Doheny was a full-fledged convert to oil, but Canfield was not. According to Henry Ailman, another transplanted New Mexican who worked alongside Doheny, Canfield did not like working with the gas and decided to give up and go back to mining. When he did, he traded his interest in the oil well for Doheny's interest in some gold claims near San Bernardino. With Ailman as his new partner, Doheny resolved to make the oil well a success.[10]

Previously, Ailman had owned a mercantile and banking operation in Silver City, but he lost the business when a run on the bank forced it into receivership. He had tried gold mining in Pinos Altos and in Arizona before arriving in Los Angeles in May 1892. When he learned of Doheny and Canfield's efforts to strike oil, he persuaded them to sublease one of their three lots to him. Consequently, there were actually two companies at work simultaneously: the original one consisting of Doheny, Canfield, and Sam Connon, another acquaintance probably from New Mexico, and a second one made up of Henry Ailman, his father-in-law, Ira Smith, and his thirteen-year-old son. Ailman's well was about fifty feet, or two weeks, behind the first, and he recalled that both efforts succeeded in finding oil that was "far superior to the tar which we expected to be satisfied with." It was at this point that Canfield left for the mountains and Connon returned to his former job at a local bank.

Fortunately, with the fledgling company near collapse, Connon rescued the operation after he received an inheritance from his parents. Even then, there was no money to spare, and they continued to use primitive methods: a drilling rig consisting of an X-shaped chunk of metal for a drill bit, a makeshift derrick, and a horse for lifting power. This system was as precarious to operate as it was cheap, because it did not allow them any control over the drilling cable. And Doheny, who Ailman said "elected himself driller," had trouble with the rig from the start. On their second attempt to position the bit over the well, for instance, Doheny lost control of the line, and the men watched helplessly as their 300-pound bit plunged 150 feet into the hole "as though shot out of a cannon." Unamused, and clearly disgruntled at being second-in-command, Ailman had to dig out the bit, which was now buried several feet into the bottom of the well.

With some practice, however, Doheny was able to "make hole" with this Spartan outfit and got down another thirty feet in the original well, where they reached a promising flow of oil. They began collecting the oil in discarded tallow buckets belonging to the Southern Pacific Railway and had eight full barrels by the next morning. The only other person interested in their strike at this point was the property owner, J. F. Turner, who showed up to see what was happening. When Turner caught sight of the oil, Ailman interpreted the look on his face to mean, "My God, have I let a fortune slip through my fingers." Next, looking for an excuse to get the oil for himself, Turner "[found] something to kick about, trifling though it was, [and] he hopped on Ed about it." Then, Ailman recalled, "Ed's Irish and Turner's state of Maine tightwadism locked horns and words flew." In the end, Turner paid them $900 to get off the property and made them agree not to drill within 1,200 feet of his ground. Not one to give up without a fight, Doheny got around this restriction by having Carrie use her name to lease an adjacent lot. While not much of a ruse, this allowed them to get within a reasonable distance of the original well and continue their operation.[11]

Within a year of Doheny's initial discovery, the momentum of the industry had picked up, and the neighborhood surrounding that initial site was crowded with nine producing wells and four companies at work. Turner had four wells pumping, Doheny and Ailman had two, another partnership had two, and a man from Downey, California, had one. According to the *Los Angeles Herald,* these wells occupied about 150 square feet of ground along both sides of State Street. In addition to the increasing number of wells, the technology was also advancing; the well-financed companies like Turner's were using standard drilling rigs and steam boilers. As yet, however, none of the wells produced much oil.[12]

In reality, production was the least of the oilmen's worries. In fact, it was almost a curse when Doheny and Ailman obtained a steady flow of oil with no market, which forced them into the street to scramble for customers among the local businesses. In this early period, there were only two big companies and a handful of smaller ones using fuel oil in their operations, and that supply came under contract from an oil company in Newhall, northeast of Los Angeles. Ailman complained that "no one would admit that there was anything near the city except thick road stuff." Finally, the manager of a small plant that ground up bone for fertilizer seemed interested. The fertilizer plant had been getting some light oil from other sources but needed a heavier product, and the Los Angeles oil seemed like an ideal substitute.

Now, however, Doheny and Ailman's dilemma changed instantaneously when they had to turn down their first large contract for lack of production. Luckily, they came up with a way to dramatically step up the pace of their operation. According to Ailman, they already had a steam burner which was sitting idle because their oil was too thick to use with a conventional burner, and they could not afford anything else. A tour of the fertilizer plant, however, had given Ailman a chance to see a different system—the one that worked with the heavier oil. When he realized he could duplicate the design on their equipment, he took Doheny aside and said to him, "Ed, we have no oil to sell. We will burn it ourselves." His invention worked as planned and enabled them to hook their burner to a spudding rig, using a five-inch rubber belt and a thirty-inch pulley, and get down to 260 feet in their first well. With a thirty-foot derrick above the hole, they were pumping three to four barrels of oil a day, as much as any well in the field.

With the combination of better equipment and a steady infusion of experienced drillers from the eastern oil fields, the shallow wells in central Los Angeles dropped down as far as 500 feet, and the need for capital grew proportionately. This transformation proved the value of the city field and brought in a crop of new investors. One of those newcomers offered Doheny a much larger engine if he would provide the derrick and the drill cable for a new company. Doheny jumped at the chance and found a third party to loan him the money for the material. Apparently, in haste, Doheny left Ailman out of the deal, although he belatedly offered to make him the company's new engineer to smooth things over.

While this operation clearly represented a step forward, it was still on the struggling end of the scale. Whether from inexperience or inferior equipment, Ailman recalled, they could not get a straight hole, and Doheny wore himself out trying to make the drill "crooked proof." All that

Ailman could say in retrospect was that the companies that were drilling deeper "wiped out our baby outfit." When that happened, Doheny and Ailman went their separate ways. Eventually, Ailman retired from the oil business with nothing to show for it except for his unheralded role as one of the pioneers of the Los Angeles oil industry.

All in all during these early years, oil production in the city remained an extremely risky proposition. Contrary to the general impression that Doheny's first well sparked an immediate oil boom, there was an extended period of slow and painful growth before the industry took off. The city experienced a roller coaster of activity between 1892 and 1899, and it was not until the end of the century that Los Angeles, and Southern California, in general, experienced the oil fever commonly associated with Doheny's efforts. Far more accurate for the early period was a comment in the *Los Angeles Times* in 1894 reminding readers that Doheny faced "hard work to make a start in the oil business at a time when nobody had any confidence in it, being forced to scrape together and mortgage everything he owned."[13]

That effort paid off, however, as Doheny climbed to the top of the local industry by year's end, with nineteen wells out of a total of 155. His company had a production capacity of 350 barrels a day but averaged about half of that due to a lack of demand. Overall, the Doheny Oil Company was regarded as "one of the most productive and best equipped groups in the district." In fact, Doheny was doing much better than that, since his closest competitor, another local partnership, had only nine wells capable of producing 175 barrels per day. Those two companies accounted for almost half of the oil produced in the city.[14]

In addition to the production of his own company, Doheny and his partner, Sam Connon, were the principal shareholders in the newly formed Metropolitan Oil Company, which had the single best producing well at 100 barrels a day. Even more remarkable in light of Doheny's previous financial straits, he and Connon put up $20,000 apiece to form the company along with three other investors. Since business was still not that good, Doheny had obviously located a source of capital. Whether it was from a local bank or a private party is unknown, although it was probably the former. Either way, this source made all the difference in the world.[15]

Despite this dramatic improvement, the oil industry was still struggling to find its way in a community wary of its presence. In particular, there were environmental concerns that left petroleum advocates pleading for a chance to prove themselves. And for better or worse, Los Angeles had been undergoing a fundamental change since the 1880s from being a passive seaside resort to becoming a modern commercial and manufacturing

Los Angeles Oil District, ca. 1885. Security Pacific National Bank Photography Collection, Los Angeles Public Library.

center. What it lacked was a cheap source of fuel. Doheny's efforts, therefore, contributed to the forward movement of the city, as long as the residents were willing to accept certain changes. "Oil derricks outlined against the western sky," wrote the *Los Angeles Times,* were not as pretty as orange trees but they were more profitable. Likewise, the *Los Angeles Herald* believed that "the hour of deliverance is at hand." [16]

The people living in the oil district were not so sure. Almost as soon as the derricks started going up, the nearby residents sought to halt the industry in its oily tracks. Throughout the summer and fall of 1894, especially, the homeowners around Second Street Park rose up in rebellion, launching one attack after another against the oil producers before the City Council. Doheny, among others, met each charge with the same defense: that the oilmen were putting ten dollars into the area for every dollar they took out and that the citizens of Los Angeles would be the ones to profit from the industry. "Smoke, noise, and dirt," said another oilman, "are the three necessary evils to the growth, expansion, and upbuilding of our beautiful city." And, he continued, if the aesthetic tastes of every citizen had to be taken into account and every nuisance wiped out, "our city of the living [would] be turned into a veritable city of the dead." [17]

Nevertheless, the oilmen had to admit that concerns about public health and safety were warranted even though they considered them overstated. This particular admission came in response to a suit filed in Federal Court by eight local residents seeking an injunction against the industry. Begun in October 1894, the suit listed every oil producer in the city and singled Doheny out from among sixty-one individuals to be the principal defendant in the case. The bill of complaint presented a graphic description of living conditions near the wells, emphasizing the "noxious vapors, smoke, noisome smells, fumes, stenches and noises which disturb, affect and impair the health of . . . [the residents] and deprive them of the comforts and enjoyments of life." For these reasons, the plaintiffs demanded municipal control of the oil industry, a prohibition on nighttime work, and at least $5,000 in damages for their suffering. In the meantime, city representatives passed a preliminary curfew on nighttime drilling activity and assigned a local police officer to enforce sanitation and safety laws within the district, but left the larger issue of control up to the courts.[18]

To meet this particular challenge, Doheny took the lead in forming the Oil-men's Protective Association in November 1894 as a cooperative attempt to govern the local industry. Focused solely on the problems outlined in the citizens' complaint the Protective Association appointed a special committee to see that the oilmen controlled spills, cleaned up their lots, and reduced the smoke from their boilers. They even offered to grade the streets with their own asphalt to make transporting oil by wagon less hazardous. The threat of real legislation inspired the producers to seek out the worst offenders and "prosecute any oil man who maintains a nuisance."[19]

This voluntary effort by the oilmen elicited a corresponding compromise from the residents: in January 1895, they offered to drop their suit if the oilmen agreed to strict boundaries on the south and west sides of the oil field to keep the derricks out of new residential areas. However, this was the one thing the oilmen absolutely refused to consider. Without any definable limits to the oil field as yet, they wanted the freedom to follow the oil no matter where it took them, and despite warnings to proceed with caution, some of the producers talked "rather wildly about the powerlessness of the courts to interfere with their business."[20] When the court dismissed the nuisance suit on April 30 without explanation, it supported the oil industry's wish to have free rein over the city after all. Although some regulations were necessary for public health and safety and some neighborhoods received protection, the Los Angeles Superior Court struck down most restrictions on the geographical growth of the oil industry. According to the *Los Angeles Times,* these were "righteous" decisions designed to ensure the industrial health of the city, if not the environment.

And until the city field had been fully explored, there was little anyone could do to stop the oil producers from conducting their business, as one attorney put it, "as though they were in the middle of the Sahara Desert."[21]

In spite of their victory in court, some of the oilmen still wanted to come up with a way to drill and pump wells that met everyone's concerns. The initial idea was to use electric motors to run the oil machinery. As before, Doheny was the first one to put an idea to the test. This time, he worked in partnership with A. P. Maginnis, an official of the Southern California Railway—the western end of the Atchison, Topeka, and Santa Fe—who was also involved in the oil business. Skilled at public relations in his railroad work, Maginnis appealed to the City Council in March 1895 for permission to set up a large generator to conduct an experiment, believing that "electricity will do away with all the offensive features" of oil production. The Council approved the proposal, and Doheny reconfigured one of his drilling rigs to operate with an electric motor and used it for several months as the public watched with anticipation. Unfortunately, the results were never satisfactory, and Doheny abandoned the attempt in mid-September.[22]

This incident was important because it was one of the first collaborations in a long history of mutual investments between Maginnis and Doheny. Maginnis held a number of positions with the Santa Fe Railway and its subsidiaries. In 1895 he was the claim agent for the Southern California Railway, the manager of the Pacific Land Improvement Company (the real estate arm of the Santa Fe), and the community liaison officer of the Elsinore, Pomona, and Los Angeles Railway Company. Outside of his official duties, Maginnis operated several oil wells in Los Angeles in partnership with K. H. Wade, the general manager of the Southern California Railway.[23] These men were Doheny's first contacts with the railroad at a time when the prospect of converting coal-burning locomotives to oil-burning engines had every oilman in California panting in anticipation. Doubtless, his relationship with two railroad executives gave him a decided advantage. Wade, in particular, had been instrumental in setting up the first California experiments between the Santa Fe, the Southern Pacific, and the Union Oil Company to use fuel oil in locomotives. After a successful test in October 1894, Union Oil thought it had an open field to supply the Santa Fe. But the deal fell through in February 1895 when Wade discovered he could get cheaper oil from the Los Angeles city field, with Doheny as the principal supplier of the Southern California Railway.[24]

Although Doheny's precise role in these events is unclear, there is no doubt that he had been determined to sell oil to the railroads from the

THE MARCH OF THE DERRICK.

Have we any guarantee that it will stop at Sunset Park?

The March of the Derrick. *Los Angeles Times,* May 24, 1900.

beginning. During a promotional trip to San Francisco in the fall of 1894, at the time Wade was working with Union Oil, Doheny met with officials of the Southern Pacific in San Francisco about supplying them with fuel. Apparently, he made a favorable enough impression that the Southern Pacific set aside a locomotive in Los Angeles and equipped it with oil burners to test the local fuel oil. Perhaps this was his part in Wade's campaign, or vice versa. It is also possible that Doheny hoped to play the two railroads against each other in a bid for his services, convinced as he was that the heavy crude oil from the Los Angeles wells would be a much cheaper fuel than coal. In recounting the details of his San Francisco trip, for instance, Doheny stressed that he "was prepared to say now that oil can be profitably furnished to the Southern Pacific at $1 a barrel, and that this would approximate coal at $3 per ton," which was much less than what the railroad paid at the time. Confident that the oil resources of the city would inspire further development, Doheny proclaimed that "one of the greatest industries on the Pacific Coast is building up right here on Second Street in Los Angeles," adding that it would also be easy to get "all the money wanted for any kind of oil well proposition." He even suggested a plan for a new company that would move oil by pipelines, from the city field to a central depot, for easy delivery along spur lines to the various railroads. He also envisioned a major pipeline to the coast, "where a huge storage tank could be placed on a dock, so that the oil barges may load direct from it." Clearly, Doheny could see where the industry was headed as early as 1894 and was determined to take a leading role in its development.[25]

While Doheny concentrated his efforts on fuel oil, he also promoted early attempts to refine heavy crude into lighter products through the Pacific Oil Refining and Supply Company, one of the first companies to try to build a pipeline and storage network in the city. The work began with E. A. Edwards, a recent immigrant from the Ohio oil fields, who built the refinery and designed a system for treating the by-products of asphalt, the company's main product. Eventually, Edwards was able to distill the local crude into at least four distinct grades, ranging from heavy stove oil to a small amount of light material similar to eastern illuminating oil.[26]

Despite its success, or because of it, the Edwards refinery, located just a few blocks from the central oil district, became the most visible symbol of the oil industry's threat to the environment. Acting under increasing pressure from the community, the City Attorney drafted an ordinance to outlaw oil refineries within the city limits and threatened to close down the existing operation. In December 1895, Doheny and Maginnis stepped in to save the company with a plan to relocate the refinery to a lot adjacent to the Southern California's track along the bed of the Los Angeles River. There they intended to make extensive improvements in the plant and machinery so that Edwards could work the local oil "for all there is in it."[27]

As with their earlier bid for an electric franchise, Maginnis lobbied City Hall on behalf of the refinery and summarized the continued plight of the industry in a letter to the Council: "I am not able to understand why the oil men, who have done more for Los Angeles than any other people, should be so continually persecuted. We have paid out about $10,000 in litigation and have never yet lost a case, which shows that we have been wrongfully accused and annoyed unjustly. The oil men have distributed in your city over $600,000 in an effort to give you cheap fuel . . . and in return we have been met only by lawsuits and injunctions." Maginnis noted, in particular, that the parties interested in the refinery had a monthly payroll of over $18,000 and represented a capital investment of over $90,000. In conclusion, Maginnis dismissed the local opposition to the refinery as the work of a "wealthy and influential member of the Standard Oil Company" who feared local competition, and asked the Council not to pass the anti-refinery ordinance without investigating the situation.[28]

Two weeks later the city leaders approved the plan to relocate the refinery on a provisional basis "as a test to use the latest improved appliances." On March 25, 1896, Doheny and Maginnis reorganized the company as the Asphaltum & Oil Refining Company, with financial help from Sam Connon and H. L. Williams, one of Edwards's original investors. Each of them put up $2,500 in return for 250 shares of stock, which accounted for half the capital stock of the company. A fifth investor, Theodore Clark, added $10,000 of his own. Once in operation, the refinery was able to process about 330 barrels of oil a day, which placed it second out of the five refineries in the Los Angeles area, behind the Union Oil Company's 400-barrel plant. Presumably, the Doheny-Connon Oil Company supplied all of the crude oil.[29]

Even as the local industry grew more sophisticated, however, there was still the fundamental problem of defining the limits of the field. More precise information would reduce the hostility of residential groups, but definition was even more important from a marketing perspective, since many potential customers feared that the local field was nothing more than a small pocket of oil that could dry up at any time. To clear up the issue, the Chamber of Commerce hired Professor W. L. Watts, a field geologist with the California State Mining Bureau, to make a special study of the oil fields in Southern California—and the Los Angeles district, in particular. As of March 1895, the city field was still confined to a few square blocks around Second Street Park radiating out from Doheny's first well. Now, some 200 wells were crammed into the area with as many as four or five per lot. But with production cut back for lack of customers, Watts hesitated to make any predictions about the supply, although he did not believe that the field would hold out for long at full capacity. He estimated current daily output at 300 barrels and thought that was about a quarter of the field's potential. From surface indications, Watts did not hazard a guess about geographical boundaries; he merely advised the oilmen to keep moving in all directions and see what happened. Contrary to his intended

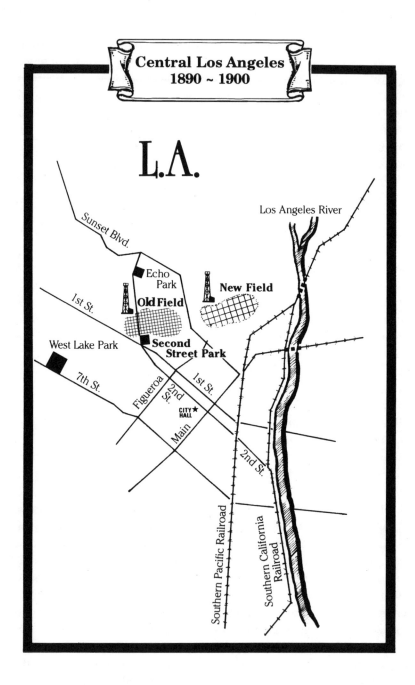

Central Los Angeles
1890 ~ 1900

L.A.

Los Angeles River

Sunset Blvd.

Echo
Park

New Field

1st St.

Old Field

West Lake Park

Second
Street Park

1st St.

7th St.

Figueroa

2nd St.

CITY ★
HALL

Main

2nd St.

Southern Pacific Railroad

Southern California Railroad

mission, therefore, Watts reinforced the conflict between the oilmen and their neighbors and heightened consumers' fears of committing themselves to an uncertain supply.[30]

As before, Doheny stepped forward with a plan. He organized a new company, the Producers Oil Company, to act as a clearinghouse for the entire field through a centralized storage and pipeline system. By creating a cooperative storage system, Doheny intended to stabilize both the supply and the price of oil so that customers would negotiate long-term contracts for fuel. According to a report in the *Los Angeles Herald*, Doheny wanted to create a "common reservoir" of oil that could be held or sold depending on the conditions of the market. Ideally, this would prevent individuals from "selling haphazard" and undercutting the price and would put the oil producers "in a position to talk business to consumers." During the previous year, for example, the price of oil dropped from $1.40 a barrel to $.85, when a dollar a barrel was the accepted minimum to make a profit.[31]

Incorporated on January 3, 1895, Producers Oil Company began with twenty-seven oilmen from the city field, representing over half of the supply. Although many observers hoped that the company would stabilize the market, it never operated as advertised. Despite Doheny's claims, many small producers were very suspicious of the company from the start, because almost all of the initial shareholders were Doheny stalwarts. These included Charlie Canfield, who had recently returned to the oil business, George Owens and Sam Connon, who were Doheny's current partners, and Frederic Northrup and Charles Sumner, who were directors of the Metropolitan Oil Company. Doheny's overwhelming domination of Producers Oil Company left the impression that it was nothing more than a scheme to gain control of the whole market.[32]

This suspicion appeared to be justified by the activity of the Union Oil Company, the largest operation in the state at the time. In response to the low prices and turbulent conditions in Los Angeles, which had begun to affect sales in the outlying regions, Union Oil tried to exert some control over the city. Previously, Union had stayed out of the Los Angeles field, believing it to be inconsequential, but by the end of 1894, Los Angeles oil was becoming a problem for the company. At the same time that Doheny was organizing Producers Oil Company, Union Oil made a direct proposal to the Los Angeles oilmen to buy up the local surplus of light fuel oil and market it on their behalf. Early the next year, Union officials reached an agreement with about twenty producers of light oil, although they accounted for only about 8 percent of the total output of heavier crude.

In the course of these dealings, Union Oil representatives let it be known that they were willing to drastically cut their own prices "in order to convince local producers that it is useless for them to compete with the big corporation."[33]

For several months, the price of oil remained at seventy to eighty-five cents per barrel, while everyone awaited the completion of the pipeline and storage facilities being constructed by Doheny and a few other large companies. By the summer of 1895, however, conditions in the field were worsening by the day, and the depressed market allowed the financially strong companies to feed off of their weaker competitors at will. Under those circumstances, an attitude of fear and desperation took hold of the small producers, which led them into a drilling frenzy in a futile effort to save themselves. Of course, it only hastened their demise. With some 400 wells pumping and forty more being drilled, the price of oil dropped with every additional barrel. At this pace, the oilmen were putting down about fifteen wells a week and eating up a new city block each month. The nine blocks that now made up the Los Angeles field were so crowded that the oil derricks touched at the base. A report on the field for the end of August estimated current production at 3,500 barrels of oil per day, when the market could not absorb 1,200. Small producers with no storage capacity and no financial reserve sold their oil for whatever they could get, which drove the price below thirty cents a barrel.[34]

To understand this suicidal behavior, we need to know something about the "rule of capture," which dominated the philosophy of oil production. Essentially, according to legal interpretation, oil could be claimed only when it reached the surface: "Whatever gets into the well belongs to the owner of the well, no matter where it came from." Thus, as one Los Angeles producer explained: "The main reason for the operation of so many wells now is that every oil well owner knows that if he doesn't pump the fellow next to him will get all the oil in the locality. There isn't a cent of money being made, but they are all pumping to prevent their neighbors from pumping up what don't belong to them strictly."[35] The result was that nothing in the market was secure, and companies with long-term contracts at fifty to seventy-five cents a barrel watched helplessly as their customers reneged on agreements when the price dropped by half. At this point, with no stable market price, no firm commitments, and no way to ship oil to potential customers outside the city, the local oil producers were, in the view of the *Los Angeles Times*, no better off than a "hungry man on a desert island with diamonds in his pockets." Over time, the situation paralyzed the market when the surviving oilmen refused to make any more contracts, stopped drilling, and decided to let the surplus play out before they started over again.[36]

With the complete demoralization of the oil market in the fall of 1895, the time was right for another attempt to get the producers to work together for their mutual benefit. From all indications, the Producers Oil Company had not yet done anything to slow down the process of disintegration. In fact, Doheny had aggravated it by soaking up as much of the cheap oil as he could get, perhaps feeling no sympathy for the individuals who refused his help. By this time, however, there was another organization on the rise as an alternative. The new group was the Los Angeles Oil Exchange, which was headed by Rufus H. Herron, a recent immigrant from the oil fields of western Pennsylvania. Like other transplants from the eastern fields, Herron was well-acquainted with the situation facing the Los Angeles producers. In particular, Herron had been in Pennsylvania during the Great Shut-Down Movement of 1887 to 1888, when the local producers not only joined a protective association but did it in cooperation with their archenemy, Standard Oil. Standing together, if only for a short time, they exerted some positive control over the chaos of the oil fields. For a full year, the association successfully held back drilling and production, eliminated the surplus, and brought the price of oil back up to an acceptable level. When it was over, the independents and Standard Oil went back to fighting each other but not before proving that, under certain conditions, small and large producers could work together profitably.[37]

With this background, Herron seemed a more benign benefactor than Doheny, and his effort effectively divided the field into competing camps: on one side were the pioneer oilmen allied with Doheny, while on the other were the rest of the producers, mostly newcomers, who were upset at having been "lured on with long yarns of how various firms were going to store our oil for us." The conditions of the market, however, made it very difficult for the Oil Exchange to promote their brand of cooperation. Although the leaders of the Exchange claimed to have at least seventy-seven out of one hundred possible producers in their organization, actual participation was less than half that number, and even those members were split into competing groups. Ideally, each company was supposed to sign a three-year contract to market their oil through the Exchange, but as of October 1895 only thirty producers had done so. As it happened, the producers were never willing to sign binding agreements but merely promised to allow the Exchange to handle their oil.[38]

The condition which actually brought the field together was an increasing glut of oil that so overwhelmed the storage system in December 1895 that it forced a district-wide shutdown. By this time, the *Los Angeles Times* could report that the "climax of defeat" had come to a majority of the well owners. With no storage and no market for their oil, producers could keep only a fraction of the city's 300 operating wells pumping.[39] Now conditions were right for the Oil Exchange to have an effect on the market. Over the next six months, a combination of production cutbacks and the failure of many weak companies stemmed the tide of oil. And using its own tank steamer, the Exchange organized several bulk sales of oil to consumers in San Francisco. The combined effect of these factors helped turn the market around and lift the price up from forty cents in December to $1.25 in June.[40]

Despite the lack of detailed evidence for these events, it is clear that Doheny was able to continue operating throughout this period because he had a larger customer base than any of his competitors. By the end of 1894, he was supplying fuel oil to a number of local businesses, including a brewery, a cold storage plant, and a packing company. He also had a contract to provide oil for the steam-generating system at City Hall, after offering to refit their burners for free and promising them a $500 reduction on the annual fuel bill they normally incurred using coal. Ironically, the members of the City Council were probably warming themselves on cheap local oil while they debated the nuisance complaints against the oilmen. Overall, Doheny's success at winning these long-term contracts left him vulnerable to any sudden changes in the oil market, especially when his aggressive marketing strategy won him a major contract to supply the Southern California Railway.[41] In this case, Doheny's friendship with A. P. Maginnis and K. H. Wade helped him to secure the railroad's business, but the work turned out to be a mixed blessing in the end. The contract began in early 1895 and called for Doheny to deliver 20,000 barrels of oil a month and keep a full month's reserve in storage. The railroad paid him $1.05 per barrel. Taking an estimated cost of production of fifty to seventy cents a barrel and adding 10 to 15 percent for delivery, Doheny had fashioned a contract with the Santa Fe that left him a reasonable, but not excessive, profit.

Not all his arrangements were so rational, however. Hoping to extend his domination of the market, Doheny took on additional contracts during the oil glut at a much lower rate; this left him desperate to buy oil at thirty to forty cents to avoid the prospect of taking a financial loss on every barrel. By March 1896, it would have cost him as much as seventy to eighty cents a barrel for any additional oil to cover contracts he had made at half that amount. Those contracts cut deeply into the earnings from his arrangement with the railroad. To make matters worse, the production of the wells, as Watts had warned, began to drop off as much as 10 percent a month as the field started to play out. And with the market price edging one dollar a barrel at the well, Doheny's margin of profit was razor-thin.[42] At the end of the oil glut, consequently, with shrinking supplies and rising prices, Doheny was hard-pressed to fill the railroad contract and keep up with the rest of his obligations. Simply put, Doheny got caught short when the price of oil started to rebound.

Given these constraints, the financial consequences of Doheny's situation were not long in coming. On the first day of August 1896, the *Los Angeles Times* reported the collapse of the Doheny-Connon Oil Company, adding that the "immediate cause of the failure was due to bad business management and extravagance." Doheny's largest creditors, especially the Farmers and Merchants Bank, forced the move. The following day the paper backed away from their attack on the management of the company, citing "unfounded rumors" as the source of the earlier quote. To avoid bankruptcy, Doheny and Connon voluntarily assigned their property to W. A. Morgan, a representative of the bank, "in order to provide funds for immediately suspending development and paying off all labor and other claims." The receiver was confident that, by maintaining daily operations without the burden of expansion, "the regular production of the property will enable its owners to liquidate all liabilities in good time."[43]

Obviously, this was not an event Doheny elaborated upon in later years, except during one interview in 1905. At that time, he charged that a combination of oil well owners—presumably the Oil Exchange—had been formed to "bust [him] up in business" because he had the "temerity" to take contracts at rates that were well below the market price for a barrel of oil. As far as it went, this explanation is in accord with the facts available. What it does not clear up is Doheny's rationale for taking contracts that put him increasingly at risk. Either he was supremely confident in his ability to find oil and did not believe that the field was vulnerable to exhaustion or he simply counted too much on his ability to control the market by gathering all the production into the Producers Oil Company. Unfortunately, he attributed the underlying problem to politics rather than management. Specifically, Doheny considered himself a victim of his political sympathies during the 1896 presidential campaign, in which he had supported the candidacy of William Jennings Bryan. Supposedly, the Farmers and Merchants Bank of Los Angeles had been part of a nationwide effort by Republican financiers to "strengthen their position in case of [some] commercial and financial disaster ... which might occur if Bryan was elected, and they were not extending their loans." This program included an attack on Democratic loyalists. Thus, Doheny was notified that the bank was "able and willing to extend aid to their friends" but could not abide those who supported William Jennings Bryan. Hearing that, Doheny told the vice-president of the bank that he understood but that he could not "change the opinions of a life time after a few minutes conversation." Instead, as he recalled, he persuaded the bank "to name a trustee to whom I would deed the property in order to fill my contracts." Afterward, he hoped to get his company back.[44] Thus, by portraying himself as the victim of jealous competitors and political enemies—a tactic he would use again— Doheny was able to sidestep any discussion of the problems he created at the time. Perhaps, given the intense feelings generated by the presidential election, he was put at a disadvantage because of his political affiliation, but that had nothing to do with what led him into trouble in the first place.

A final note about Doheny's political activity is that he had recently joined the Silver Republican Club, a group of pro-Bryan Republicans formed in the months before the election—a curious place for a lifelong Democrat, unless he was actively recruiting his business associates for the opposition. Doheny was also one of thirty delegates chosen to represent Los Angeles County at a conference held by the provisional committee of the Silver Republicans, and he continued this work despite any conflict it caused. In July 1897, for example, when Bryan addressed the Silver Republicans of Los Angeles, Edward and Carrie Doheny were there, along with A. P. Maginnis and several other oilmen, seated prominently in front of the honored guest.[45]

Political sympathies notwithstanding, Doheny's problems in 1896 were financial and had resulted from a too-rapid expansion of his organization. Afterward, with the company in receivership, Doheny worked in vain for several months to turn the situation around. One of the first things he did was to move outside the central district in an attempt to find new territory. As it was, the central oil district was approximately 800 feet wide, north to south, and one mile long, east to west. The wells along the northern and southern boundaries had not been good producers while those on either end of the field sat along an area where the oil strata dropped off so steeply that it cost too much to drill for the deeper oil. Since the bank was unavailable as a source of capital, it is not clear who put up the money for the wildcat well. Nevertheless, in November 1896 Doheny started drilling three-quarters of a mile beyond the western boundary of the oil zone. Undeniably aggressive, he was not known for being careless. Thus, his reputation as a "cautious exploiter" led many observers to celebrate prematurely the expansion of the field. Unfortunately, Doheny missed the oil sand by a quarter of a mile and ended up with water instead of oil. He made a few more attempts closer in with no more success. Eventually, by the summer of 1897, a new flush field had come in on the east side of the old district, which sent the market into another period of overproduction. By then, however, Doheny had already given up and moved on.[46]

In making this decision, Doheny was following the lead of the Santa Fe Railroad, which was determined to establish an independent source of oil. Apparently, before the new field opened up, some of the strongest members of the Oil Exchange, which had broken apart by this time, had stepped in to make up the difference between what the railroad needed and what Doheny could supply. In doing that, these individuals deliberately raised the price of oil as high as possible. When it reached $1.67 a barrel in March 1897, the Santa Fe balked, converted a number of engines back to burning coal, and sent Doheny out to Orange County, near the city of Fullerton, to open up a new district. Once established there in December 1897, Doheny sold out what was left of his Los Angeles holdings to John A. Connon— Sam's brother—for $1,000.[47]

Actually, Doheny's decision to move into Orange County had been well planned, since he had taken out several oil leases in Fullerton at least a year in advance. In June 1895, for example, Doheny obtained a lease for two pieces of property in Fullerton from the Olinda Ranch Company; the lease included an option to purchase 2,700 acres for $51,000. To maintain the lease in the meantime, Doheny had to drill at least one well before January 1896, suggesting that some of his financial problems in Los Angeles might have come from prospecting in Fullerton—that is, if he was working for himself at that point. It also seems likely that the Santa Fe was underwriting his lease hunting in Orange County and perhaps even his wildcat work in the city.[48]

The only thing that is clear is that Doheny's financial difficulties in no way imperiled his relationship with the Santa Fe. Certainly, it made him more dependent on their largesse. On the other hand, the railroad seemed to need his expertise just as much. Consequently, on December 5, 1896, the president of the Santa Fe Railroad approved a contract between K. H. Wade and Doheny that extended their arrangement. Essentially, the five-year contract obligated Doheny to develop the Fullerton leases that he had obtained, along with others held by Wade, to supply the Southern California Railway. The railroad also agreed to pay him to investigate other prospects "with a view of acquiring and developing the same" on their behalf. And for the life of the agreement, the railroad expected to have the benefit of his "knowledge and experience" at all times and required him to "personally direct and superintend the work of development and production of oil in the lands covered by [the] leases." According to this agreement, which was clearly defined as not being a partnership, Doheny was responsible for providing the drilling machinery (engines, boilers, cables, and oil and water lines), while the railroad would take care of the well casing, oil derricks, pumps, material for storage tanks, transportation facilities, fuel, and labor costs. The cost of fuel to operate the equipment would be divided between the two parties, with the railroad paying a two-thirds share. After deducting for royalties paid to the landowners, the railroad agreed to buy two-thirds of the net from Doheny at one dollar per barrel. Doheny received the other third of the oil in payment for his work and had the option of selling it, as well, to the railroad for the same price. Because this was not a partnership, however, Doheny did not have a proprietary interest in any of the leases or materials furnished by the railroad, and if the Santa Fe needed to move faster than Doheny's resources would allow, it retained the option of bringing in a third party.[49]

When Doheny headed to Fullerton in March 1897, therefore, he went with the full support of the Santa Fe behind him. But even with that help, opening a new field from scratch took time, and it was slow going in Fullerton for many months. Meanwhile, back in Los Angeles, the opening of the eastern extension of the field ushered in another period of overproduction that forced prices back down below fifty cents a barrel by the end of the summer. This situation allowed the railroad to maintain operations and buy up a three-months' reserve of fuel oil, about 65,000 barrels, to tide them over while Doheny built up their properties in Orange County. More than anything else, the continued volatility of the market reinforced the Santa Fe's determination to secure its own supply of oil. Seven months into the work, when Doheny had two wells producing a total of fifty barrels a day and two more ready for the pump, W. G. Nevin, who took over the Southern California after Wade's death in March 1897, boasted that the railroad was now "practically independent" of any action by the local producers and expected to be totally self-sufficient by the spring of 1898.[50] Despite Nevin's confidence, Doheny did not save the Santa Fe from the vagaries of the market as early as anticipated, but his work was impressive nonetheless. When he completed the first wells in October 1897, they met only about 5 percent of the railroad's current demand. By the following

August, he had ten wells that produced about 200 barrels a day, or roughly 20 percent of total consumption. From there the pace of development increased steadily until the fall of 1900, when Doheny had nineteen wells that produced as much as 100 barrels a day each, bringing the Santa Fe close to the independence it desired.[51]

Apart from his work in Fullerton, Doheny was also experimenting in the western section of the district near the mouth of Brea Cañon. In July 1899, he formed the Brea Cañon Oil Company—with a coterie of Santa Fe investors, including Maginnis, Nevin, and C. N. Sterry, a Santa Fe attorney from Los Angeles—to handle the properties. Early appraisals of the Brea Cañon had been enthusiastic and the company's first well produced several hundred barrels of oil a day for the first six months, when most of the wells throughout Southern California yielded well below half that amount.[52]

Having fulfilled his primary obligations to the Santa Fe in Fullerton, Doheny began to range outside of the Los Angeles Basin and soon migrated to Bakersfield in Kern County. As with every preceding oil discovery in California, there were obvious signs that oil existed along the Kern River, but for many years, no one cared to look. One person who did was Thomas Means, an old rancher whose property sat along a bend in the river about seven miles outside of Bakersfield. Most folks considered Means a lunatic and a pest on the subject of oil and dismissed his rantings about having a fortune in oil at his doorstep. Means did not want to do the work himself, but he badgered the locals to come out and take a chance on his property. Finally, in the spring of 1899, two local men, Jonathan and James Elwood, took him up on the offer and drilled the first well. Having scouted the area on his own, Doheny was familiar with Means's story and was quick to move in as soon as he heard about the new well. In a race with John B. Treadwell, his counterpart for the Southern Pacific Railway, Doheny secured a lease on the Means ranch and bought up additional tracts along the river to determine the direction of the oil pool.[53]

Then, on May 23, 1899, Doheny incorporated the Petroleum Development Company as an independent operation outside the purview of his Fullerton contract. With an initial capital stock of $50,000, Doheny was the principal shareholder with $20,000. Naturally, several Santa Fe officials invested, as well, and most of Doheny's oil went straight into the engines of the Southern California Railway. This time, Doheny really did help set off the next oil boom, as the Kern River field expanded to include some twelve square miles of land, more than forty oil companies, and 134 wells by the end of its first year. Most of the producing outfits were small operations with three or four wells apiece, but sitting at the top of the list were the two companies allied with the railroads. At this point, Treadwell had nineteen wells, Doheny had seventeen, and both were drilling as quickly as possible.[54]

Although the Santa Fe was Doheny's principal customer in Kern River, the railroad did not step in immediately and take over the operations as they had in Fullerton. In fact, the Santa Fe was still rather cautious with respect to the oil situation. Where the Southern Pacific was in the process of converting all of its locomotives to burn oil, the Santa Fe decided to maintain some coal engines just in case oil production fell off or was deliberately withheld. Before making a complete switch to fuel oil, the Santa Fe wanted to have an extensive storage system paralleling their lines and a headquarters in place at Bakersfield. Thus, the railroad continued to encourage Doheny's efforts without making it a new policy.[55]

In fact, both the Brea Cañon and Petroleum Development oil companies appear to have operated as independent companies, unlike the Fullerton properties. And there is no indication that the Santa Fe representatives who invested in these companies had official funds at their disposal, despite the fact that their efforts clearly fit the railroad's expansion plans. One example will suffice. In April 1897, Doheny and several of his associates bought some land in Fullerton in their own names, although they intended to use it for oil to fill the Santa Fe's contract. In this case, they purchased forty acres of land for $2,000, developed it for two years, and then sold it to Nevin for $10,000 in March 1899. At that point, it was clear that Nevin bought the land on behalf of the Santa Fe Railroad.[56]

Although there is room to speculate about the personal involvement of the railroad officers, there is no doubt that Doheny was able to take advantage of his work for the Santa Fe. Relying on the income from the Santa Fe's oil field in Fullerton and his position as the railroad's oil expert, Doheny not only escaped potential disaster in Los Angeles but expanded his own operations along with those of his benefactors. Taking full advantage of the latitude of his contract, Doheny went into the Brea Cañon and then moved on to Bakersfield, pulling the railroad along behind him to each destination. Once established in Kern River, he relinquished his contract in Fullerton and forged ahead into Mexico, using the profits from the Petroleum Development Company to support his latest investments. When Doheny decided to close out his Fullerton contract in October 1900, he had produced more than 200,000 barrels of oil for the railroad. As of August 31, Doheny had been paid $58,846 for the oil he sold to the Santa Fe. Out of that, he spent about $14,000 for machinery, leaving the remainder for living expenses and other investments. In the end, the Santa Fe valued his share of the two years remaining on his contract, assuming a 23 percent annual reduction in output, at $127,126 and offered him a cash payment of $67,500. From an initial investment of $300,000, Doheny estimated the value of the Fullerton operation at $2.5 million. Sustaining Doheny's development work over the first three years meant that the railroad had paid an average price of $1.64 a barrel when the market rate was no more than one dollar, and often much less. But president E. P. Ripley considered it a vital investment since it had protected them from what he described as "combinations formed among the producers to squeeze us."[57]

In addition to his work in Southern California, Doheny also had a contract to supply all the Santa Fe's oil for their Mojave-to-San Francisco line. Once again, the railroad relied on Doheny's expertise and confidence and signed the contract when he had only one small well, producing thirty barrels a day, while the railroad needed at least a thousand barrels. While waiting for him to build up production in Bakersfield to cover the new contract, the Santa Fe shipped its own oil up from Fullerton and bought cheap oil in Kern River during the first months of flush production. By the following year, Doheny had met the demands of the contract with approximately twenty wells in production and found himself with enough free time to explore for oil in Mexico. As prospects increased below the border, Doheny negotiated an end to his relationship with the Santa Fe in August 1901, when he submitted a proposal to sell the Petroleum Development Company to the railroad. The details of his appraisal illustrate just how well he was doing in Kern River. He estimated the total worth of the company at $3,150,100, based on the following assets: 1,500 acres of oil land; thirty wells, which produced an average of fifty barrels a day each; 40,000 barrels of oil in storage; and $225,000 in oil-well machinery, tanks, and other supplies. Using the Santa Fe's own estimate of its oil requirements, he valued the remainder of his contract for 30,000 barrels a month at $900,000. At the time, Doheny was actually producing at least 45,000 barrels a month, out of which the railroad took its 30,000 barrels at $.96 each when the market rate was $.38. And since he had only 40,000 barrels in storage, he must have been selling the rest of it to the railroad for storage depots along their lines. In terms of profitability, Doheny noted that oil could be "produced and delivered on board the cars from the Petroleum Development Company's wells at less than fifteen cents per barrel." This left him with a profit of seventy-one cents per barrel on his contract. Certainly, once assured of the supply, the Santa Fe was happy to take that savings for itself. Finally, based on his own geological experiments, Doheny offered an "ultra-conservative" estimate for the company's oil reserves at 100 million barrels—enough oil to run the entire Santa Fe system west of Albuquerque "for over 50 years." Taking everything together, Doheny asked for $1.8 million for the Petroleum Development Company. The Santa Fe disputed some of Doheny's calculations and countered with an offer of $1.25 million, which Doheny accepted. Even though he now had to split the proceeds with five minority stockholders, he was due about $850,000 for himself.[58]

After having started with nothing but an idea and some determination nine years earlier, Doheny left for Mexico a millionaire in 1902. Although he had displayed an extraordinary amount of skill and ambition over these years, his initiative might not have counted for much had it not been for his connection to the Santa Fe Railroad. With that as his safety net, Doheny proceeded relatively risk-free into a market that others found inherently unstable. Still, his promotional efforts to overcome the railroad's reluctance to convert to oil and his tireless work to open up new fields were good indications that he would be equally successful in his later adventures south of the border.

In closing this chapter, before going on to Doheny's work in Mexico, we need to take a final glance at his domestic life during these years. For lack of information to the contrary, Edward and Carrie must have continued their married life in Los Angeles much as they had in New Mexico. All that is known for sure, aside from Carrie's role in leasing oil property, is that they shared the tragedy of losing their daughter, Eileen, in 1892 and the consolation of having another child, Edward Jr., the next year. And in the summer of 1896, when Doheny was forced to take stock of his company and his career, Carrie was the one who persuaded him to go back to Wisconsin and see about his parents. Once there, learning that everyone but a brother had died in the twenty-four years since he had left, Doheny took his brother back to Los Angeles to live with him, adding to an already extended family that included his in-laws, Mariah and Martin Barber, who had come to Los Angeles in 1893. Barber worked for Doheny through the 1890s and eventually became general superintendent of the Santa Fe's oil development in California.[59]

It is certain, though, that Edward and Carrie's relationship had been deteriorating during these years and reached the point of divorce sometime around 1898. At the time, divorce was still a relatively unusual and drastic response to a failing marriage, and there must have been a serious and justifiable reason for the breakup. Carrie moved north to San Francisco and later had a house built in Oakland where she reportedly lived quite well on a $500 per month alimony settlement. Edward remained in Los Angeles and became engaged to Carrie Estelle Betzold, known as Estelle, a twenty-five-year-old telephone operator. Rumor had it that it was Estelle's voice that first captured his attention. However they met, Edward and Estelle were married in a civil ceremony in August 1900. The wedding took place in Albuquerque, New Mexico, aboard a private rail car belonging to A. P. Maginnis, as part of a business trip and train holiday that included Mr. and Mrs. Maginnis, Charles Canfield and his wife, and a few other guests.[60]

Upon returning to the West Coast, however, the newlywed couple received the news that Carrie had died. Newspaper accounts of the tragedy quoted Miss M. Morgan, who had been Carrie's companion for the preceding ten months. According to Morgan, Carrie asked her to order some fluid to recharge the household batteries, along with some medicine, from the local drug store. When the supplies were delivered to the house, Carrie answered the door, took the package, and disappeared into her bedroom upstairs. A short time later, Morgan was startled "by a violent screaming." Rushing to Carrie's room, Morgan found her "in terrible agony." Morgan said that Carrie was able to tell her that she mistook the battery fluid for the medicine and had swallowed some before she realized her error. This would have been a curious mistake, however, since the bottle of battery fluid had "Poison" written on it in conspicuous red letters. The coroner determined that Carrie had actually poured herself a large wine glass full of the solution—at least six ounces—and drank all of it, which would have required several gulps at least. Because the battery fluid caused her to vomit almost as soon as she got it down, her death was not immediate, and she suffered for several days before finally succumbing to the toxic mixture. In the end, however, the coroner did not challenge the story of an accidental poisoning. All that Morgan could add in the way of explanation was that "Mrs. Doheny has been a sufferer from nervous troubles for a long time." Incidently, there was no mention of Edward Jr. in all of this. Presumably, young "Ned," who was then about seven years old, remained with his father after the divorce, suggesting that Carrie had either been judged unfit for the task, or had chosen to let the child go.[61]

Given the circumstances of her death and the likelihood that she deliberately took her own life, Carrie Lou Ella Doheny was no longer a subject for discussion in the Doheny household. Edward never mentioned her again, at least not in public. The Dohenys (Edward, Estelle, and Ned) remained an intensely private family, and none of their closest friends, even those who had known Carrie, betrayed their confidence. For her part,

Estelle and Edward Doheny, ca. 1900–1905. Archival Center, Archdiocese of Los Angeles, Papers of Carrie Estelle and Edward L. Doheny.

despite some obvious insecurities, Estelle rose to the challenge of managing a wealthy household with determination, if not enthusiasm.[62] For reasons unknown, she would never have any children, although there was every indication that she accepted Ned as her own, and most people believed he was. Estelle devoted herself to philanthropic work, book collecting, and the oil business. From the beginning, she served as a close and trusted adviser to her husband and eventually became one of the first female directors of a major oil company when she joined the boards of several Doheny corporations in the early 1920s.

3 THE BIRTH OF THE MEXICAN
OIL INDUSTRY, 1900–1910

During the 1890s and early 1900s American business saw some of its best opportunities in the development of foreign industry. Aptly characterized as a "spillover" into undeveloped areas, this process involved heavy investments in mining, agriculture, and railroad construction to secure raw materials for burgeoning American factories. Creating foreign markets for American products was an inherent but less important element of this activity. Because of its proximity and seemingly stable government under President Porfirio Díaz, Mexico received an unprecedented share of this new American business, and investors operated as though there were no firm border between the two countries.

Doheny began exploring for oil in Mexico just as this process reached its height at the turn of the century, and his efforts have been interpreted as an extension of his California activities. However, even the proponents of the spillover analogy question whether it is anything more than a general definition, and Doheny's experience in Mexico challenges some of the basic elements of the model and reflects the idiosyncrasies of this type of entrepreneurial activity. Since Doheny became involved in Mexico while he was still operating in California, he might have been planning to link the two sides of the business. Certainly, his intention to supply oil for the Mexican Central Railroad, one of the largest and most important American investments in the country, seems to fit the phenomenon described above, but once in Mexico Doheny operated altogether differently.[1]

First of all, Doheny sold out his California properties in 1902 in order to concentrate solely on Mexico. Thus, his move was not the result of excess capital and did not stem from the need for additional oil to supplement his California supply; quite the opposite was true. Considering his recent success in opening up prolific oil fields in Southern California just as the industry was taking off, Doheny's decision to leave is an anomaly. He should have taken advantage of his position to dominate the next phase of development; instead, he gambled on Mexico. Thereafter, Doheny tried to create a Mexican market for fuel oil and did not reenter the American market until massive overproduction forced a spillover back into the United States a decade later. Even when he returned in 1908 to oil exploration in California, after establishing his Mexican business, there was no connection between the two enterprises. Thus, Doheny's venture in Mexico was the inverse of what would normally happen and reflected his desire to build a new, large-scale industry virtually free from direct competition.

The highlights of Doheny's first years in Mexico have been portrayed as a relatively straightforward progression. First, he went to furnish oil for the Mexican Central Railroad. Then, at a crucial moment, the railroad reneged on its contract and left him without a market. Ultimately, he survived by selling asphalt for street paving until he brought in several large gushers in 1910 and began selling oil abroad. Missing from standard accounts is a sense of the dynamic conditions of the Mexican oil industry at its inception and the complex work Doheny performed in financing his companies, building a market, and defining his long-term goals. Like California, Mexico had been the scene of periodic attempts to establish an oil industry for almost forty years before Doheny arrived. One of the earliest reports from the 1860s noted that prospectors were already locating oil springs on both coasts as well as in the valley of Mexico. In May 1865, for example, several American residents of Mexico, along with a number of New York capitalists, obtained oil lands and exclusive refining rights from the government and were convinced of the "inconceivable value" of Mexican oil. A few years later, a Pennsylvania oilman exclaimed that the surface indications of oil around Juan Felipe, situated along the Gulf Coast in an area Doheny would eventually control, were a virtual Niagara Falls compared to anything back home and "must be seen to be believed." An official report on the resources of Mexico in 1891 noted the abundant "deposits of asphaltum, liquid petroleum, and bituminous coal." What no one realized, though, was how challenging the physical conditions of working in Mexico could be, where the long distances, hostile climate, and lack of infrastructure had left the petroleum wealth of the nation relatively untouched.[2]

By the early 1890s, however, economic activity of all kinds increased dramatically under President Porfirio Díaz, as his tight political rein and desire to modernize the country opened the floodgates of capital investment. The foreign business community, aided by a few Mexican investors, spurred a desire for internal improvements similar to those in the United States, including a dramatic increase in the demand for heating and illuminating oil. When available, these petroleum products came from the United States at a prohibitive cost. But the rising demand for oil, coupled with the reports of the prodigious number of petroleum exudes, inspired new attempts to exploit the resources of the country. When Doheny and Canfield made their first prospecting trip to Mexico in May 1900, there were several petroleum companies already hard at work. The largest and most well established was the Waters-Pierce Oil Company, which did not produce oil but sold refined products on the local market. Under the aggressive leadership of Henry Clay Pierce, the company had been supplying processed oil to Mexico for over twenty years through its ties to the Standard Oil Company in the United States. In this way, at least, by implanting a desire for petroleum products, Pierce was perhaps the true pioneer of the industry.[3]

Eventually, Pierce also turned to importing crude oil from the United States and refining it in Mexico to escape the import duties on refined products. At this time, using native crude was still considered impractical, but Pierce was well aware of the various efforts to discover a suitable supply of Mexican oil. In March 1900, for instance, a Waters-Pierce official reported on the progress of two well-funded English companies that were exploring the oil deposits in Papantla, Veracruz, as well as a third group of investors hard at work in Oaxaca. There were also reports in the *Mexican Herald,* the advocate of American business interests, claiming that the fuel question in Mexico was being answered by a "strong combination of leading Mexican gentlemen," who had acquired a large tract of land on the Pacific coast. After receiving a barrage of "bogus reports regarding oil finds," however, the paper stopped printing them indiscriminately but maintained that the oil supply in Mexico was no longer in doubt.[4]

Doheny and Canfield arrived in the midst of this activity in the spring of 1900, having been persuaded to examine the oil prospects of the country by A. A. Robinson, the president of the Mexican Central Railroad. Robinson had headed up the engineering department of the Santa Fe, then became a vice president and general manager of the railroad. In 1893, Robinson had resigned from the Santa Fe to become president of the Mexican Central, and based primarily on the Santa Fe's experience, Robinson eventually decided to use oil on the Mexican Central, hoping to develop a native supply in Mexico. As Doheny recalled, Robinson "knew of my connection with the development of oil in Los Angeles and was anxious for me to undertake the discovery of petroleum anywhere along the lines of his railroad in Mexico."[5]

Apparently, Doheny did not take the proposition too seriously in the beginning and asked Canfield to join him on what they assumed would be no more than a paid vacation: "Having succeeded beyond our utmost expectations, we went to Mexico for a rest, deciding that we could rest better while prospecting." But Robinson was serious enough to promise Doheny that he would "facilitate in every way possible our efforts to develop [any oil property] and make a contract with us, if we were successful, to purchase the oil for fuel for the Mexican Central Railway."[6]

Robinson's offer was too good to pass up. Here was a chance to combine raw adventure in Mexico with the promise of the same sort of financial arrangement with the railroad that Doheny had enjoyed in California. Furthermore, having prospected in Mexico during his mining days, Doheny did not doubt its potentially vast resources. The first expedition took place in the spring of 1900, with the oilmen prospecting from the back of Robinson's private car. By this time, they had been joined by A. P. Maginnis, who was an old friend of Robinson's and was probably responsible for bringing Robinson and Doheny together. When this preliminary scouting trip revealed promising oil exudes along the Central's line into Tampico, Doheny worked for several months buying up as much of the surrounding territory as he could lay his hands on.[7] Doheny's enthusiasm for the project was clearly evident in a September 1900 letter to a prospective investor: "Without wishing to make it appear that we are extravagant in our ideas, we do not feel at all timid about saying that the Mexican lands which we have acquired have all the earmarks of containing within their limits oil territory equal in oil value per acre, and many times greater in extent, than the Bakersfield district in California."[8]

Doheny and Canfield incorporated the Mexican Petroleum Company of California on December 18, 1900, to develop their newly acquired properties. The list of directors included Maginnis, who would become the first superintendent; W. G. Nevin, a director of the Santa Fe's California oil properties and the general manager of the Santa Fe lines west of Albuquerque; E. D. Kenna, the general solicitor for the Santa Fe and one of the Southwest's best corporation lawyers; H. M. McIntosh, a Chicago capitalist who had financial interests in California real estate; and Russell J. Waters, a former bank president and a current Republican congressman from Los Angeles. The remaining list of directors and investors read like a "Who's

Who" of Santa Fe officials and Los Angeles businessmen, including Santa Fe president E. P. Ripley and chairman of the board Aldace F. Walker, as well as a host of financiers, attorneys, and judges. There was even a respectable contingent of local oil men that Doheny had fought in the mid-1890s, including his old nemesis from the Oil Exchange, R. H. Herron. Typically, oil companies used inflated capitalization figures to impress unsuspecting investors, but this was a close corporation with no intention of propagandizing its work. Clearly, they were not giving away any secrets when they listed the capital stock at just $225, a token $5 apiece for the initial 45 investors.[9]

For the next several years, in fact, Doheny struggled to keep information about the company's progress from leaking out to the press, but the Spindletop blowout in Beaumont in January 1901 made that almost impossible by creating a climate of speculation. In the months that followed, Texas oil fever spread as far south as Tampico, Mexico, where the residents were convinced that the Mexican Petroleum Company was hiding a fortune on its 465,000 acres outside of the city. When drilling began on April 30 near the Ebano station on the Mexican Central line, there was no denying the local interest. One Tampico reporter was certain that "oil in Mexico means gold, and if one-half of the hopes of the company now in the field are realized it means that Tampico and the Gulf Coast of Mexico will see an era of prosperity never before witnessed in the history of the republic." However, in spite of the number of oil speculators and lease hunters prowling around town during the summer, the Mexican Petroleum Company put up what were described as "immovable barriers in the way of a rubber-necked public" by withholding information about their work.[10]

Doheny was more forthcoming with the Mexican government when he sought and received a formal ten-year concession to legitimize his operation. Under the terms of the agreement, the government would suspend the import duties on certain building materials and exempt the company from all federal exactions except the stamp tax. In return, Doheny promised to meet certain development targets and agreed to sell oil to the government at ten percent below wholesale. A few days before this concession took effect, on May 14, 1901, Doheny struck oil at Ebano. At fifty barrels a day, this was not the gusher Tampico residents had been hoping for, and Doheny waited seven months before telling the local press that the company had a producing well.[11]

In the meantime, the foremost problem was to implement the plans for selling this oil to the Mexican Central. According to Doheny, he had been offered a specific contract with the railroad in August 1900, several months before he incorporated the oil company. Supposedly, the railroad agreed to purchase oil from him at $.90 to $1.20 per barrel, depending upon its point of delivery, while he agreed to convert the locomotives to oil burners at his own expense, maintain them with fuel oil, and cover any reconversion costs if he failed to keep pace with demand. But, as Doheny recalled, "the first effort on the part of the oil company to put this contract into effect was met by the statement of the chairman of the board of the Mexican Central that the contract had been abrogated." And in 1901, the chairman was none other than Henry Clay Pierce, the only man possibly threatened by Doheny's presence in Mexico.[12]

Doheny blamed Pierce for scuttling his plans, but the situation was not as simple as he made it out to be. There was no question that the Mexican Petroleum Company had been formed to sell oil to the railroad, but there was some doubt about the nature of that commitment, and Doheny seems to have become involved with the Mexican Central at the wrong time. In March 1901, a group of American investors linked with the Standard Oil Company and including Henry Clay Pierce, started buying up shares of Mexican Central and soon controlled 55 percent of the stock. With that control, they elected a new board of directors and took over the management of the railroad. Apparently, Robinson tried to block the takeover but ultimately failed. When it was over, Robinson was still president of the company, but ten out of seventeen members of the board had been replaced, and Pierce had been elected chairman. To make the line more profitable, Pierce noted that his efforts would be directed "to the physical betterment of the property and increasing its traffic through the development of the resources of Mexico."[13]

When the immediate plans of the new management did not include the use of Ebano oil on the Mexican Central, Doheny blamed it on Pierce's treachery. But if Doheny had actually had an enforceable contract with the railroad, Pierce would not have been able to cancel it without some legal consequence. Previously, Doheny had never hesitated to go to court to protect his rights, yet he apparently accepted this devastating turn of events without so much as a whimper. Since such a reaction would have been uncharacteristic for Doheny, it is probably that his supposed contract was not a signed agreement but a long-term objective based on Robinson's desire to use Mexican fuel oil. That understanding might have fallen victim to the machinations of Henry Clay Pierce, who was regarded as a brilliant but unprincipled businessman who "liked to pull fast ones." But there were also larger financial considerations at work. Specifically, a report from the Mexican Central in November 1901 revealed that the railroad still planned to use oil but that it had "no way of securing the much desired fuel at a moderate cost." From the railroad's perspective, Doheny's production was as yet inadequate, and imported oil from Texas or California was too expensive.[14]

Doubtless shocked to find himself without a guaranteed market for the first time in a decade, Doheny singled out Pierce for blame and overlooked his own miscalculation. But this episode forced him to widen the net for potential customers by becoming more outspoken on behalf of the business, reminiscent of his early experience in Los Angeles. In August 1901, for example, Doheny explained to the local press that he and Canfield had revolutionized the fuel situation on the West Coast by discovering the great oil fields of California and proclaimed that "we are going to do the same thing for Mexico." Nevertheless, Doheny was still worried that the Mexican Petroleum Company might somehow be unfairly associated with unscrupulous oil promoters and tried to keep specific information to a minimum. As he explained it:

> The Mexican Petroleum Company does not feel disposed to furnish material and advertising for professional boomers. On the strength of our developments many persons attempt floating oil propositions imposing bogus stock upon uninformed persons. People familiar with the nature of oil fields know that one man might have a valuable claim and another, with adjoining land, a claim absolutely without value. When the time comes the Mexican Petroleum Company will make a statement to the public as to what it expects to do. At present the less given by the newspapers the better.[15]

Still, he could not stall an eager public for long, and, a few weeks later, on his return trip to California, Doheny revealed that the company had no fewer than 600,000 acres in its possession in the Tampico area. Obviously, his earlier silence had been necessary to keep the oil boomers at bay until the company had all the property it needed; with that accomplished, Doheny announced that he needed about 600 men to clear the land to make way for the drilling crews. To date, the company had more than a million dollars invested in the operation, and, Doheny added, "we have not been in the habit of using money to no purpose." But he was not yet willing to state what it was. Instead, he offered a compromise: the "Mexican public will demand that we explain some of the plans of our work, and by October we are confident that there will be something of unusual interest to give out regarding what we have found up there."[16]

Doheny missed this deadline by a couple of months, but in December he formally announced that Mexico—not just his company—had an oil well producing about 400 barrels per day. Actually, the *Mexican Herald* had already published several reports, going back to October, stating that the Mexican Petroleum Company had oil in paying quantities, and within two weeks of those reports, at least five new companies had formed to develop oil prospects. Although none of them was in the Tampico area, Doheny was careful not to tip his hand.[17]

As before, he also made a point of assuring everyone that, unlike these other companies, his operation was not putting any of the public's money at risk, and he went out of his way to discredit stories that the company had been selling stock in the market: "We have no small investors in our company. The men interested in our concern are involved to the extent of $5,000 and over, none less. Some of us have invested $200,000 in the enterprise. We do not want any man to invest his savings with us. The oil business is too uncertain for the laboring man to tamper with." Then, "as a way of placing the company right in the minds of the public," Doheny said he would repurchase the shares of any stockholders who were dissatisfied with their investment and offered to pay fifty cents a share for any returned stock plus a ten percent profit on the investment up to that point. All of this was intended to validate his longstanding claim that the Mexican Petroleum Company had not been using the names of wealthy investors to promote a swindling scheme aimed at the unsuspecting public.[18]

Why Doheny felt that he needed to allay the fears of people who had not been offered shares in his company in the first place seemed inexplicable until he revealed that he had just returned from a lengthy visit with President Díaz. At that meeting, Díaz told him that he did not want to see Mexico exploited by the kind of stock manipulation taking place in the Texas oil fields. With that concern in mind, Doheny directed his comments primarily at the capital, where several of Díaz's associates, and eventually the president himself, were shareholders in the Mexican Petroleum Company. Apart from the potential problem of speculators, Díaz was so afraid that Standard Oil was interested in producing oil in Mexico that he made Doheny promise never to sell his oil holdings to Standard Oil without giving the Mexican government the first option to buy him out.[19]

Thus, even though he knew the situation was more complicated, Doheny may have accused Pierce of interfering with his contract with the railroad as a way of substantiating his independence from the oil trust. It is also possible that Doheny's promise to Díaz kept him from selling the company when the Mexican Central postponed its conversion to fuel oil.

In later years, Doheny would recall that the loss of his anticipated arrangement with the Mexican Central was so devastating that it scared several of his largest stockholders into pulling their money out of the company. This was part of the reason that Doheny sold the Petroleum Development Company in Bakersfield to the Santa Fe in April 1902. But as the situation continued to worsen into the summer, at least one of Doheny's investors suggested that they sell a half interest in the company to either Standard Oil or Waters-Pierce to give them the leverage they needed to break into the market. Obviously, Doheny resisted, not so much because of his promise to Díaz but from an increasing determination to find a market in Mexico beyond the railroad.[20]

The depth of the company's financial plight during this period is impossible to fathom, and the actual number of shareholder defections is unknown. But it is clear that the large capital expenditures tested the nerves of Doheny's associates and threw him back on his own resources a number of times. Nevertheless, he retained a pool of seasoned investors who were not likely to run at the first sign of trouble. Typical of this group was Richard C. Kerens, the individual who suggested that Doheny cooperate with Pierce. Based in St. Louis, Kerens had been instrumental in promoting a number of western railroad lines, including a partnership with Colis Huntington in the Los Angeles, Pasadena, Glendale Railway in 1890. Kerens had also invested heavily in mining property, including the Pacific Gold Mining Company of Pinos Altos, New Mexico, which had leased its mines to Doheny in 1890. The following year, Kerens had been appointed by President Benjamin Harrison to an intercontinental railway survey commission that conducted a lengthy investigation of the railroad systems of fifteen Latin American nations. When he finished that project in 1900, Kerens joined the initial group of investors in the Mexican Petroleum Company. Kerens's daughter was married to E. D. Kenna, the Santa Fe Railroad attorney, who was also on Doheny's board.

Kerens was perhaps most important, though, for his political influence. He had served on the Republican National Committee from 1888 to 1900 and worked closely with the powerful Mark A. Hanna during the two McKinley campaigns. Despite the fact that they had some obvious political differences, Doheny's friendship with the "political boss of Missouri" provided links to prominent Republican politicians and businessmen, which accounted for much of his early success. Finally, Kerens also made it his mission to meet on friendly terms with Henry Pierce, to the point of inviting him out on a private hunting trip the next time they were both in Mexico.[21]

With that kind of support, Doheny had no reason to panic as long as he could find a market for Mexican oil. In reality, though, heavy petroleum of the type found at Ebano had a limited range of uses: it could either be burned as fuel oil or refined into asphalt. Thus, with the collapse of the Mexican Central plan, there was only one alternative. The question was whether Doheny could break into the asphalt business. As it stood, the industry in Mexico was dominated by the Barber Asphalt Paving Company, a division of a larger asphalt trust that controlled the paving business in the United States and elsewhere. Barber had already done some work in Mexico and had just negotiated additional street contracts for several of the largest cities when Doheny arrived on the scene. Fortunately, though, Barber's position was not absolute. The failure of several companies to complete their projects more than ten years earlier had produced an official inquiry into how these contracts had been assigned. In particular, plans for covering streets in Mexico City had been on hold for ten years—until 1899—at which time the city council appointed a commission of lawyers and engineers to devise stringent guidelines for prospective bidders. With the new rules, the paving commission hoped to prevent fly-by-night companies from entering the bidding process altogether. Henceforth, officials would accept bids only from companies that were presently engaged in the paving business and could prove that they had satisfactorily laid pavements in at least two foreign cities.[22]

When the council offered new contracts for Mexico City in 1900, there were only three companies apparently qualified to submit proposals: the Barber Asphalt Paving Company of New York, the Assyrian Asphalt Company of Chicago, and the Neuchâtel Asphalt Company of London. When the British company failed to meet the submission deadline, the council began an exhaustive review of the two remaining bids, including an analysis of every aspect of each company's previous work. Initially, the commissioners declined both offers. The Chicago company could not substantiate its claims about past work, and although Barber Asphalt had documented reports on its work in New York, Chicago, New Orleans, and Newark, the company had used imported material from Trinidad and charged premium prices. Lacking an alternative, however, the commission negotiated a 15 percent reduction in fees and reluctantly accepted Barber's bid to pave seventy-five streets in the capital.[23]

These negotiations ended a month before Doheny arrived in Mexico and would have been part of his investigation of the local market. Clearly, challenging Barber's position in an open contest would be difficult, and if other cities adopted the same rules as had the capital, it would be impossible. However, if Doheny could overcome the prejudice against new companies, he stood a chance of competing against the established operators by undercutting the price, and his trump card was his six new wells at Ebano. Instead of having to import raw material from Trinidad or even California, as Barber had to, Doheny could produce asphalt from Mexican oil. By the spring of 1902, the Ebano wells had literally paved his way into the asphalt business in Mexico.[24]

What really cleared his path, however, was the collapse of Barber's parent organization, the National Asphalt Company. At the time, Barber was the leading subsidiary of at least twenty companies that accounted for almost all of the asphalt work done in the United States. But after losing several big-city paving contracts to independent asphalt companies, the trust was placed in receivership in December 1901. The trust also lost a protracted legal battle over the possession of a pitch lake in Venezuela, supposedly the most valuable asphalt deposit in the world. Despite assurances that the financial difficulties of National Asphalt would not affect Barber's work in Mexico, local officials were justifiably worried. And Doheny had been given an opportunity that he could not afford to pass up.[25]

The first order of business was to find a way to compensate for his lack of experience. Knowing that he had price and accessibility in his favor, Doheny decided to bring in an established company from California to act as a reputable spokesman for the quality of his Ebano material. With that arrangement in place, Doheny formally incorporated the Mexican Asphalt Paving and Construction Company on June 18, 1902. The investor group included the same core of individuals who had formed the Mexican Petroleum Company: Charles Canfield, A. P. Maginnis, Russell Waters, and Charles Wellborn, a Los Angeles attorney and long-time associate of Doheny's who had taken over for W. G. Nevin after his death in January. Joining them were J. A. Fairchild and E. W. Gilmore, the co-owners of the Fairchild & Gilmore Asphalt Company, with offices in San Francisco and Los Angeles.[26]

Two weeks later, Fairchild & Gilmore wrote up a promotional letter touting Mexican Asphalt. Without identifying themselves as directors of Doheny's company, they stated that they had been in the asphalt construction business for over fifteen years and were familiar with every type and grade of commercial asphalt. After testing samples from Ebano, they proclaimed it "superior to nearly all of the other brands of refined asphaltum which are at present offered in the market to contracting firms laying asphaltum pavements." While they previously had relied upon California asphalt exclusively, they were prepared to switch to the Mexican product as soon as it was available: "We have the utmost confidence in its quality and superiority and do not hesitate to recommend its use wherever asphaltum pavements are to be laid." Within a few months, officials in Mexico City were experimenting with Ebano asphalt, despite a fair amount of interference from the established companies.[27]

Along with this promotional campaign about his paving material, Doheny also released more information about the overall extent of his operation, much of it coming through A. P. Maginnis. In August 1902, for example, Maginnis pulled out all the stops in an interview for the *Mexican Herald*:

> I am convinced that there is a larger supply of oil in the Republic of Mexico than will be found in the states of Texas and California combined. . . . Everyone knows what the discovery of large quantities of oil means for the future of Mexico. . . . I tell you I see such a brilliant future for Mexico as no man dreamed of a few years ago. I have no fears of contradiction when I say that our own property alone will be pumping 200,000 barrels a month within a year. . . . For almost two years now we have worked quietly and with as little publicity as possible. We were not in the promoting business. We were sure we had a rich commercial enterprise in our hands, and then too there were other lands which we had not yet acquired and we didn't want to talk too much. But now we have everything fixed up. We have found oil. We have the field and the market, and we don't mind taking the public into our confidence for the sake of its own information.[28]

Doheny gave a more concrete appraisal of the company's assets a few months later. At that time, they had eight producing wells at Ebano with a combined capacity of 600 barrels per day, or 18,000 per month. With the completion of the four wells being drilled, Doheny thought that the company could produce 1,000 barrels per day and expected to reach 5,000 barrels by January 1904, shy of Maginnis's prediction but impressive, nonetheless. In total, the Mexican Petroleum Company had invested $4 million in their properties and was about to add another $500,000 to build about 95,000 barrels of tank storage and a six-mile railroad spur to connect the oil camp with the Mexican Central line. To complete the job, the company had about 30 American and 350 Mexican laborers working as hard as they could. With respect to marketing his product, Doheny acknowledged that, although asphalt "adds greatly to its commercial value, our aim is to dispose of the bulk of our oil for fuel."[29]

For all of its preparations, however, the Mexican Petroleum Company had not yet sold a single barrel of oil. Ironically, the first prospective

Mex. Pet Co's Steel traction-wagon hauling 2 wagon loads of casing and a 40 H.p. boiler

Drilling Work at Ebano, ca. 1903. Archival Center, Archdiocese of Los Angeles.

customer was the Waters-Pierce Oil Company, which sent some of their managers on an inspection tour of Ebano in January 1903. They were escorted around the property by Herbert G. Wylie, another Los Angeles well driller, who had been in control of Doheny's operation at Bakersfield and who had taken over Maginnis's position as superintendent in Mexico the year before. Wylie was proud of the job he was doing at Ebano and told Doheny that the Pierce people "were astonished at the progress made here during the past few months and at the amount of work now being carried on." Having convinced them that "the next six months would be the decisive period in our work here," Wylie expected Pierce to wait until then before making any decision. He also suspected that they "had in mind the purchase of the property, rather than the production." In the meantime, Waters-Pierce requested sixty barrels of test oil for their refinery.[30]

In addition to giving promotional tours of the Ebano facilities, Wylie was also responsible for explaining the large sums of money spent at the camp to the stockholders of the company. Apparently, the grumbling about excessive capital expenditures was still a problem, and Wylie was on hand at the January 1903 annual meeting to give an accounting of his work. Wylie extended the same challenge to the shareholders that he did to prospective customers: come and see for yourself. He was certain that anyone who had been to Ebano in the past and revisited it now would approve every penny spent on improvements, and he personally assured Doheny that recent investments would "commend themselves to any one who will give them consideration."[31]

Doheny was thoroughly convinced that Mexican Petroleum had "the most complete oil camp in the world." The company's own railroad ran from the Ebano station of the Mexican Central line to the company's refinery and out to the wells. Their oil-burning engine, the first in Mexico, was a working advertisement for the business. The camp also had a twenty-two-mile water line to the Tamesi River fitted with high-pressure pumps and boilers. An existing thirty-barrel-a-day refinery, used to make samples of Ebano asphalt, was being replaced by a large asphalt plant that could handle up to 12,000 barrels of oil a day. Alongside the refinery, the company was building a cooperage plant capable of turning out 1,000 barrels a day in which to ship the asphalt to market. In addition, the company had all the sundry elements necessary run a self-sufficient operation: machine shop, blacksmith shop, saw mill, electric plant, ice plant, and warehouse. The whole camp employed a workforce of 50 Americans and 700 Mexicans.[32]

Clearly, there was a lot going on at Ebano; even if Doheny had not begun to promote his activities, it would have been hard to keep his business under wraps any longer. In fact, as he laid the groundwork, several other companies came in behind him. Although not on the same scale, these other efforts were usually tied in some way to one of the competing railways in Mexico. In Guerrero, for example, the management of the Mexico, Cuernavaca, and Pacific Railway had experienced oilmen looking for oil along its tracks, and the Southern Pacific purchased a number of wells in Sonora for its Mexican subsidiary. Among the more outlandish schemes was a proposal from a Texas company to run their excess production from Beaumont through a three-inch pipe to Mexico City. As impractical as this was, it reflected a desire by many businessmen in Mexico to have access to foreign oil to make up for the slow pace of domestic production.[33] Because the duty on imported oil made such plans impractical, businessmen began to work for a repeal of the law.

The campaign to remove the tax originated in 1901 with the American Smelting and Refining Company, part of the Guggenheim empire. American Smelting already used oil at its New Jersey plant, planned to burn Beaumont oil in a new smelter in El Paso, and wanted to import Texas oil for their plants in Monterrey and Aguascalientes. Disclaiming any special privilege, the company's chairman, David Guggenheim, argued that removing the import duty would benefit every industry in Mexico. The petroleum age was here to stay, Guggenheim asserted, and the Mexican government needed to encourage its use from every available source. Guggenheim's appeal was well-founded but failed to account for the nascent oil business in Mexico, which had the support of the Díaz administration. Besides, there was no guarantee that eliminating the import duty would actually lower oil prices in Mexico for other consumers. Most Mexicans, especially those in government, believed that the Standard Oil Company controlled Texas oil and fully expected the oil trust to take advantage of any change in the law. And, according to a former employee, Waters-Pierce was already cheating on the duty by importing refined oil that had been colored with just enough crude—about 10 percent—to pass inspection. After the company had paid the lowest duty rate for this oil, the additive was removed, at virtually no cost to the company, and the resulting refined product was sold at full price. If this was true, then reducing the oil import duty would simply add another layer of profit for the Standard Oil organization.[34]

Rather than reducing the oil duty, the Mexican government did all it could to encourage efforts to produce oil in Mexico, including the addition of a new law in January 1902 which offered the same privileges to any producer that Doheny had received in his concession six months earlier. The major difference was that, whereas Doheny had asked only for tax abatements and a reduction of import duties on industrial materials, the new recipients received óne-year permits to explore for oil on vast stretches of public land. Once they had located and developed an oil prospect to the point of producing at least 2,000 liters, or about 12 barrels, of oil per day, they would receive an official concession to fully exploit the source. Moreover, the first company to discover oil in a specific territory could establish an exclusion zone of up to three kilometers from the center of the well to keep out competitors.[35]

Needless to say, Doheny was not happy about a law that allowed others to come in under better conditions than he had received in 1900, especially when he had been promised an exclusive right to the privileges he had negotiated. He was particularly irritated with Weetman Pearson, the famous British contractor, who had come to Mexico on a major construction job and ended up rivaling Doheny in the oil business. Whereas Doheny and Díaz met cordially on a few occasions, Pearson and the Mexican president became close personal friends. And when Pearson received liberal concessions to begin exploring for oil in 1901, Doheny resented him for it.

Certainly, Doheny was not wrong in perceiving a change of allegiance within the Díaz government. In fact, his conflict with Pearson signaled an increased friction between American businessmen and President Díaz over preferential rights to European investors in Mexico.[36]

Initially, Díaz's modernization policy favored heavy American investments in basic industries and led businessmen to feel that their money and property were safer in Mexico than in the United States. But the result exceeded Díaz's expectations, as United States investors began to control major sectors of the economy. By the early 1900s, American capital made up 70 percent of the total foreign investment in Mexico. In the years leading up to the revolution in 1911, Mexican leaders concluded that this overwhelming presence of American economic power threatened their nation's stability and increased the likelihood of attempted political or military intervention by the United States. The most aggressively anti-American among Díaz's advisers was his finance minister, Jose Yves Limantour, who not only sought out European investments but seemed to have a special antipathy to Doheny's oil business. Doheny recalled that, for whatever reason, Limantour "tried to create an atmosphere of dislike, almost contempt, for our efforts."[37]

It was also clear to many observers that it was not simply the weight of American investment that was cause for concern but the mercenary attitude that came with it. Even the *Mexican Herald,* the advance agent of the American business community, acknowledged a tone in Yankee capitalism which was hard to endure:

> If there is in all the Mexican republic one American who makes his home there with any other ultimate object than the dollar, he is the exception that proves the rule ... Americans in Mexico want to make money and make it fast ... From our early years we have associated Mexico with treasure. Romance, beauty, chivalry, tragedy—all have figured in our imagination, but first and foremost has been treasure ... In general your American is for amassing wealth in Mexico and bringing the wealth home. There are Americans in Mexico who represent all that is best in Americanism, but unfortunately their modest incandescents are too often outshone by the sixty-candle arc lights of the bad Americans.[38]

Fortunately, except for Limantour, most Mexican officials tended to congratulate Doheny for his efforts to develop the native oil industry. Of course, he had been actively campaigning on behalf of his work from the very beginning, escorting prominent Mexican and American visitors to

Ebano on a regular schedule. On one trip in early 1904, Doheny invited the congressional representative from Jalisco, Tomas Moran, to inspect the development of the oil field. Moran was duly impressed with the facilities and even more so with "the energy, determination, and perseverance of Mr. Doheny and his associates." At one point, Moran was accidentally splashed with oil from one of the wells and was immediately advised that he "had been baptized in oil" and would henceforth be an oilman. If this was not a planned event on the tour, it should have been, considering Moran's reaction: "I believe I will be one," he recalled later, "as my experience at Ebano has converted me to the belief that we have lots of oil right here in Mexico." Moran, who went on to invest in the company, was certain that Americans like Doheny would always be welcome in his country.[39]

No doubt, many other Mexican leaders received similar treatment and came to the same conclusion, and Doheny missed no opportunity to convert officials from outside of Mexico, either. A month before Moran's visit, Meredith P. Snyder, the Democratic mayor of Los Angeles, equated what he saw at Ebano with what had occurred in Los Angeles a decade earlier, and there was no doubt in Snyder's mind that oil had been "the salvation of California." In 1906, as the annual convention of the International Institute of Geologists met in Mexico City, Doheny personally escorted a trainload of government officials and geological experts on an inspection tour of the oil wells.[40]

Clearly, Doheny had everyone's attention and was doing everything he could to convince them of the practical applications of oil. Apart from its use as fuel, it could pave the roads and provide gas for lighting, heat, and other domestic purposes. As Doheny incorporated all of these elements into his campaign to market Ebano oil, he actually benefitted from the temporary shelving of his agreement with the railroad. If nothing else, it forced him to concentrate on asphalt and gas production as the most visible signs of progress in Mexico. Mexico City was the obvious place to begin this process, and, in January 1904, Doheny brought in P. C. Smith, another California partner, as the chief engineer of the company. Doheny also hired an experienced contractor from the Sicilian Asphalt Company of New York to oversee paving operations. The latter had directed the paving of Fifth Avenue and Wall Street and was expected to put the new company on a thoroughly professional level. Finally, in what was one of the best decisions of Doheny's career, he picked Harold Walker, a young attorney from New York, to become the general manager. Walker was the son of former Santa Fe chairman Aldace F. Walker, one of the original investors in Mexican Petroleum. After his father's death, Walker went to Mexico in 1903 to in-

Promotional Visit to Ebano, ca. 1905. Archival Center, Archdiocese of
Los Angeles.

vestigate the value of the oil company stock, and that initial contact led to
a thirty-year association with Doheny. Walker was a graduate of Columbia
Law School and had worked for a New York law firm before he took control
of the asphalt company, and he soon became the principal attorney for all
of Doheny's Mexican operations.[41]

By the time Doheny began work in Mexico City in 1904, about 370,000
square meters of asphalt had been put down by the Barber Asphalt Company over the previous two years. By February, Doheny's Mexican Asphalt
Company had contracts for another 100,000 meters in the capital and additional work in Guadalajara. As he anticipated, this work proved to be a

bargain for everyone involved. For example, with the four successive contracts Mexican Asphalt had with the city of Guadalajara, the company laid a total of 145,000 square meters of paving over a four-year period, for which it received approximately $1,140,000 in fees, or $7.85 per square meter. Then, in 1908, the company put down an additional 50,000 meters of pavement at $9 per meter. By contrast, the Barber Asphalt Company had been charging $11.00 to $11.50 per meter.[42]

In addition to the cost benefits of having his own oil supply, Doheny was able to save even more money because of a new portable asphalt plant invented by his partner, P. C. Smith. The Smith Asphalt Preparer, touted as the "latest and most improved asphalt plant that has yet been devised," was simply a compact asphalt mixer mounted on a freight car, which eliminated the need to set up a temporary site at every job and enabled the company to go to work almost immediately. Smith also adapted oil burners to the elements used to heat sand and asphalt prior to mixing. Previously, it took time to heat up coal, and fuel was wasted as the coal continued to burn while it cooled down. Now, using oil, the fire could be lit instantly and extinguished at the beginning and end of a paving run. The Smith oil burner not only saved time and fuel but required only two men to produce 800 square meters of two-inch wearing surface per day, well above the production of any permanent plant in Mexico City.[43]

Given these economies, Doheny continued to win contracts to pave hundreds of streets in Mexico City, Guadalajara, and Tampico. He sent Ebano asphalt to several major American cities, such as New York, New Orleans, and Los Angeles. His success using native material even prompted the Mexican Congress, in 1908, to pass a law requiring the use of Ebano asphalt for any future paving work in the capital as a way to foster sales and growth of home products and industries. Asphalt production had become a profitable, if secondary, branch of Doheny's business.[44]

Doheny's prospects for the fuel oil business brightened considerably in the fall of 1904, when the Mexican Central Railroad finally consented to test his product. After three years of financial reorganization, the Mexican Central was completing an aggressive development program to modernize the road and expand its mileage. The railroad had not kept up with capital improvements and found itself falling behind its competitors. In addition, although gross earnings had been increasing over the years, the profit margin had been eaten away by a declining exchange rate between Mexican silver and American gold. Although these conditions affected every line in Mexico, the Central seemed the hardest hit. Poor performance and the failure to pay dividends prompted the 1901 takeover that made Henry

Pierce chairman of the board. To pay for the revitalization program, however, the new board assumed $20 million in bonded debt in 1902 and 1904 just to make basic improvements in track and rolling stock. With this added burden, the declining peso, which dropped in value from $.49 in 1900 to below $.40 in 1903, became a constant threat. The impact of the devaluation was so severe that the Mexican government subsidized the interest payments on railroad bonds and even passed a decree in 1903 allowing all the lines to increase their rates by 15 percent to cover their currency losses.[45]

In light of these factors, it was no wonder that the Mexican Central backed away from a conversion to fuel oil and remained skeptical of Doheny's claim that his Ebano wells could produce all the oil it needed. By September 1904, however, Pierce anticipated a surplus for the year and realized that he needed to complete his program of improvements before the first set of bonds reached maturity in 1907. This was the time to make the transition to oil.[46]

If Pierce needed to justify the decision to proceed cautiously along these lines, he had only to point out the experience of the Tehuantepec Railroad, a newly reconstructed railway owned jointly by the Mexican government and Weetman Pearson. In 1899, Pearson had won a contract to rebuild an existing two-hundred-mile-long railway across the Isthmus of Tehuantepec in conjunction with a harbor construction project at Coatzacoalcos. With that work underway, Pearson got interested in oil after an unplanned layover in Laredo, Texas, in April 1901. By chance, this was just a few weeks after the Spindletop gusher came in, and, catching oil fever along with the rest of the population, Pearson returned to Mexico a determined man. After acquiring oil properties on the Isthmus, Pearson set out to duplicate Doheny's recent success at Ebano by supplying the Tehuantepec engines with his own oil. The railroad ordered six oil-burning locomotives based on Pearson's assurance that he was certain to find an adequate supply of petroleum.[47]

Unfortunately, none of Pearson's wells on the Isthmus met his expectations and never approached the requirements of the Tehuantepec Railway. This set Pearson's oil company off on a spate of wildcatting across southern Mexico, but to no avail. Although the new engines were a great success, the oil had to be imported by tank steamer from Beaumont, and, by early 1905, Pearson thought he might have to seek out oil lands in Texas to fulfill his obligations to the Tehuantepec. Pearson's failure was a good object lesson for the Mexican Central, as it was considering making the conversion to fuel oil, but Doheny claimed to have the oil that his British counterpart lacked. Since he had proved the utility of the fuel on his own engines at Ebano, Doheny felt that the Mexican Central was being either overly cautious or deliberately evasive.[48]

In the meantime, Doheny hedged his own bets. All the major railroads in Mexico were testing his oil simultaneously: the Mexican Central, the Interoceanic, and the Mexican Railway, Ltd. Previously, the Mexican Railway Company had been importing coal briquettes from Wales, while the Interoceanic and the Mexican Central received almost all their fuel from coal fields in the United States. The Interoceanic had actually been experimenting with fuel oil since the fall of 1902, when officials requested 100 barrels of Ebano oil and tested it against a similar amount from Texas. Doheny's liaison with the railroad thought that "it [would] be easy to close a deal" if the tests proved satisfactory, but for some reason they were still experimenting two years later. The Mexican Central began its tests in 1903, although it was initially interested in using the oil for heating and rolling iron in its manufacturing plant.[49]

Curiously, the first engine tests were not made with fuel oil; instead, they were made with a combination of coal dust and asphalt, a mixture concocted by P. C. Smith of the Mexican Asphalt Paving Company. Because the Mexican Central's coal came from as far away as Philadelphia and Baltimore, it contained a lot of dust by the time it had been jostled all the way to Mexico. Smith's solution was simply to mix the coal dust with about ten percent asphalt to produce an excellent fuel that, unlike oil, did not require any modification of the burners or the fire box.[50]

Although Smith's idea was cheap and practical, it left the railroad dependent on imported coal. Unfortunately, the quality of Mexican coal was inferior and the cost of producing it prohibitive—a combination of factors, according to one mining historian, that literally "drove consumers to oil or imported fuel." But transporting coal from the United States or Great Britain introduced its own set of problems. The 70,000 tons that the Mexican Central imported from the Northeast every month left the railroad vulnerable to any number of hazards along the route, from traffic jams to labor strikes. Importing was also a major source of financial strain, since the company had to set aside a large number of cars to haul the coal and had to pay for it in American currency.[51]

And yet, the only thing worse than sticking with a bad situation would have been a desperate leap into a more precarious one, as the Tehuantepec's predicament showed. That railroad had survived because it was a short, two-hundred-mile line with only a handful of oil burners. The Mexican Central, on the other hand, was more than fifteen times as large, and an equivalent miscalculation could have been catastrophic. Doheny, of all people, knew the consequences of pressing for large oil contracts before he was ready to handle them, and, at one point during the summer of 1904, he admitted that the Mexican Petroleum Company was also unwilling to make any fuel oil contracts "until it is in a position to carry them out without fail."[52]

Up to that time, Doheny was producing a small but steady supply of oil. It was enough to get the asphalt business started and keep the storage tanks full, but nowhere near the thousands of barrels a day that the Mexican Central would require. Doheny made a huge step forward in April 1904, however, when the company drilled its first official gusher, which blew in at 1,500 barrels per day and gave him the proof he needed that there was an extensive reservoir of oil at Ebano. If nothing else, it at least impressed his stockholders, who tripled a request for $250,000 in bonds once the gusher had been flowing for two months.[53]

Doheny needed the money to dredge out an existing gully between Mexican Petroleum's railroad line at Ebano and the Pánuco River, some ten miles to the south. The new well actually sat in the middle of this gully and was vulnerable to periodic flooding. Doheny wanted to create a permanent canal, in part to protect the well, but also so that oil could be loaded directly onto barges and steam tugs and sent down the waterway to the river and out to the port of Tampico. A system like that would make the company completely self-sufficient. With additional storage facilities and a fleet of ocean tankers along the Gulf, Doheny believed, they would have "free access to the markets of the world."[54]

Apparently, it was at this point in January 1905, rather than earlier, that Doheny was perceived as a potential threat to the Waters-Pierce Oil Company. In fact, there was a great deal of speculation going on that an oil war was brewing between the two American companies over the gasoline market in Mexico. While it was true that Doheny could manufacture gasoline as a by-product of topping fuel oil and making asphalt, it was a small percentage of the final product. Nevertheless, to keep him from putting what he had on the market, Waters-Pierce lowered the price of gasoline for its industrial customers, mostly mining companies, who might be tempted to switch suppliers. One mine owner stated that a Waters-Pierce agent made repeated offers to lower his fuel bill if he would promise not to sign a contract with Doheny. The mine owner refused to be cornered in this fashion and was surprised to receive an unsolicited price cut anyway.[55]

Since Ebano fuel oil was usually taken straight from the well, however, a better alternative would be to tie up Doheny's oil with a contract to supply the Mexican Central as soon as possible. Perhaps that was one of the reasons, along with the economic factors discussed earlier, that the Mexican Central made its first real test of Ebano oil at precisely this time. In spite of his motivation, though, Pierce could not hurry along a review process that seemed to take forever. Doheny, at least, was running out of patience, as the Mexican Central conducted second and third trials on the oil between February and May 1905 and two other railroads pursued similar experiments.[56] Although the tests went fairly well, a lot of foot-dragging occurred behind the scenes, as the railroads negotiated the terms of their proposed contracts, and Doheny was uncharacteristically pessimistic in early May when he vented his frustration to the press:

> There is one great source of wealth down there as to which myself and associates have been sorely disappointed. I refer to fuel oil. There is absolutely no demand for it. The railroads won't have it except at a prohibitive rate, and they will not use it for power. For the last four years we have been producing and storing it, and haven't sold a barrel. A single well belonging to us has given forth half a million barrels in a year. There is enough belonging to us to supply the demand of the world, and yet it is about the most valueless stuff imaginable under existing conditions.[57]

Doheny's assertions to the contrary, the railroads still had legitimate concerns about the quality, if not the quantity, of the oil. For one thing, its high asphalt content made it harder to burn than either California or Texas fuel oil. For another, the Ebano oil gave off a tremendous amount of smoke. California oil had been a real improvement over coal because it was a clean-burning fuel. Mexican oil was just the opposite. This issue was an insurmountable problem for the Mexican Railway, because their passenger trains passed through a number of tunnels along heavy grades. Under such conditions, the smoke and gas thrown off by the oil burners could be deadly if a train got stuck in one of the tunnels. On flatter routes and on freight trains, in particular, the smoke was not a concern.[58]

There were also doubts about Doheny's claims that he could meet any demand. As it turned out, almost as soon as he committed himself to supply the Mexican Central, he revised his calculations and notified the other railways that he might not have enough oil to supply all three lines after all. In September 1906, he cut off negotiations with the Interoceanic Railway, forcing it, for the time being, to abandon efforts to convert to oil; in October, he did the same with the Mexican Railway. The latter company turned instead to Pearson and agreed to use the residue from his new refinery at

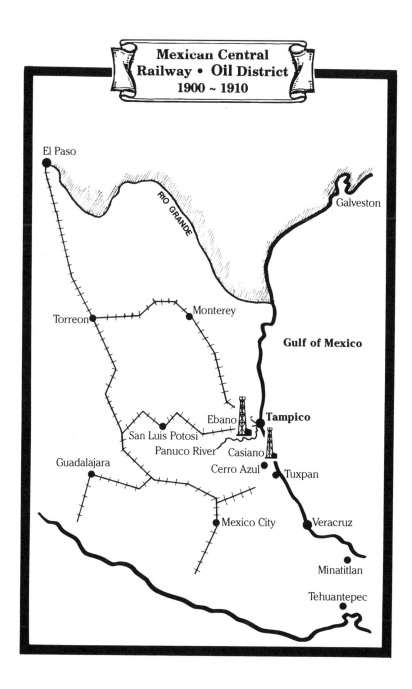

Mexican Central Railway • Oil District 1900 ~ 1910

El Paso

RIO GRANDE

Galveston

Torreon

Monterey

Gulf of Mexico

Ebano

Tampico

San Luis Potosi

Panuco River

Casiano

Guadalajara

Cerro Azul

Tuxpan

Mexico City

Veracruz

Minatitlan

Tehuantepec

Minatitlán, Veracruz, as fuel oil. This material burned more cleanly than did Ebano oil and proved an ideal fuel for the Mexican Railway. Curiously, the Tehuantepec Railroad continued to burn Texas oil, as part of a larger strategy to set aside all of Pearson's production for an assault on the refined oil market in Mexico.[59]

Doheny's hard-won contract with the Mexican Central was a fifteen-year agreement that called for approximately 45 million barrels of fuel oil and promised a 20 percent reduction in fuel costs from those of coal. At the time, Doheny could manage only 2,000 barrels per day, or about a quarter of what the railroad would require with all of its locomotives burning oil. But the Mexican Central planned to convert its engines in stages and counted on Doheny to increase production proportionately. Starting with twelve operating oil burners in December 1905, the railroad's officials hoped to convert an average of seven locomotives per month over the next two years, to reach a total of 170 by October 1907. After that, they would convert the remainder of their 200 to 300 coal engines at the rate of a dozen a month until they were finished. From 1908 to 1910, the Mexican Central demanded an average of about 6,250 barrels a day, or enough for more than 200 engines using 30 barrels a day. Even at this rate, however, the railway ran into supply trouble and had to return to using coal on some of the lines.[60]

Still, as promised, the Mexican Central posted significant savings on fuel costs and operating expenses. Initially, the railroad reported an increase in maintenance repairs per locomotive—from $1,862 in 1905 to $2,360 in 1906—attributed to the cost of converting them to burn oil. At the same time, the company reported a fuel savings of approximately $4,200 per year for each oil-burning engine. Since fuel costs made up about a third of the railroad's operating expenses, this was a major improvement. The difference between using oil and using coal was clearly shown in a detailed report by the *Wall Street Journal*, comparing the 1907 financial statements of the Mexican Central and the National Railroad of Mexico. According to this analysis, the Mexican Central reported a 10 percent increase in gross earnings and a 16 percent reduction in fuel costs. The National, on the other hand, saw a 13 percent gain in gross income, negated by a 26 percent increase in the cost of coal. So, although Doheny could not meet all of their expectations, the leaders of the Mexican Central had little to complain about with respect to the benefits of using Ebano fuel oil.[61]

Another beneficiary of this improved efficiency was the Mexican government, which by this time was a majority shareholder in the largest of the nation's railroads. As part of a plan initiated by Finance Minister Limantour in 1902 to offset financial problems and the threat of bankruptcy for the major railroads, the government quietly purchased railroad stocks until it achieved a dominant position on the boards of the major lines. Then, beginning with the National Railroad and the Interoceanic, the railways were merged under government supervision. In 1906, the government formed the National Railroads of Mexico Company, which held an option on Mexican Central stock and integrated it into the national system a few years later.[62]

Given that the Mexican government's objective was to improve the economic performance of the railroads, Doheny's fuel oil contracts were an essential element of success. Eventually, he would supply oil for trains running on 85 percent of the railway mileage in Mexico. Years later, when he was accused of monopolizing the profits from Mexican oil, Doheny cited the benefits of his fuel oil contract with the government as evidence to the contrary.[63]

It was precisely the potential for substantial profits, however, that led the Díaz government to briefly consider a plan to take control of the coal and petroleum industries along with the railroads. Beginning in August 1905, at the same time the government was buying its way into the railway business, a committee of Mexican lawyers and engineers submitted such a proposal to the minister of development. At issue was Article 10 of the 1884 mining code, which stated that coal mines and oil wells were the exclusive property of the owners of the surface land. The committee wanted to amend the law to allow for expropriation by the government under certain circumstances. In particular, they sought to regain control of Mexico's petroleum resources by defining oil production as a public utility. Thereafter, the property owners would be compensated based on a percentage of the value of the oil extracted from their land but would lose direct control of the oil itself.[64]

Questions over the legal merits of this proposal inspired a series of debates in the fall of 1905 among the best lawyers in the nation. One of the things that was clear from the start was that the argument over oil did not necessarily arise from the fear that foreigners would steal away the nation's natural resources. More worrisome from the government's perspective was that "the owners of the soil [had] not been displaying sufficient energy in exploring for such deposits or in working them when discovered." To the surprise of many observers, however, the legal experts upheld the existing law and did not sanction any move toward nationalization. While this seemed like a definitive answer to the question of subsoil

Doheny on Horseback, at Ebano, ca. 1905. Archival Center, Archdiocese of Los Angeles.

rights, the debate turned out to be a prelude to a more determined attack on foreign ownership during the revolution.[65]

Nonetheless, petroleum's growing importance as a public utility was most evident in the area of manufactured gas. Once again, Ebano oil could be run straight from the wells into the fire boxes of locomotives. But when it was topped, it yielded a small percentage of gasoline and kerosene, and, when further refined into asphalt, Ebano oil furnished another 20 to 30 percent in gas oil. Having banked a good deal of his future success on the asphalt business, Doheny took the next step in deciding to manufacture city gas from the residue. Consequently, in the fall of 1906, Doheny obtained a concession from the Mexican government allowing him to manufacture and distribute crude-oil gas in Mexico City and its suburbs. Next, he organized the Mexican National Gas Company to carry out those plans and brought in an experienced manager from Los Angeles, expecting to have the Mexico City operation running within a year. Instead, it was almost three years from the date of the contract before he began in earnest.[66]

The delay was related mostly to the large capital expenditures necessary to construct the plant and install gas lines and meters but also to a change in management along the way. When he was finally ready to move ahead in the spring of 1909, Doheny purchased the land for the gas plant and then went to New York in July to buy $480,000 worth of gas supplies, including over thirty miles of gas pipe, oil tanks, gas meters, and appliances. At this point, Doheny still seemed confident that gas would be running through the lines by the end of the year, but, as one delay led to another, the company risked losing the goodwill of the residents who, according to a local reporter, were "impatiently waiting for the time when [they] will be connected up to the supply." In May 1910, the company promised to have the job completed within a matter of days, and Doheny made his fifty-second trip to Mexico to supervise the long-awaited connection of the gas lines. However, no sooner was the company in business than it was overwhelmed by demand, and Doheny once again found himself unable to fully support a market he had created.[67]

But Doheny had been hard at work on a permanent solution to his oil supply problem when he opened up a new petroleum zone in the Huasteca, the Indian name for the border area between the states of Veracruz, Tamaulipas, and San Luis Potosi, which would be known as the "golden lane" in later years. Doheny and Canfield had actually prospected there in 1900 and were extremely impressed with the number of exudes and the amount of visible oil. Although the property was unavailable initially, it was subsequently leased to the Barber Asphalt Company as a potential source of paving material; Doheny was able to acquire it in 1906, when Barber sold the Huasteca leases to him after having taken possession of a large asphalt deposit in Venezuela the previous year.[68]

Like many places in Mexico, natural asphalt could be dug out of the surface in the Huasteca as a result of constant oil seepage. Unlike the Ebano product, however, the oil was a good deal lighter and offered excellent prospects for further refining. For this reason alone, Doheny recalled, "We made up our minds that we wanted that property, wanted it badly, and wanted it right away." Once he had it, Doheny incorporated the Huasteca Petroleum Company on February 12, 1907, to develop the area. Four days later he organized a new holding company, the Mexican Petroleum Company, Ltd., of Delaware, to finance the various components of his oil business in Mexico.[69]

These new arrangements were necessary because developing the Huasteca property required another massive capital investment. Where the wells at Ebano had been found within easy reach of the Mexican Central line, the initial Huasteca drilling site was twenty to thirty miles inland from the Gulf and required a combination of canoe trip and horseback journey to get through the jungle. Setting up drilling machinery was an incredible undertaking in itself. The best way to get the oil out was to construct a seventy-mile-long pipeline that ran from the wells to Tampico. Added to that, when Harold Walker negotiated the government concession to develop the Huasteca properties in 1908, he obligated the company to construct another pipeline to Mexico City, about 190 miles to the southwest. Walker agreed to the Mexico City pipeline as part of the plan to provide oil for the gas company. But many engineers, including some on Doheny's staff, thought that pumping heavy crude oil onto Mexico's central mesa was impossible; in any case, it could never be a cost-effective operation. Doheny disagreed, citing the successful California pipeline that ran from Bakersfield to San Francisco. Although that line climbed just 800 feet, Doheny believed it was only a matter of adding enough pumping stations to lift the oil 8,000 feet onto the mesa. Extrapolating from California, he calculated that it would take five to seven percent of the oil moving through the line to operate the necessary machinery.[70]

In December 1910, the Huasteca Petroleum Company allocated $3 million for the Mexico City pipeline and planned to have oil flowing as soon as possible. They intended to deliver a minimum of 20,000 barrels a day to be used by the Mexican National Gas plant as well as a large number of other crude oil consumers. The pipeline was also needed to relieve congestion on the Mexican railways, which prevented them from carrying any more than half of the oil traffic. Then, just as these plans got underway, the company gave up on the project without offering an explanation. Perhaps the idea was as impractical as its critics claimed, but the work might also have been considered too dangerous to attempt during the opening disturbances of the coming revolution.[71]

Meanwhile, work on the shorter pipeline from the new field to Tampico had gone ahead out of absolute necessity. While Doheny had been putting together the plans for his first well at Casiano, the Pearson company started drilling at Dos Bocas, less than fifteen miles to the north. Then, in July 1908, the Dos Bocas well came in so violently that it caught the drilling crew off guard. As the first jets of gas and oil shot from the well, they were ignited by the flame under the steam boilers nearby. Instantly, the well became a raging inferno, and it burned for the next two months with such ferocity that some said a person could read a newspaper by its light seventeen miles away. When the well finally burned itself out, it was still churning up 25,000 barrels a day of hot oil and saltwater into what was described as "an immense cauldron in which the water and oil boils up in great wave-like upheavals." Supposedly, Pearson lost several million barrels of oil in the catastrophe, although many people believed the well had been mostly gas. In either case, Dos Bocas put the Mexican oil fields on the map and alerted Doheny to the danger that lay ahead.[72]

Clearly, he was not going to make the same mistake. But if he drilled a well even close to the size of Dos Bocas, which he fully expected to do, it was certain to overrun any storage system in a matter of days. Still, because he needed the oil as soon as he could get it, Doheny gambled a bit by constructing a pipeline and storage system at the same time that the drilling crews started a number of wells. By the end of 1909, he had five drilling rigs in operation and two completed wells whose combined production of 1,200 barrels a day went into one 55,000-barrel tank. At that point, all the sections of eight-inch pipe needed to complete the line had been distributed along the route, but only about ten miles of it were ready for oil. This initial stretch was crucial, though, since it ran from the wells toward the edge of the Tamiahua Lagoon, an inlet from the Gulf, where the company had three steel barges ready to load. Two more 55,000-barrel tanks were also under construction at the northern end of the pipeline in Tampico, with additional tanks to be added to the three pumping stations along the route.[73]

With these preparations underway, the company drilled in its first big well, Casiano No. 6, on July 26, 1910. The well started producing at 8,000 barrels a day and reached 14,000 barrels two weeks later when it was completely shut in. The two 55,000-barrel tanks were full, and the pipeline was still a month from being finished, despite some 2,000 workers being pressed to the limit. Then, on September 11, the crew on Casiano No. 7 struck oil. This second gusher came in suddenly at 60,000 barrels per day before the crew had cemented the well casing in place. When Herbert Wylie, by now the Huasteca superintendent, tried to close in the well, the internal pressure lifted the casing off the bottom, allowing the oil to escape and work its way into seepages around the well, which created oil springs as far as 300 feet away from the derrick that produced 3,000 barrels a day on their own. Fearing another Dos Bocas blowout, Wylie opened the gate valve as much as necessary to stabilize the well, which left them with a flow of 25,000 barrels a day. By September 17, with the completion of the pipeline, a potential disaster had been averted. Nevertheless, the company had to shut in production on all of the other wells, stop drilling, and devote all its resources to handling the oil from Casiano No. 7.[74]

Even at a reduced flow, the big well filled the Huasteca pipeline to capacity from the start, forcing the company to begin a parallel line almost immediately to double the volume. In the meantime, Doheny needed to move the oil as quickly as possible. He began by signing a larger contract with the Waters-Pierce refinery which took a million barrels of oil out of storage at once and another 1.5 million over an extended period. Doheny also hoped that his sales and gas operations in Mexico City would draw off even more oil, but he was still left with a large and growing surplus.[75]

Given the market constraints in Mexico, American oil producers had been anticipating the inevitable overflow of Mexican crude across the border for several years. At the time, there was no specific duty on Mexican oil except for a countervailing tax against Mexico's import fees. With increasing production, American producers believed that President Díaz was planning to remove import duties on foreign oil as a way to force the United States to respond in kind. As one fearful oilman put it, "There is a flood of oil in Mexico, enough to fill the Rio Grande, ready to be poured into this country when that duty is repealed. It is dirty oil but it is dangerous." When the United States Congress deliberated tariff reform in March 1909, the independent oil producers of Ohio went so far as to send a delegation to Washington to lobby against any possibility of Mexican oil being put on the free list. In fact, the independents wanted the United States to place a formal duty on Mexican oil as "the most dangerous threat" to the small producer in America.[76]

In response to the outcry against Mexican oil, Doheny wrote a letter to the Senate stating that there was nothing to fear since he was still struggling to meet his contract obligations. At the time, he was producing 7,000 barrels a day, while he owed the National Railways of Mexico 10,000 and the other producers combined did not make up another 1,500. Under those circumstances, the only crisis was in Mexico—not in the United States. Besides, Doheny continued, "if we should, fortunately, be able to produce more than they [the railroads] need or take, it might be sold to the U.S. in the east for road-working purposes, [but] it certainly cannot be imported into the U.S. for refining purposes." Ironically, Doheny and his fellow producers were appealing to the Mexican Congress to adjust the duty on American oil to keep Texas oil from flooding south.[77]

To settle the argument, the Taft administration sent its chief geologist, C. W. Hayes, to survey the situation. After interviewing Doheny and Pearson and a taking personal tour of the oilfields, Hayes concluded that, while Mexican oil production was bound to increase, "the quality is such that it cannot compete under present conditions in the markets of the United States or Europe." Furthermore, with almost all of the Mexican oil in the hands of large producers and under contract for years to come, there was little chance for small operators to move in and upset the market, as usually happened in the United States. Relying on Hayes's evaluation, the Senate voted down the proposed duty on Mexican oil in June 1909. But the advent of the gusher era in Mexico the next year disproved most of Hayes's assumptions and generated new waves of fear from American producers.[78]

However, Hayes was right to see that the Mexican oil industry would remain in the hands of a few very large companies for the foreseeable future. It was certainly obvious that Doheny's operations literally defined the situation from 1901 to 1910, and there was no reason to believe that this would change any time soon. In the first decade of oil production, Doheny's Ebano wells had accounted for 10.5 million barrels out of a total of 12,290,775, or roughly 85 percent of the national output. The remainder came from the only other companies of any consequence—Weetman Pearson's oil company and the Oil Fields of Mexico, a company started by another Englishman, Percy Furber. Between them, they averaged 700 barrels a day from 1904 to 1910.[79]

If Doheny's dominant position was not enough to discourage imitators, the early experiences of the other two companies revealed the obstacles awaiting anyone foolish enough to try and come in behind them. Pearson's story, in particular, was an object lesson on how to lose a fortune in dry holes and disappointing wells. "It is to be doubted," one oil reporter wrote in February 1910, "if any corporation in the long and romantic history of the oil trade had expended such enormous sums of money to so little advantage as have the Pearson interests in the Republic of Mexico."[80]

Having tried and failed to locate oil in Tehuantepec in the early 1900s and having lost Dos Bocas in 1908, Pearson, like Henry Pierce, was still getting most of his oil from Texas. Perhaps for that reason, he decided to challenge Waters-Pierce for a share of the refined oil market in Mexico. At first, to avoid a fight, Pearson hoped to divide the trade by mutual agreement, but the two could not agree on a percentage split; supposedly, Pearson wanted half the market and Pierce insisted on two-thirds. The Englishman retaliated with a direct assault on the market, which touched off an oil war between the two companies. In the heat of the battle, Pearson tried to force a merger with Waters-Pierce but failed in the attempt. At that point, as one reporter noted, "there is little pretense on either side that the war is not one of extermination, with no mercy extended or expected."[81]

Ultimately, Pearson gained the upper hand when he created a new Mexican company known as the Compania Mexicana de Petroleo "El Aguila," S.A. (a Mexican company dealing in the Eagle brand of refined oil). El

Aguila, or the Mexican Eagle, assumed control of Pearson's holdings north of Veracruz and was devoted exclusively to serving the domestic market with native crude and refined oil. Having thus reconstituted itself as a domestic company, El Aguila began to attack the "foreign" character of the opposition. It also strengthened its direct ties to the Mexican government through its directors, including Governor Enrique C. Creel of Chihuahua, Governor Guillermo Landa y Escandon of the Federal District, and Colonel Porfirio Díaz Jr. Next, the company inundated the public with effective, and sometimes shameless, appeals to native sentiment: "Down with the Trusts," went one advertisement, pointing out Pierce's ties to Standard Oil. "Even the Pope has issued orders that only Aguila Oil shall be used," stated another.[82]

With approximately 20 percent of the retail market in hand by 1909, Pearson was still importing oil from Texas and losing money on every barrel. Failing in his efforts to secure oil in the Huasteca, Pearson turned to Percy Furber, whose Oil Fields of Mexico Company seemed to be having better luck producing oil near Papantla, Veracruz. Furber had started out in 1900, at the same time as Doheny, after taking control of a company associated with Cecil Rhodes. Several years of legal battles kept him from drilling until 1904. Unfortunately, while Furber had a number of active wells, he had no large producers. Nonetheless, Pearson was either so convinced of the worth of Furber's property or so hard up for oil that he formed a partnership with the Oil Fields of Mexico Company in 1909. In exchange for all of Furber's output, Pearson agreed to complete a railway and pipeline from the wells to the coast at Tuxpan, which still left him loading his oil onto boats and shipping it down the coat to his Minatitlán refinery. As with all his experiences to this point, however, Pearson's run of bad luck continued, and the Furber wells proved to be of little value.[83]

Throughout this process, Doheny played no active role in the battle between the retail companies beyond his limited contract with the Waters-Pierce Refinery. While there had been some early talk about a possible three-way contest for the local petroleum market, Doheny had no plans to move further into the refining end of the business. But given his complaints about Pearson's relationship with the Díaz administration, he could not help being drawn into the contest when he rejected an offer to sell oil to El Aguila.[84]

In the end, Pearson's position changed overnight when, in December 1910, he brought in the biggest Mexican gusher to date. The well, known as Potrero del Llano No. 4, sat on a separate tract of land between two of Doheny's properties, about twenty-five miles south of Casiano. Once again, the well ran wild for almost two months before the company brought it under control at an estimated flow of 100,000 barrels per day. Now more than ever, this monster well reflected the complete transformation of the Mexican oil industry. In the nine years from 1901 to 1910, Doheny had produced over 10 million barrels from his wells at Ebano. In the fifteen months from September 1910 to December 1911, Casiano No. 7 produced 10.5 million barrels while flowing at less than half its potential. If opened all the way, Pearson's Potrero No. 4 could produce the same amount in three months. By 1911, Mexico was drowning in oil. Henceforth, the full development of the Mexican oil industry would depend on the ability of the major companies to transport their growing production to as many customers as could be found, no matter how far away (see Appendix A).[85]

In looking back over the period from 1900 to 1910, which formed the introductory phase of the Mexican petroleum industry, it is clear that Doheny was primarily responsible for the direction the industry would take. As a result of his past experience in California and his financial backing, Doheny succeeded where others feared to try. In reviewing his work with Canfield, Doheny noted that:

> Our lifetime spent at prospecting and our experience in developing oil in the vicinity of the exudes in California, constituted in us the proper frame of mind to fully appreciate the evidences of petroleum which existed in Mexico, and which undoubtedly had been seen by thousands of natives and perhaps a great many intelligent Mexicans and foreigners, who, however, by reason of not having had the proper experience which we had, were not sufficiently impressed to undertake the task of developing oil there, which task did not prove light, even though we went into it with health, strength, enthusiasm, and practically unlimited cash resources, and a great belief in our own judgment and good fortune.[86]

Unquestionably, the "practically unlimited cash resources" were crucial to success and allowed Doheny to control the fuel oil trade in Mexico, after negotiating the nearly insurmountable barriers to entry. By both necessity and design, Doheny developed the Mexican Petroleum Company on a massive scale when he purchased more than 500,000 acres of oil land and invested over $4 million at Ebano in advance of the market. If he had maintained his primary operation in California, instead, and only entered Mexico on a limited basis, the development of the Mexican oil industry might have looked more like the chaotic scramble that took place in the flush fields of both California and Texas. But it was Doheny's persistent attempt to distance himself from the Spindletop phenomenon that set the ground rules for entering the Mexican market. It was certainly true, as one American oil reporter observed, that "the individual with a $3,000 bank roll and a 40-acre lease would be a piker in Mexico."[87]

Compared to Doheny's specialized knowledge and established financial backing, Weetman Pearson's perseverance and personal wealth served him well. With Doheny dominating the fuel oil trade through native production and Henry Pierce controlling the sale of refined products using imported oil, Pearson eventually adopted a combined strategy of using native production for the refined oil market. Pearson's decision, like Doheny's, evolved as much from the type of oil he found as from any predetermined plan. Had Pearson initially located an extremely heavy-grade fuel oil similar to that from the Ebano wells, he might have used his considerable influence with the Díaz government to challenge Doheny's position as the chief supplier for the National Railways. Instead, he found a higher-quality oil at Tehuantepec which could be refined in competition with Pierce's imported product. Overall, these three options comprised the only possible marketing strategies for Mexican oil during this introductory phase of the industry.

The irony was that, once the Casiano and Potrero gushers came in, any strategy aimed at dominating a sector of the domestic market was totally inconsequential. The story of the growth of the Mexican oil industry after 1911 is one that centers on the direct competition between Doheny and Pearson to move their oil, crude or refined, into an international arena. As Doheny concluded in June 1911, "Mexico has reached its market limit . . . We must go abroad to sell."[88]

4 RETURN TO CALIFORNIA, 1908–1912

With the Mexican Petroleum Company operating at a steady profit by 1908, Doheny turned his attention once again to the California oil industry. Despite a six-year absence, Doheny's reputation as one of the state's oil pioneers and his intimate knowledge of the region's petroleum fields enabled him to quickly re-establish his position as a powerful independent producer. There were also new legends about his exploits in Mexico which made him seem almost invincible and his success in California the second time around happened so quickly that it was almost as though he had never been gone. The reasons why this was so reflect the elements that transformed Doheny from a good oilman into a masterful executive. Having tested his organizational skills in Mexico, Doheny returned to California with the confidence that he could prevail under any conditions.

His development as a businessman progressed incrementally from the moment he and Canfield dug out their discovery well in Los Angeles in 1892. Although he expanded rapidly on his own, it was his work for the Santa Fe, as oil consultant and manager of their oil properties, that first put him in control of a complex operation. When he went to Mexico in 1900, Doheny scouted out the initial drilling locations like the veteran prospector that he was, but he had to think on a much larger scale than ever before. With those properties in hand, Doheny turned over the oil camp to his managers, A. P. Maginnis and Herbert Wylie, and assumed the enormous responsibilities of securing capital and establishing a market for Mexican oil. After he sold out his California company to the Santa Fe in 1902, Doheny divided his time between bimonthly trips to Mexico and promotional activities which took him from Los Angeles to New York. All the while, the operations of the Mexican Petroleum Company expanded under a growing contingent of able subordinates. This process accelerated dramatically when he returned to California, requiring Doheny to direct the affairs of two large organizations, one domestic, and the other foreign.

Doheny's path to the top rank of American business leaders began in the late nineteenth-century—an environment that offered enormous monetary rewards for hard work and practical experience. But as the economic landscape changed in the early 1900s, many individuals with backgrounds and educations similar to Doheny's failed to keep up with the fast-paced world of new management and organizational techniques. Although Doheny never relinquished a certain level of autocratic control which typified the former era, he had to develop a modern corporate structure to stay competitive in the new age. Since there are no reflections of his own to guide us, we have no clear answer as to how Doheny made this transformation.

Certainly, he learned a great deal from all of his associates over the years, but there were also a few key alliances that account for Doheny's ability to adapt to the demands of modern business. His long-standing relationship with the officers of the Santa Fe Railway, for example, provided him with a number of excellent tutors. In particular, there appears to be a striking similarity between Doheny's cautious, but progressive, policies and those of E. P. Ripley, the president of the Santa Fe. Because there is no evidence of a personal tie between the two men, Ripley's influence is a matter of conjecture. But, even watching from a distance, Doheny would have been introduced to the fundamentals of big business from a man with an unassailable reputation as an executive. Before Ripley assumed control of the Santa Fe in 1896, it had fallen into disrepute, and according to one railroad historian, Ripley "turned a bankrupt ruin into one of the most profitable carriers in the nation through careful, controlled expansion, rapid modernization, and a concern for economic development of its territory."[1]

Doheny's work had been part of this process for its first five years and it was for the purpose of modernizing the railroad that he encountered Ripley in 1897. After having supplied fuel oil to the Southern California Railway for several years, Doheny's position as the Santa Fe's oil expert drew him into that corporate environment and made the rest of his career possible. In a 1905 interview Doheny acknowledged this relationship, without mentioning Ripley by name, when he noted the critical role of the railroad's investments in oil lands and companies in advance of the other roads. Without a doubt, Doheny asserted, the Santa Fe had been the "father of the fuel oil business" in California. And it was just as true that Doheny succeeded in Mexico by taking that railroad network with him.[2]

Another important experience was Doheny's tenure as a director of the Union Oil Company from 1902 to 1904, a position that gave him a closer look at the inner workings of one of the most well-established operations in the state. It was also no small token of his stature among California oilmen that Union Oil's board of directors sought his advice in the first place and contravened an internal policy against selling any treasury stock to get his assent. In doing so, Union's chairman, Lyman Stewart, held no illusions about acquiring the services of a powerful and ambitious individual like Doheny. Stewart did not presume to wield any influence over him and recognized that Doheny "was not the type of character to be dominated or dictated to." Nevertheless, Stewart shouldered the responsibility for inviting Doheny into his company because he "wanted the benefit of his counsel." Doheny must have appreciated the gesture, since his only recorded contribution was a resolution he put forth to raise Stewart's salary as president to $1,000 a month. The parsimonious Stewart objected to the move and asked for $3,000 a year. Doheny persuaded the board to approve the larger sum anyway.[3]

Doubtless, all of these influences contributed to Doheny's ability to establish his fuel oil business in Mexico and to his desire to return to California. Notwithstanding the importance of these corporate sources, Doheny also succeeded because he had extremely capable partners, beginning with Charles Canfield. While Doheny and Canfield went together to Mexico in 1900, Canfield continued to build up his California interests after Doheny sold out to the Santa Fe Railroad in 1902. Over the next five years, Canfield made periodic trips to Ebano and New York on behalf of the Mexican Petroleum Company, but he concentrated his efforts in the Kern River and Coalinga oil fields, where he earned a reputation similar to Doheny's as one of the most capable independent producers in the state. Canfield also honed his executive abilities through close contact with the top officials of both the Santa Fe and the Southern Pacific railroads. Although Canfield was in no way Doheny's proxy during this period, he charted the way for his partner's eventual return.

For that reason, and because they reveal several heretofore neglected trends in the historical development of the California oil industry, Canfield's activities are worth examining in some detail. Of particular note were his continuous efforts to establish a united front among the independent producers in response to the flush field conditions after 1900, a situation that mirrored the one that had almost ruined the Los Angeles district five years earlier. By 1902, massive overproduction and cutthroat competition in Kern River sent the price of oil below twenty cents a barrel. At the beginning of this downward trend in the summer of 1900, Doheny and Canfield joined the first attempt to create an independent organization to control the field and protect the local producers from the growing menace of the Standard Oil Company.[4]

There had been unsubstantiated rumors in the 1890s that the oil trust was lurking in the shadows of the Los Angeles oil district hoping to capture the local market, but nothing had come of it. Five years later, there were better reasons to believe the threat in Kern River. In fact, in 1900, Standard Oil acquired the Pacific Coast Oil Company as its official California subsidiary and, consequently, was in the market for crude oil across the state. Moreover, a Standard Oil agent had been prowling around Bakersfield at the same time that the local producers were hashing out the details of a cooperative plan. At a crucial moment in the negotiations, the agent announced that Standard planned to step into the picture, buy up the surplus oil, and put it into storage. The agent literally scoffed at the puny efforts of the local oilmen to band together in the face of the threat. He claimed that the group would "go to pieces" in a matter of weeks, noting that the oil trust "had gone up against cooperative societies before and vanquished them." The Standard Oil Company, he boasted, "had met fraternal bodies, but had never met defeat."[5]

Many small producers naturally reacted to this challenge with resignation, but there were others who believed that they could not only learn from past mistakes but take some lessons from the tactics of the great monopoly, itself. "John D. Rockefeller's brains cannot be concealed," one stalwart noted, "and the public will surely take advantage of them." Neither Canfield nor Doheny, however, seemed the least bit concerned with Standard Oil. Canfield took the heretical view that the trust ought to be encouraged to come in and set up the storage and pipeline facilities necessary to stabilize the situation. Let them "build the tanks, lay the pipe, and find the market," Canfield thought, while the independents furnished the oil.[6]

In reality, Standard Oil was in no better position to control the California market than any other large company, and the belief in its monopoly power came from assumptions that the oil business on the West Coast mirrored that of the rest of the nation. Actually, for much of the early 1900s, the state's petroleum industry remained an isolated market revolving around the sale of heavy fuel oil instead of refined products. Standard Oil was a latecomer to this region, with little opportunity and no inclination to produce oil for itself. And Standard's national strategy of dominating the refined oil trade emphasized the weakest segment of the California industry. Although the Standard Oil Company of California, formed in 1906, would eventually catch up over the years and expand to gigantic proportions, the initial decision to hold back from acquiring oil lands and entering production cost it a significant share of the market.[7]

In 1905, however, prompted by Theodore Roosevelt's "trust-busting" campaign and Ida Tarbell's recent exposé of Rockefeller's empire, the Bureau of Corporations went hunting for Standard Oil on the West Coast. When asked about the situation by federal investigators, Canfield explained the unique characteristics of the California market which prevented Standard Oil from wielding its traditional level of power. No corporation, Canfield believed, could really control the local industry:

> There are too many fields easy of access to market that can be developed by individuals every day. There are thousands of them in the state today which can be opened up and every one of them are a menace to the market and you can't stop them. The water ways belong to everybody, and many of those fields are right adjacent to tidewater. Every man that has a piece of land with oil on it can drill a well, as they have been doing throughout the state. I think there are easily a hundred operators who are ready to sell oil on the market, and people are going to buy oil where they can get it cheapest.[8]

Nothing made that situation more evident than the dismal performance of the initial Kern River cooperative, formed in September 1900. Known as the Producers' Oil, Storage and Transportation Company, this organization supposedly had commitments to handle three-fourths of the oil from the field. Unfortunately, fear and self-interest remained the bane of any attempt to stabilize the market, and the combined effect of increased production, falling prices, and rampant speculation began eroding the level of trust within the organization from the start. Although Doheny participated in the planning stages of the cooperative, his work in Mexico dominated his attention, and he was not an active member. Canfield, who was president of the company, was also occupied on several fronts, and nothing much came of the attempt to organize.[9]

Then, with the local situation almost out of control by the summer and fall of 1901, five large independents, including the Canfield Oil Company, merged to form the Associated Oil Company, which subsequently took in dozens of smaller operators. Canfield was also the first president of the Associated and recalled that it was only after running the price of oil down to fifteen cents a barrel that the producers took this step. Short of that,

Canfield believed, "half of us would have been bankrupt." Instead, the Associated acquired the oil properties and contracts of its members and attempted to regulate production accordingly. This stabilized the market to a degree and provided enough oil for the new company to secure a fuel oil contract with the Southern Pacific Railroad. Soon thereafter, Canfield also brought in the Chanslor-Canfield Midway Oil Company, which had a contract to supply oil for the Santa Fe.[10]

By heading up the Associated Oil Company, Canfield took his place within the inner circle of businessmen who controlled the development of the San Joaquin Valley, and he helped establish one of the major components of the oil industry in California. Doheny, on the other hand, disappeared from the scene entirely once he sold the Petroleum Development Company to the Santa Fe in 1902. The irony of Canfield's position was that, through its role as the major supplier of oil to the major railways, the Associated Oil Company became as powerful in reality as Standard Oil had been in the imagination of the independent producers. While Associated Oil never monopolized the West Coast petroleum market, it controlled about 70 percent of the fuel oil business in these early years and was able to dictate terms to the small producers who joined and punish those who refused.[11]

Along the way, Canfield found himself caught between the Southern Pacific and the Santa Fe as they fought to control the production and transportation of fuel oil. And with both railroads purchasing oil lands and forming production companies of their own, the Associated's position was never secure. In 1903, for instance, a dispute over shipping charges between the oil company and the Southern Pacific cost Associated Oil a measure of control over its own operations. Believing that the railroad charged exorbitant rates to ship oil from Kern River to the coast, the Associated threatened to build its own pipeline between Bakersfield and San Francisco. In response, E. H. Harriman, the new head of the Southern Pacific, negotiated a long-term contract with the oil company in exchange for approximately forty percent of its stock. Harriman paid double the market price for his shares and received a contract for 10 million barrels of oil at twenty-five cents a barrel. Harriman managed to stop the oil company's rebellion, but, in doing so, he upset the balance between the two railways.[12]

When Harriman assumed control of the Southern Pacific in 1901, he started to modernize the road and streamline its finances in the same way Ripley had reorganized the Santa Fe. Both efforts naturally included a growing interest in petroleum. From the start, the Southern Pacific had an advantage with its large holdings of public land in California which cut across the newly opened petroleum district. Colis Huntington had sold off a good deal of this in the 1890s, but Harriman knew enough to maintain control of strategic oil properties. The Southern Pacific also formed the Kern Trading & Oil Company to produce fuel oil in addition to its contract with Associated Oil.[13]

These moves further strained the relationship between Harriman and Ripley over the expansion of their western lines. But given the existing level of tension, Harriman hoped to avoid a conflict over oil resources which could be mutually harmful. Before he purchased his Associated stock, for instance, he tried to assure Ripley that he wanted the oil shares as a wedge to keep the Associated directors in line, not as a lever to squeeze the Santa Fe out of the picture. In fact, Harriman offered Ripley a chance for the Santa Fe to join him as a one-third partner in the stock purchase. Ripley was not interested at the moment and said he would need a one-half share, in any case, but he left the door open for further negotiations. Then, when Harriman went ahead on his own, Ripley started to worry. More threatening was Harriman's silent campaign to purchase small amounts of Santa Fe stock in his own name. Since Harriman's tactics in gobbling up competitors were notorious, Ripley had to respond.[14]

With this turn of events, Ripley believed that a significant portion of the Santa Fe's oil supply had been put at risk and that his shipping contract with the Associated, which generated over $1 million a year in revenues, was in jeopardy as well. Apparently, Harriman was not scheming for any particular advantage in this case, but Ripley had to be sure that he had an impregnable supply of oil. At first, Ripley contemplated a rate war with Harriman to divert traffic away from the Southern Pacific, but he decided instead to attack the oil issue head on. Specifically, Ripley wanted to purchase an oil reserve large enough to break the market if Harriman moved against the Santa Fe. "If we had a surplus of oil which could be put into the market," Ripley believed, "we would then have both the oil and the transportation, and would be in a position to demand our share of the business upon threat of making the business worthless."[15]

Ostensibly, the Santa Fe purchased Doheny's old company for precisely this sort of contingency. But by 1904, the Petroleum Development Company's wells at Bakersfield were being invaded by water. The situation was not irretrievable, but it required recasing the wells, which drastically reduced the company's output, forcing it into the market to purchase oil to make good on contract obligations. Doheny had initially estimated that the company's property contained 100 million barrels of recoverable oil, and the Santa Fe had expected to draw down that supply at one million barrels per year. Now, after correcting for the presence of water, the rail-road had to cut its expectations by half.[16]

To shore up his position, Ripley negotiated a separate deal with Can-field, outside the purview of the Associated Oil Company, for the Santa Fe to purchase half of the Chanslor-Canfield Midway Oil Company's undevel-oped property in the Midway field. In this way, Ripley would have access to prospective oil lands potentially more productive than all of the prop-erty the Associated had under its control. Canfield thought the Midway property contained at least 500 million barrels. Having learned its lesson with Doheny, however, the Santa Fe lowered its expectations by more than half, estimating that there were about 200 million barrels in the ground, 120 million of which would be recoverable. This was enough to meet their needs for many years to come. And, as Ripley concluded, it "put into our hands a weapon which the other side cannot afford to trifle with."[17]

With his strategy set, Ripley then threatened to open up the field on his own if he did not receive satisfactory treatment from the Associated Oil Company. In return for abandoning these plans, the Santa Fe obtained a five-year contract for oil at twenty-five cents a barrel and a guarantee that its shipping arrangements with the oil company would continue as before. Although Ripley's primary objective in gaining control of the Mid-way property had been to strengthen his hand against the combined threat from the Associated and the Southern Pacific, he also saw it as a way to secure the field against an invasion by the smaller independents. He thought the Santa Fe's strong presence in the field would be "a good thing for everyone concerned and a step in the direction of getting the business into a comparatively small number of hands." And he had no doubt that these undeveloped lands could easily become a "thorn in the flesh of the railroads as well as the Associated" if not conservatively controlled.[18]

Although this was clearly a boon to the Santa Fe, Ripley's decision to use the Chanslor-Canfield Midway Oil Company to bring the Associated to heel left the Midway shareholders fuming when they realized that he was not going to develop the property after all. And they were particularly angry with Canfield, who seemed to be playing both sides of the field. Under the circumstances, Canfield and a few other Midway stockholders having positions with Associated Oil were persuaded to sell the other half of the company to the Santa Fe. In the end, the railroad paid $1.75 million for the entire property, giving Ripley everything he wanted. Canfield, on the other hand, compromised his relationship with the Southern Pacific and ended up on very bad terms with several members of the Associated's board. As a result, he resigned as a director in 1910 and filed suit against

Associated Oil for interfering with the renewal of the Santa Fe's oil contracts. For Doheny, at least, a large share of the proceeds from the Midway
sale probably went straight into the pool of capital available for his work
at Ebano.[19]

Interestingly, the effects of having railroad executives as principal
shareholders of the large oil companies in California were never addressed
during the federal government's investigation of the state's oil industry.
The independent producers did their part to focus public attention on
the issue when they loudly accused the major oil companies of conspiring
with the railroads. But the federal agents seemed oblivious to any claims
that were not somehow related to Standard Oil. That the investigators
were more preoccupied with the oil trust than blind to actual conditions
was revealed by their observation that "the complicated relations of the
railroads to the oil business [were] clearly fraught with mischievous
possibilities."[20]

Given the confusing arrangements between contesting parties, it was
almost impossible to tell who benefitted from any particular piece of business. A few sources, however, confirm the collusion between the railroads
and the large oil companies. During one negotiation, for instance, Ripley
offered to pay several cents a barrel above the market rate for oil if the oil
company agreed to make at least 40 percent of its shipments to San Francisco on the Santa Fe. In this instance, the excess payments on a proposed
three-year contract for 110,000 barrels a year netted the Associated at least
$25,000 to $30,000 annually, which Ripley acknowledged, "to all intents
and purposes," was a "rebate on [the Associated's] freight." Previously, in
the late 1890s, the government had accused the Santa Fe of having granted
$400,000 in rebates to the Colorado Fuel and Iron Company in a case
that led to the resignation of Paul Morton, President Roosevelt's secretary of the navy and a former vice-president of the Santa Fe. Still,
in 1905, the Bureau of Corporations refused to delve into the relationship between the Santa Fe, the Southern Pacific, and the Associated Oil
Company.[21]

It was clear that, despite its stated goals, the Associated Oil Company
was not a panacea for the problems of the market. The very fact that there
were still hundreds of small companies pumping out oil despite the depressed conditions belied the ability of the large companies to handle
the situation. To protect themselves, the Associated, Union Oil, and Standard Oil (Pacific Oil Company) all tried to capture and store as much
surplus oil as they could while a plague of independent producers descended on the district. In fact, California had become a haven for insolvent

organizations precisely because oil was so easy to find. According to statistics for 1907, 96 percent of all the wells drilled in California produced some oil, compared to 79 percent for the country as a whole. And from 1907 through 1919, about 92 percent of all wells in California struck oil, compared to the national average of 73 percent. The result was rampant overproduction by those without the financial resources to handle the oil.[22]

In the fall of 1904, Pacific Oil finally refused to keep buying heavy crude oil when there was no end in sight, thus abandoning its suppliers to the market. This decision precipitated another moment of truth in the oil district and brought a new organization into existence, the Independent Oil Producers Agency. Ultimately, the Agency exerted enough control over the situation to sign a new contract with the Associated Oil Company for several million barrels of oil at a minimum of eighteen cents a barrel, which absorbed the production of seventeen small companies. The Associated also agreed to accept up to 90,000 barrels of oil a month in additional storage from new Agency members as long as the total did not exceed 500,000 barrels a month for purchased and stored oil combined. A few years later, the independent producers in Coalinga, at the northern section of the district, formed a second Agency that contracted with the Associated Oil Company to sell at least 14,000 barrels a day between 1907 and 1909.[23]

To summarize, the California oil industry after 1902 was shaped by a steady process of consolidation, which placed most of the business into the hands of several large marketing companies and several regional producers' agencies that bargained on behalf of many, but by no means all, of the smaller independents. Canfield played a major role in this process from 1902 to 1905, but his direct involvement in the California operations began to decline by the latter part of the decade. This was partially due to his worsening relationship with the Associated Oil Company, but Canfield also deliberately withdrew from the field after the death of his wife in January 1906, which, according to his son-in-law, took "the joy of planning and developing" out of his life. Thereafter, until his own death in August 1913, Canfield retreated from much of his previous activity in California, although he continued to make trips to Mexico and elsewhere as the first vice-president of the Mexican Petroleum Company. Nevertheless, when Doheny returned to the West Coast as a producer in 1908, he entered a market shaped by Canfield's efforts. He emphasized this contribution in a later tribute to his partner: "If the development of the oil industry has meant anything to California and the nation at large, then to Mr. Canfield much of the praise for the tremendous work belongs. On that industry our state's prosperity has to a great extent been founded, and in Mr. Canfield's life is to be found the big chapters of the story of that industry's growth."[24]

To cope with the financial and organizational responsibilities required to handle the simultaneous development of his expanding operations in Mexico and California, Doheny turned to several other individuals. Two of the most important were T. A. O'Donnell, who assumed the primary role in California, and Norman Bridge, who served effectively on both sides of the border as company treasurer. Thomas A. O'Donnell grew up in the Pennsylvania oil fields in the 1870s and was the master of every detail of the business by the time he arrived in Los Angeles twenty years later. He first went to work for the Union Oil Company, but Doheny soon hired him to oversee the drilling operations on his wells in the old Los Angeles city field. A few years later, O'Donnell and Max Whittier, another pioneer driller, formed their own company and put down more than sixty wells by 1897, when they went off in different directions. By 1908, when Doheny needed his help once again, O'Donnell had become one of the best drilling contractors in the state and a mainstay of the industry.[25]

In contrast to O'Donnell, Dr. Norman Bridge did not know a thing about oil when he started in the business. While struggling to build up a medical practice in Chicago in the 1870s, Bridge occasionally gambled on investment schemes that robbed his bank account as well as his conscience. Through deliberate restraint, he concentrated on his medical career to become a professor of medicine at Rush Medical College, later associated with the University of Chicago, and an attending physician at several local hospitals. After contracting tuberculosis, Bridge moved to Los Angeles in 1891 to recuperate. As one of the city's most influential physicians, Bridge directed several tuberculosis sanatoriums and participated in a wide range of civic and cultural organizations.[26]

When oil fever took hold of Southern California in the late 1890s, Bridge succumbed to temptation once again and made some ill-advised investments that taught him a lesson: "If one wished to go into the oil business," Bridge observed, "it ought to be with people who understood it, and who had a reputation for success at it." Adopting this strategy led him to put up $5,000 as one of the original investors in the Mexican Petroleum Company in 1900. Three years later, he was on the board of directors and headed for a prominent role in the oil business. When the stockholders of the company blocked Doheny and Canfield's initial plan to expand into the Huasteca district in 1906, Bridge helped them form a private syndicate to get the project underway. E. P. Ripley was the fourth member of that group, although his responsibilities with the Santa Fe kept him a distant and silent partner. Bridge, on the other hand, went into the work full force and, at the age of sixty-one, changed careers to become an oilman. This was not, he wrote, without some "strain of soul," because he was deeply concerned about the unseemly aspects of big business. In the end, he consoled himself with the thought that at least in the oil industry he could help make a "great addition to the wealth of the world without hurting anybody." He felt even better about his partners, "the two masters" of oil exploration, and he was soon hacking his way through the Mexican jungle with Doheny and Canfield in pursuit of oil lands and leases. On those occasions, Bridge made up for his lack of practical experience with good humor, intelligence, and reliability.[27]

Finally, there were two other men, J. C. Anderson and J. M. Danzinger, who made up the core of Doheny's California team. Anderson began by acquiring leases for him in 1907 and became the manager of all of Doheny's West Coast properties a few years later. Being Doheny's brother-in-law, he was perhaps the closest of his associates. Similarly, Danzinger had been an attorney for the Chanslor-Canfield Midway Oil Company and was Canfield's son-in-law at the time he went to work for Doheny.[28]

Thus armed with talent, Doheny renewed his California interests when he incorporated a series of producing companies between 1908 and 1910. These included the American Petroleum Company, centered in Coalinga; the Niles Lease Oil Company, located in the Salt Lake field in Los Angeles; and the American Oilfields Company, concentrated in the Midway field. There were also two subsidiary companies, Midland Oil and Midland Oilfields, designed to develop smaller properties in the Midway and Sunset districts. All of these companies operated almost exclusively on proven oil land, rather than prospects, which virtually assured their success from the beginning.[29]

The decision to purchase only proven acreage reflected a change in Doheny's character which did not go unnoticed among the old hands of the industry. In reviewing the development of the new American Petroleum Company, one oilman could not help but wonder about the difference: "It is noted that E. L. Doheny, who is the principal owner of the company, has changed from being one of the rankest wildcatters in the west to one of the most conservative operators . . . It is said that in the early days when his fortune was small he was willing to risk it on a single throw, but now that he has become immensely wealthy, he is pursuing the policy of making investments in only such land as is sure to bring a return much smaller than he hoped to be able to obtain when he was operating as a wildcatter."[30] Although this observation overstated Doheny's former exploits, it was entirely correct about his maturation as a businessman and entrepreneur. But his more sophisticated approach did not make him any less controversial or dangerous to his fellow producers.

To the contrary, Doheny's reemergence in California upset the delicate balance between the big marketing companies and the independents, because he could afford to pursue his own goals. This was immediately apparent when he made a separate contract with the Associated Oil Company in October 1908 which called for an average of 4,200 barrels of oil a day over a five-year period, or about one-third of the entire contract for the Coalinga Agency. Doheny's advantages angered the Agency's directors and made life uncomfortable for T. A. O'Donnell, who was an original member of the group. In his own defense, O'Donnell stated that he "tried in every way" to stop Doheny's negotiations with Associated Oil but that they were too far along to terminate. He was successful, however, in getting Doheny to admit that he had been wrong in not joining forces with the independent producers. Having "now realized his mistake," as O'Donnell put it, Doheny offered to surrender his contract when he joined up. Instead, the Agency's directors decided to allow Doheny to keep the contract for himself if he brought in all of his excess oil.[31]

The Agency based this decision on an improving market that coincided with Doheny's return to California. During a profitable interlude between 1907 and 1909, demand for crude oil briefly exceeded production and brought the price up from twenty-five to fifty cents a barrel. Meanwhile, oil stocks dropped to their lowest point in the decade. Having stayed abreast of the local situation, Doheny entered the market at precisely the right time, and his initial production helped shore up the reserves of both the Associated and the Agency when they needed it most. However, this proved to be an illusory benefit when Doheny and a few other well-financed companies brought in several large wells in both Coalinga and Midway, again flooding the state with oil. The subsequent depression lasted for more than five years, until the fuel oil demands of the First World War caused a turnaround in local conditions.[32]

Within a short time, Doheny's large production made him a vital element in any attempt to control the market, but, less than a year after agreeing to join the Coalinga Agency, Doheny balked at the low price they offered him for his oil and refused to sign a long-term contract. Instead, he arranged to sell all of his oil to the Associated Oil Company, which immediately imperiled those Agency contracts that were based on his surplus. At the time, the oil lands of the American Petroleum Company made up one-fifth of all the property under Agency control. Doheny was thus

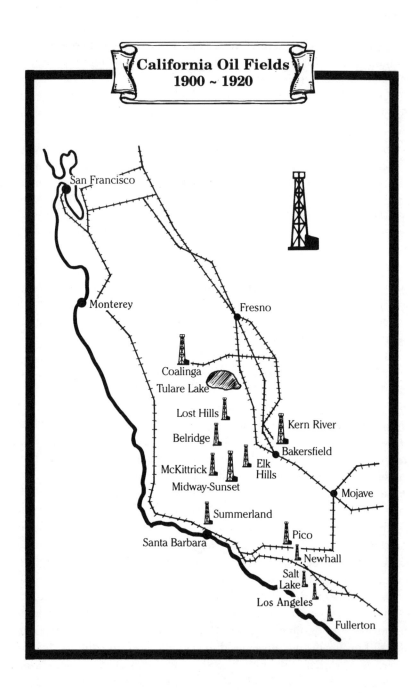

California Oil Fields
1900 ~ 1920

San Francisco

Monterey

Fresno

Coalinga
Tulare Lake

Lost Hills

Belridge

Kern River

McKittrick

Elk
Hills

Bakersfield

Midway-Sunset

Mojave

Summerland

Pico

Santa Barbara

Newhall

Salt
Lake

Los Angeles

Fullerton

both the most important ally and the most dangerous competitor of the independent operators in the San Joaquin Valley.[33]

As before, however, there were other self-interested champions willing to save the local producers. In this instance, Lyman Stewart came forward and offered to make Union Oil the exclusive sales agent for all the oil produced by both of the independent agencies, prompting the Coalinga and Bakersfield producers to merge into one large group. Thereafter, the newly reorganized Independent Oil Producers Agency, headquartered in Bakersfield, signed a long-term contract with the Union Oil Company. Through these arrangements, the Agency kept struggling producers in business while Stewart transformed Union Oil into one of the strongest marketing companies in the state. In particular, he used the Agency's oil to meet the demands of a six-year contract to deliver fuel oil via tank steamer for the construction of the Panama Canal. In later years, Union continued exporting large amounts of California oil throughout South America and the Pacific.[34]

Doheny's intentions were more problematic, and speculation about his motives spawned numerous unsubstantiated rumors about his plans. One supposedly reliable source claimed that Doheny had merely cooperated with the Agency so that he could learn about its plans and then trade that information for a favorable deal with the Associated. A similarly conspiratorial theory suggested that Doheny was plotting to take over control of the Associated for himself. If nothing else, the situation drew out a vivid portrait of Doheny's image among his contemporaries: "It is conceded that Mr. Doheny has the nerve force and brain to handle the Associated Oil Company's affairs, but it is well known that the temperament of the man would forbid success. Mr. Doheny is high strung, a quick thinker, imperious, but he lacks temperamentally, the qualifications of the diplomat, his methods are direct and his actions incisive, judging by past actions he cannot be politic, suave, ingratiating, and achieve results by those milder manners and methods which are certain to be necessary in the future management of the Associated."[35] These strident qualities accounted for much of Doheny's success, and he clearly preferred to run things when he could, but there was no evidence to suggest that he intended to take over the Associated Oil Company. Nevertheless, his aggressive tactics and tough reputation were cause for concern among the independents.

With his companies operating in every major oil field in the state, Doheny's influence grew with each new well. This was especially true for the American Oilfields Company, which began operations in the Midway district in February 1910. Drilling on proven oil land under the best of circumstances led to nearly instant success. Beginning in April 1910 with a production rate of 400 barrels a day, the company had increased its output to over 5,000 barrels a day two months later. And Doheny could have doubled that amount, since he actually drilled two 5,000-barrel wells in May but shut them in and cut back development for lack of adequate storage. Clearly, Doheny had no desire to flood the market with oil if he could avoid it, and he hoped to leave the oil in the ground for as long as possible.[36]

These plans went awry, however, when the Midway-Sunset field produced several large gushers in the spring and summer of 1910. This development began in March, when Union Oil drilled in its famous Lakeview No. 1, which produced about 16,000 barrels a day for eighteen months before it stopped flowing. Typically, almost half of that oil went to waste while drillers tried to control the well. Then, in mid-July, Doheny unexpectedly hit a big gusher of his own: American Oilfields No. 79 started at 10,000 barrels a day during its first two weeks and increased to more than 20,000 barrels a day through August, with most of the oil going into storage. The next month, Norman Bridge released a statement to the stockholders of the company proclaiming that American Oilfields was "now producing more oil than any other single oil company in the world," with a daily production of over 25,000 barrels for the first week of September. Incredibly, that record stood for only ten days, until the Huasteca Petroleum Company drilled in Casiano No. 7. At that point, with his California and Mexican wells combined, Doheny was producing crude oil at an astonishing rate.[37]

The effect of the gushers on the Midway field was instantaneous. A four-hundred-percent increase in production, from 2,095,000 barrels in 1909 to 10,436,000 for 1910, made it the most rapidly growing oil district in the state. Doheny's American Oilfields Company accounted for twenty-five percent of the total, with more than 2 million barrels of its own. Coalinga grew at a modest rate of 25 percent, from 14,795,000 to 18,388,000 barrels, for 1910 but had the largest production of any district in the state. The American Petroleum Company produced about 10,000 barrels a day, or roughly twenty percent of Coalinga's annual total.[38]

Because of Doheny's looming presence in the market by 1910, the Independent Oil Producers Agency had to find a way to cooperate with him. To do that, the members made an open bid to bring him into the Agency on his own terms. What Doheny demanded, and received, was a three-year contract for a minimum delivery of 1 million barrels of oil a year at a guaranteed price of fifty cents a barrel. Initially, the members of the Agency agreed to these special privileges because, as one observed, they saw "too many advantages with Doheny in the Agency to complain." Certainly, there was an argument to be made for gaining control of Doheny's oil before he used it against them.[39]

However, Doheny had also been looking for a way to improve the situation in anticipation of the threatened overproduction from the Midway field, and he thought he had found it in a plan to market California oil in Arizona. This project began in March 1910 and involved L. P. St. Clair, the head of the Agency, and W. L. Stewart, the new president of Union Oil. Doubtless, Doheny's assurances that this new venture would be a success helped the Agency decide to give him his special concessions. Industry analysts, at least, regarded the plan as a "master stroke for the future of the Independent Agency." As he conceived it, based on his recent experiences in the Huasteca, Doheny planned to construct an eight-inch pipeline from Kern County to the mines and smelters in Arizona, along with a possible extension across the border to Cananea, Mexico. This 700-mile line would be built along the tracks of the Santa Fe Railroad to facilitate the transportation of construction material and labor. To coordinate the work, Doheny, St. Clair, and Stewart formed the California-Arizona Pipe-Line Company on March 23, 1910. Although Doheny was supposed to handle the marketing work in Arizona, it was obvious to most observers that, given his other obligations, he was unlikely to devote the necessary time to see the project through.[40]

Without a doubt, those constraints forced him to abandon the effort, especially after 1911, when the political situation in Mexico demanded almost all of his attention. Nevertheless, the idea lingered for quite some time, and, as late as February 1912, the Agency was still paying Norman Bridge's expenses for work "connected with an investigation of the possible expansion of the fuel oil business in Arizona." But any concerted effort to push the pipeline project must have been unlikely at this point, since the Agency was also hunting for customers anywhere it could find them, including extensive efforts by President St. Clair to secure long-term contracts in South America in conjunction with Union Oil.[41]

In conclusion, given the tremendous increases in production already underway in the oil fields, the Independent Oil Producers Agency based the special concessions it gave to Doheny and a few other large companies on a fundamental misreading of the market. According to an Agency director, the contracts had been made at a point when the "conditions in the oil business looked rosy" and the Agency "confidently expected to get in excess of fifty cents per barrel for all its production." At that point, in 1910, the independent producers had visions of controlling the oil production of the entire state. But in the middle of a subsequent oil glut, with prices dropping below thirty cents a barrel by 1911, the Agency had to use the proceeds from almost half of its sales contracts just to make the payments to the companies that had gotten special terms. With no room to grow and no desire to renege on its obligations, the Agency pleaded with the large companies to adopt a "true Agency spirit" and accept a reduction of their contracts instead of insisting on their "pound of flesh."[42]

Doheny's response to this plea was not recorded, but there were numerous reports indicating that he was not brimming with the spirit of cooperation. In particular, American Oilfields had been accused of breaching its contract with the Agency through various efforts to contract with outside parties. Still, Doheny had played a vital, albeit sometimes antagonistic, role in the early history of the Independent Oil Producers Agency and kept most of his California companies affiliated with the organization for many years to come. His direct participation in the Agency lasted for less than a year, from May 1910 to April 1911. After that, O'Donnell served as Doheny's proxy at all of the stockholders' meetings over the next few years. Although Doheny was reelected to the Executive Committee in April 1912, he no longer attended the meetings.[43]

By this time, Doheny had once again become a significant factor in the California oil industry. Furthermore, in contrast to what happened in 1902, when circumstances forced him to sell out, Doheny's California operations moved forward under separate management even as the Mexican side of the business absorbed the bulk of his energy over the next few years. Despite the rapid success made in just four years of work, the outlook for Doheny's Mexican operations eclipsed even the brightest prospects for California oil. Although Doheny's capacity to juggle the financial and strategic policies of the two separate enterprises showed remarkable vision and executive ability, this was only a prelude to future demands that would tax the resources of his organization to the limit and require every ounce of Doheny's skill.

5 CREATING AN INTERNATIONAL
OIL COMPANY, 1912–1915

With the advent of the gusher era in Mexico in 1911, everyone wanted to get in on the action. According to a promotional advertisement in *The Oil Age*, Tampico had become the "new storm center for oil investments and land speculation" and was likely to be the world's leading oil port within the next five years. As it was, Tampico had already developed from a languid, backwater port into a burgeoning distribution center for crude oil, if not a full-fledged boomtown. By this time, most of the exported petroleum was bound for the new refineries that were springing up along the Gulf coasts of Texas and Louisiana, although delivery routes reached as far north as Boston and across the Atlantic to London. Without question, Doheny and Pearson dominated this business, as they would for the rest of the decade, but they were joined by subsidiaries from every major oil company in the world along with an increasing number of independent operators.[1]

According to one report, there were twenty oil companies actually engaged in production in Mexico in the fall of 1911 and at least two to three times that number operating as promotional fronts to sell prospective oil lands. Almost all of this activity centered on an area in the Tampico district some twenty-five to forty-five miles inland from the city. Specifically, the new oil zone ran along both sides of the Pánuco River near the small towns of Topila and Pánuco, where producers could send their oil out by barge without having to build railroad or pipeline facilities. Doheny's 450,000-acre property at Ebano sat like a separate kingdom to the northwest of these small lots. The big wells drilled by Doheny at

Casiano and by Pearson at Potrero del Llano were in the Huasteca district 75 to 100 miles to the south.

By contrast, the companies operating along the Pánuco fought over small leases of a few thousand acres, and most of the wells averaged less than 100 barrels per day. Of the better-run operations, there was the Mexican Fuel Oil Company, controlled by the Texas Company, which had a total production of 400 barrels a day, and the East Coast Oil Company, owned by the Southern Pacific Railroad, which had an impressive gusher near Topila capable of producing 6,000 to 10,000 barrels a day. The problem for the latecomers, however, was not the lack of oil but the impossibility of securing adjoining tracts around an oil well to protect it from competitors. Consequently, the small parcels of land in the area between Topila and Pánuco became the bargaining chips of land speculators, and strategic properties within a few hundred feet of a producing well became the "sweeteners" added to deals for larger properties away from the river. It was the revolving trade for these leases that kept the market humming and gave the area its notorious reputation.[2]

The competition for land in the oil districts south of Tampico was not nearly as vicious because of the Herculean efforts required to transport oil out of the area. Consequently, the Tamiahua district, west of the Tamiahua Lagoon and the port of Tuxpan, stayed primarily in the hands of the Huasteca Petroleum Company, except for the tract containing Pearson's Potrero well. Farther south, Pearson still held oil lands in both the Tehuantepec and Tabasco districts, but he had abandoned his efforts to develop the properties.

Along the Pánuco River, however, things moved quickly. By the end of 1912, Everette DeGolyer, an American geologist working for Pearson's Mexican Eagle Company, counted eighty-nine oil companies at work in some capacity. American operators led the list with fifty, followed by the British with twenty-one and the Mexicans with thirteen. DeGolyer also estimated the total amount of money invested in the oil fields so far at $175 million. Once again, the Americans were first with $97.5 million, the British second with $75 million, and the Mexicans third with $2.5 million. For the most part, this money represented the value of the leaseholds rather than direct investments in plant and equipment, since only Doheny and Pearson had yet to build up any infrastructure. As it stood, 252 wells had been drilled in the Tampico district; sixty-four of those were producing oil, with the five largest accounting for 90 percent of the total output.[3]

Still, the speculators and small operators continued to pour into Tampico over the next few years, pushing the number of oil companies listed in Mexico to almost 200. Of the fifty that were actually producing oil, most were either direct subsidiaries of the large companies or independent outfits working on their behalf. For the period up to 1913, the list of major organizations included the Continental Mexican Petroleum Company (General Petroleum, California); Corona Petroleum Company (Royal Dutch Shell); East Coast Oil Company (Southern Pacific Railroad, which sold its Mexican production to the Texas Company in exchange for fuel oil in Texas); Interocean Oil Company (U.S. Asphalt Company/Barber Asphalt Company); Magnolia Petroleum Company (Standard Oil New York); Mexican Gulf Oil Company (Gulf Refining Company); Penn Mex Fuel Company (South Penn Oil Company/Standard Oil); and the Tampico Company (Texas Company).[4]

Doheny not only helped usher in the new age of Mexican oil when he drilled in Casiano No. 7 in September 1910, but he completed the process when he exported the first load of Mexican crude out of Tampico in May 1911. And that shipment, 32,000 barrels of Huasteca oil headed to Texas for the Magnolia Oil Company, confirmed the growing fear among Gulf Coast producers that their days were numbered. Doheny's action initially set off another round of complaints about the "Menace of Mexican Oil," as one article put it. But this time, before the independent producers could mobilize in self-defense, a curious thing happened: Mexican crude turned out to have a positive effect on the Texas oil market. Instead of driving out local producers, it allowed them to substitute the Mexican product for fuel oil, while refining their lighter-grade oil into more profitable products. Before long, the influx of Mexican oil was "hailed with delight" and demand increased dramatically. The problem now was getting it there.[5]

By the end of 1911, Doheny was producing about 42,250 barrels of oil a day with the output of Casiano No. 7 cut back to less than half its potential. At the same time, the company's sales contracts called for about 26,650 barrels a day, equal to the shut-in flow of Casiano No. 7 by itself. These contracts were with the National Railways of Mexico, Standard Oil (New York and New Jersey), the Waters-Pierce Refinery, the Santa Fe Railway, Gulf Refining Company, and the Mexican Petroleum Company's asphalt and gas subsidiaries in Mexico City. Unfortunately, without his own shipping facilities Doheny could not take advantage of potential American customers waiting for Mexican oil and was in grave danger of drowning in his own production. Already, the company's storage facilities were 95 percent full with over six million barrels of oil in steel tanks and concrete reservoirs.[6]

This was a critical moment for Doheny's Mexican business, since he was turning down large contracts for Mexican oil in Texas and in the East for lack of transportation. Yet he desperately needed those sales to soak up his vast production and generate revenue for additional capital improvements. Facing a short-term financial bottleneck that limited his ability to keep pace with the market and threatened the profitability of his business, Doheny had no choice but to take the Mexican Petroleum Company public to raise the necessary funds—a decision not easily accepted by the directors of the company.

Prior to the rapid development of the Huasteca property in 1909, Doheny had operated almost entirely with internal financing. Until 1904, the bonded debt of the company had been limited to $250,000, used to finish the storage facilities at Ebano. Then, as the plans for drilling the Casiano wells took shape in the summer of 1909, the company needed money to construct the pipeline to Tampico. To complete that project, the directors approved $2 million in Huasteca Petroleum Company, Coast Pipe Line bonds, which were only marginally successful despite the attached participation certificates that returned ten cents for every barrel of oil sent through the pipeline. Less than half of the bonds were sold, and those that were proved to be an unacceptable drain on the company's cash flow with the pipeline operating at full capacity from the moment it opened.

In the summer of 1910, as both Casiano No. 6 and No. 7 were about to be drilled in, Doheny knew he needed additional funds to complete the pipeline and build as much storage as possible. To meet these escalating demands, the board of directors issued a third series of bonds for another $2 million: $250,000 to pay off the first issue and $1.75 million for the storage facilities. Up to this point, these bond issues had been aimed at a small core of stockholders and investors in California and were lightly traded on the Los Angeles Stock Exchange.[7]

Fortunately, as Doheny pressed on with the pipeline project, he received some unsolicited financial support from Mike Benedum and Joseph Trees, former employees of Standard Oil's South Penn Oil Company who enjoyed a reputation similar to that of Doheny and Canfield as two of the shrewdest oil drillers in the United States. Benedum and Trees had been responsible for opening up major fields in West Virginia, Illinois, and Oklahoma in the face of stiff opposition from several Standard Oil subsidiaries. And in every case, they managed to sell their holdings to Standard Oil for a considerable profit.[8]

In the early summer of 1910, they earned a multi-million-dollar profit from the sale of oil leases in the Caddo field of Louisiana and were looking for a new investment. Trees ended up going to Mexico to investigate Doheny's work for two Pittsburgh businessmen who wanted to "take a flyer in oil." Doheny arranged for him to go down to the Huasteca field, and, by amazing coincidence, Trees was standing on the drilling floor of Casiano No. 6 when it blew in on July 26. He was still trying to assimilate the experience a few days later when he wrote to Benedum and exclaimed, "Mike, You've never seen an oil well. Those things we drilled in Illinois and Caddo were just little creeks of oil. I tell you these Mexican wells are oceans."[9]

From a distance, Benedum hesitated. "I wasn't much for going in," he recalled, "but Joe was so anxious he made a deal with Doheny." That arrangement involved a cash payment for $500,000 worth of Mexican Petroleum stock and a seat on the board of directors. Harry Brown, the Pittsburgh coal man who had persuaded Trees to go to Mexico in the first place, also became a director with a somewhat smaller investment. These were sorely needed funds in the fall of 1910, as the company raced against the clock to complete the Huasteca pipeline in advance of Casiano No. 7. If anything, Benedum understated the situation when he remarked that their money must have "relieved Doheny to a certain extent."[10]

The financial pressure worsened even more, however, after they brought in the well and discovered that they could close down production by only one half. This initiated what Doheny described as a period of "very active scrambling . . . for a market for immediate delivery of oil," which included sending Benedum to negotiate a contract with Standard Oil New Jersey to buy Huasteca crude. Benedum met with Henry Rogers in New York, described Doheny's operation in detail, and testified that the oil had been thoroughly tested and proven. Knowing Benedum's reputation, Rogers did not hesitate in the least: "If that's true and I know you think it is, we want that oil." When he left, Benedum had an agreement with Rogers for Standard Oil to purchase 12,000 barrels of oil a day at fifty-two cents a barrel.

At almost the same time, Doheny met with the Mellon interests in Pittsburgh, hoping to get a contract with the Gulf Oil Company. When he and Benedum met later to compare notes, they apparently got into a heated argument over the arrangements with Standard Oil. As Benedum remembered it, Doheny was "cursing and sanding to beat the band" because he thought he could make a better deal on his own. Benedum also believed that Doheny wanted to pit Gulf and Standard against each other to bid up the price. Regardless, Benedum took the dispute personally and telephoned Rogers to say that he was through with Doheny and to warn him that he was going to have to fight for the oil with Gulf. "Leave that to me," Rogers told him. The next day, according to Benedum, Gulf Oil turned down Doheny's offer and Benedum believed his conversation with Rogers had something to do with it. Supposedly, Doheny then had to crawl back to Standard Oil and renegotiate a deal at a much lower price.[11]

There are several things wrong with Benedum's recollection of events. First, Doheny had too much oil on hand to get into a bidding war over the price. Second, instead of negotiating for a maximum amount per barrel, Doheny apparently wanted something closer to a loan in exchange for oil. And for that, he was practically willing to give away the oil. In the end, according to Doheny, the "efforts to sell oil at a reduced price in consideration of . . . large sums of money in advance, resulted in the acquisition of $650,000."[12]

Specifically, Doheny's deal with Rogers called for 6,000 barrels a day at thirty-nine cents a barrel for three years, and it could be renewed for five more at Standard's request. In return for these generous terms, Rogers paid an undisclosed amount in cash. Next, contrary to Benedum's account, Doheny also made a two-year contract with Gulf Oil to provide 2,000 barrels a day at forty-four cents a barrel. In addition, he had a three-year contract with the Santa Fe Railway for 2,500 barrels a day at forty-six cents and a three-year contract with Waters-Pierce for 2,900 barrels at sixty-six cents plus an additional 700 barrels of refined oil at ninety-three cents. Waters-Pierce made an initial payment of $250,000 to Doheny on its first million barrels, with the remaining $400,000 in advance payments divided among the other three companies.[13]

The Santa Fe Railway's interest in Mexican oil presented an interesting dilemma because of president E. P. Ripley's personal involvement with the Mexican Petroleum Company. Before he contracted with Doheny for Huasteca oil, Ripley explained to the chairman of the executive committee that, when he first invested in Mexican Petroleum, there was no thought of using the oil on the Santa Fe because of the prohibitive duty on oil imports. The recent elimination of the duty, however, made it economical to buy Mexican crude, although it put Ripley in the position of asking the railroad to purchase oil from which he would personally profit: "We have always insisted that none of our officers should occupy this dual relation, but in this case it could not be foreseen." To solve the problem, he delegated the responsibility for purchasing oil to the officers of the Gulf, Colorado, and Santa Fe Railway, who had "no other interest than to buy on the most favorable terms possible," since they would actually be using the fuel.[14]

From all indications, aside from Benedum's initial meeting with Standard Oil, Doheny made all of these contracts on his own. In fact, he and Benedum parted company immediately after their fight outside of Rog-

ers's office. Soon thereafter, Benedum and Trees sold out their stock in Doheny's company and struck out on their own, taking their profits and the
first-hand information they had gained about Mexico with them. They
capitalized on the experience the next year when they put together the
Penn-Mex Fuel Company. And true to form, they sold a majority of the
stock to Standard Oil through the South Penn Oil Company. With those
connections, Penn-Mex advanced rapidly over the next few years to become the third largest oil company in Mexico, behind Mexican Petroleum
and the Mexican Eagle. In the end, had he not needed financial help from
all quarters, Doheny might have complained that Benedum and Trees took
advantage of him from the beginning.[15]

The total of the cash advances on the contracts, the sale of preferred
stock to Benedum and Trees, and an additional sale of over 20,000 shares of
common stock on the Los Angeles Stock Exchange produced about $1.75
million, barely enough to complete the Huasteca pipeline and begin work
on the storage tanks. To make up the shortfall and keep from assuming
more debt, a committee of the largest stockholders decided to pass the
dividend on the common stock for the next six months, and possibly for
the rest of the year, which would generate another $600,000 to $1.2 million for expansion. Actually, the bulk of the company's earnings had been
going back into capital improvements anyway, although they returned
$3,239,969 on the preferred stock from February 1907 to March 1911. The
common shareholders bore the burden of expansion, except for $305,241
paid out in dividends in 1910. Ultimately, however, even these efforts
proved inadequate.[16]

To finally put the company on a strong financial base, Doheny went to
New York in the spring of 1911 to ask for a $12 million line of credit from
the investment bankers at William Salomon & Company. The money
would be used to consolidate the outstanding bonds, buy back the Huasteca participation certificates (which cost the company $2,800 a day), and
purchase a small fleet of tank steamers. To investigate the proposal and
value the assets of the Mexican Petroleum Company, Salomon sent Ralph
Arnold, a young consulting geologist from California who had worked for
the U.S. Geological Survey, to Mexico in June. Arnold and his assistant,
V. R. Garfias, made a thorough examination of the property and came back
with an estimate so low that it almost ruined Doheny's plans. Specifically,
Arnold was unwilling to credit Mexican oil lands with more potential than
what he could see in front of him. The current state of geological knowledge about the Mexican oil fields was extremely limited, and Arnold had
little to go on except his observation that "no commercially productive

well has been drilled farther than one-fourth of a mile distant from some
sort of surface evidence such as seepages, asphalt deposits or gas emana-
tions." Arnold did not assume that no wells would be found in the outlying
areas; he just refused to credit them with anything but nominal value until
proven. However, he seemed to take caution a bit too far by categorizing
probable oil land within a quarter-mile of a surface indication as "speculative," making his estimates particularly low. He valued the Ebano and Casiano fields at $1.2 and $2 million, respectively, and credited $9.5 million for
seventeen other probable sites combined. After accounting for the pipelines, refinery, oil camps, and storage facilities, Arnold estimated the value
of the company at $20,122,817.

Doheny was justifiably frustrated, if not angered, by Arnold's "ultra-
conservative" appraisal. And it was certainly true, as he noted, that since
the Huasteca company made forty-one cents a barrel profit from its current sales, the proceeds from Casiano No. 7 alone would exceed Arnold's
estimate in less than six months. In his rejoinder, Doheny wrote that "we
not only do not accede to the approximate valuation given to the properties, but we do not agree with the opinion of the geologist as to the area of
land, at the different localities, which will prove to be oil-containing."
Then, Doheny invited the bankers to come to Mexico and judge the property for themselves.[17]

At least a dozen East Coast financiers accepted his offer and descended
on the properties of the Mexican Petroleum Company in the fall of 1911,
with a number of geologists and oil experts in tow. By the end of December, a new appraisal was submitted by Dr. I. C. White, the state geologist
for West Virginia. Previously, White had earned widespread acclaim as the
main proponent of the anticlinal theory of oil and gas accumulation, which
fundamentally proved the value of geological knowledge in hunting oil. In
Mexico, where the sources of oil were more obvious, White followed the
same procedures he had used to determine the value of Pennsylvania oil
lands, where proven oil property sold for $800 to $1,000 per barrel of daily
settled production—an amount which returned two or three times the
initial investment. To ensure that his Mexican estimates were "entirely
within conservative lines," White reduced this figure to $300 per barrel,
although that still left his numbers four times greater than Arnold's. As for
the prospective oil lands, White calculated the original cash value of the
Ebano field at $6 million and used that number as the basis for everything
else. But to be absolutely certain of his estimates, he assumed that only half
of the thirty undeveloped properties would prove viable, and then he further reduced all of his figures by 40 percent to come up with a final value

of $50 million for the probable oil lands alone. Excluding both the Mexican Asphalt Paving and Construction Company and the Mexican National Gas Company, White believed that the Mexican Petroleum Company was worth $73,624,000.

For Doheny, the disparity between Arnold's nominal value for prospective oil land and White's $50 million was the difference between success and failure, and the West Virginia geologist was duly enshrined into the pantheon of company heroes for his faith in Mexican oil. Incredibly, even White's conservative estimates grossly undervalued the potential of the company, given that the largest oil well in the world, Cerro Azul No. 4, would be located on one of those prospective properties four years later. But White at least hinted at such a possibility in the final comment of his report: "The Mexican oil fields," he concluded, "appear to be the greatest and richest the world has ever seen."[18]

White's declaration still did not make instant believers out of all of the bankers, but it did confirm the belief of George G. Henry, Doheny's major ally. Henry, a former vice-president of the Guaranty Trust Company, was Doheny's only friend on Wall Street in 1911. Barely thirty years old, Henry was young and ambitious, and he recognized an opportunity in Mexican oil when everyone else hesitated. Doheny recalled that, after he had made his initial pitch to the young banker, Henry was able "to pierce through the veils of ignorance, of novelty, of doubt." Doheny added that, "where others had been blind, George Henry saw." For the next six years, until his death in 1917, Henry guided all of Mexican Petroleum's financial arrangements as Salomon's representative on the board of directors.[19]

For their initial transaction, Salomon & Company underwrote a $4 million bond issue in early April 1912, which paid down the existing debt and put a million dollars into Mexican Petroleum's treasury for future needs. Then, on April 20, 1912, the bankers placed the company on the New York Stock Exchange. As one of the first oil companies to be accepted on the exchange, "Mexican Pete" (listed as Mexpet) was an instant success, and over the next decade it became one of the most heavily traded stocks and a bellwether for oil shares in general. The dramatic political events occurring simultaneously in Mexico during this period also made it the most volatile issue on the market.[20]

This situation began in 1908 when Porfirio Díaz announced that he was going to retire after more than two decades of dictatorial rule. Having raised the hopes for democratic reform among Mexicans of all classes, Díaz dashed them again when he reneged on his promise to allow an open presidential election in 1910. Instead, hoping to cut short an incipient political reform movement, Díaz jailed his chief rival, Francisco Madero, and had himself reelected in another staged contest. Madero was released on bond and fled north to San Antonio, Texas, where he prepared for an open rebellion against the Díaz government, ultimately forcing the aging dictator from office in May 1911. Díaz took refuge in France but left behind a fractured and divisive atmosphere among his opponents. An interim government took over after Díaz's departure and held another election in the fall, which Madero won by a wide margin.

When Madero assumed office as the new president of Mexico in November 1911, his triumph unwittingly set the stage for several years of bloody fighting, as an array of ambitious regional leaders, disgruntled military officers, and angry peasants rose up against him from all sides. Although no single group had the power to overthrow the central government, their competing demands robbed Madero of any chance to consolidate his position. The oil companies were rumored to be part of this process, and the Standard Oil Company, the "Lucifer of the corporations," was under suspicion of having conducted an anti-Díaz propaganda campaign because of his opposition to the oil trust. Supposedly, Standard hoped to soften up American public opinion to accept a new government in Mexico.[21]

Although Wall Street avoided taking sides, the political turmoil in Mexico threatened to shake up the market when Mexican Petroleum appeared on the New York Stock Exchange in the spring of 1912. While the mixture of revolution and profit-taking inherent in Mexpet stock kept some investors at bay, the added risk made it all the more enticing for others. According to one market analyst:

> If any recent tip has been more widely circulated than the advice to buy Mexican Petroleum common I do not know of it. Both in and out of the street the advice has been given to "load up," and, judging by the extent of recent transactions, that advice seems to have been taken by a considerable number of those who have received it. It takes courage in these days . . . to commit oneself to an investment based on property in that country. Not only that, it requires an unusual combination of optimism and courage to inaugurate a market campaign in a security of this kind at a time when holders of some Mexican securities are suffering a loss of income as a result of the disturbed condition in that country.[22]

Obviously, Doheny had little choice about the timing, but he did not believe the situation would last very long or threaten the foreign companies operating in Mexico. Like most Americans, he underestimated the level of political disaffection in Mexico and was overly optimistic about prospects for peace. Mexpet's record on the Los Angeles exchange reflected this general attitude, since the value of the common stock more than doubled over the course of the Madero rebellion. And confidence ran so high among American investors in the summer of 1911 that many believed the revolution was "now probably a thing of the past." Other observers attributed Mexican Petroleum's continued advance through the beginning of 1912 to Madero's ability to "run his government with a firm hand and also to the high character of the principal American operators in the field and the moral influence of their financial strength." This faith in the Mexican government slipped a bit when Madero's countermeasures proved to be feeble efforts in comparison to those of his predecessor. "Madero," wrote the *Oil Age*, "is too gentle a ruler for the turbulent breeds whom Díaz ruled with an iron hand; but it is hoped that the federal forces may yet be able to bring about peace."[23]

More troubling was Madero's intention to tax foreign businesses in Mexico, especially the oil companies. Industry spokesmen responded to the prospect of reform with preemptive arguments against the need for a fundamental change in Mexican society and government. These sentiments revealed an underlying fear of the future without the immutable rules of the Díaz era: "[The oil companies] are aware that they have obtained valuable concessions in a foreign country without much trouble and on liberal terms and they are willing to accede to what is just . . . [however] it is by no means likely that the matter of taxation would have come up even now had it not been for the revolution. Things had been running along smoothly under Díaz, at least as far as the companies were concerned. There had been no need for special taxation on the oil industry. With the revolution everything was changed."[24]

Even appeals such as this, however, failed to have an impact, and Madero insisted on a petroleum tax of at least three cents a barrel. The oil companies grumbled about the precedent but admitted that any tax up to five cents a barrel could be absorbed without effect. In this instance, Madero's halfhearted attack seemed like a prudent decision not to kill "the goose that laid the golden egg."[25]

Nevertheless, as the reports of chaotic conditions in Mexico grew more insistent by the summer of 1912, it was difficult to remain calm. For the most part, the oil press dismissed alarmist opinions with assurances that Madero would "eventually hunt down the last insurrecto and establish a stable government." And the oil companies themselves continued to "pursue their way calmly and confidently." Although the oilmen did not complain too loudly about the limited demands placed upon them by the Madero government, they recognized that the altered political environment after the overthrow of Díaz contained the seeds of a more forceful reaction against the foreign oil companies. For the time being, they were thankful for what they had gotten.[26]

However, as Madero tried to assume the mantle of power as a moderate reformer, he became the first victim of change. Madero lacked both the charismatic appeal and the military muscle needed to hold the country together, and he was also unable to recognize the political enemies who were operating within his own administration, including close advisers, military commanders, and even the Ambassador of the United States. As one historian concluded, "All, save Madero, must have gagged on the stench of treachery." It was not surprising, therefore, that fifteen months into his presidency Madero was removed from office by General Victoriano Huerta, one of several military holdovers from the Díaz administration. What was shocking, however, was Madero's assassination outside the gates of the federal prison in Mexico City on the night of February 21, 1913.[27]

As so often happens in such circumstances, Madero achieved the kind of stature in death that had eluded him in office. As a martyr to the cause, his name became a rallying cry for the competing factions to take arms against General Huerta and the threat of another iron grip on Mexico's political future. Unfortunately, the reaction against Huerta was yet another temporary union among predominantly local and often antithetical factions. When that coalition broke apart, it resulted in a civil war that took several years to run its course.

Although the oil zone sat to the side of the major theater of military operations, Tampico and the surrounding oil camps were a financial magnet for both the established government and the local rebel groups, who needed money and supplies to keep their troops in the field. As the revolution progressed, the oil companies endured successive rounds of federal and state taxes on production and exports as well as random forced loans and protection payments extorted by enterprising rebel organizations. To head off the "destructive tax legislation," in June 1913 the oil companies formed the Mexican Oil Association, headed by C. W. Hayes, vice-president of El Aguila, to negotiate their position with the Huerta government. Although the Penn Mex and the East Coast Oil Company joined this effort, Doheny was conspicuously absent, perhaps because the Association only succeeded in calling greater attention to the industry.[28]

Fortunately, the same economic factors that made the oil companies such an attractive target also made them immune to wanton destruction, since no Mexican leader could afford to choke off a steady source of income. The United States government also refused to sanction military intervention on behalf of the American oil companies, although company representatives used the threat of such action in dealing with the Mexicans. Under the circumstances, very little physical damage occurred in the oil fields, but they became an important element in the ideological war over the role of foreign business.

Yet the sporadic rebel attacks in the oil zone were not inconsequential. They slowed down the growth of the oil industry, frequently interrupted field work, and occasionally forced oil camps to shut down for their own protection. And each occurrence sent out waves of fear that reached both Washington and New York. Naturally, reports of random violence eroded the former sense of confidence that the oil zone would be spared the ravages of civil war. This change in attitude was most apparent on the financial market, where the fluctuating value of Mexpet shares served as a barometer of anxiety about the safety of the oil wells. After reaching a high of $84¾ in the fall of 1912, Mexpet common dropped to $44¾ a year later. Thereafter, the stock wavered in response to every crisis but fell to its lowest level when Doheny and his directors decided to suspend the quarterly dividend in November 1913 because of their own uncertainty about the political situation in Mexico. To no one's surprise, Mexican Petroleum stock dropped another twenty points in four days of panic selling and continued to fluctuate by almost that much in an afternoon, depending on the conditions.[29]

The first mention of serious trouble in the oil region came in May 1913, when anti-Huerta raiders on the Gulf Coast burned the railroad bridges between Tampico and Monterrey to cut off transportation links to the United States and telegraph lines to Mexico City. Another group tried to intercept the pay shipment to Ebano but had to settle for a few hundred dollars and a complement of horses, saddles, and rifles taken from the camp. Similar incidents occurred across the oil zone, raising fears about an impending attack on Tampico. Sure enough, a rebel group infiltrated the city on December 10 and fought with federal troops before retreating into the countryside three days later. Expecting the worst, about 500 American residents took shelter aboard American warships anchored in port. In this instance, the federal troops managed to drive off the rebels without incident. While the government soldiers often appeared totally inadequate to the task, they were still the only security Americans had against the rebel forces, and thus far no foreigner had been harmed, and no oil company had sustained any property damage. But President Wilson jeopardized that protection when he made it clear that he had no intention of recognizing the legitimacy of the Huerta regime, despite the fact that other nations had already done so. His decision came as a major blow to the Mexican Petroleum Company and other businesses that were solely dependent on federal troops to guard their interests in the field.

In light of this attitude, the real concern for the oil companies was to avoid getting caught on the wrong side of any particular engagement, leaving them to deal with each situation as circumstances warranted. This was a strategy for survival, not for making friends, and it often led to simultaneous alliances with one group in Tampico and another in the oil fields. In March 1914, for instance, Herbert Wylie and his nephew, J. Oswald Boyd, the superintendent of the Ebano camp, could not return from a trip to California because of unfriendly relations with the rebel troops in Tampico after they allowed government soldiers to stand watch over the company's oil properties. And this was not the first time Boyd had been advised to beat a hasty retreat "as a matter of wisdom." With the formal recognition of General Huerta in doubt, the situation grew even more ambiguous. Over time, however, the ad hoc policy allowed for a subtle interplay between contending sides which proved more effective than relying on either the Mexican or the American government for protection. Besides, it was apparent that any appeal to President Wilson was likely to fall on deaf ears.[30]

This did not mean that Wilson had no intention of intervening in the Mexican situation; he just refused to do so on behalf of American business interests. Instead, Wilson based his opposition to Huerta on personal distaste for the general's complicity in Madero's murder. Wilson declared in private that he would never "recognize a government of butchers." This attitude had a profound effect on American policy over the next year and resulted in a diplomatic stalemate between the United States and Mexico, as other nations recognized Huerta's de facto control while Wilson waited for an opportunity to get rid of the man. From his perspective, Wilson was engaged in a type of moral diplomacy which gave him the right to intervene at any point to plant the seeds of democracy.[31]

Wilson thought he saw such potential in the reform movement of Venustiano Carranza, the governor of Coahuila, who had assumed nominal control of the rebel forces in Mexico. Carranza came from an established family, had a good education, and projected a studious persona guaranteed to catch the eye of the American president. Wilson was particularly beguiled by the "Constitutionalist" banner under which Carranza waged war against the Huerta dictatorship, calling for free elections and a popularly constituted government. But Carranza's hold on the rebellion was tenuous at best, and his position at the head of the movement was under attack by Francisco "Pancho" Villa, the wily guerrilla leader from Chihuahua, and Emiliano Zapata, the champion of the peasant rebellion in the central state of Morelos. Still, Carranza's success represented the best chance for positive change in Mexico, and Wilson was determined to help, despite a warning from Carranza that any intervention by the United States, regardless of its motive, would be judged a hostile act.[32]

Undeterred, Wilson seized upon a minor diplomatic squabble involving Mexican troops and American sailors at Tampico in April 1914 to manufacture an incident worthy of a military reprisal. Admittedly, Wilson told a reporter after the fact, "it was a psychological moment" and not a great crisis, but that was all he needed. The American community in Tampico at first prepared for an invasion, after the senior naval officer in command announced an attack, but then was left confused and frightened when he changed his mind and aborted the evacuation of more than a thousand Americans from the city. A week later, ostensibly to stop the flow of arms—headed to Huerta's forces—into that port, Wilson decided to send troops ashore in Veracruz rather than in Tampico. With that campaign underway, the Navy ordered its three gunboats out of the river at Tampico to keep them free from attack, leaving the American civilians to fend for themselves and their property.[33]

The worst moment came when a crowd of enraged citizens surrounded a local hotel and threatened the 150 Americans holed up inside. They were saved by an intrepid German commander who intervened on their behalf. With the help of British and German ships, along with the private vessels of some of the oil companies, including Doheny's private yacht, hundreds of American refugees made it out of the city and onto the American gunboats in the Gulf. As if their ordeal had not been bad enough already, the refugees were then evacuated to Galveston against their will, where they sat in bureaucratic limbo for a month before they were allowed to return to Tampico. "The feeling of every American coming out of Tampico," as one survivor testified later, "is that he was deserted by his country."[34]

When the whole affair was over, Tampico was in the hands of the revolutionary forces, and the Americans were left to deal with a group of people whom they alternately feared and ridiculed. The rebel troops guarding the Huasteca terminal station, for example, lacking the accoutrements and demeanor of trained soldiers, were described in the oil press as little more than "comic opera pirate[s]."[35]

On a larger scale, the invasion and occupation of the port of Veracruz allowed the United States to take false credit for Huerta's resignation in July 1914. But a protracted battle of wills between Wilson and Carranza over the ultimate withdrawal of American troops went on for months. By the time the marines left in November, the rebel forces had splintered into contending factions, leaving Carranza's leadership as First Chief of the revolution in doubt and Wilson's objective of free elections in shambles. Furthermore, the intervention heightened tensions between Americans and Mexicans of all political persuasions and threatened to create an anti-American backlash that had not been present before. Still, there was little agitation against foreign business in Mexico and no evidence of any "long incubating resentment against American economic interests."[36]

Wilson, like most progressives, defined the enterprises he would support according to his own moral calculus and had no use whatsoever for the oil companies. Commenting on the causes of social unrest in Mexico, Wilson criticized the foreign business community in general for wielding disproportionate power, thereby creating the conditions for revolution. But he went out of his way to disparage American interests, in particular: "I shall fight every one of these men who are now seeking and who will then be seeking to exploit Mexico for their own selfish ends. I shall do what I can to keep Mexico from their plundering. There shall be no individual exploitation of Mexico if I can help it."[37]

In June 1914, Doheny responded to these attacks in his annual message to the stockholders of the Mexican Petroleum Company by dismissing the allegations of exploitation leveled against the "grasping corporations owned and controlled by foreign capitalists." Referring to his initial acquisition of oil land in 1900, Doheny assured his shareholders that he had never stolen anything from the Mexicans. On the contrary, he maintained, "every land owner who sold us land during the early years of our operations was the envy of his neighbors, and was convinced that he had made a good bargain." Furthermore, Doheny stated that he had paid at least the going market rate—and usually a lot more—for every acre of land the company owned and that, during those negotiations, the Mexicans had been "shrewd traders" capable of dealing sharply on their own behalf. They had not been hapless victims of his personal greed. Doheny pointed out that his Mexican attorneys, who doubted the success of his oil business, thought he paid far too much for the land. Certainly, Ralph Arnold would have agreed with them.[38]

Doheny also attacked the idea that all foreign companies exploited Mexican workers and treated them with contempt. Without denying that such abuse occurred in many organizations, he blamed it on an erroneous stereotype of the Mexican as an indolent peon who needed to be pressed into service. From his own experience, Doheny considered native workers to be very satisfactory employees who performed "with as much fortitude and much more good humor" than their American counterparts. And in return for their dedication and loyalty, the Mexican Petroleum Company paid its Mexican employees twice the standard wage for industrial labor. In addition, he continued, the company provided adequate housing, modern sanitation and bathing facilities, and schools for the children, and it also prohibited consumption of alcohol on company property. Mexican Petroleum also maintained a store to provide basic foodstuffs and necessary items for the oil workers, and, although such company stores were generally notorious for overcharging workers and stealing business away from local merchants, Doheny emphasized that the Mexican Petroleum outlet did not sell goods at a profit and stocked only daily necessities. Wherever possible, he wanted his workers to spread their bimonthly wages among the local shops and businesses as a boon to the local economy.

Doubtless, Doheny painted the rosiest picture he could of labor conditions, but there is no denying that his companies provided a relatively decent working environment. In particular, the oil company employees fared much better than those in the mining industry, where conditions ranged from barely adequate to deplorable. But the well-ordered world that Doheny described was not the norm, either, for the petroleum industry by 1913. The first generation of oil workers, who had moved from the hacienda to the oil camp, did not experience an abrupt change in lifestyle or habits. In the beginning, the company was not yet on a rigid work schedule, and workers had some control over their daily activities. These allowances disappeared, however, as the company put its five oil camps, refinery, and loading wharf into full operation to meet the demands of a fully diversified industry. Large-scale oil production for export necessitated a highly stratified, time-conscious labor system that led to increasing discontent from the native work force.[39]

At that point, workers chafed under an economic system that gave the highest rewards to the foreign employees and a small core of skilled Mexicans. For the most part, the common workers were left with little in comparison. Over time, most Mexican oil workers, skilled and unskilled, began to see themselves as being caught in an ever-tightening economic vise, as the rampant inflation of the oil zone and the precarious nature of industrial life combined to erode any sense of security. They eventually solved the problem through unionization, which gave the oil workers an opportunity to link up with the larger political elements of the revolution. Obviously, Doheny did not concede any of these factors in 1914, and the argument over the impact of the foreign oil companies on Mexico has continued unabated.[40]

It is enough to point out that the economic significance of the oil industry in Mexico became all the more apparent as the corrosive effects of the revolution ate away everything else around it. And during the darkest days of the conflict, the oil companies represented one of the only bright spots in the economy. Incidentally, Doheny received an unusual testimony to this effect in a poignant letter from Porfirio Díaz Jr., written from his home-in-exile in France in 1915: "Some time ago I wrote to our friend Mr. Norman Bridge telling him that owing to the difficult circumstances in which I find myself on account of the dreadful condition of my poor country, I am now obliged to sell my shares of the Mexican Petroleum (preferred). The little I had in Mexico has been either stolen, dreadfully damaged or ruined by the bandits, and of what is left, nothing produces, and for my living I am compelled to sell the only [thing] that has been left, that is my shares."[41]

Without question, even under the worst conditions during the initial period of civil war, the Mexican Petroleum Company continued to earn a reasonable return despite losing much of its domestic business. The railroads, in particular, suffered repeated attacks by rebel bands who tore up the tracks and destroyed rolling stock. Internal conditions on the Mexican railway system were so bad that the National Railways took as little as 400,000 barrels of oil on their yearly contract of 3.5 million. The total sales of Mexican Petroleum during the first years of the revolution were as follows: 8,662,700 barrels in 1912; 12,325,228 in 1913; 8,231,348 in 1914; and 6,287,528 in 1915. The company also experienced a 22 percent drop in export sales, from 7,602,058 barrels in 1913 to 5,933,488 in 1914, and a further decline of almost 25 percent, to 4,457,147 barrels, in 1915.[42]

With the exception of the National Railways, most of these reductions in sales came from conscious corporate decisions to curtail activity in response to increased disturbances in Mexico. According to Doheny, those conditions "caused the management to refrain from extensive contract undertakings," which included not renewing several agreements that expired in 1913 and 1914. This was due in part to fears that shipments could be cut off at Tampico at any time and also because the company lacked sufficient storage facilities outside of Mexico to ensure a safe supply of oil for its customers. It also had to do with the political situation itself, since in

April 1915, an unidentified official of Huasteca Petroleum, presumably Herbert Wylie, stated that, for the past two years, "we have been marking time, so far as taking on any new or large contract is concerned, preferring to run along as we were, rather than to direct attention and possibly invite hostile attacks by too big a showing of business and earnings."[43]

Although these deliberate reductions represented a significant percentage of oil sales, the company still earned a profit each year. But the disposition of those funds further underscored the extreme caution taken by the management after 1913. Net profits for the years 1912 to 1915 were $2,849,771 for 1912; $5,182,767 for 1913; $2,718,021 for 1914; and $2,888,101 for 1915. Of these amounts, the company returned in dividends $1,923,545 in 1912 and $2,173,100 in 1913, or roughly 67 percent and 42 percent of net income, respectively. After suspending dividend payments for the next two years, the company had $11,260,808 in total surplus (cash and investments) by the end of 1915, or roughly twice the figure for 1913. And given the potential for chaos during the civil war, Doheny held an ever increasing amount of that money in a cash reserve that grew from $167,000 in 1913 to as much as $7 million by 1918.[44]

Clearly, Doheny hoped to be able to cover any unforseen disasters and to fund the bulk of his expansion plans entirely out of retained earnings. As it was, no emergency developed, leaving him with a margin of safety he had never known before. In general, these conservative policies won the company a solid reputation on the New York Stock Exchange and shares of Mexpet common increased in value after the initial shocks in 1912 and 1913. By employing sound business principles, as one director put it, Doheny finally proved "that the stock is an investment, [and] not purely speculation."[45]

Now was the time to complete the plan for a large-scale transportation and storage network that was first begun in 1911. Since that time, there had never been enough storage to meet the capacity of the wells or enough ships to meet the demand of the Gulf Coast market. This left the major companies to fight over the available charter vessels. Doheny's efforts to acquire the necessary tankers for the Mexican Petroleum Company were, he admitted at the time, "unremitting and unsuccessful." In the first months of 1912, for example, there were only six vessels available to carry oil out of Tampico: one small tanker belonging to the Texas Company, three British tankships, and two tank barges, one each from Germany and Belgium. Doheny chartered a British tank steamer to supply the Magnolia Petroleum company at Sabine, Texas, and filled a German ship chartered by Standard Oil for deliveries to Perth Amboy, New Jersey. Various smaller shipments went aboard another British vessel to the Gulf Refining Company at Tampa, Florida.[46]

In March 1912, Doheny placed his first order for two large tankers for the Huasteca Petroleum Company from an English shipyard. Later that year, he incorporated the Petroleum Transport Company (of Maine) to take over the shipping operations and contracted for more tankers and oil barges. The Huasteca Company's first big ship, the *Herbert G. Wylie*, arrived at the Gulf Refining Company dock at Port Arthur, Texas, with its initial load of oil in February 1913. Wylie, who was on board for the maiden voyage, announced that the company was ready to enter the marketing end of the business with full force and was not confining its efforts to any specific area: "The Huasteca Company will sell oil and deliver it wherever profit is visible. I consider the European market attractive, and while I am not saying that our fleet is being assembled for any particular line of distribution, yet I will say that the European market for Mexican crude is attractive and the Huasteca Company is selling oil."[47]

Before Doheny could extend his reach that far, however, he had to complete the existing work on plans for a distribution network in the United States, which included a number of sales outlets along the Atlantic Coast and an American refinery. He paid for it by selling another 14,660 shares of common stock instead of tapping the company's well-stuffed surplus account. In searching out potential sites, Doheny and Canfield had investigated the oil terminals along the Texas and Louisiana coasts in 1912 and finally settled on the old Destrehan Plantation on the Mississippi River, twenty-two miles above New Orleans. As the location for a new refinery and storage depot, Destrehan had many advantages. In particular, the property had more than a mile of river frontage and extended back far enough to reach the tracks of the Illinois Central Railway, providing direct access to markets throughout the southeastern and midwestern states.

Doheny's new 6,000-barrel-a-day refinery specialized in Mexpet (also a brand name for Mexican Petroleum's products) road oil and asphalt, which were marketed from a southern sales office in New Orleans. Mexpet road oil was sold primarily to cities and railway companies that used it to control the dust along their lines. The asphalt needed no introduction, since it had been used for years on the East Coast with excellent results. Within a short time, the company was making deliveries as far north as Milwaukee, and in 1915, it added another station at Tampa, Florida, which included facilities for bunkering large ships and served as a distribution center for rail deliveries from Destrehan.[48]

To promote its operations along the eastern seaboard, Mexican Petroleum set up a main sales office in New York City and smaller outposts in Boston, Portland, Maine, and Providence, Rhode Island. Since oil was cheaper and cleaner to use than coal, this area became a prime location for securing industrial customers. In Portland, the largest purchaser was the International Paper Company. In Providence, the Jenckes Spinning Company kept Mexpet's three delivery trucks busy throughout the day. Mexpet also had smaller contracts with the American Woolen Company, the Manville woolen mills, D. Goff & Sons textile mill, and the Loutitt Home Hand Laundry Company.

Apart from economy, the conversion from coal to oil provided unique benefits to each of these customers. Goff & Sons, for example, ran their boilers at full capacity only for half of the day but needed a minimum level of steam around the clock. Previously, the coal fires had to be banked at night, which consumed fuel during non-production hours. Converting to oil allowed the company to shut the burners off completely, except for one fifteen-minute interval, and still maintain the required amount of steam without any waste of fuel. Abandoning the use of coal at the laundry achieved a minor revolution by setting loose for other tasks a large group of workers who had been needed to pick the soot off the collars and clothes handled at the plant.

To control these northeastern marketing and distribution centers, Doheny organized another subsidiary in 1915, the Mexican Petroleum Corporation of Maine. That company took over the existing outlets and added one more—at Carteret, New Jersey, located along the west side of Staten Island Sound. There, they constructed an oil storage depot and a large deep-water wharf capable of handling ships of any size. In addition, they employed a fleet of tugs and barges to supply Mexpet fuel oil to ocean liners at their respective piers anywhere in New York Harbor. By the end of the year, Doheny had fuel oil contracts with the International Mercantile Marine for its ships going from New York to California via the Panama Canal and with the Eastern Steamship Company for several of its lines, as well as a large contract to deliver crude oil to the Atlantic Refining Company in Philadelphia.[49]

Negotiations for transatlantic business began in the spring of 1914, when Doheny met with Lord Pirrie, Chairman of the Board of Harland & Wolff, one of Britain's largest shipbuilding and engineering firms. Pirrie headed an investment syndicate representing almost all of the major companies: Cunard, White Star, American, Red Star, Atlantic Transport, Dominion, National, and Leyland. And these organizations represented dozens of smaller steamship lines around the world. In April 1915, Doheny and Pirrie agreed to form the British-Mexican Petroleum Company to handle fuel oil sales in western Europe. This was an incredible opportunity, since the British investors involved were linked to a variety of manufacturing and railway enterprises in addition to their shipping interests. Although the first draft of the incorporation papers was ready by the summer of 1915, the agreement had to be put on hold when World War I diverted everyone's attention, and the company did not begin operations until 1919.[50]

The ability of the war to alter present circumstances was particularly evident when Doheny, Herbert Wylie, and George Henry returned from England on the final voyage of the Cunard liner *Lusitania,* before it was torpedoed by a German U-boat on May 7, 1915. During the trip, Doheny was still conducting business as he and Wylie inspected the *Lusitania*'s engines and boiler rooms in preparation for turning it into one of the first commercial vessels to burn oil. Doheny then outlined his plans for the British-Mexican company to Leonard Fanning, a well-known journalist for the oil press, as the *Lusitania* steamed into New York Harbor for the last time. Fanning wrote that two English companies would be formed: one to build tank stations and refineries throughout Europe and another to handle oil deliveries from Tampico. The Mexican Petroleum Company had a half-interest in the latter and a one-third share of the refining and sales operation. Mexican Petroleum would also receive a twenty-five-year contract for crude oil as soon as the parties signed the agreement.[51]

Doheny explained these arrangements to his stockholders a few months later and gave some specific reasons for taking the company's business so far afield. First of all, Doheny believed that they now owned "the greatest of all oil properties" in the world, which had already produced 50 million barrels of oil from a handful of wells. And since so many other wells were either closed in or seriously cut back, production could be increased five-fold at a moment's notice. This excess capacity demanded an extraordinary effort to find outlets for the oil. Ordinarily, Doheny would have preferred to push his operations in the United States, but he anticipated that the growing production from the mid-continent oil fields would choke off that option. The combined effect of these conditions, Doheny continued,

> moved the officials of your Company to seek and develop a market for its petroleum-fuel product as largely as possible in an entirely new field, where it would not come into destructive competition with the production of other regions, but by supplying a new want, create a new and large

market for fuel-petroleum ... Our new associates who own the patent rights for the construction of the most successful internal-combustion engine for maritime uses, and who also are interested in freight carrying vessels which ply the seven seas, have agreed to construct all their new boats as oil-users.[52]

He characterized the arrangement between Mexican Petroleum and the British investors as a coalition between the "most influential fuel-consuming interests of the world for maritime uses" and the "largest area of proven bonanza oil territory under one ownership and control." Barring the intervention of "unforeseen insurmountable obstacles," Doheny envisioned the creation of a market that could handle not just the output of the Mexican Petroleum Company but the surplus petroleum of the entire world. He concluded that the introduction of oil as a maritime fuel "will as surely revolutionize the character of ocean travel as did the introduction of steam displace, to an enormous extent, the sailing vessels of former times."[53]

Although dramatic, the impact of liquid fuel on the maritime industry was actually a long time in coming, and serious efforts calling for the adoption of oil fuel on both merchant marine and military ships had been going on for at least a decade. Russian ships had started using oil in the 1870s, and the Shell Oil Company had been operating oil-fired tankers since 1900. Yet, by the summer of 1914, less than 5 percent of the world's merchant ships used oil for fuel. At the same time, however, under conditions of war, the naval forces of both the United States and Great Britain were converting to oil burners as quickly as they could. Fuel oil solved the military's need for speed, efficiency, and clean operation, while the continual sinking of coal-fired vessels cleared the way for modern oil-burners in the postwar years.[54]

As early as 1904, the United States Navy had released a report based on its own extensive experiments which detailed the superior results of fuel oil versus coal. But due to the unreliability of the supply, the navy had been unwilling to use oil except for "special purposes and in particular localities." At the time, the navy concluded that the commercial demand for petroleum products was so large that only about 3 percent of the world's requirements for marine (merchant and military) fuel could be offset by using oil. By the early 1910s, however, almost all of the military ships under construction had oil burners.[55]

The British Navy had been following the same path, and Weetman Pearson—now Lord Cowdray—made an aggressive bid to tie up his excess production from Mexico with the British Admiralty. Like Doheny, Cowdray hoped that his newly founded Eagle Transport Company would capture a major share of the oil-bunkering business that was just beginning to refashion the maritime fuel industry. The sixty oil tankers under construction in Britain during the summer of 1912 provided evidence of this transformation.[56]

Naturally, both Doheny and Cowdray wanted to promote this situation with their respective governments. In December 1913, Cowdray even tried to get the Royal Navy to invest in the Mexican Eagle Oil Company. But British officials had no interest in propping up Cowdray's enterprise at a time when Mexico was in turmoil. Furthermore, the Wilson Administration was hypersensitive about British relations with the Huerta regime and looked upon the British government as a pawn of Lord Cowdray. Then, when the British acquiesced to American control in Mexico in November 1913, they had no desire to prove Wilson right by signing an agreement with the Mexican Eagle. Given these constraints, the British Admiralty turned to the newly formed Anglo-Persian Oil Company and signed a long-term contract for naval fuel in May 1914. In the meantime, the British purchased fuel oil from the United States, and especially from Texas distributors, to meet their current demand. While heavy Mexican crude offset these shipments, it did not meet British fuel oil standards on its own.[57]

Doheny also understood the importance of tying Mexican oil to the fuel requirements of the United States Navy and hoped to fund some of the expansion costs for the Mexican Petroleum Company through an arrangement with the government. In 1914, he made a proposal to the Navy Department to supply it with 7,000 barrels of Mexican crude per day at 40 percent below the market rate. In return for this discount, Doheny wanted a $2 million loan to purchase oil tankers and storage facilities in Louisiana or Mississippi. The navy declined the offer. But having already acknowledged a future dependence on oil, the federal government was also in the process of setting aside designated oil lands in the western United States for emergency use.[58]

In particular, the navy pinned its hopes for a future supply of petroleum on the control of public land in California. Unfortunately, the disposition of this land, withdrawn from the public domain in 1909 and 1910 and established as a naval reserve two years later, was already being challenged in federal court by the Southern Pacific Railway and a number of oil companies with prior claims to the property. Although the American Oilfields Company had a few leases in dispute, Doheny was only marginally involved in these early fights, and there was nothing to suggest his later role in the controversy over the Elk Hills oil reserve. For the time being, he concentrated on the development of his other properties in California and Mexico and redoubled his efforts to promote the use of fuel oil as a vital component of both military and industrial efficiency.[59]

6   THE PAN AMERICAN

PETROLEUM & TRANSPORT

COMPANY, 1916

Having completed the marketing arrangements for the Mexican Petroleum Company by the summer of 1915, Doheny was ready to push his way into the front ranks of the international oil trade. With the eastern half of the organization in place, he needed only to bring his California properties into the mix. Up to this point, Doheny had been forced to set aside his West Coast operations to deal with more immediate problems in Mexico—a surfeit of oil and an unsettled political situation. But as early as 1912, just before Mexico fell into the chaos of the post-Madero civil war, he made the first move toward a consolidation of his California businesses. Then, a few years later, as the dust of the Mexican revolution started to settle, Doheny made a bold move to take control of the California oil market. Although he ultimately failed in the attempt, the episode revealed much about Doheny's overall strategy and ambition, in which he employed methodical tactics in pursuit of almost limitless objectives.

He began in the spring of 1912, when he created the California Petroleum Corporation to recapitalize his West Coast operation. Although selling stock in the new holding company generated needed cash for Doheny, it also worked as a financial reward for the associates of William Salomon & Company, who had just finished placing the Mexican Petroleum Company on the New York Stock Exchange. And because a number of investment bankers and stock brokers made a quick profit floating California Petroleum, it received unwanted attention from the start. The details of the transaction were made public in a larger government investigation of Wall Street practices in 1913. Directed by Arsene Pujo, a subcommittee of the House Banking and Currency Committee took up allegations that a "money trust" existed among the members of the nation's financial establishment. Near the end of those hearings, the subcommittee called George Henry to testify about the mechanics of the California Petroleum deal as an illustration of the problem.[1]

For the most part, Henry's testimony confirmed suspicions that a few large organizations controlled and manipulated the stock market and the public's money to their own advantage. In the case of California Petroleum, an original banking group made up of William Salomon & Company, Hallegarten, and Lewisohn Brothers paid Doheny $8,215,662 for approximately 175,000 shares of stock in the new company: 100,000 shares of preferred and 75,000 shares of common. Then, with Doheny out of the picture, Salomon distributed the issue in three phases. First, it sold $5 million worth of stock (50,000 preferred and 25,000 common) to a syndicate in London which listed Calpet (the trade name of the company) on the Paris exchange. Next, Salomon sold the same amount to a sub-syndicate made up of preferred customers in New York, Chicago, and Detroit, in which each participant received a specified allotment of shares to be purchased at $91½ for the preferred and $40 for the common. Finally, having earned $1,784,328 in cash from the preceding sales, Salomon held back 25,000 shares of common for itself as profit for putting the deal together.[2]

With the stock distributed in this manner, Henry directed the brokers at Lewisohn to make a market for the new issue on the exchange. They began by trading the stock at $40 to $50 a share on the curb market for the first week. Then, just before it went on to the big board, Salomon released an appraisal of the property, conducted once again by Ralph Arnold, stating that the stock was worth over $100 a share. Despite his earlier dispute with Doheny over the value of Mexpet properties, Arnold was still the leading geologist in California, and his opinion mattered. This time, he was genuinely enthusiastic about the new company.[3]

With this sort of advance billing, it was no surprise that Calpet had a sensational opening on the exchange, and it was all the brokers could do to hold back the tide and keep the stock from going up too quickly. As it was, it closed out its first day at $72, with a volume of 52,200 shares traded. Over the next three weeks, the entire issue turned over three times, with 362,270 shares traded out of a total of 105,729 shares outstanding. Lewisohn's effort to place a floor under the stock accounted for most of those trades, and, between October 5 and October 21, the brokers sold 172,000 shares and repurchased 149,000. According to market experts, a firm could expect to buy and sell 100,000 shares of a new issue for every 20,000 it placed in the market.[4]

Samuel Untermeyer, a wealthy Wall Street attorney acting as counsel for the subcommittee, accused Henry of simply manufacturing a false market for the stock. As Untermeyer saw it, the brokers boomed the stock and then relied on a series of manufactured trades to drive up the price. To the contrary, Henry insisted that they had only been responding to inordinate public demand, not creating it, and that they had actually lost money trying to steady the price. To keep the stock in bounds, however, Henry admitted that they had someone on hand everyday to give "buying orders on a scale down and selling orders on a scale up." Untermeyer interpreted this as a ruse to make the stock appear active; Henry considered it essential to "give the stock a real market." In the end, the committee saw it as yet another example of "unwholesome speculation and manipulation."[5]

Regardless of the promotional activities of the investment bankers, the demand for California Petroleum was not wholly artificial. Certainly, based on the previous performance of Mexican Petroleum, a new Doheny company was bound to attract attention, especially when Mexpet common, which entered the market at $62¾ six months earlier, was trading at over $90 when Calpet first appeared. And, except for the Texas Company, whose stock was expensive and lightly traded, Doheny had the only oil stocks on the market.[6] In general, as one writer explained a few years later, investors came to expect marvelous things from Doheny and claimed to see a special sort of luck where he was concerned: "Mr. Doheny goes in where good judgment justifies a reasonable expectation of success and comes out saturated with richness, staggering under a heaped up load of results ... A truly scientific person would be compelled to define 'Doheny luck' as good sound sense plus a gorgeous abundance not anticipated."[7]

Doheny's choice of an Irish shamrock for the Mexpet logo suggested that he, too, had come to believe in his own good fortune. But such confidence seemed misplaced in the case of the California Petroleum Corporation, which came together just as the oil market hit another downturn. Although it was never in financial difficulty, the company failed to meet the high expectations of its investors. A snapshot of the industry in July 1913 showed that Calpet's producing subsidiaries, American Oilfields and American Petroleum, were among the strongest independents in the state. At that time, American Oilfields, which operated in the Midway oil district, was the largest and most important member of the Independent Oil Producers Agency. Of the 129 companies belonging to the Agency, American Oilfields alone produced 264,906 barrels of oil that month, or roughly 27 percent of the Agency's total production. In comparison, the next largest company was Nevada Petroleum, at 75,000 barrels a month, while the remaining companies averaged about 5,000 barrels apiece. The situation in Coalinga, where American Petroleum produced 186,317 barrels on contract with the Associated Oil Company, was not quite as strong. Still, American Petroleum accounted for 12 percent of the Associated's business. Overall, for the month under review, the combined production of the two companies made California Petroleum—at 451,223 barrels—fifth among the seven largest producers on the West Coast, after Union Oil at 843,871 barrels, Standard Oil at 751,906, Kern Trading and Oil Company (Southern Pacific) at 678,302, and Associated Oil Company at 564,840. Santa Fe (formerly a combination of Chanslor & Canfield Midway Oil and Petroleum Development) and General Petroleum Company were right behind, with 397,143 and 362,559 barrels, respectively.[8]

Facing another oil glut, however, Doheny used the cash received from floating Calpet to build an extensive storage network and cut back production to just meet his contract obligations. Planning for the future, though, he continued to buy up prospective oil land outside of the San Joaquin Valley. In doing so, Doheny was able to open and close various fields according to the market and, thus, gain control of a strategic combination of proven, but undeveloped, properties. This left him free to rely on his long-term contracts to the Independent Oil Producers Agency and Associated Oil during the bad times, and to open up new "freelance" properties, outside the control of either marketing organization, when prices went back up.[9]

At the other end of the scale, the remaining members of the Agency were almost always out of step with the market. They sold oil at a loss during times of depression and produced too much when conditions started to improve. Although their ability to upset the situation at almost any point gave them a negative power, the small independents survived on the sufferance and superior market intelligence of the large companies. Supposedly, the IOPA had been formed to keep the independents in line, but the small producers defied efforts at full control and continued to pose a danger to themselves and to the fortunes of the state. For that reason, the worsening conditions in 1914 inspired another plan to reorganize the independent oil companies into a stronger combination.

This latest idea came from Mark L. Requa, a San Francisco mining engineer and president of the Nevada Petroleum Company. As a frequent writer and public speaker on oil issues, Requa was a well-known figure on the West Coast. He was also a long-standing critic of the small-minded attitude of the independent producers. In fact, he wanted to get rid of them altogether. Outlining the problem to the assembled membership of the IOPA in July 1914, Requa was blunt, if not insulting:

> I am telling no secrets when I say that to the average producer of oil a continuation of existing conditions spells ruin, nor do I exaggerate in saying that unless conditions are changed, the oil properties in the hands of the average small company are, relatively speaking, without value. We are exhausting one of the State's greatest assets without any adequate return . . . The individual producer, from early ignorance, creates a condition that spells financial suicide. He immolates himself upon the altar of his own ignorance and short-sighted avarice and blames his troubles, not upon himself, where they belong, but upon the marketing companies that merely buy his product at prices set by himself in competition with his neighbor.[10]

The marketing companies, by contrast, stood above the fray and prospered accordingly. The Agency, Requa believed, needed to do the same: "It seems to me obvious that we can do no better than emulate the example set for us. Let us determine the value of what we have and thereafter so weld together the various units . . . to reap the benefits that are justly ours." But instead of relying on cooperative association alone, Requa proposed the creation of a new company made up of independent producers who would exchange their individual properties for stock in a new corporation. By cutting overhead and other duplicated costs, including the salaries of the people responsible for the crisis in the first place, the new organization would be able to approach Standard Oil, Associated Oil, and Union Oil on equal, if not better, terms. Of course, many people thought that it would be "utterly impossible" to convince the officers of the existing companies to give up their meal tickets for stock in the new corporation, but Requa believed they were facing a life or death situation that demanded a drastic solution.[11]

The first step, to which the Agency members reluctantly agreed, was to conduct a thorough appraisal of each member's assets. Requa warned that "this valuing will mean a complete investigation of your records and the collecting of all available statistics concerning your property." Unfortunately, despite fifteen months of work, Requa discovered that the producers did not have anything to reveal but their own incompetence; there was no reliable information about the historical development of the various California oilfields and almost no financial data for any particular organization. Of the 130 companies under review, no more than a half dozen had adequate records. Despite his own suspicions, Requa was thoroughly appalled at the "dense ignorance" of oilmen about basic business concepts. Most of the independents did not even know how much it actually cost them to produce a barrel of oil, so it was a wonder that they had stayed in business as long as they had.[12]

In a previous investigation, Requa had determined that most California oilmen based their production expenses on the direct cost of pumping oil from an existing well, without considering previous outlays for exploration, the price of materials, or additional factors such as interest and depreciation. When those elements were added in, he estimated that the true cost of producing a barrel of oil was approximately thirty to thirty-five cents—almost as much as the normal bulk price for oil at the wells. Requa suggested that, by figuring costs the way they did, some producers were deliberately fooling the public about the health of their companies and living off of the lie. Thus, to rationalize the production cycle and promote the public interest, Requa became an early advocate for mandatory standards of cost accounting for oil companies.[13]

In the meantime, the best he could do was to assemble the accounting data and production curves for Doheny's companies in Coalinga and Midway and extrapolate from them to find a suitable base for Kern River, Orange County, and a handful of smaller fields for which he had no information at all. By its very inadequacy, Requa's valuation of the independents' holdings reinforced his call for a massive reorganization of the Agency itself. Consequently, in 1915, Requa, along with L. P. St. Clair, the head of the Agency, and T. A. O'Donnell, vice-president of California Petroleum, met with W. L. Stewart, president of the Union Oil Company, to discuss a merger.[14]

Up to this point, Doheny had deliberately been absent from these discussions, although it became clear later on that, from the beginning, he and George Henry had been behind the effort to roll the independent companies into a competitive organization. In fact, in 1914, William Salomon hired Ralph Arnold to evaluate several potential combinations among Union Oil, Associated Oil, General Petroleum, and California Petroleum. While Doheny tried to stay out of public view for as long as possible, there was growing suspicion within the industry that he was the power behind the merger effort in California.

Thus, in line with Doheny's plans, Requa hoped to purchase a majority share of Union Oil on behalf of the Agency. Instead, because of a number of intervening factors, he settled for an option on the United Petroleum Company, the principal holding company through which the Stewart family controlled the larger organization. But there was trouble from the start when Andrew Weir, an English investor who owned a large share of the company's stock, opposed the deal. Weir was also a major shareholder of the General Petroleum Company, which was in serious financial trouble at the time, and his presence made for a messy combination of interests and personalities.[15]

To complicate the situation even further, a group of disgruntled Union stockholders opposed to any merger filed suit in federal court to dissolve United Petroleum and wrest control from the Stewart family. The actions of this insurgent group, led by John Garrigues, the former treasurer of the company, threw a pall over any plans for the future. Garrigues was a strident critic of the Stewarts' management decisions and characterized Union's arrangements with the Agency as a series of "invidious contracts" that imperiled the health of the entire company.

O'Donnell recalled that Garrigues had repeatedly tried to browbeat and intimidate the Agency's executive committee during negotiations with Union Oil. And Garrigues was notorious for having made some statements about the Stewarts during a news conference that were so libelous that the local papers refused to print them. Not surprisingly, Garrigues interpreted the proposed sale of the company to Requa as an underhanded way for the Stewart family to inflate the value of its stock and cheat everyone else. Though the merger documents stipulated that all shareholders would participate in the deal equally, Garrigues managed to rattle the nerves of Union stockholders by bringing the legality of the holding company itself into question.[16]

A similar, but less volatile, struggle occurred within the ranks of the Doheny organization as his participation in the California merger became better known. Doheny first tipped his hand in this regard in September 1915, when he informed the stockholders of Mexican Petroleum that he wanted to form a seven-year voting trust so that the company could take advantage of war-time changes in the European market. Ostensibly, a trusteeship made up of Doheny, Herbert Wylie, and J. M. Danzinger would better serve the interests of the company by being able to take immediate action without seeking stockholder approval at every turn. In the context of Doheny's simultaneous efforts in California, however, many shareholders interpreted the move as a possible threat to their capacity to control the future of the company. Just prior to the annual meeting in December 1915, anonymous petitions appeared in New York brokerage houses urging stockholders to hold firm against Doheny's proposal. Although these messages usually wound up in the wastebasket, they raised eyebrows about management's plans. In the end, this short-lived rebellion was inconsequential except as an indication that not everyone was comfortable with Doheny's ulterior motives.[17]

The first public information about Doheny's intentions came to light on December 10, 1915, when he announced that he was forming a $100 million petroleum and transport company and that it would be the greatest enterprise of its kind in America. At this point, Doheny's efforts and those of the IOPA were finally recognized as one and the same. That revelation led to increased speculation among industry analysts that Union Oil, Associated Oil, and the General Petroleum Company would all come together under the Doheny umbrella, along with the Agency itself. At least W. L. Stewart confirmed that Requa's option for United Petroleum shares was on behalf of the new Doheny company. By the middle of January 1916, the *San Francisco Examiner,* which had been following Requa's progress in some detail, reported that Doheny's Mexican Petroleum Company would be the nucleus of the largest oil combination in the world.[18]

Apart from that with Union Oil, any direct connection with the other companies was less certain and subject to speculation. The clearest statement came from L. P. St. Clair, who confirmed the negotiations between the Doheny interests, Union Oil, General Petroleum, and the IOPA and claimed that "the situation looks encouraging for a definite conclusion of the transaction." The *Wall Street Journal* was just as certain that the Associated Oil Company had to be included in any combination.[19]

In support of that position, the *New York Times* reported that Doheny held a short-term option on $20 million worth of Associated stock owned by the Southern Pacific Railway. But for reasons not stated, Doheny allowed the option to lapse at the end of the January. According to William Sproule, the president of Associated Oil, there was "absolutely no truth in the report that negotiations are in progress with Mr. Doheny or anyone else for a change in control of the Associated Oil Co." Nevertheless, a subsequent report noted that Sproule, who also had assumed control of the Southern Pacific in 1914, viewed the oil company as an unnecessary burden for the railroad and had been trying unsuccessfully to find a buyer.[20]

At the same time, Requa's negotiations with Union Oil ground to a halt, after he spent a month in New York trying to work out an acceptable arrangement with an investment banking committee. Requa's option called for Doheny to make a $1 million cash payment toward the purchase of $4 million of United Petroleum stock owned by the Stewart family. United Petroleum sat at the top of a pyramided structure, where it controlled the shares of the Union Provident Company, which in turn controlled the $34 million of outstanding stock of Union Oil. Perhaps the impending stockholder suit against this holding company arrangement caused Requa to give up his option before the deadline of February 15, 1916.[21]

By the end of 1915, there had also been a dramatic change in the West Coast oil market, which allowed Union Oil to earn a sizable profit for the year and quieted many of its critics. To their credit, the Stewarts took advantage of the situation to voluntarily dissolve United Petroleum prior to any court ruling and, hence, regained the support of most shareholders— except for Garrigues, of course, who was unceremoniously dumped from the board of directors along the way. In October 1916, a Los Angeles court formally ordered the liquidation of the holding company as an unlawful form of control, but by then the crisis had long since passed.[22]

For the first time in five years, oil consumption outpaced production on the West Coast, and the contract price rose above seventy cents per barrel. These improvements, coupled with the congenitally short memory of most oil producers, forced the marketing companies to shelve any merger plans for the moment. The members of the Agency, on the other hand, stuck with long-term contracts at less than fifty cents a barrel, did not see any immediate benefit from these changes. For that reason alone, Doheny was still planning to combine the members of the Agency into a single entity in order to eliminate the competitive deficiencies of the independent companies. But once having renegotiated their contracts at higher prices, the recalcitrant producers turned him down and voted to maintain the Agency as it was, with California Petroleum firmly ensconced at the center.[23]

In the light of improved conditions, Doheny's plans were seen as too ambitious and threatening to his fellow oilmen. No doubt, he had been thinking on a scale that challenged the imagination of his most ardent supporters and scared the devil out of his enemies. Had the merger gone through as planned, it would have been an amazing accomplishment. As of December 1915, the combined assets of California Petroleum, Associated Oil, Union Oil, and General Petroleum totaled $214,778,310. A company of that magnitude would have been more than twice the size of Standard Oil of California, which had $98,543,332 in assets, and roughly three-quarters the size of Standard Oil New Jersey, with $281,903,777. By adding the Mexican Petroleum Company to this California combination— at $63,051,445—to say nothing of the smaller members of the Agency, Doheny would have been able to compete one-to-one with the Rockefeller dynasty.[24]

In retrospect, Doheny might have been able to complete each of these mergers by taking them one at a time, but trying to capture three different organizations simultaneously was virtually impossible. Yet Doheny and Requa took advantage of a particular moment in the development of the California oil industry when such an idea was given serious consideration. Unfortunately, despite having purchase options for all the major prospects, they simply ran out of time before the market turned around once again, due largely to the unforeseen consequences of the war in Europe. In the end, Doheny accepted the circumstances in California for what they were and refocused his attention on Mexico, where he still had an opportunity to push his company to the forefront of the industry.

Even with his California plans falling down around him, however, Doheny still needed a way to consolidate his existing operation. To do that, he incorporated the Pan American Petroleum & Transport Company of Delaware on February 2, 1916. Although capitalized at $150 million, the company's initial capital stock was approximately $40 million, divided between $10 million preferred and $30,494,750 common. Acting as a pure holding company, Pan American Petroleum derived its income from its constituent companies in the following proportions: 45 percent of Mexican Petroleum common; 75 percent of Mexican Petroleum preferred; 97 percent of the Petroleum Transport Company common; 59 percent of Caloric Company common (a South American marketing subsidiary based in Brazil); 66 percent of Caloric preferred; and 100 percent of Buena Fe Petroleum, a small California subsidiary.[25]

In return for financing this new organization, Wall Street gained a sizable constituency on the board of Pan American Petroleum. Doheny retained active control of the company's management, with 60 percent of the members of the board under his command, but investment bankers filled out the remaining positions. The outside directors included Thomas Cochran Jr., president of the Liberty Mutual National Bank; Edward R. Tinker Jr., vice-president of the Chase National Bank; Eugene Meyer Jr., of Eugene Meyer and Company; and two partners from William Salomon & Company.[26]

In a letter to Salomon & Company at the time of incorporation, Doheny justified their faith in the new organization by claiming that Pan American Petroleum would soon control "the largest area of proven oil territory in the world under one ownership." As it turned out, this was no idle boast. In fact, just eight days later, the Huasteca Petroleum Company drilled in Cerro Azul No. 4, the largest oil well in the world at the time. In this instance, Doheny had literally been banking on the new well coming in when it did, having drilled down to the cap rock the year before. At that time, the company suspended operations in the face of increased political turmoil in Mexico and did not obtain permission to resume drilling until after Carranza received de facto recognition by the Wilson administration in October 1915. Meanwhile, after gauging the pressure in the well, they knew they had another tremendous gusher on their hands when they went to work again in February.[27]

Doheny was so confident that the well would be a prize that he had a photographer camped out in the jungle with cameras, moving-picture equipment, and a portable darkroom to record the event. With everything in place, the drilling crew hit a large pocket of gas on February 9, which gave further indication of what was to come. Early the next morning, the bit plunged through the protective layer of rock, the drill cable went slack as the pressure of the gas lifted the tools back up the casing, and the well began to rumble and roar with volcanic ferocity. Taking that as their final cue, the drilling crew ran for their lives but managed to get only about twenty feet away before the well erupted in an explosion of gas that shot the 4,000-pound string of tools straight out of the hole. When they came down, they were 125 feet away from the well and a mere nine feet from the photographer, who, in an understandable moment of panic, missed filming the initial blowout.

Over the next few days, however, as the well spewed out a column of oil 600 feet into the air, the photographer captured the dramatic images of Cerro Azul that appeared under the caption "World's Greatest Oil Well" in almost every major newspaper in the country. To celebrate the occasion, George Henry hosted a lavish dinner in New York in Doheny's honor, featuring a motion picture of Cerro Azul blowing at full strength before it was brought under control. As incredible as it seemed, the maximum flow of the well was estimated at more than 260,000 barrels a day—more oil, as Herbert Wylie pointed out, than was produced by the entire state of California.[28]

Of course that much production, all at once, again overwhelmed the company's infrastructure, despite its best efforts to prepare for a large well. In this instance, the crew had a complete valve system installed on the pipe before they drilled in the well and had storage tanks set up for a half-million barrels of oil. But when the gas pressure blew the drilling tools out of the well, they ripped apart the valve, the derrick, and everything else in the way. As a result, there was no way to shut in the flow, and the well ran wild for seven days before the crew was able to screw a new valve over the casing and bring it under control. In the meantime, they burned off what

World's Greatest Oil Well, Cerro Azul No. 4, February 1916. Archival
Center, Archdiocese of Los Angeles.

excess oil they could while the rest overran the storage facilities and saturated the ground for two miles around the well. Other preparations paid
off handsomely, however—especially the twin eight-inch pipelines from
Tampico. Those lines had been only about fifty feet short of the well when
the company suspended the initial drilling campaign in 1915 and were
easily completed once the new gate valve was in place.[29]

Obviously, Doheny had been incredibly shrewd to have all of this work come together as it did, and, in his deliberate attempt to showcase the well, he even managed to have Dr. I. C. White on hand when Cerro Azul roared to life. As before, White had been chosen to appraise the property for the investment bankers, and he followed the same procedures that he had used four years earlier, allowing $300 a barrel for the settled daily production of the Ebano and Casiano properties and $500 a barrel for Cerro Azul. He raised the number for the new well because the old figures had been proven to be even more conservative than he had intended in 1911. Previously, White had appraised the Ebano field at $2 million and Casiano at $10,674,000. By 1916, however, those properties had already returned net earnings of $2,080,349 and $12,810,861, respectively, and were still producing oil at approximately the same rate without any water.

The prospects for Cerro Azul were even brighter, since White found that the basin around the well was ten times bigger than the one around Casiano and that the adjacent oil seepages were 100 times as large and much more active. Furthermore, White noted that Cerro Azul sat in the middle of a 52,000-acre tract of land that the company held in fee, unencumbered by government concessions. This virtually eliminated the likelihood of competitive drilling, since the nearest boundary line was more than five miles away. Taking all of these factors into consideration and using Casiano as a yardstick, White predicted that Cerro Azul would produce at least a billion barrels of oil.

Assuming a settled production of 200,000 barrels a day, White calculated the value of the new well at $100 million, or just ten cents a barrel for oil in the ground. White added $12.6 million to that amount for Ebano and Casiano combined and $19,721,000 for the remaining camp property, fixtures, and machinery. Because Cerro Azul by itself exceeded the value of White's previous estimate for all the undeveloped oil lands, he tripled his initial figure to arrive at $162 million for properties held in reserve. Consequently, according to these calculations, which were still relatively conservative, the Mexican Petroleum Company was worth $294,321,000, or four times its 1911 value. After a detailed examination of the oil fields, White predicted the probable future production of the company at 5,140,500,000 barrels of oil, or sixty-eight years at 200,000 barrels a day. Given these extraordinary numbers, White admitted that his greatest difficulty in presenting his estimates was making them "small enough to appear reasonable."[30]

Just when Doheny hoped to capitalize on this vast productive capacity, however, the political situation in Mexico worsened once again. Ironically,

Cerro Azul's fantastic potential made many investors increasingly nervous about the situation. In particular, the rebel activities of Francisco "Pancho" Villa, who lashed out against the United States for its recognition of Carranza in the fall of 1915, made conditions even more volatile than they had been before. Villa believed that the Wilson Administration's decision to recognize the Carranza government was based on a secret pact that granted concessions to the Americans and compromised Mexico's sovereignty. An attempt at such a plan had been made by Mexican and American representatives, but Villa was mistaken about Carranza's complicity in the scheme. Believing as he did, however, Villa tried to compromise the relationship between the United States and Mexican governments through various acts of terror, including the murder of a number of American civilians and businesspeople.[31]

By January 1916, the rumors of possible intervention by United States troops led many investment houses to discourage customers from buying shares of Mexican Petroleum. The best policy, according to one, was simply to "lie low and await developments." But tensions increased dramatically after the infamous raid at Columbus, New Mexico, by Villa's forces on March 9, 1916, and they reached the breaking point when Pershing's Punitive Expedition crossed into Mexico in pursuit of the rebel forces a short while later. All of this looked like some sort of bizarre conspiracy to one reporter, who noted that the periodic instability in Mexico managed to "stifle enthusiasm whenever it seemed likely to creep out." The whole situation was so fraught with danger that, for a time during the early spring of 1916, it almost crowded out the war news from across the Atlantic. In Europe, according to this same observer, it would take a deliberate attack by a German submarine to cause a sudden change of events, "but the case of Mexico is entirely different. Any hour may bring forth a crisis."[32]

The effect of this situation, combined with the merger-induced speculation about the disposition of Doheny's California operations, ratchetted up the activity in Mexican Petroleum common on the New York Stock Exchange. The anticipated merger caused both Doheny companies to take a dramatic jump in December 1915: Mexpet common went from $96 to $125, and Calpet common went from $29 to $39. At the beginning of 1915, Mexican Pete had been as low as $51, and California Petroleum had been down to $8 in July. In terms of total volume, Mexican Petroleum consistently led the market as one of most active stocks. For example, on the final trading day of 1915, 95,700 shares of Mexpet changed hands, a volume second only to that of U.S. Steel, and the stock closed at $123. It started the new year at $127 with 102,200 shares trading hands, having doubled its opening price from three years earlier. Then, from its high point on January 4, the price dropped as low as \$95 by the end of February. On average, there were over 31,000 shares of Mexican Petroleum traded every market day from January through March. California Petroleum also enjoyed a brief resurgence, when it opened the year with a volume of 36,000 shares, although at \$38, the price was disappointing.[33]

Apparently, the Mexican political situation not only tempered the market's enthusiasm for the newly formed Pan American Petroleum company but commanded much of Doheny's attention. And those constraints, coupled with the failure of the West Coast merger, led him to resign his position as president of the California Petroleum Company in April 1916 and sell off his stock holdings in the company. Although Doheny did not completely cut his ties to Calpet, retaining a seat on the board of American Petroleum, he reduced his responsibilities as much as possible. Herbert Wylie and J. M. Danzinger stayed on as directors for each of the subsidiaries, while T. A. O'Donnell became the new president of California Petroleum.[34]

Doheny did not retire from California as much as he freed himself to be more creative and spontaneous in making smaller investments across the state, when he had the time, and many of these subsequent acquisitions were initiated in partnership with California Petroleum. In that way, Doheny was able to assume an entrepreneurial role once again and concentrate his efforts in the newest oil districts. To begin, he created the Fairfield Petroleum Company to operate wells in Kern County and to hold new producing properties in Texas. Next, he formed the Pan American Petroleum Investment Company to purchase \$2 million worth of oil lands on the Bell Ranch in Santa Barbara County, considered by most experts to be one of the choicest pieces of oil territory in the state. At the same time, in the fall of 1916, he formed the Pan American Petroleum Company of California to acquire 6,000 acres and thirty operating wells from the Bard Oil and Asphalt Company. Finally, he set up the Doheny Pacific Petroleum Company to control smaller holdings from North Midway to Simi Valley. Although some of the funding for these purchases came from corporate sources, most of the money came directly out of Doheny's pocket. Once again, Doheny was taking advantage of changing conditions in the California oilfields, which placed a premium on increased production, rapid drilling, and the acquisition of new territory.[35]

For its part, California Petroleum became a corporate orphan within the Doheny organization after 1916 and maintained a weak but steady position in the market behind the Associated Oil Company, Union Oil, and

Standard Oil. Over time, the gap between it and the others widened as the top three companies developed into fully integrated operations. Apparently, the failure of the merger froze Calpet into position as a large producing company only. In terms of overall growth for the rest of the decade, the total assets of California Petroleum rose by a scant 2 percent, while Associated Oil increased by 21 percent, Union Oil by 67 percent, and Standard Oil by an aggressive 253 percent. For the same period, net earnings went up 82 percent for California Petroleum, 314 percent for Associated Oil, 429 percent for Union Oil, and 465 percent for Standard Oil. The return on assets (net earnings/total assets) averaged just 7 percent for California Petroleum, 13 percent for Associated Oil, 16 percent for Union Oil, and 22 percent for Standard Oil. Having begun in 1913 with such bright prospects, investors were left to wonder what had gone wrong. The company was either incredibly conservative or seriously mismanaged, and no one seemed to know which was the case.[36]

Initially, the company's poor earnings were a consequence of two factors: its long-term contracts with the Agency, and a decline in production caused by water seepage in Kern River. Consequently, its total monthly output, which included several Doheny companies half-owned by California Petroleum, fell slightly in 1914 to 415,055 barrels, dropped sharply to a low of 276,041 barrels in 1917, and recovered to 486,400 barrels by 1919. Its share of the state's total production varied accordingly: 4.8 percent in 1914, 3.4 percent in 1917, and 5.8 percent in 1919. Calpet actually had considerable capacity tied up in its reserves, and, when those properties came on line in the early 1920s, oil production doubled almost immediately. At that point, one market expert suggested that "the company evidently enjoyed a sagacious management from the beginning."[37]

Although California Petroleum's overall position among the large oil companies remained about the same, there was a marked consolidation of the market into the hands of the top organizations. Primarily, this involved the emergence of Standard Oil California, whose share of total production went from 13 percent in 1914 to 25 percent in 1919. Standard's rapid growth also accounted for the rise in the combined output of the seven largest companies over this same period—from 48 percent to 71 percent of the total. Calpet remained part of that group but at the lower end of the scale. And despite Doheny and Requa's best efforts, the smaller independents grew even more dependent upon the marketing giants.[38]

In the end, however, the dramatic improvement in the West Coast oil market after 1916 helped inaugurate a national role for the California oil industry. While the formal entry of the United States into the European war gave the state its first chance to export oil outside of the region, it was even more important for giving the leaders of the local industry a national forum from which to promote their own interests. In particular, Requa, O'Donnell, and Doheny were soon headed to Washington as industry representatives, charged with coordinating the nation's petroleum supply during the war. While Doheny benefitted most from circumstances that highlighted the value of Mexican fuel oil over the California product, local oilmen still had a chance to make a case for their state. In this way, at least, the preceding few years had been excellent preparation for a situation that demanded a cooperative effort on all fronts. And after twenty years in the oil business, Doheny got a chance to become one of the titans of the industry.

7 THE VISION OF PEACE:
FUEL OIL FOR THE WAR

By the time Doheny formed the Pan American Petroleum & Transport Company in 1916, he was considered to be one of the nation's most enterprising businessmen. His reputation on the West Coast, in particular, had reached legendary proportions. According to one author writing in 1918, there were hundreds of men in California's history who had risen to wealth through mining, real estate, and other ventures, but there was "only one Doheny." What made him unique, the author continued, was his varied talents as "a manager, an executive, a promoter, a stock salesman, a banker, a capitalist, a financier, a diplomat, an expert on manipulation, an authority on transportation, a professor of chemistry, a wizard at geology, and a magnate of sorts."[1] Apart from the obvious hyperbole, this was a reasonable assessment of Doheny's career or, at least, of what he was about to make of it. Another writer went further, suggesting that "what the name of Rockefeller is to the oil refining industry, the name Doheny is to the oil producing industry . . . It was he who, like a modern Moses, struck the supposedly dry sands of California with his rod until the valuable fluid gushed forth and it was he who drilled in the tangled jungles of Mexico and unloosed 'gushers' such as the world had never seen before."[2]

Certainly, after two decades of work, this was not undeserved praise, and at sixty years old, Doheny was ready to assume a prominent role in the nation's business affairs. But such a position required some fundamental changes in his responsibilities and in his outlook. Although he had been accumulating power and wealth for some time, Doheny had been completely absorbed in building his oil companies. But now that he had an empire to protect, he needed to widen his sphere of influence to meet a variety of challenges, and Doheny took advantage of the United States' participation in the World War to make it happen.

At the time America entered the war in the spring of 1917, business and industrial leaders of all types were becoming vital participants in the effort to bring the nation up to full strength. The demands of the war also made the security of the Mexican oil industry a primary concern for national defense and reinforced the strategic value of the California oil fields for the future. According to a recent study of the international oil industry during this period, there "is no time when business competition is so heavily politicized as in war, which for business means a covert struggle for advantage under a publicly emphasized desire to serve the national interest." Without question, Doheny took advantage of America's role in the war to propel himself and his company into national prominence. And as the next two chapters will show, it was almost impossible for him to draw a clear line between duty and opportunity during a national emergency.[3]

From the very beginning of the European conflict, there was every indication that oil would play a prominent role. In the fall of 1914, for example, an article entitled "Gasoline and the War" noted that oil had already become more important than food or ammunition. "It has been an axiom of war since wars began," the author wrote, "that an army travels on its belly ... As it is now, an army travels on its gasoline." The possession of oil, therefore, was essential to the prosecution of modern warfare. And right from the start, the United States served as the principal source of petroleum products to the Allied forces, especially for the fuel oil demands of the British Admiralty. American refineries along the Gulf Coast were particularly important in this trade, and heavy Mexican crude was used to replace the lighter products needed for the European theater. Mexican oil played an even larger role as an industrial fuel for American factories in the Northeast, where Doheny's companies dominated the business.[4]

The war effort became the perfect advertising medium for fuel oil, and Doheny wasted no time taking advantage of the situation. The first issue of the company magazine, the *Pan American Record*, announced the arrival of "the century of oil" and went on to explain that every marvel of modern technology would be nothing but a "Jules Verne dream" without fuel oil. Thus, the primary lesson to be taken from the battlefields of Europe was that the current fight was merely a prelude to an even greater conflict in the years to come: "Scientific method will be applied more and more in every domain of human activity, and in this titanic economic struggle that is approaching, only those best equipped will survive the 'storm and stress' period. Quick transportation is the very essence of success, and the highest speed is only possible for the consumer of oil. If you are not driving your machinery with oil, make the change now; in a few months it may be too late."[5]

This statement encapsulated the twin goals of Doheny's marketing strategy during the period: the industrial application of fuel oil and the conversion of the world's shipping fleets to oil. Obviously, as suggested above, the emphasis on marine transportation was especially important, and Doheny advertised his fuel oil as though it were a tonic for the travails of modern commerce. Each succeeding issue of the *Pan American Record*, in fact, repeated the warning that the real contest between nations would not begin until the economic competition after the war. "For years we have prepared for this development both on the Atlantic and Pacific coasts," one article maintained, "and our oil in Mexico and California is especially suitable for marine fuel." With a new era at hand, according to another, "coal will remain for commercial sloths; oil will be the fuel for those who observe those clearly defined laws that lead to success."[6]

During the preparedness campaigns leading up to America's participation in the war, the *MexPet Record* gave the following warning: "End of war in Europe will mark the beginning of the world's greatest struggle for commercial supremacy. The liberated tonnage of Germany will join with war-freed vessels of all the world in searching out cargoes in all seas and all countries. The ships that use fuel-oil will be first to every port because they will be swiftest on the voyage. The ships that are prepared will get the cargoes. Be prepared by having your ships fitted to burn Mexpet Fuel-Oil."[7]

Statements of this type were not just simple advertisements for a product; they were sophisticated arguments aimed at the political leaders in Washington. In this case, the message was clear: the United States and its commercial agents could reshape the world by using Mexican oil as their source of power. Another example of this approach can be seen in a full-page illustration entitled "The Vision of Peace," which portrayed a multi-ethnic group of people gazing heavenward at a bank of clouds shaped like the Western Hemisphere. Where California and Mexico would be located in these cloud formations, there were oil derricks pouring their contents on the troubled waters of the world. The sense of irony in this scene is palpable, since oil would do as much to roil those waters as to calm them. Nevertheless, from the company's point of view, oil was a commercial and civilizing agent that no nation could afford to neglect.[8]

An earlier statement in the *MexPet Record* was even more direct: "Transportation is the most important thing in the world and fuel-oil is

The Vision of Peace. *Pan American Record*, March 1917.

the most important factor in transportation. Therefore the nation that controls fuel-oil controls the world." The company even published a revised version of the song "Rule Britannia," rendered as "Rule Petroleum!" to dramatize the point: "The Muses, still with Freedom found, Shall to thy happy yachts repair; Blest oil! with matchless power crowned, To rule the sea and guard the air. Rule, Petroleum! Petroleum, rule the waves! Fuel-Oil is not for slaves."[9] Taken together, the foregoing statements not only provided a marketing outline for the fuel oil business, but they gave Doheny a political agenda for the war. In the first place, aside from pushing the development of his own transportation network, he had to convince the American government of the strategic value of the Mexican oil fields, and he had to stop the Mexican government from implementing a nationalist attack against the industry.

He put his plan into effect on the eve of America's entry into the war, when he pledged his Mexican oil properties, and his fleet of oil tankers, to the United States government. Actually, such offers of personal service and business assistance were not uncommon in the spring of 1917, and Doheny's motives were unquestioned. In fact, the *Los Angeles Times* took comfort in knowing that one of its citizens, and "one of the country's most influential figures in the oil and financial world," would make such a sacrifice. Doheny prefaced his gesture by saying that "every citizen of the United States should loyally support the President in this crisis, and the world should understand that the President has the united nation behind him." To that end, he sent a formal announcement to President Wilson on Feb. 7, 1917, offering the use of Pan American Petroleum's tank steamers, 5 million barrels of fuel oil stored at Tampico, and any other aid the government might need. The *New York Times* considered it "one of the most gratifying offers" made at a time when firms were volunteering everything from rubber to steel.[10]

On the West Coast, Doheny also led a movement aimed at strengthening the navy's defensive posture in the Pacific. Specifically, he started a fund with $10,000 of his own money to build up the Naval Militia of California. Taking advice from naval officers who considered the current fleet inadequate and understaffed, Doheny and other like-minded businessmen wanted to put 100,000 men into the Naval Reserve and then enlist them into active duty with financial inducements from private donations. In this regard, Doheny's efforts were similar to the work being done by the National Security League, which focused attention on military preparedness, expanding the armed forces, and promoting a plan for universal military training. The latter organization, "bankrolled by big capitalists," operated military training facilities around the country aimed specifically at the business class. Although California was one of the last places to catch war fever, at least a dozen corporate officers of Pan American Petroleum spent time at the preparedness camp at Monterey in the summer of 1916, including E. L. Doheny Jr., who went on to serve as a Naval Reserve officer during the war.[11]

Up to this point, Doheny's efforts had been consonant with those of other business leaders concerned about American security, but soon after the United States formally entered the war in April 1917, he made a contribution to the California State Council of Defense that went well beyond the bounds of normal activity. In fact, Doheny shocked state officials when he presented the governor with $100,000 worth of weapons consisting of "nearly a million rounds of ammunition, almost enough high-power rifles to arm a regiment and enough modern machine guns to equip three batteries." At first, Doheny stated that the material had been on order for some time and had only just arrived, but as it turned out, the weapons had been cached somewhere in central California for a much longer period. Doheny's previous support for military training facilities lent some consistency to his claim that he had purchased the weapons as a precaution in case of war. And, considering that the National Guard and regular army units were likely to be withdrawn from the region under that condition, the chairman of the Defense Council stated that "the value of Doheny's contribution is almost incalculable."[12]

The worsening political situation in Mexico suggested another rationale for Doheny's unusual stockpile, although no state or federal official was inclined to explore the possibility. During the first years of the revolution, the foreign oil camps had been armed for their own protection but they quickly discovered that this only made them more vulnerable to banditry. Then, when Carranza came to power, the oilmen were forced to discontinue the practice altogether and rely upon the government for protection against the rebels. In addition, the Wilson Administration placed a formal embargo on all arms shipments to Mexico. It seems likely, therefore, that Doheny's gift had been a supply of weapons intended for the oilfields before the policy changed.

According to Harold Walker, there was no inclination among American oil workers to have the region turned into an armed camp. In fact, in a confidential letter to the secretary of the interior, Franklin Lane, in November 1916, Walker stated that "self protection and national safety demand that no American bullets shall go to a country that will misuse them . . . and turn them against Americans. . . . If the de facto government does not get ammunition the bandits will get none." To do otherwise, Walker concluded, increased the likelihood that "one of those American bullets is apt to get me."[13]

This attitude casts serious doubt on a more provocative interpretation that links Doheny's actions with alleged attempts by American citizens to instigate a counter-revolution against the Carranza government. For those critical of American business interests in Mexico, Doheny's name, like

Rockefeller's, become synonymous with such activity. While there is no denying that Doheny was actively involved in trying to manipulate the political situation in Mexico—or at least the North American interpretation of it—there is no proof that he was personally involved in direct efforts to overthrow the government. Unfortunately, it is almost impossible to sort out the facts on this issue, even though the State Department was aware of the various accusations against the oil companies and military intelligence officers had tried to assimilate information from all sources. In one instance in March 1918, a postal censor intercepted a letter from a man in Mexico City offering to supply the Mexican News Bureau with "documentary evidence" that Doheny's weapons had been intended for a rebellion against the Carranza regime in Lower California.[14]

The letter alleged that Doheny promised to give full financial support to Esteban Cantu, the insurgent Governor of Lower California, if he would start a military uprising on the Mexican mainland designed to "force radical concessions from the Carranza Government." According to an official report, Cantu was well known along the border for having a tight political grip on his state and a loose set of morals. Aside from licensing all types of vice operations, however, he was seen as a friend and protector of American property owners in Mexico. Thus, Cantu's indiscretions were tolerated because of his businesslike efficiency, which, in the opinion of a recent historian, allowed him to run Baja California Norte "as if it were a subsidiary of General Motors." Furthermore, Cantu's opposition to federal control from Mexico City made him the subject of incessant talk about the possible annexation of Lower California to the United States. In reality, Cantu flaunted his relative isolation from the political pull of Mexico City for his own reasons and had no intention of playing into the hands of the Americans. But he thrived off the annexationist sentiment in California and Arizona, nonetheless.[15]

Since he had no business interests in the region, it is doubtful that Doheny was involved in these plots, although a well-armed rebellion in the far West might have relieved governmental pressure on the oil zone. Unfortunately, as will become more apparent with his later activities, Doheny fell into the habit of throwing money at almost any project even remotely aligned with his interests in Mexico. However, in the absence of factual evidence for support, all that can be said for sure is that there was enough intrigue among business interests in Mexico to support any number of conspiracy theories.

With America's entrance into the war, however, Doheny did not have to resort to promoting armed rebellion to advance his cause. Instead, as a member of the newly appointed committee on petroleum resources, he had a legitimate access to power through the Council of National Defense. Headed by A. C. Bedford, the new president of Standard Oil New Jersey, the committee was charged, by Bernard Baruch, the director of the War Industries Board, with managing the nation's petroleum supply. To carry out that order, Bedford chose a select group of leading oilmen to help him coordinate the industry: Doheny, G. S. Davison of Gulf Oil, J. W. Van Dyke of Atlantic Refining, C. F. Lufkin of The Texas Company, H. F. Sinclair of Sinclair Oil & Refining, and J. H. Markum, an independent producer.[16]

Naturally, the members of the petroleum committee relished the opportunity to blend their own goals with those of the nation at large. Bedford, for instance, hoped to repair Standard Oil's public image by creating a cooperative arrangement between the federal government and the industry in general. According to Mark L. Requa, who had been appointed as the Fuel Oil Controller for the United States Fuel Administration, Bedford had a vision for a new order within the oil industry which demanded public confidence and widespread publicity. "He had seen the old order go down before adverse public opinion," Requa recalled, and "realized that for better or worse a new order had come and he conformed to it." The oil committee, therefore, provided the perfect opportunity to reshape the industry and place it on the leading edge of America's war effort. It was also a larger reflection of the type of activity that Requa and Doheny had been involved in on the West Coast.[17]

For Doheny, at least, this was the perfect time to advance Mexican oil as an essential resource for the United States, and he anticipated a profitable working relationship between his company and the government. "There are few corporations in the country," he said, "whose business is more necessary for war-like operations than the Pan American Petroleum & Transport Company." Oil tankers, in particular, were a "sine qua non of success." With five of its ships in the service of the British Admiralty by the fall of 1917 and another five carrying Mexican crude to the Gulf and Atlantic refineries, the company claimed a prominent role in the Allied effort. Already, its shipments of oil from Tampico had more than doubled, from 702,650 barrels in July 1916 to 1,608,305 barrels a year later. And, month after month, as the Allies seemed always to be running out of fuel, the company stressed the transportation problem: "WE HAVE THE PRODUCTION; WE NEED THE TANKERS."[18]

From his seat on the petroleum committee, Doheny pressed the issue at every opportunity. "The big problem that confronts the government so far as oil is concerned," Doheny told a West Coast reporter, "is that of keeping the shipment of the Mexican oil supply up to the maximum":

> The Allies are dependent upon the Mexican output. There would be no trouble in giving the Allies all the oil they need if we had the tankers, but the government has had to withdraw so many boats for other branches of the trans-Atlantic service that there is a threatened shortage of tank ships. Our United States supply is on the ragged edge of being just sufficient for our needs. Four million gallons of gasoline [are] annually produced from the Mexican output of crude oil, and 50 percent of that quantity is exported to Europe. Our big job now is that of getting the facilities with which to convey Mexican oil to a point on the Atlantic Coast from where it can be shipped to England by the shortest route.[19]

Doheny's comments about his own business highlighted the dilemma for the petroleum committee as a whole. Somehow, out of the welter of competing companies, overlapping markets, and inadequate transportation facilities, the leaders of the industry had to provide the necessary fuel for the battlefields of Europe without hindering the supply needed for critical domestic industries and civilian consumption. Initially, the committee hoped to use its governmental authority to enforce its decisions, but within six months after it was formed, the Wilson Administration decided to turn the cooperative committees over to their respective trade organizations. Of course, given the independent nature of the business, the oil industry did not have one. As an alternative, Baruch asked Bedford if the oil group would simply reconstitute itself as a trade organization and continue working without interruption. Absent official sanction, however, there was no guarantee that the nation's oil producers, or any other group, would follow along. For that reason, the United States Chamber of Commerce suggested that all major industries form War Services Committees, controlled by the War Industries Board, to replace the previous committees of the Council of National Defense. This alteration allowed the petroleum committee in particular to retain its members and its quasi-official status without risking an embarrassing revolt from within. To further legitimize the organization, the members voted to include representatives from the smaller independent companies, and, on December 21, 1917, the new Petroleum War Service Committee held the first of forty-one meetings to carry out its mission.[20]

Aside from handling the existing crisis, the Petroleum Committee represented a providential development for the oil industry and the beginning of a psychological change among the oilmen themselves. For the first time in the industry's history, independents, wildcat drillers, and the big integrated companies sat down to coordinate their efforts. To make the change even more startling, the committee no longer met in Washington but in Bedford's office at 26 Broadway, the headquarters of the Standard Oil Company. For many oilmen, this was tantamount to dancing with the devil, but it was also an opportunity to form the sort of association that had thus far eluded the industry. Doheny's experience on the committee helped him to finally envision himself as one of the industry's leaders. Six years earlier, he had gone to New York to beg Standard Oil for a contract. Now, the main office of the Pan American Petroleum & Transport Company was just up the street, and Doheny presented himself at Bedford's door as an equal.

As for the work itself, Doheny sat on the producing and transportation subcommittees and was vice-chairman of the group responsible for allocating fuel resources among the Allies. These assignments allowed him to promote the tanker routes between Tampico and the Atlantic Coast refineries and to argue that the Mexican trade should receive priority assignments. In addition to Doheny, Herbert Wylie sat on an advisory committee to study the construction of tank vessels, barges, and other ships, and Frederic R. Kellogg, counsel for the Mexican Petroleum Company, served on a legal committee to determine the limits of the petroleum group's authority.[21]

Along with Doheny and Requa, T. A. O'Donnell was the other Californian who took on a major role as the director of domestic production, a separate position that required him to work as a liaison between the government and the independent producers. To convince wary independents that he was on their side, O'Donnell resigned as president of the California Petroleum Company and from the boards of Mexican Petroleum and Pan American Petroleum. Still, he was especially well equipped to comment on Mexico and repeatedly emphasized its importance as America's oil reserve. "We have a safety valve in Mexico," O'Donnell told a national convention of oilmen, "that is going to take care of us in time, but meanwhile we have to furnish every barrel of oil where it is."[22]

While Doheny and his associates worked to promote their business within official circles, the *Pan American Record* published desperate pleas for more tankers to be diverted to the Mexican supply routes and for more of the merchant ships to be converted from coal to oil. As it was, most of them still burned coal that had to be shipped to the coast by rail. "The Allies are crying for help," one article noted, "which we are unable to render owing to the clogged conditions of our railways and harbors." With inadequate sources of coal and an overextended rail system, hundreds of fully loaded ships were left stranded for want of fuel.

Doheny considered this a criminal waste of resources: "No oil-burning vessel need ever be delayed an hour for fuel in a port through railroad congestion." Just one Mexican tanker with 10,000 tons of fuel oil could replace 600 rail cars of coal and supply a dozen ships with round-trip passage to Europe. In 1917, alone, it would have taken 55,000 cars to equal the company's shipments of 6 million barrels of oil along the Atlantic Coast. With an adequate number of tankers, Doheny believed that Mexican oil could win the war for the Allies. However, while there was no disputing the benefits of fuel oil, there was also no way to make the conversion during the war.[23] Overall, despite these constraints Doheny was doing a brisk business by 1918. By that time, the Mexican Petroleum Company was controlling most of the northeastern industrial market, sending gasoline directly to Europe, and furnishing almost all the oil going to the South American market, where Chilean mines supplied vital raw materials for the munitions industry.[24]

At the same time, Doheny was waging a constant battle to keep his own fleet of oil tankers at a minimum level to meet the demand. When the war began, Pan American Petroleum had fourteen ships under construction. Of the five vessels built and delivered during 1917, one was immediately commandeered by the government, and four went into regular service. Construction delays on the remainder ran from five to eight months, and Doheny received three large ocean tankers out of an order of five, and one small coastal tanker out of four, by the summer of 1918. The schedule was so constrained, however, that the Emergency Fleet Corporation, the government agency responsible for controlling the shipbuilding industry, asked the petroleum committee members if they could build their own tankers. Needing every vessel they could lay their hands on, the committee members were prepared to do just that when the war ended in November 1918.

Doheny was never satisfied with the government's handling of the shipping arrangements, believing that his oil tankers should have received priority treatment, although he would have settled for having them completed according to the terms of his contract, which stated that all of his ships should have been finished by January 1918. If not, the yard was supposed to pay a $1,000 penalty for every day that the ships remained uncompleted. Given the exigencies of the war, the Emergency Fleet Corporation disregarded all previous contracts, rearranged the building program, and put many customers on hold for the duration. In the meantime, they refused to acknowledge late charges on overdue orders and insisted on adding the rising cost of building materials to the agreed-upon price of each ship. Feeling as he did about the necessity of his oil tankers, Doheny was outraged at the Fleet Corporation's tactics and demanded that the government abide by the rules. In the end, he figured the government owed him $850,000 in construction penalties and $1,555,000 in excess charges.[25]

In light of his complaints, Doheny appeared before a Senate Commerce Committee in June 1918 to testify about price-gouging and corrupt practices at the Fleet Corporation's Hogg Island shipyard. Doheny argued that his ships had been held hostage, under the threat of being commandeered, until he paid an inflated price to get them. "We allowed ourselves to be coerced," Doheny admitted, "in order to get the ships." Several oil companies had undergone a similar experience, and Doheny was not alone in complaining about the situation. F. R. Kellogg, counsel for the Mexican Petroleum Company, for example, was on hand seeking compensation for industry losses on behalf of the Petroleum War Services Committee. Ultimately, evidence taken at the hearings substantiated Doheny's charges of profiteering at Hogg Island, but such abuses had been expected and were supposed to be tolerated under the circumstances. Nevertheless, Doheny reported in his 1917 annual message to the stockholders that the unpaid late penalties and the business lost on account of the shipping problems cost the company in excess of $6 million for the first six months of the war. The only consolation, Doheny added, was the knowledge that "they were providing a vital component of the Allied effort."[26]

However, investors did not have to be satisfied with good works alone, since the Doheny companies were still doing quite well. Pan American Petroleum had gross earnings of $5,114,628 for 1917 and $8,066,727 for 1918, although deductions for income and excess profits taxes reduced net profits to $4,308,904 and $4,666,727, respectively. Gross earnings for Mexican Petroleum, on the other hand, from which Pan American Petroleum derived half its income, increased dramatically over the course of the war—from $9,668,464 in 1916, to $18,121,790 in 1917, and $26,320,546 in 1918. Net profits, subject to both United States and Mexican government taxes, were $7,153,060, $4,986,021, and $6,699,444, respectively, for the same period. The company sold 7,850,194 barrels of oil in 1916, 16,736,000 barrels in 1917, and 18,500,000 in 1918. The selling price per barrel increased from $.85 in 1916 to just over a dollar a barrel in 1917, and reached $1.42 in 1918. Rather than being a reflection of the bulk price of crude oil in Mexico, this growth represented increased sales of refined fuel oil and gasoline from the company's topping plant in Tampico and the refinery at Destrehan, Louisiana. The 25 percent drop in net profits between 1916 and 1917 represented a massive investment in ships and transportation facilities, which more than doubled the operating expenses, from twenty to forty-five cents a barrel. In 1918, the government's excess profits tax reduced proceeds by an additional $5 million. Under protest, the company also paid several million dollars a year in taxes to the government of Mexico.[27]

Although Doheny anticipated an unparalleled growth in the fuel oil business for the coming years, he was deliberately cautious in his remarks to the shareholders in July 1918, when he reminded them that "the revenue received by the stockholders is the result of an investment of large sums of money, in a very precarious enterprise, in a foreign country, where success depends not only on the good judgment of the management, but upon the good will and fair treatment of the Government and people where the business is carried on, and of the home Government of the Company where the capital originates and most of the facilities for operation are produced."[28]

Doheny argued that the taxation programs of both the United States and Mexican governments needlessly threatened the future of the company, since both nations received risk-free benefits from Mexican oil production. Moreover, because the legitimate investors had not yet recovered their initial capital, none of the company's earnings should be taxed as profit until the original investment had been paid out. Actually, this was a common refrain within the industry in protest to any government tax plan. According to Doheny, the oilmen were "only too anxious to support the Government in every possible way," but the popular idea that oil production could be treated like any other industry with a stable cost structure and regular output was completely false. "It is 100 percent wildcatting today, as it always has been," he insisted. "If you cut off the incentive to prospect" through taxation, "you automatically stop the supply."[29]

While there were inordinate risks involved in doing business in Mexico, there were also enormous profits to be made, as well, as indicated by the rise in Mexpet shares during the war years and after. Between 1916 and 1920, more than 5 million shares of Mexican Petroleum common traded hands each year, putting it in league with U.S. Steel, Crucible Steel, and Anaconda Copper at the top of the list of industrial stocks. As noted earlier, the price fell from $129 to $67 during the political crisis in Mexico ignited by the Pershing Expedition during 1916 and early 1917. Thereafter, the stock climbed as high as $264 and, by October 1919, was a market sensation. That dramatic increase was an indication of both the financial health of the company, as measured by its economic importance during the war, and the prospect that Mexican oil would become even more important in the future.[30]

What the company still needed, however, was the clear and unambiguous support of the American government. Certainly, it was not from a lack of trying on Doheny's part that the company had not yet secured this guarantee. In fact, as we have seen, he used every method he could think of to link the American war effort, the nation's future oil supply, and the anticipated competition on the high seas after the war to the possession and protection of the Mexican oil fields. To supplement the work of the War Services Petroleum Committee and the constant editorializing of the *Pan American Record*, Doheny also enlisted the help of Mark Requa, the National Fuel Oil director, to request that the government use, and protect, Mexican oil as the only means to preserve the dwindling petroleum reserves in the United States.

Specifically, Doheny sent a letter to Requa in March 1918 laying out all the arguments in favor of Mexican oil, and he had it privately published and distributed around the country as a policy statement. Doheny's main point was that the nation's current domestic oil resources were inadequate to the demands of the war. Mexican crude was already being substituted for shortages on the West Coast and to compensate for the declining production of many older fields elsewhere. Although Doheny admitted that new fields would be discovered to take their place, he was certain they would not be opened up in time to make a difference in the war. To rely upon prospective oil lands at the present time, Doheny asserted, "would be to invite disaster to our arms in the great impending struggle."[31]

A few months later, Requa wrote to Frank L. Polk, Counselor for the State Department, to summarize the nation's oil situation as it related to Mexico. For the first six months of 1918, Requa reported, United States production, excluding that of California, had been approximately 635,000 barrels a day, with another 40,000 barrels a day withdrawn from storage. Imports from Mexico averaged 90,000 barrels of oil a day, and Mexican oil also supplied an additional 40,000 barrels a day directly to Europe and South America. If the Mexican supply were cut off for any reason, the United States would have to make up for it with stored oil out of an available stock of 100 million barrels, or about an eighteen-month supply. If the war lasted well into 1919, as many people anticipated, and the demand continued to rise, the government would have to begin rationing oil, something that had been avoided thus far.[32]

Even without the information gleaned from Doheny, Requa believed this situation to be absolutely true as a result of his frustrating attempts to purchase oil in the Mid-Continent field. Requa had attempted to purchase a few million barrels of fuel oil as a winter reserve for the military. To his surprise, he came up empty-handed and concluded that "any surplus quantity of fuel oil is apparently nonexistent at the present time." Even if he had located the oil, it would have still been impossible to get it delivered to its destination on the East Coast, since the pipelines and railways were filled to capacity. The situation convinced Requa that conditions were grim at best: "We have insufficient transportation facilities; we have insufficient refining facilities; and we have not a reserve of fuel oil any place throughout the United States upon which to draw in compensation for the loss of this Mexican source of supply." That was precisely the point Doheny had been trying to make since the beginning of the war.[33]

Later critics, knowing that the war lasted only until November 1918 and that the United States found itself facing an oil glut in the early 1920s, have argued that oilmen like Doheny deliberately lied about conditions to gain control of foreign supplies and public oil lands in the United States. President Wilson's secretary of the navy, Josephus Daniels, perhaps the most skeptical of the lot, attributed every argument about the shortage of domestic production to industry propaganda. But official estimates of the nation's oil supply tended to be very low during these years and were supported by reports written by both Ralph Arnold and I. C. White for the United States Geological Survey.[34]

For Doheny, there was more than enough evidence to suggest that the United States would be making a major economic blunder if it let the Mexican oil industry slip from its grasp. Doheny reemphasized the scramble for oil that was sure to come after the war, a struggle the Wilson Administration seemed unwilling to acknowledge. Quoting from the head of the British Board of Trade, Doheny pointed out that Great Britain already had a stated policy "to acquire as large a control as possible of the world supply of petroleum," especially in the Middle East. Consequently, Doheny drew a parallel between British interests in the Anglo-Persian oil fields and the American presence in Mexico. Clearly, with both Britain and Germany scouring the globe for petroleum, Doheny believed that the United States "must avail itself of the enterprise and ability and pioneer spirit of its citizens to acquire and to have and to hold a reasonable portion of the world's petroleum supplies." America's future as a world leader depended on the possession of Mexican oil, and it was up to Doheny to convince the administration to follow his lead.

8 PROMOTING AN OIL POLICY
FOR MEXICO, 1917–1920

No matter how hard Doheny tried to make Mexican oil a vital part of the nation's war effort, he could never be certain of the government's protection without a commitment from President Wilson. While Doheny tried to create a groundswell of public support for a stronger Mexican policy by advertising the strategic importance of his business at every opportunity, he worked even harder to find a way to appeal directly to the president. Doheny and his associates already had access to a variety of government officials in Washington, including Secretary of State Robert Lansing, who were equally frustrated at Wilson's apparent antipathy to the plight of American property owners in Mexico. Yet, not even Lansing, a consistent friend to business, was willing to allow the Mexican situation to interfere with America's obligations in Europe and Wilson's primary focus.

Despite rhetorical comments to the contrary, Woodrow Wilson was not antibusiness in any real sense of the term. In fact, a review of his administration's economic policies for Latin America reveals a clear determination to bolster American influence throughout the region. During the war, the Commerce Department, in particular, went to extraordinary lengths to have American firms take over the communications, banking, and shipping businesses formerly controlled by British interests. Although these policies were criticized for being overly bureaucratic and did not receive the full support of the financial community, they were aimed at strengthening business ties with Latin America in order to promote economic growth and a healthy political environment.[1]

Previously, Wilson had claimed that "there is no man who is more interested than I am in carrying the enterprise of American businessmen to
every quarter of the globe." Furthermore, he believed that "concessions
obtained by financiers must be safeguarded by ministers of state, even if the
sovereignty of unwilling nations be outraged in the process." As president,
however, Wilson had to set aside this conviction in favor of his concept of
political self-determination, no matter how contradictory it seemed. And,
as a progressive Democrat, Wilson attacked loosely defined special interests
at home and abroad. Consequently, he could not risk any policy that might
make him out to be "a tool of unscrupulous businessmen."[2]

Given that the public opinion of oil companies was low, Wilson's political considerations were especially sensitive to the Mexican petroleum industry. Having already been stung by two failed interventions in Mexico—
in 1914 and 1916—he had no desire to try again, regardless of the reason.
Still, despite these obstacles, Doheny and others with business investments
in Mexico continued to approach the State Department with their complaints. But in response to Wilson's apparent indifference to their plight,
their methods grew increasingly oblique. They relied primarily on the services of Chandler P. Anderson, a lawyer and former counselor in the State
Department, who worked as a business lobbyist in private practice. Anderson had served in every administration from McKinley's to Wilson's and
was a skilled practitioner of international law and dollar diplomacy. After
William Jennings Bryan resigned as secretary of state in 1915, Anderson
had stepped in briefly as acting counselor to the new secretary, Robert
Lansing. Unfortunately, as a Republican, Anderson was never offered a
permanent post. But he remained close to both Lansing and Frank Polk,
who became the counselor, and continued to work for the department
on a limited basis—enough to give him access to departmental files and
confidential material on Mexico. Thus, Anderson's unique position allowed him to straddle the line between private and public interests, and he
served as a useful buffer between the two. In particular, he both articulated
and restrained the opposition to Wilson's Mexican policy.[3]

Anderson's first contact with the Doheny organization came in January
1917, when he met with Harold Walker to discuss the dangers posed by the
Carranza government. Subsequently, in the spring and summer of 1917,
Anderson worked to stiffen the State Department's response to Mexico on
behalf of several oil and mining companies. This was a crucial time, just
after America's entry into the war, when Wilson was prepared to give up
the protection of American investments in return for Carranza's promise

to resist German efforts to start a conflict between Mexico and the United States. Fearing that Carranza would confiscate foreign-owned property if given the chance, Walker hired Anderson to persuade the State Department to explicitly link the sanctity of American investments with full diplomatic recognition.[4]

The threat of confiscation emanated from the Mexican Constitution of 1917, which represented a sharp break with the past in challenging the legitimacy of all foreign-held property and concessions, especially subsoil rights to minerals and oil. To review, the Mexican law dealing with this issue had followed the traditional Spanish interpretation that gave total control of these deposits to the crown. After independence, subsoil rights rested with the Mexican government. In 1884, the government of Porfirio Díaz adopted a new mining code to attract foreign investment which gave control over subsoil deposits to whoever owned, or controlled, the surface land. A public legal debate over the issue of nationalizing the oil lands took place in 1905 but failed to change the law. Finally, the principle of private ownership of petroleum deposits was reinforced once again by a subsequent law in 1909, although the legal authority of that decision crumbled along with Porfirio Díaz in the opening act of the revolution.[5]

With Carranza in power, but not unchallenged, Mexican leaders from all sides gathered in 1916 to write a new constitution. Article 27 of that document reclaimed ownership of all mineral deposits for the nation. As a statement of ideology, the antiforeign elements of the new constitution marked the apex of the rebellion against the Díaz era and struck the first blows for economic independence. The essence of Article 27 stated that the Mexican nation owned all lands within its territory and had the sole right to create, or dispose of, private property at its discretion. Existing private property was subject to regulation and to possible expropriation in the public interest. Henceforth, landowners were to be Mexican citizens by birth or naturalization, and only Mexican companies would be allowed to acquire land and obtain concessions to develop mines and oil wells. Foreign enterprises could have access to the same privileges as long as they became domestic corporations and waived their right to protection from their respective governments. Finally, foreigners would be excluded from owning land within 100 kilometers of the frontier and 50 kilometers of the coast, an area that encompassed almost the entire oil zone from Tampico to Veracruz.[6]

Speaking at a conference on international relations in 1920, Frederic Kellogg of the Mexican Petroleum Company described the essence of the new constitution in this way:

The situation was precisely the same as though the State of Massachusetts should come to a man who for seventeen years had owned the house in which he lived, and which he originally bought and paid for, and in the title to which there are no defects, and say to him, "We have decided to take over the ownership of your property. If you desire to do so, you may still occupy the house, but only upon condition that you pay the government such rental as we may now fix, subject to any increase hereafter that we may see fit to make, and that you comply with such other conditions as we may impose."[7]

To American property holders, this idea was so abhorrent that it was unthinkable. Foreign investors had been invited into Mexico by the government, and the revolutionaries had no right to infringe on former legal agreements. Such action was, they felt, an attack against the basic principles of civilization.

In taking up the oilmen's fight, Anderson tried to see the situation from their perspective, but he was never as bellicose as most of his clients. Instead of calling for war, Anderson wanted the United States to devise a legal solution to the Mexican problem in the form of a treaty that would bar the retroactive application of the constitution. Secretary Lansing agreed with that approach and gave Anderson a free hand to work on such a document. In the end, however, Anderson fell back on the standard elements of dollar diplomacy by drafting a proposal offering Carranza a loan to be repaid out of the tax receipts on foreign-owned businesses in return for a guarantee of property rights. Additionally, to ensure Mexico's support of the Allied effort in the war, Carranza would have to allow American military protection of the oilfields. Although Lansing agreed to these ideas in principle, he was unwilling to commit the necessary forces to make them work and did not want to provoke Carranza into a reaction that would require a military response. For these reasons, Lansing also opposed a formal loan to Mexico but said that the administration would not stand in the way of any private arrangements made with American bankers. Essentially, in Anderson's words, Lansing wanted property owners to "find some way to acquiesce and tide the thing over for the present."[8]

For his part, Carranza no doubt needed money to put down local rebellions against the government and rebuild his country, but he refused to respond to American ultimatums. During the war, in fact, he deftly played the foreign powers—the United States, Great Britain, and Germany—against one another, kept his economy afloat by taxing foreign corporations and their exports, and maintained relative independence despite attempts by both Axis and Allied powers to trip him up and grab the oil zone for themselves. In not submitting to intervention by any of the major powers or making concessions for a loan, the Mexican government "succeeded in turning the tables and in exploiting their rivalry for its own ends."[9]

Nevertheless, Lansing's desire to have the oilmen take care of their own problems did not mean that the Wilson Administration could afford to completely abandon its citizens in the oil zone, so the United States Navy maintained two ships in Tampico harbor throughout the period from 1914 to 1920. Although this was not much of a military deterrent, it gave a psychological boost to the American community and kept alive the hope that more was on the way. The ships also watched over the 10 million barrels of oil stored along the river and gave limited protection to the oil flowing out to the Allies. "Their removal under any circumstances," Harold Walker believed, "would jeopardize the whole terminal and supply."[10]

In reality, the commander in charge of the naval group was more or less an observer charged with evaluating the political situation but without the authority to act on what he learned. The confusion and frustration of that dilemma were aptly summarized by Captain Louis Richardson in the fall of 1917: "I know the foreign business men and their characters; also the leading Mexican military and civil officials ... I am on most friendly terms with all parties. The difficulty of forming a correct estimate is caused by the fact that each one tells you things that are not facts with the view of getting you excited and influenced in his favor or he tells you as a fact the thing that is only a day-dream. My task is to weigh all rumors, the character of the man and the personal interest or motive and try to arrive at a correct idea of what the situation really is."[11]

Richardson's predicament was best illustrated by his relationship with William Green, the superintendent for Huasteca Petroleum. Having served with the United States Army in the Philippines, Green was described as "two hundred and fifty pounds of effective dynamite" who had the nerve and cunning necessary to deal with the political factions and petty bandits of the oil zone. Harold Walker once described Green admiringly as a consummate practitioner of "jungle diplomacy." Certainly, Green was not afraid to get his hands dirty in the process and was never far from the action. When Richardson pleaded with him on one occasion to "get into the attitude of trying to help the Mexican government pacify the oil district," Green scoffed back, "The trouble with you, Captain, is that you are honest, whereas in Mexico the crookeder you are and the better you get away with it, the more you are respected." Though he claimed to seek authority from Doheny for every move, Green admitted there were "inconsistencies" in his reports to the home office. Naval intelligence officers considered him unreliable and possibly dangerous.[12]

Chandler Anderson faced a similar situation in Washington, where the web of activity against Carranza was made up of representatives from an array of regional strongmen looking for any signal, and a little money, to begin a rebellion. Almost without exception, American business interests encouraged this activity to some degree in the hope that a spark might catch fire and draw the United States into the conflict. And the Americans were not alone in this desire, as Anderson recorded after a meeting in May 1917 with officials from the British Embassy and the Mexican Eagle Oil Company. The "general impression of these men," he noted, "seems to be that the great mass of the Mexican people would welcome intervention by the United States." Apparently, the British had been working on their own plans for a coup and were simply looking for a little support to put it into effect. In this instance, they hoped to set up Madero's former finance minister as the new president of Mexico. Eventually, Lord Cowdray, president of the Mexican Eagle, discouraged these efforts and fell into line behind President Wilson's lead. Afterward, Cowdray hired Anderson to lobby for the British oil interests along with his other clients.[13]

By virtue of his position, Doheny never publicly advocated a specific plan for dealing with Carranza, although Anderson observed that Doheny was a "very intelligent and forcible Irishman, who in spite of his democratic politics is exceedingly outspoken in condemning the administration in its Mexican dealings." His preference, Anderson continued, "would be to have Carranza eliminated, but he realizes that the president is not likely to agree to this." Doheny approved of Anderson's plans to at least force Carranza to eliminate the objectionable provisions of the constitution as a prerequisite for recognition. In the meantime, Doheny's representatives were aware of the various intrigues afoot and did what they could to push the process along.[14]

With President Wilson's mind fixed on the war in Europe, however, the United States granted full recognition to Carranza in September 1917 without demanding any of the terms that Anderson recommended. After hearing the news of this decision, Walker called Anderson to ridicule what he called Wilson's "great and good friend" appeal to Carranza. He also told him that the Mexican leader had responded to Wilson's favor with an announcement that he was going to send federal troops into the oilfields to drive out the rebels and bring the area under the control of the government. This eventuality was the oilmen's worst nightmare, and they assumed that the radical demands of Article 27 were sure to follow.[15]

Moreover, Wilson's comments implied that, as a way of making up for past sins, he was finally ready to acknowledge the right of the Mexican government to handle its internal affairs as it saw fit. In a subsequent address to an audience of Mexican newspaper editors, Wilson stressed his disinterested role in the World War and said he was ready to show a similar attitude toward Mexico "by any act of friendship that you may propose. . . . Some of us, if I may say so privately, look back with regret upon some of the more ancient relations that we have had with Mexico long before our generation; and America, if I may so express it, would now feel ashamed to take advantage of a neighbor." The problem with the Monroe Doctrine, Wilson went on to say, was that "we did not ask whether it was agreeable to you that we should be your big brother." And although that policy offered protection from outside aggression, Wilson noted that it did nothing to protect Mexico and its neighbors from the United States. "When you reflect how wonderful a storehouse of treasure Mexico is," the president concluded, "you can see how her future must depend upon peace and honor, so that nobody shall exploit her."[16]

Meanwhile, the situation in the oilfields was growing more chaotic and dangerous by the day. To offset the inertia in Washington and to accede to Lansing's wishes, the oil companies had been conducting their own foreign policy designed to keep the Carranza forces at a distance. Primarily, this was the work of rebel troops under the control of Manuel Pelaez, a self-appointed protector of the oil zone, whose family leased oil lands to the Mexican Eagle Oil Company and had as much to lose from Carranza's campaign as did the foreign operators. As one observer noted, Pelaez not only "took kindly to the oil business, he learned to take from it as well." And from the beginning, Pelaez demanded arms and money from the oil companies in return for his protection.[17]

Initially, the Huasteca Petroleum Company hoped to use Pelaez's occupation of the oilfields as the foundation for direct intervention by the United States. In one report, Walker noted that "the company I represent has always understood the plan of the United States forces to be the immediate occupation of Tampico and the protection of the oilfields by an expeditionary force of at least 1,000 marines or soldiers" and that "our work and agreements with Pelaez have all been made with such an expedition in view." A few months later, however, the American consul at Tampico warned the State Department that it should not read too much into this support, since "Pelaez does not pretend that he will take up arms with the United States in case of war or intervention."[18]

However, Pelaez said all the right things when he subsequently listed the aims of his rebellion: he opposed the "idiocy" of the new constitution, derided the "insane foolishness" of Carranza's supporters, and promised to uphold the rights of foreigners by protecting the oilfields. And even though Pelaez was committed to keeping Mexico neutral during the war, he was not inclined to prevent belligerents from using Mexican oil in the fight. This last point was the most important, since Carranza's neutrality was predicated upon treating oil as contraband. The oil producers believed that this was a clear sign that Carranza had fallen under the sway of German agents who wanted to destroy, or tie up, the oil properties in any way they could. In June 1917, Walker sent a detailed memo, "The Allies' Oil Supplies," to the State Department in an effort to make this point as forcefully as he could. Domestic oil production in the United States could be increased only slightly, Walker stated, while the Mexican Petroleum Company and the Mexican Eagle could double their output of 50 million barrels per year at a moment's notice "if they are only guaranteed protection of their governments." This was becoming even more imperative, he thought, since "we have to count on the real hostility of the de facto government of Mexico, which is notoriously playing with the Germans." Somehow, Walker concluded, they had to "make the American and British Governments see it."[19]

In the interim, the oil companies acquiesced to Pelaez's demands with the full knowledge and approval of Robert Lansing. Financially, Pelaez kept himself in the field through a series of forced loans against the oil companies, which they supposedly paid under duress, but there was a dispute over whether the oil companies should, or did, supply the weapons and ammunition that he requested. Although this was not a policy anyone wanted to publicize, Lansing told Chandler Anderson in April 1917 that he was entirely willing to have Pelaez supplied with weapons "so long as the matter was not brought to the attention of the government." Moreover, Lansing told Anderson that he "could rest assured that the Administration would not prosecute anyone who was assisting Peleyas [*sic*] so long as he remained friendly to the foreign interests in that region."[20]

For obvious reasons, the oil companies denied that they provided Pelaez such support, although the possibility that they did provides another speculative explanation for the previously mentioned stash of arms that Doheny had hidden away in the California desert. Walker at one point made this admission:

> It is within the knowledge of the Counselor of the State Department that in the month of February, 1917, pressure was brought to bear upon the

Huasteca Petroleum Company from important sources, to make a shipment or shipments of rifles and cartridges to the Pelaez forces; and that
the [company] would have nothing to do with such procedure without the
request and consent of the State Department, and opposed the proposal
for reasons then explained, principal among which was the evil effect of
strengthening any Mexican rebel faction with military supplies. It did not
then; it did not before; it has not subsequently, ever delivered arms
or munitions of any sort to forces in rebellion against the Carranza
government.[21]

Nevertheless, just two months later, Doheny handed over his stockpile of
rifles and ammunition to the governor of California.

Naturally, Carranza's supporters in Mexico and the United States accused the oil companies of trying to overthrow the government. But the
oilmen protested that they were only giving what money was necessary to
protect the oil supply, and they denied giving weapons. Doheny's position,
as cabled to William Green, was to "pay only what is unavoidable to save
property of the company and lives of employes [sic]." The congruence of
interests between the oilmen and Pelaez, however, left the lines of authority
open to political interpretation.[22] Harold Walker, for example, conceded
that this was an "anomalous" situation but defended Pelaez to the State
Department whenever possible. He even remarked to one official that he
had Manuel Pelaez to thank for the fact that he could buy gasoline for his
car in September 1917 at the same price as he had in March. Still, he had
no illusions about Pelaez's ultimate loyalty: "While Pelaez has a chance to
keep on living, he will of course protect the oil for his own interest; but if
he is beset and his life endangered (there is of course a price on his head
now) he will do what every Mexican has always done with the Golden
Goose—kill it, to leave his enemy a dead goose. You or I would do the
same."[23]

Taking all of this into account, it seems unlikely that the oil companies
made a deliberate business decision to live with this level of uncertainty.
At the very least, with Article 27 hanging over their heads, Pelaez's actions
kept Carranza from asserting control in the district and gave the oilmen
time to work on the Wilson administration.[24] Unfortunately, the president's decision to grant full recognition to Carranza completely frustrated
their efforts, although Doheny refused to abandon his attempts to change
Wilson's mind. Following on the heels of this defeat, he proposed to form
a publicity bureau designed to "educate the American people about the
conditions in Mexico and to bring pressure to bear upon our government

in the hope of stiffening up its policy for the protection of American interests." When he heard it, Anderson shuddered at the thought of a plan designed to publicly flail the president for his position on Mexico; he gave it no hope of changing Wilson's mind and was certain that it would force Carranza to retaliate. At the same time, Anderson thought the oilmen would be burning their bridges behind them and would not be able to go back to the State Department for protection. Moreover, Anderson knew that such a campaign from his clients would end his already tenuous relationship with the administration.

Curiously, Anderson also admitted that he was inclined to give the president the benefit of the doubt. In fact, he thought it was possible that Wilson's recognition policy had been designed to give Carranza enough rope to hang himself, so that the United States could say it had done everything possible before intervening. His analysis was "that the President was either sincerely desirous of the ultimate success of the Carranza government, or that he was simply waiting for an opportune time to make an excuse by its failure for intervention." For the moment, Anderson could not decide which way the president was headed. Nevertheless, he clung to the hope that Wilson might yet be "planning the acquisition of Mexico by the United States." So, as long as there was even the remotest possibility of intervention along these lines, Anderson recommended that Doheny regulate his activities so as to "assist the President in this policy rather than start a campaign of criticism."[25]

On September 20, therefore, scarcely a week after this discussion, Doheny announced a plan not for a publicity bureau but for an academic study of recent Mexican history: "I should like to see a great file of materials relevant to the Mexican problem gathered both from printed sources and from interviewing those who are well informed." From such an archive, Doheny wanted to have two books prepared and published. The first book would be "a comprehensive and living statement setting forth the fundamental facts and forces [that] would be useful to public officials of the United States if carefully supported by verified tables of facts and figures." The second would be "a human interest story of the industrial and social life of the Mexicans [that] might help the American public better to understand the special conditions existing in Mexico." Without resorting to propaganda, Doheny also thought that "such a story might tell something of the conditions under which American pioneers entered Mexico to engage in various kinds of business, what they have done, and what have been the economic and social effects produced by their activities."

Ultimately, Doheny hoped that this material, once divided into specific subject areas, would support several scholarly monographs suitable for use at the university level:

> The time has come, I believe, in the history of our country when it is important that our thinking men and women should have actual knowledge of, and give increasing thought to, the relationships of our industrial life to those of other peoples, and the influence of those relations upon the material life and welfare of our own and other countries. Increasingly the pioneers of American industry are reaching out beyond our own boundaries to take up work of various kinds. The mass of our people whose interests are circumscribed by local and internal matters should understand the meaning of this work upon their own. Otherwise we are all at the mercy of the superficial sensationalist and the designing demagogue. The truth shall be made to prevail.[26]

With this outline as a guide, Doheny donated $100,000 to form the Doheny Research Foundation and appointed George Scott, a specialist in international law and a former research associate at the Carnegie Institution, to head the project. Previously, Scott had been working in Washington with Harold Walker and Norman Bridge to devise a suitable publicity campaign. With Scott in charge, Doheny asked only that he be kept apprised of the foundation's progress. In a press release, Scott emphasized that, given the current political climate in Mexico, it was Doheny's desire to provide President Wilson "with information such as a thoroughly disinterested group of investigators can gather."[27]

Doheny had actually been involved in a similar project once before—in 1915. At that time, he had given $20,000 to organize a committee of twelve college presidents to "study Mexico in the interests of humanity." Presumably, he had hoped that Wilson would appreciate the effort and be receptive to the message. Unfortunately, the project foundered in its early stages because it was too dangerous to send researchers into Mexico during the civil war. The committee did sponsor one report on the educational system in Mexico which called for more humanitarian efforts by the United States, although there was an implicit assumption that Mexico could not progress politically and economically without submitting to American tutelage.[28]

It was obvious that Doheny was advancing from a familiar pattern in setting up this new research operation in 1917. But it is also true that his latest effort emerged alongside a similar one devised by President Wilson to study the political situation in Europe. At the same time that Chandler

Anderson was convincing the oilmen to adopt a more progressive strategy, he was working with Robert Lansing to organize a program to prepare United States negotiators for the impending peace talks at the end of the war. Anderson had hoped to direct the project, but Wilson did not want the State Department involved. Instead, the president set up an independent group known officially as the "Inquiry," directed by his close friend Colonel Edward House and funded by some discretionary accounts available to the White House. Colonel House briefly considered using Anderson for the section dealing with international law, right about the time that Doheny wanted to start his publicity bureau, but then rejected him on the basis of a security check. In that report, the attorney general had characterized Anderson as "a bright and shining example of pretty much everything you don't want."[29]

One of the hallmarks of Wilson's plan was its reliance upon academicians rather than government personnel to provide an independent analysis of the social and political problems associated with a peace settlement in Europe. Clearly, Doheny's Mexican project was conceived as a sympathetic reflection of Wilson's Inquiry. But what is most interesting is that both efforts were taken to be serious and important in the academic community. There were no charges, outside of Mexico, of course, that Doheny's money and position would unduly influence the results of his survey, and absolutely no indication that the Wilson Administration viewed his project as illegitimate. From every indication, the Doheny Research Foundation's study of the Mexican revolution fit in as one more component of the work being performed by a large segment of the nation's scholars and intellectuals. In fact, a fierce competition developed among the wartime agencies for their services. Many of the people hired for the Doheny Foundation moved to the War Trade Board or some other agency at the end of their contracts and regarded the two experiences similarly. And once the Inquiry broadened its focus to include Latin America, the two organizations collaborated where possible with information and personnel.[30]

South of the border, the editor of a pro-German newspaper in Mexico used the Doheny project as effective war propaganda by claiming that Doheny and other American capitalists had given a million dollars for a study whose "sole object" was to "blacken our country in foreign parts by making a false and malicious report." President Carranza believed that the Doheny researchers were "trying to find out things that [were] none of their business" and that this supposedly impartial investigation would be followed by military and political intervention, as had happened in the Philippines.[31]

While Doheny's motives were certainly not unbiased, there was no denying the legitimacy of the work. And on this score, at least, Doheny did what he said he would do: he wrote the checks as Scott requested them, gave several interviews about his experiences in Mexico, and was otherwise invisible. The research team itself, which numbered as many as fifteen, was drawn from the ranks of the best universities and would not have tolerated direct interference in any case. To further validate the project, Doheny and Scott persuaded the University of California at Berkeley to act as the host institution for the work. Berkeley designated each of the scholars as official research associates, which gave them access to the library, staff, and office space. The president of the university, Benjamin Ide Wheeler, told Doheny that he sheltered the project because he was convinced of the "scientific disinterestedness" of the foundation and the high caliber of its members.[32]

With these arrangements in place, the researchers went to work to answer one fundamental question: What's the matter with Mexico as an orderly, self-governing community? Taking that as their guide, the members pursued their research from November 1917 through the summer of 1918. During that time, they collected the factual material that Doheny requested and conducted more than 500 interviews with American businessmen working in Mexico and former Mexican officials from the Díaz and Madero administrations. Surprisingly, these interviews did not reveal any universal desire for military intervention. But they almost all reflected an overwhelming disgust with Wilson's conciliatory policy of "watchful waiting," which seemed to aggravate the conditions under which Americans suffered in Mexico. Doheny and his associates were especially blunt about their desire to see the country freed from Carranza's radical program. Robert Cleland, a historian from Occidental College who was put in charge of analyzing the mining and petroleum industries, noted that, "almost without exception," the oilmen anticipated direct American intervention in the northern section of Mexico to protect their interests.[33]

To afford some level of objectivity in their reports, the researchers tried to get into Mexico, but the Mexican government barred them from entering the country. It was clear that Carranza opposed the investigation because of Doheny's support. In contrast, the government permitted a section of George Creel's Committee on Public Information to operate in Mexico during the same period. That group distributed American war propaganda throughout the country in an effort to dispel pro-German sentiment in Mexico and worked openly without interference. A handful of Doheny scholars slipped into Mexico surreptitiously but were unable to do any thorough or consistent work. And, even if they had been invited in, the almost complete absence of documentary material on economic and social conditions in Mexico would not have changed anyone's opinion or the level of analysis.[34]

In their finished reports, which covered major topics such as government, industry, education, health and sanitation, the researchers were not inclined to support military intervention in Mexico. But like most Americans, they also believed that the United States ought to play a vital role in Mexico's future. Although the resumption of normal commercial relations was high on the list of desirable reforms, foreign businessmen were not exonerated for their past behavior. Blatant abuse of the Mexican people was not to be tolerated, but neither was Mexico's recent attempt to restrict the superior talent and skill of American investors.

In the end, there was nothing in the reports that Doheny could not endorse or appreciate. And despite its inherent biases and evidentiary problems, the work represented the most thorough study of Mexico to date, just as he had hoped it would. Unfortunately, with the end of the European war in November 1918, the pressure to keep the Mexican situation under wraps no longer existed, and there was no need to remain quiet about the president's policy. Thus, almost as soon as the researchers concluded their studies, Doheny refused to see the project through to publication. This decision left George Scott thoroughly disillusioned about Doheny's motives but, nonetheless, convinced of the academic quality of the work. Scott tried to get the University of California to fund the final stage of the enterprise, but the regents turned him down, as well. Over the next few years, however, former members of the foundation published a half-dozen scholarly monographs on Mexico which partially fulfilled Doheny's original aims. But Doheny's unwillingness to pay out a few thousand dollars more to complete his two books, after putting in $120,000 up to that time, reinforces the conclusion that this had really been little more than an elaborate diversion in the larger scheme of oil-related propaganda.[35]

In December 1918, a new organization, the National Association for the Protection of American Rights in Mexico, was formed. This group was backed almost exclusively by the large oil companies, and it took an aggressive approach to informing the American public about the latest conditions in Mexico. Like that of the Doheny Research Foundation, the mission of the NAPARIM was to collect as much data as possible about foreign enterprises in Mexico and to present these data to government officials and the American public. The difference was that the NAPARIM distributed its reports in the form of short propaganda pamphlets and newspaper articles, with no presumption of academic objectivity.[36]

The NAPARIM also sponsored a Senate investigation of the political situation in Mexico in 1919, headed by New Mexico Senator Albert B. Fall, a consistent opponent of Wilson's ideals. As noted in chapter 2, Fall and Doheny both had been in Kingston, New Mexico, in the mid-1880s but were not personally close until this collaboration over Mexico. In well-publicized hearings before a subcommittee on United States-Mexican relations, Fall delved into the "outrages" inflicted on Americans by the Carranza government. It was obvious from the beginning, as Harold Walker noted, that the oil interests were no longer worried about the "danger of criticizing the Carranza authorities in public or private."[37]

In the months prior to the Fall investigation, the reading public had already been treated to numerous stories purporting to reveal the true motives of the oilmen. In July 1919, L. J. de Bekker, a writer for the *New York Tribune*, produced a series of articles for *The Nation* entitled "The Plot Against Mexico," which charged the oilmen with all manner of evildoing. Then, just prior to the start of the Fall hearings, Samuel Guy Inman, an American missionary representing a coalition of Christians opposed to an aggressive foreign policy in Latin America, published a book entitled *Intervention in Mexico*, which repeated many of the charges that de Bekker had laid out. Inman was the first person called to testify before the committee, and he became a political lightning rod for Senator Fall.[38]

From Inman's perspective, the Mexican problem in the United States sprang from five basic sources: a lack of knowledge about Mexican geography and history, ignorance of the internal political currents of Mexico, the difference between Anglo-Saxon and Latin psychology, the impossibility of separating the Mexican question from American political and economic life, and the fact that the American people did not get the truth about conditions in Mexico. This was the Doheny program in almost every respect, and Inman even praised Doheny's financial support as a first step along the road to understanding. But he also supposed—not incorrectly—that the Doheny reports advocated the vocational rehabilitation of Mexico through increased contact with American business, and Inman warned his readers that nothing would be worse than to turn Mexicans into worshipers of "crass materialism." Inman offered a cogent argument for leaving Mexico alone. He believed that the country was in the midst of a true social revolution and that the situation was not going to be resolved by any action on the part of the United States. "We might as well stop fooling ourselves,"

Inman concluded, that Americans would wake up one morning to find that the Mexican problem had been solved "by a shuffling of the political cards."[39]

But that was precisely what the Fall Committee hoped to accomplish. As a counterpoint, the Committee called Doheny to center stage as the star witness for the oil industry and the business community, in general. During his testimony, Doheny explained the plight of American firms struggling to conduct normal business in Mexico in the face of Carranza's antiforeign demands. He maintained that radical taxation policies and the provisions of Article 27 inhibited profitable oil production in Mexico and threatened to eliminate ownership of private property altogether. The real problem, from his perspective, was Carranza's belief that he could wipe out the contracts and agreements of the last fifteen years with impunity. Nevertheless, in spite of his intense dislike for Carranza's policies, Doheny stated that he was not an interventionist but stood "in an absolutely neutral position with reference to the political affairs in Mexico." All he could really do was to complain. On this matter, Doheny's personal preference for a new government in Mexico conflicted with the realization that a direct military invasion into the oil zone might prompt Carranza or Pelaez to destroy the wells as a desperate act of defiance. The oilmen, as one industry observer noted correctly, were stuck "between the devil and the deep blue sea."[40]

Recently, it has been suggested that the oilmen miscalculated the political equation in Mexico. Supposedly, they would have been better off joining with the Carranza forces rather than continuing their support of Pelaez, since rebel exactions in 1919 almost equaled the tax demands of the central government and Pelaez's raids on the oil camps caused considerable damage. Logically, the oilmen had less to fear from Carranza's Article 27, to which he was not personally committed, than they did from Pelaez's continued rebellion. And, according to this view, "if the oilmen really had a choice of tax men perhaps they would have chosen Carranza," suggesting that Pelaez never gave them the luxury of choosing.[41]

Yet, there was an ideological component to the oilmen's case that defied logical explanation. The only thing that was clear, even under the most chaotic circumstances, was that the oilmen understood Pelaez and his basic desire for money and power, whereas they were never sure about Carranza and Mexico's "confiscatory" constitution. Therefore, they resisted his physical possession of the oilfields with every means at their disposal. Certainly, this was a fundamental misreading of Carranza's intentions, which were nationalist but not anticapitalist. Likewise, the oilmen misunderstood

Woodrow Wilson's support of the Carranza government and viewed it as a basic disavowal of their rights. Overall, the situation worked to defeat the bottom-line pragmatism of business, which would have had the oil companies settle for what they could get out of the new government and move on.

In the background, the specter of the Bolshevik Revolution rampaging across the world stage confused the issue even more, and suggesting a link between the revolutions in Mexico and Russia was an effective argument, even if it tended more toward hysterical fantasy than proven fact. This was a current theme during the Fall Committee hearings and the subject of many NAPARIM pamphlets. In "Plow With Petroleum," for example, published in 1920, the "Argonauts of oil" referred to the attack on their legal rights by the "Bolshevistic-Carranza government" in Mexico and asked readers if they were in favor of having their government declare "a firm, definite policy toward the protection of American citizens, whether they be in Mexico, Siberia, or Keokuk."[42]

Perhaps because of the extreme rhetoric from all sides, the ideological contest in Mexico produced a political stalemate between 1915 and 1919. While it is true that the oilmen could not remove Carranza or his obnoxious constitutional policies, they did not acquiesce to them, either. They paid what taxes and duties they could not avoid and held firm against Article 27. Needing money, Carranza compromised to the degree that he did not insist on implementing what he could not defend, and he succeeded in gaining United States recognition and enough tax revenue to successfully keep Mexico out of the hands of the foreign powers. Pelaez waged a successful guerilla war in the Huasteca district, which earned him a share of the oil wealth and kept the central authorities out of his home territory.

Overall, the one who benefitted most was Woodrow Wilson. More than anyone else, Wilson understood that the best strategy was simply to leave the situation alone. By not adding the United States military into the equation, a mistake he had made earlier at Veracruz and with the Pershing Expedition, he forced the three other groups into a rough balance of power, with definite limits on how far any single group was willing to push its agenda. This was a noisy, sometimes destructive, and occasionally deadly stalemate, but it left Wilson free to try his hand at settling the European conflict. That he ultimately failed in that endeavor should not obscure the fact that it was his Mexican policy that gave him the opportunity to try.

These were short-term gains, however, made possible by the enormity of the German threat. Afterward, the scorecard looked drastically different for the contenders in Mexico. In the spring of 1920, Carranza was forced from office and ultimately assassinated by his political opponents under the leadership of Alvaro Obregón. Pelaez, who rose briefly with the Obregón regime, failed to develop the political vision necessary to survive on a larger field and was eventually forced back home to an involuntary retirement. Only Doheny and the oil companies were left to fight for, and profit from, another day. Yet that was more a victory for oil, itself, which because of the World War had become a strategic commodity valuable enough to ensure its own survival. Mexican oil, in particular, was about to enter the period of its greatest influence—the early 1920s.

9 DOMESTIC POLITICS AND INTERNATIONAL RELATIONS: IRELAND AND JAPAN, 1920–1921

With the increasing size and importance of his oil holdings in Mexico and the United States, Doheny found his political influence growing in proportion to his economic power. Although he did not emerge as a figure of national importance until 1920, he had been a prominent Democrat on the West Coast since the late 1890s. From the beginning, Doheny's devotion to the party was rooted in his Irish-American heritage, faith in the Catholic church, and his long years on the Western frontier, which had made him a sympathetic follower of William Jennings Bryan. Over time, however, his financial success eroded the logic, if not the sentiment, behind those positions, and, by the early 1920s, he found himself at a political crossroads. Had his ideas been totally mercenary, Doheny would probably have given up on the Democrats in 1916, when Republican presidential candidate Charles Evans Hughes emphasized the Mexican crisis as a major campaign issue in opposition to Woodrow Wilson. Instead, Doheny's significant financial support in California helped Wilson achieve an improbable victory in his bid for reelection.

At the end of the war, however, Wilson's internationalism and his refusal to entertain the Mexican question at the Paris Peace Conference angered Doheny to no end. Thereafter, although he played a prominent role at the Democratic convention in 1920, he broke with the party on a number of fronts. Much of his disaffection came from his growing friendship with Albert B. Fall, one of Wilson's harshest critics and the newly appointed secretary of the interior under Republican Warren Harding. As an intensely private individual, Doheny did not aspire to elected office, but, in the early 1920s, he allowed himself to be seduced by the idea that he could play a large role in shaping national and international events beyond his immediate interests in Mexican affairs. And it was his own patriotic commitment to Ireland and the United States, coupled neatly with his financial interests, which led him along a circuitous path into the controversy over the naval oil reserve in California. Ironically, when the details of those supposedly corrupt dealings became public knowledge in 1924, both political parties abandoned him.

Prior to 1920, Doheny was known for having "strong convictions on the questions of the day," but he usually kept them to himself, and his only forays into the political limelight were brief and largely ceremonial. For instance, in 1912, Doheny tried unsuccessfully to become a presidential elector for Woodrow Wilson after supporting conservative Democrat Champ Clark through the state primary. Then, in 1916, Doheny was chosen as an elector and earned the praise of state officials for pushing the Wilson campaign to victory in California. There was even a brief mention of Doheny as a suitable candidate for the Senate in 1916. Apparently, believing that the next Senator would come from the southern part of the state, northern California Democrats suggested Doheny as a compromise candidate. But, as one political observer pointed out, Doheny's only real qualification for the job was a "pocketbook [that measured] up to Bourbon expectations." Whether Doheny had such aspirations is doubtful, but his wealth made him an attractive, if unlikely, prospect nonetheless.[1]

A few years later, after having spent almost all of his time in Washington and New York during the war, Doheny enjoyed a solid reputation among many admirers. In 1920, he went to the Democratic national convention in San Francisco as a delegate at large from California and served as a member of the resolutions committee. And in return for his previous efforts, Doheny was nominated as the state's choice for vice-president. According to Isidore Dockweiler, California's representative on the national committee, this was intended as "a graceful tribute by the party in return for California's electoral vote in 1916, when Doheny headed the ticket."[2]

More than a favorite son, however, Doheny had support from a number of state delegations, and, according to a party leader from Missouri, his name had "been persistently mentioned in Washington" as a candidate for the office. One unnamed Californian in Washington, most likely Franklin Lane, Wilson's former secretary of the interior who had gone to work for Doheny after leaving the cabinet in 1919, believed that "the Presidential campaign with Doheny on the ticket would doubtless develop the fact that during the war he was one of the world's most useful citizens." This individual also predicted that both national conventions would be full of surprises and considered it "within the realm of probability that this many-sided man ... might emerge from the San Francisco convention as its nominee for president of the United States."[3]

At the convention, itself, rather than basking in the glory of past achievements, Doheny became involved in a struggle over the issue of Irish nationalism, which compromised his position among many delegates. At the center of this controversy was Eamon De Valera, the newly elected president of the Irish Republic, formed in January 1919 after Irish nationalists declared their independence in defiance of British control. Shortly thereafter, as the situation in Ireland erupted into another civil war, De Valera fled to the United States seeking financial and political support for the cause. He found an overwhelmingly receptive audience almost everywhere he went, especially among the Irish-American community in California. Having been a major financial contributor to the nationalist movement all along, Doheny also supported De Valera's mission in America.[4]

During the summer of 1920, De Valera presented proposals to both political parties for a plank in their respective platforms recognizing the Irish Republic. Not surprisingly, the Republicans turned him down, but he hoped for better luck in San Francisco. Appearing before the resolutions committee, De Valera asked for a straight vote in favor of Irish recognition, but the members rejected the Irish plank by thirty-one votes to seventeen. Initially, no one among the group who voted for the measure, including Doheny, was willing to take up the issue as a minority statement to be presented to the full convention. But after a meeting of Irish supporters outside the convention hall got so heated that the police had to be called in, De Valera accepted a compromise resolution that stood some chance of success. Although seven members of the committee signed the amended plank as a minority report, Doheny was the only one willing to present it to the delegates.[5]

Under the circumstances, this was a brave act, since Doheny not only faced an unsympathetic audience but had to speak on the heels of the venerable William Jennings Bryan himself. Having never before addressed a mass audience, Doheny showed his nervousness as he proceeded haltingly into his speech and even forgot part of the text. He began by asking the members to indulge his "weak voice and inexperience," but he made no excuse for his intention to speak in favor of Ireland's struggle for freedom. One sympathetic observer thought he did better than that when he reported that Doheny "went through like a Sinn Fein soldier and proudly marched up to the speaker's platform and presented the document." The task at hand, Doheny said, was to firm up the party's weak statement of sympathy for the "aspirations of Ireland for self-government." The revised plank read that "mindful of the circumstances of birth of our own nation," the party would support "recognition without intervention in all cases where the people of a nation have by the free vote of the people set up a republic and chosen a government to which they yield willing obedience." In the end, the delegates refused to endorse the Irish cause and voted down the minority plank 665 votes to 402. For Doheny, however, the experience at the convention took him deeper into the Irish nationalist movement, where he started to see himself as a statesman as well as a businessman.[6]

And so, Doheny must have felt an even greater sense of accomplishment in his subsequent nomination as a vice-presidential candidate. After choosing James M. Cox of Ohio to be their standard-bearer, the convention accepted suggestions for the second place on the ticket, and Lorin Handley, a delegate from Los Angeles, offered Doheny's name for consideration. Still boasting of the state's role in the last election, Handley remarked that California was "perfectly willing to yield the Presidency to Ohio, but not the glory of electing the last Democratic President of the United States." Their reward, Handley asserted, would come through the vice-presidency, since California wanted not only to elect Governor Cox but "to elect with him a great patriot to stand by his side to make humanity's fight." Because Doheny's life was "a typical romance of American improved opportunity," Handley believed that it was an example of success that every citizen could appreciate. Thus, Doheny was put forward as "the man out of the West who can reach the hearts and the souls, not only of the Democrats of the West, but of the great free-thinking people of the West." When Handley finished, a representative from Massachusetts came forward to second the nomination, believing that, if the party wanted to win in November, it needed to balance Cox's political record with Doheny's success in business, and portraying Doheny as "a self-made man . . . who is needed in this hour of reconstruction."[7]

As far as political parties and their conventions are concerned, there was really nothing exceptional in Doheny's nomination; scores of other individuals—of greater and lesser utility—had been given similar moments of glory. Certainly, there was limited support for putting a sixty-four-year-old oil magnate on the ticket; the prize ultimately went to the much younger, and far more charismatic, Franklin D. Roosevelt. For Doheny, however, this was another indication that he had some unique qualities to offer and that there were people willing to make use of his potential in both subtle and overt ways.[8]

One of the most influential of these was Franklin Lane, who now worked as a legal advisor for the Pan American Petroleum & Transport Company. As the head of the Interior Department, Lane had been a lonely voice for private enterprise among a choir of strict conservationists. And because of internal conflicts and the inadequacy of his government salary, Lane had contemplated resigning his office several times during the war years but promised Wilson he would see the crisis through. Then, having been "literally forced out of public life by my lack of resources," as Lane put it, he accepted a $50,000-a-year position with Doheny, hoping he could at least make enough before retirement to get out of debt and remove the financial burden from his family.

As it turned out, Lane had little more than a year to live and spent most of his months on the Doheny payroll seeking treatment for a heart condition that ultimately caused his death. He also spent time in the Pan American Petroleum offices in New York and at Doheny's home and ranch in Los Angeles getting to know his benefactor. Although Lane had always been a staunch advocate of the oil industry and wanted to see the federal government give the oilmen free rein to manage the nation's petroleum resources, he was an ambivalent cheerleader for big business. As his career revealed, he gave little thought to personal wealth and admitted to having spent the years since his boyhood fighting "Wall Street rascals." But for some reason, he felt that Doheny was different, if no less wealthy, than his Eastern counterparts.[9]

Lane, who described himself as a "wild cross between a crazy Irishman, with dreams, desires, fancies, and a dour Scot," was not an active member of the Irish-American community and often lamented the less charitable aspects of the Irish temperament. But he understood the power of the Irish independence movement in the United States and almost certainly had a hand in supporting Doheny's appearance at the Democratic convention on behalf of the cause. Sometime later, Lane presented Doheny with an Irish flag, noting that it stood as a symbol for the divine aspirations of a people "to whom most of the arts were known when England and America were forest wastes, whose women have made the world beautiful by their virtue, and whose men have made the world free by their courage." No doubt inspired by Lane's faith and encouragement, Doheny seemed more willing than ever to live up to that ideal.[10]

At the same time, during the fall of 1920, De Valera broke with the leading members of the Irish nationalist movement in America, the Friends of Irish Freedom, to form his own group called the American Association for the Recognition of the Irish Republic. The divisive issue was whether the money collected in the United States ought to be used to influence American politicians to support a diplomatic solution for Ireland or whether the funds should be sent directly to Ireland to support the revolutionaries in the civil war. De Valera advocated the latter strategy and forced the break with the existing nationalist party. On November 17, the members of the AARIR elected Doheny national president of the new organization.[11]

Lane obviously paid a good deal of attention to the Irish situation and must have been alarmed at Doheny's prominent role in the more radical organization. Within a few weeks of Doheny's taking office as the head of the AARIR, Lane wrote him with a plan designed to put some distance between Doheny and the armed struggle in Ireland. Lane claimed to see an opportunity for Doheny to bridge the ideological gap between the Irish and British leaders by offering to mediate a peaceful end to the conflict. Lane began by claiming that the time was ripe "for some practical man, preferably an outsider, to do something for Ireland—and why should you not be that man?" Then he continued:

> You have made a great fortune and achieved a great name in the business world. You would have done great things for Mexico, altogether unselfishly, if the chance had come—and may be it will come yet. But there is no reason why you might not do something internationally for your Father's land which you love so dearly. Service for Ireland cannot be rendered by stirring up the Irish here or embittering our people further against England. Hatred will not solve this problem . . . Lloyd George is willing to talk terms now. There must be a go-between. He must have the confidence of the Irish. You have that. He must also have access to the British Ministry. You have that, or easily can get it. Isn't it worth trying? . . . You would have to speak to Lloyd George as a known partisan of the Irish cause, but not as one committed to a program. You would be the vehicle through which the Irish would learn the best they could hope for, this side of war. You would go on oil business. No one in the world would have the slightest idea, either here or there, what you were trying to do until something was done. It would be fatal to the English and to Irish pride to have it thought that they could not speak together. But we know that they cannot. Both need a friend.[12]

The effect of this kind of an appeal can hardly be overstated. And Doheny seemed to be heeding Lane's advice when, over the next few months, he subsidized a national fund-raising drive for the relief of Ireland. In this instance, Doheny advanced the group $250,000 to set up collection committees across the country, and he contributed heavily thereafter.

Ultimately, the effort generated over $5 million to alleviate suffering in Ireland caused by the ongoing political conflict. As the state chairman for the American Committee for the Relief of Ireland, Doheny appealed to the citizens of Los Angeles to meet their quota. He asked them to forget politics and religion for the moment so that they could see the real situation in Ireland, where thousands of "hungry, naked, sick women and children and old people . . . [looked] to the United States as their last hope." Any who had the means, but was unwilling, to help would have "no excuse to give his conscience for turning a deaf ear to weak humans in terrible distress."[13]

While the move to provide humanitarian relief to Ireland produced an unqualified success in the United States in the spring of 1921, there were also secret, high-level talks, of the type Lane envisioned, going on between De Valera and Lloyd George to put an end to the fighting. Soon after forming his new American organization in December 1920, De Valera had returned to Ireland and was eventually arrested by the British authorities in June 1921. The British, however, knew that there was no way to sue for peace with the Irish leader in jail, so De Valera was granted an unexpected release and an invitation to meet with Lloyd George. Over the course of several months, the two men hashed out their respective goals for Ireland, with De Valera holding out for something more than dominion status.[14]

Doheny's link to the truce between the combatants in July 1921, and the subsequent signing of an Anglo-Irish Treaty in December, can only be surmised. Certainly, there is no evidence to suggest that Doheny participated in any of these talks. But if he followed Lane's advice to act discreetly as a bridge between the two leaders, there is room to speculate about his influence. If nothing else, Doheny must have had some method of contacting De Valera because of his position as president of the AARIR. Along those lines, Lloyd George's biographer notes that, in the early months of 1921, the prime minister "secretly attempted, through several intermediaries, to reach some common ground with De Valera," although the effort failed at the time. And in at least one instance, the British ambassador to the United States, Sir Auckland Geddes, wrote to the foreign office on December 8, 1921, two days after the signing of the treaty, that Doheny "was attempting to take credit for creating the conditions which made it possible."[15]

The Anglo-Irish Treaty and the subsequent creation of the Irish Free State granted a degree of independence and self-determination for Ireland great enough to satisfy the desires of most of the moderate nationalists. Indeed, the principal leaders of the AARIR, especially Doheny, considered the Irish Free State to be as close to a republic as Ireland was going to get for some time and celebrated its creation as the logical end of their own movement in the United States. Upon hearing the news of an agreement, Doheny noted that Ireland's friends in America had been working to "get them not to be too extreme. . . . The accomplishment of the Irish Free State is what I have hoped for. I have had the utmost faith that the conference would result in it. I have believed that Lloyd George and his Ministry were sincerely working for a settlement, and knew that the aims of De Valera and his associates were the same."[16]

In the days that followed, however, Doheny's position led De Valera to make an angry and permanent break with him. Once having negotiated the truce, De Valera would have nothing to do with the treaty, which he considered a weak-willed surrender to the British Government. Instead, De Valera called for a resumption of the civil war in Ireland. Believing that the treaty was the right solution, Doheny resigned his position as the head of the AARIR early in 1922, in a clash with a more militant faction within the organization.[17]

On a completely different level, the negotiations over the Anglo-Irish Treaty introduced other issues concerning American security in the North Atlantic and the naval rivalry between Britain and the United States. In fact, while the Irish question was being negotiated, the world's major naval powers prepared to meet in Washington, D.C., at a disarmament conference to determine the balance of naval power for the postwar decade. In advance of that meeting, in September 1921, the executive committee of the AARIR met in Chicago to discuss a proposed clause in the Irish treaty giving Britain the right to install naval and air force stations in Ireland. Seeing a hidden agenda in the British plans, the committee sent a letter to President Harding, with a copy to be delivered to the members of the American delegation, warning them of the danger. The committee saw no defensive component to these demands and believed that recent comments by British military and government officials indicated that the North Atlantic would be the battlefield of the future. "Against what nation or nations," the committee asked, "are these aggressive naval and aerial plans and provisions directed?" In their minds, the British scheme for Ireland constituted "a menace to the security of the United States."[18]

It is interesting to note that the head of the anti-De Valera faction in Boston wrote a letter to the secretary of state claiming that Doheny's share of the British-Mexican Petroleum Company made him a partner, and co-conspirator, with the British Government. And his large fuel oil contracts based on Mexican oil production made him a vital link to any British naval operation in the Atlantic. "Undoubtedly," the letter continued, "through

Mr. Doheny's activities, England has been given an advantage over America," which constituted a "serious menace" to American security. The writer even called for a congressional investigation of this relationship so that, in case of war, the United States could nullify Doheny's contract with British shipping companies.[19]

The American government had, in fact, been using the Irish situation as a wedge to achieve concessions from Britain all along, but this had little to do with any planned military installations in Ireland. Rather, the State Department used the civil unrest in Ireland as a lens to focus attention on their desire to force Great Britain to relinquish its strategic alliance with Japan. The real potential threat to American security came from the direction of the Pacific Ocean not the Atlantic. Thus, Secretary of State Hughes linked the Irish question to the latter issue and told the British ambassador that a resumption of the Anglo-Japanese alliance would bring together anti-British elements in the United States calling for the support of the insurrection in Ireland and possible congressional action to recognize the Irish Republic. Looking years into the future, the British were unwilling to gamble against America's rise as the preeminent Western power, and they acquiesced to Hughes' demands.[20]

Doheny's role as the head of the AARIR and that organization's concerns over British naval policy also provided him with an indirect link to the larger issues of American security beyond his concerns with Mexico, and his position as a prominent Californian carried him into the debate over various plans to offset the Japanese threat in the Pacific. All of these elements converged after the election of Republican Warren Harding in 1921 as the new president of the United States. Despite having been briefly considered as a possible member of the opposing ticket, Doheny was warmly received by the new administration, with Secretary of the Interior Albert Fall being the most conspicuous of his Republican friends. Two days after the election, Doheny wrote to Fall that "it is in sackcloth and ashes that I come to your feet to beg forgiveness and admission among the ranks of the sane people of the Country." He asked Fall to understand, "as most of my friends do, why I thought it best to remain regular." What those reasons were Doheny did not say, but he had obviously come to despise the Democratic candidate, James Cox. According to Doheny, Harding won because he "undoubtedly convinced the people that he was a safe man to be the country's president." On the other hand, Doheny continued, "the vituperative and dastardly dishonest campaign of Cox surely had the reverse effect."[21]

Doheny was referring here to an incident that happened late in the campaign, when one of Harding's nastier critics dredged up an old rumor about the Republican candidate's ancestry. Essentially, the claim was that, several generations back, the Hardings had come from the West Indies and that Warren Harding was, therefore, a mestizo. Although Cox and the Democratic National Committee denounced the information as slanderous, pamphlets detailing the race issue found their way by the thousands underneath voters' doors, onto commuter trains, and into hotel lobbies through the efforts of energetic, and anonymous, volunteers. Having stated that he "never heard a dirtier argument," Doheny gave $25,000 to the Republican party to have the pictures of Harding's parents printed in all of the New York City newspapers to dispute the claim.[22]

Aside from the underhanded tactics, Doheny noted that the voters' decision was also a reaction against "the fallacies and fatal consequences of Wilson's League of Nations." And Fall, as Doheny reminded him, was owed a debt of gratitude from the American people for his work as a member of the "Senate oligarchy" responsible for defeating the League. When it was over, Doheny believed that the election of 1920 "was a greater cause for rejoicing than the signing of the Armistice on November 11, 1918, or of any other event or day since the eventful day in 1776 which gave birth to this Republic. . . . The United States must, and now will be preserved, as the inspiration to progress for all the world by maintaining an independent and tolerant individualism among its citizens, and nationalism among the nations of the world, rather than promoting socialism with all its degrading effects, and internationalism with its danger of complete annihilation of Americanism."[23]

Once in office, the Harding Administration used the Washington Disarmament Conference in November 1921 as the first test of its ability to handle foreign policy in a new era. And given the climate of opinion at that time, recent appraisals have given the president high marks for pragmatism in negotiating a realistic treaty between the naval powers which at least temporarily reduced tensions around the world. In brief, the United States, Great Britain, and Japan agreed to stop all major ship construction at current levels, established a 5:5:3 naval ratio among the powers, negated the Anglo-Japanese alliance, and made mutual concessions not to fortify islands and outposts in the western Pacific to reduce the possibility of an unintended confrontation. All in all, this seemed like a simple, cost-effective strategy, and it was extremely popular at a time when the American public refused to sacrifice tax relief to pay for additional military obligations. Nevertheless, modern scholars, knowing what came later, have characterized the debate over the disarmament package as "shallow, cursory, and largely uninformed." Thus, without much reflection, the arms agreement was "steamrollered" into law.[24]

Another reason for this legislative coup was that a significant contingent of naval officers, primarily those responsible for war plans in the Pacific, were left entirely outside of the process. By and large, this group opposed almost every provision in the treaty, but their objections were never considered in the rush to push an agreement through Congress without debate. This tactic, and the political mindset behind it, made it quite clear to naval officers in the field that they could not appeal to Congress or to the public for additional support. In particular, the head of the General Board of the Navy, recently returned from the Asiatic Fleet, was absolutely "convinced of the Japanese menace," but his views, along with those of the War Plans Division, itself, were ignored because they deviated from what the politicians wanted to hear.[25]

As we know now, however, the fears about Japan were not mere illusions used to prop up the military budget. In fact, Japanese-American relations were at such a low point in 1921 that, one British naval expert concluded, "the situation in the Far East was so ominous that well-informed observers believed war between the United States and Japan to be only a question of time, and no long time at that." A memo on Japanese preparedness in April 1921, from the Office of Naval Intelligence, also concluded that "there seems no question that Japan is preparing for any eventuality that may occur and that America is the country she has in mind."[26]

Without question, the Japanese Navy focused its attention almost exclusively on the United States. But the Japanese were also engaged in a similar internal dispute over the need for a strong position at the disarmament conference. Consequently, while the treaty was hailed as a political victory for Congress and the president by stopping the call for increased military spending, it was also seen as a "godsend" by the Japanese naval minister, who knew that his country's economy could not support an arms race with the United States. However, the Japanese navy also had a corps of officers who reacted violently to the restrictions of the treaty: "As far as I am concerned," said Vice-Admiral Kato Kanji, "war with America starts now. We'll get our revenge over this, by God!"[27]

In hindsight, the conference turned out to be a temporary bandage for a festering problem on both sides of the Pacific. As one American naval officer noted after reviewing the nonfortification provisions of the treaty: "It is thus seen that our statesmen at Washington did not achieve great ends without making concessions . . . [and] our hand is weakened in the Far East by this abdication of potential strategic position."[28] Although navy leaders had to accept the domestic political decisions made at that conference, they did not allow them to completely hinder preparations for a Pacific strategy. Recognizing the inevitable limitations placed on President Harding, the Navy Department, under Secretary Edwin Denby, "moved with circumspection," as one historian put it, to do as much as possible to strengthen the Pacific Fleet.[29]

Some plans were as simple as sending oil-burning ships to the Pacific and coal-burning vessels to the Atlantic to take advantage of the cheapest source of fuel in each region. But these obvious moves were actually designed to cover more controversial changes along the lines of creating one grand fleet instead maintaining two equally divided forces, as mandated by former Navy Secretary Josephus Daniels. For years, critics argued with Daniels—to no avail—that one large fleet rather than two inadequate ones would be far more intimidating, especially to the Japanese. Once free of him, Daniels's opponents implemented their plans for redeploying the most powerful ships to Pacific waters. However, this strategy was limited by the inadequate shore facilities in the region. Existing plans to fully equip and protect bases in the Philippines and Guam had been scuttled by the disarmament treaty. For a line of defense against Japan, the navy would have to make do with commercial harbors in the western Pacific. Only the base at Pearl Harbor, Hawaii, had the capability of becoming a first-class naval station, but it was relatively undeveloped at the time.[30]

Although Pearl Harbor was too far away from Japan to replace the need for bases farther west, it would be the central staging area for the Pacific Fleet and was the key to stopping any Japanese strike against the American mainland. Given this anticipated role, an official inspection in 1919 concluded that Pearl Harbor's current facilities were "entirely inefficient" for peacetime operations and "totally inadequate" for an emergency. The base needed longer piers, deep draft docks, and most especially fuel oil depots to meet even minimal standards. Implementing this Pacific strategy in the face of public apathy toward defense requirements made it necessary that fleet changes and other modifications be conducted as quietly as possible to avoid alerting the media and Congress to what was happening, at least until it was too late to do anything about it. An essential element in the success of this plan was that Navy Secretary Denby, unlike his predecessor, encouraged his subordinates to take the initiative in coming up with new ways to accomplish these goals.[31]

Controlling the navy's oil supply was also an integral part of this process. To streamline administrative responsibilities and assure a sufficient supply of oil for the fleet, Denby transferred operational control of the naval petroleum reserves in California and Wyoming to the Department of the Interior. Since the Interior Department was already supervising public oil lands through the Bureau of Mines and the Geological Survey, it would save the navy needless duplication to have it administer the reserves as well. Along with this exchange of control, Denby authorized the secretary of the interior to use the royalty oil accruing from wells on the reserves as payment for the construction of fuel storage tanks at Pearl Harbor. Without sufficient funds to bring the base at Pearl Harbor up to operational standards, and with the certain knowledge that Congress would not give him any more, Secretary Fall decided to do the next best thing: trade the oil that he had in hand already for the storage tanks and dock facilities that he needed at Pearl Harbor. From the beginning, there were critics in the Navy Department who questioned both the loss of control over the petroleum reserves and the legality of transferring authority to Fall. But the utility of the trade could not be denied. The next problem was finding someone willing to take the navy's oil in payment for such a massive construction project.[32]

In November 1921, as the Washington Conference got underway, Fall set to work on the plan. His first move was to ask Doheny if he could get an estimate of what it would cost to put up thirty 50,000-barrel tanks at Pearl Harbor. As the former head of the Mexican lobby in the Senate, Fall knew the extent of the Mexican Petroleum Company's storage facilities in Tampico and trusted Doheny's opinion. Furthermore, to protect the government from private wells operating along the perimeter of the naval reserve at Elk Hills, Doheny had already been awarded the right to drill several dozen offset wells on a small strip lease within the reserve itself— contracts won through competitive bids approved by Secretary Daniels before he left office. Thus, Fall had reason to believe that, in a similar contest, Doheny would win the additional leases necessary to pay for the work at Pearl Harbor. Yet, when Doheny reported back to Fall on November 28 with an estimate of $3.5 million, or just under 3 million barrels of royalty oil, he stated that he was not interested in doing work that required outside construction contracts and complicated negotiations with the government.[33]

Doheny changed his mind, however, after he received a visit from Rear Admiral John K. Robison a few weeks later. During the war, Robison had been Edward Doheny Jr.'s battleship commander. Afterward, the young Doheny kept in touch with Robison and had spoken many times of his father's oil operations in California. With this mutual connection, Robison and the senior Doheny had met socially on a few occasions. Then, in October 1921, Robison was appointed by Secretary Denby to become the Chief of the Bureau of Engineering, the office in charge of the naval oil reserves. Prior to that, he had been working in the Office of the Chief of Operations on wartime plans for the navy's shore stations, where he had spent most of the previous year completing a report on the "problem in the Pacific." For Robison, therefore, the oil supply was of paramount importance.[34]

When the two men met again in December 1921, Doheny mentioned that he had been attending some of the sessions of the Disarmament Conference, and Robison let him know that the administration had called the conference specifically because of Japanese conduct in the western Pacific, "with the idea of trying to bring about a crushing of this Japanese movement toward supremacy." Robison also revealed that the Naval Intelligence Department had reports that Japan was prepared for "mobilization along the Oriental frontier" and for maneuvers "toward our borders." Knowing that Doheny had initially turned down Fall's invitation to bid on a contract to provision Pearl Harbor with oil, Robison made it quite clear that, if the navy did not complete these preparations in time, the United States would be at Japan's mercy. Without that supply, Robison declared, "our navy could easily be overcome."[35]

Having seen firsthand the result of invasions in Europe, Robison warned Doheny that a similar attack by the Japanese along the California coast would be just as catastrophic as the German invasion of Belgium, producing "a reign of terrorism that would be indescribable." Doheny recalled that Robison "got me very much worked up over it and told me in a very earnest tone of voice that it was up to me to give him such assurance that at least one company would bid on this [Pearl Harbor] transaction." Then, Robison recounted Lord Curzon's statement that the "armies of the Allies float[ed] to victory on a tide of oil." Amending it for the current crisis with Japan, Robison insisted that America could only maintain its position by "floating to security on a tide of oil on the Pacific."[36]

Supposedly, Doheny's previous objections to the project were swept away by Robison's dramatic presentation. And once again, as had happened with Lane during the Anglo-Irish dispute, someone was appealing to him to make a great personal commitment not just as a patriot but as the only person in America uniquely suited to the task. Nothing in Doheny's recent experience caused him to refuse the request. That night, Doheny promised Robison that the navy could count on an offer from his company to do the work at Pearl Harbor. Furthermore, Doheny told him, "we would not figure on any profit in [the] transaction."[37]

And so, over the next year Doheny took on several additional contracts for leasing large sections of the Elk Hills Petroleum Reserve to accomplish these ends. In addition, Doheny kept his word to give the government its best deal for the Pearl Harbor construction job. Without a doubt, the value of Doheny's prospective leases on the reserve would be worth a vast sum over the next few decades. In return, he was willing to put up millions of his own to fulfill the navy's immediate requirements.

Then, in the spring of 1922, when Congress caught wind of Fall and Denby's policies, Robert La Follette, the Wisconsin firebrand, was the first to cry foul. Initially, attention fell on the contracts made with Harry Sinclair to drill oil on Naval Reserve No. 3 in Teapot Dome, Wyoming. Those contracts were not associated with any of Doheny's work at Pearl Harbor and seemed particularly suspicious. But recalling the Ballinger-Pinchot controversy during the Taft administration, La Follette reminded his colleagues that the Interior Department had always been the preferred "sluiceway" for corruption when private interests wanted to loot the government. The "throwing open of the naval reserves" to the oil corporations was obviously a part of that pattern and they should have seen it coming.[38]

Then La Follette cited a communication he had recently received from former Navy Secretary Daniels stating that Denby's leasing policy was "outrageous and wicked" and risked the "very national existence of the United States." The senator added that he had also been "astounded" that the new head of the navy would transfer control of the reserves to the Interior Department. In La Follette's opinion, given Albert Fall's longstanding preference for the private development of public land, that was nothing but a "surrender to the burglars." Moreover, since they had left a "trail of corruption . . . in the pages of American history," La Follette insisted that oil companies could never be trusted under any circumstances. Obviously, they were at it again, using ruthless means to seize the nation's oil supply with one hand while robbing the average citizen through extortionist prices with the other. In response to these charges the oil press ridiculed La Follette as "the most warped man in public life."[39]

Admittedly, despite the hysteria, the combination of public servants, private businessmen, and government resources seemed like a certain formula for corruption when Congress took up its investigation of the matter in 1923. But what about Doheny's role in these transactions? Was the story of the Japanese menace nothing but a ruse to gain control of the navy's oil for profit? Were Doheny's claims of patriotism just a pathetic attempt to explain away his insatiable greed? Or did he take advantage of the naval reserves because he needed the oil for his companies? Having determined how Doheny could have become involved in the leasing of the Elk Hills oil reserve as a result of his desire to do his part to shore up the nation's defenses in the Pacific, is it necessary for us, today, to assume that his allegiance was only as deep as his financial interests?

In 1923, the public responded to such questions according to whether they thought that businessmen were basically honest or inherently crooked. Politicians reacted according to their previous association with the suspects. Before any of these points can be adequately addressed, however, a more sophisticated approach must be taken to determine whether Doheny's contracts with the government actually sustained or enhanced his oil interests, regardless of the other issues. If he was desperate for oil, he might have done anything to get it. But if he was not, or had less risky options, perhaps his motives were more laudable, if not more altruistic, than have been presumed.

10 SALT WATER AND REVOLUTION:
MEXICO, 1921–1923

In the three years between the end of the World War I and Doheny's acquisition of his first contract for the large oil properties in the Elk Hills Naval Petroleum Reserve in 1921, many people became convinced that the Mexican oil supply was all but exhausted. Since Mexican production reached its peak at the end of that year and declined thereafter, it is logical to assume that Doheny leased the oil reserve to offset a shrinking supply in Mexico. But, as this chapter will show, the situation was more complex than that, and Doheny never conceded that his Mexican properties were running dry. On the contrary, he engaged industry pessimists, stock market raiders, and the Mexican government in a running battle to prove his point. In doing so, he was pulled into an even wider range of activity than what has been described previously.

To begin, the dire predictions about Mexican oil were based on the rapid invasion of salt water into some of the largest wells. This process was by no means unanticipated in Mexican gushers, since it was the force of pressurized salt water beneath the oil that gave the wells their tremendous output. But that spectacular production, which had been going on for a decade, also meant that even the largest pools of oil could be exhausted fairly quickly. There was also the risk that the speed of the oil rushing into the well would pull the water layer up high enough to choke off the flow. If production were managed properly, this would not happen until most of the recoverable oil had been expelled, but there was always the danger of ruining a property through overproduction, as was the case in Mexico.

Unfortunately, all of these issues were twisted out of proportion by the contending parties, and reporters played up the seemingly unanticipated demise of wells as the beginning of the end of the Mexican oil industry. From the public's perspective, as Herbert Wylie complained, the salt water scare "has been pictured like a roaring lion going about eating up all the wells."[1] But there was no denying the fact that the oldest Mexican fields were beginning to run dry. The Mexican Eagle's largest well, Potrero del Llano, stopped production in December 1918, and Huasteca Petroleum's Casiano No. 7 went to water in November 1919, after producing one hundred million barrels of oil. In his annual message for 1920, Doheny tried to ease the anxiety of his shareholders over this situation. Losing these fields was natural and inevitable, he said, and was no more indicative of some alarming condition "than is the death of a nonagenarian or even an octogenarian indicative of a lack of sanitary or health conditions in the vicinity where he had lived."[2]

While this was obviously a correct geological assessment of the situation, it did nothing to stop various individuals from playing up the crisis and circulating rumors about the impending demise of Mexican oil. Some gloomily predicted that the loss of cheap Mexican fuel oil would force American shipping and industrial interests back to coal. Gulf Coast producers, on the other hand, tired of competing against low-priced Mexican crude as their own output increased dramatically, were ecstatic over the possibility of capturing the fuel oil market for themselves. But those concerned with America's international position worried that the loss of Mexican production would give England a distinct advantage in the global race for petroleum, since the British government had been actively supporting commercial oil ventures around the world while the United States took virtually all of its imports from Mexico.

To make matters worse, the continuing political battle with Carranza and the lack of support from the Wilson Administration had almost forced Doheny to sell his Mexican holdings to the British after the war. At that time, as the oilmen pointed out during Senator Fall's investigation of Mexican affairs, the real problem in Mexico was not the loss of the old wells but the inability to drill new ones in undeveloped territory because of the legal conflicts over property ownership and drilling permits. By presidential decree, Carranza had denied those permits to foreign-owned companies unless they relinquished title to lands acquired from the Díaz government and took new concessions and leases, based upon Article 27 of the constitution, in their place. It was at that point, in January 1919, when Mark Requa, who was still in charge of the nation's fuel resources, warned the State Department that Doheny was ready to sell out. According to Requa, representatives of Royal Dutch-Shell had been interested in the Mexican

Petroleum Company for some time, and, were it not for Doheny's promise to the government not to sell during the war, he might have done so already. Now that he was free of that commitment, he was supposedly headed to London to make a deal.[3]

He was also going to Europe as a member of a committee selected by the National Association for the Protection of American Rights in Mexico to discuss the Mexican situation with the American peace delegation in Paris. Before he left New York, Doheny told the press that he was going to Paris to ask one question only:

> Will the Governments that will be established in the many new states that will be formed out of the future great nations of Eastern Europe be permitted to ignore the vested property rights of citizens and foreigners that have been established for years; and if not, will Mexico, which is in the same category, while not a combatant in the great war, be allowed by the powers to issue confiscatory decrees and by overt acts not only to ignore vested property rights but to enact legislation that is against all law, equity and justice. . . . Vested property rights in Mexico are inalienable, no matter what the Carranza or any other government of that benighted country may declare.[4]

Despite the fact that this group of American industrial and banking interests was denied a forum at the Paris Peace Conference, Doheny gave no hint that he was ready to give up the fight. But, according to Requa, the very idea that he was thinking about it caused the State Department to suggest that either Bernard Baruch, the head of the War Industries Board, or John Davis, the U.S. ambassador to Britain, intercept Doheny when he got to London and persuade him not to sell his company to any foreign interest. And Doheny presumably received a guarantee that businessmen with interests in Mexico would not be abandoned after the Peace Conference in return for another promise to that effect.[5]

Because so little of Requa's information can be corroborated, his warning about Doheny was probably more of a scare tactic than anything else, although there was a report from a London correspondent stating that Doheny's negotiations with the Shell organization had been broken off at the last minute over the terms of the deal. Perhaps the United States government had intercepted him in time after all. For its part, Royal Dutch-Shell was still interested in Mexican oil and purchased working control of the Mexican Eagle Oil Company two months later. This was a tremendous boon for the European conglomerate, which produced approximately 27 million barrels of oil in 1918 and could anticipate adding another 17 million barrels from the Mexican Eagle. (The purchase of Mexican Petroleum, on the other hand, would have increased the amount to 21.5 million barrels.)[6]

Writing from London in March 1919, Clarence Barron, Doheny's close friend and editor of the *Wall Street Journal,* worried over the British government's oil policies. While Doheny had been publicly and privately insulted by the Wilson Administration in Washington, Barron observed that he was being "welcomed with open arms by every shipping interest in Britain." Doheny was in London primarily to complete the arrangements for the British-Mexican Petroleum Company, which had been postponed during the war. This company, co-owned by English investors and Pan American Petroleum, ultimately signed a twenty-five-year, fixed-rate contract with Doheny for Mexican fuel oil, the longest running obligation ever undertaken by an oil company at that time. Clearly, in Barron's opinion, the American government was "not alive to the Mexican situation" and had allowed itself to be outmaneuvered by the British.[7]

Early the next year, Requa, who had since become an engineering consultant for the Mining Bureau and a vice-president of Sinclair Oil, tried one more time to get the administration's attention. In a lengthy report to the chairman of the United States Shipping Board, Requa offered an extensive appraisal of domestic oil resources, which concluded that fuel oil imports from Mexico provided the only margin of safety given current market conditions and anticipated demand. As in his earlier reports during the war, Requa maintained that the geographical location of most large American oilfields and the lack of transportation facilities prevented an easy substitution of Mexican crude. In this case, the fuel oil for American shipping, as for the British, had to come from Mexico. But the salt water invasion of the old wells and the inability to drill new ones threatened that source. For that reason, Requa suggested, Carranza's legal stratagems, as well as any other "forcible interference" by Mexican authorities to hinder the oil industry, should be seen as an obvious "attack upon the national welfare of the United States" and treated as an act of war. Such a policy, Requa asserted, should be "as fixed as the Monroe Doctrine."[8]

At the same time that Requa was pleading with the United States government to recognize the impending crisis in Mexico, American producers were appealing to Carranza for some resolution to save the industry. On January 14, 1920, the oilmen sent a telegram to the Mexican president outlining the situation: "Within the last few months there has been a steady encroachment of salt water. . . . Numerous wells have ceased to produce petroleum; others are failing rapidly, and still others will be lost in the near future.... As a result of what has occurred, the Mexican petroleum industry ... faces a crisis, and is about to suffer a severe loss which can be avoided without prejudice to the rights of either side." Ignoring the issue of land titles for the moment, the companies asked Carranza to grant them provisional drilling permits to tide them over until the Mexican Congress met in September to consider the petroleum law once again. Carranza formally accepted the oilmen's proposition three days later, and news of this agreement reached Washington on January 21, the day after Requa had delivered his latest report. A few days after that, the United States Shipping Board notified the secretary of state that a scheduled conference on the Mexican oil supply was no longer necessary. For the moment, at least, the crisis had passed.[9]

Taking advantage of this lull in the storm to resolve the questions about the future of the Mexican oil supply, Franklin Lane recommended that the government send a team of oil geologists and engineers from the Geological Survey and the Bureau of Mines into Mexico to conduct a definitive appraisal of the industry. The State Department endorsed Lane's proposal and passed it on to the Mexican ambassador. After some diplomatic wrangling, Carranza also agreed to allow a scientific study of the Mexican oilfields so long as the Mexican authorities were able to deny any official knowledge of the investigation. For some reason, perhaps having to do with the upcoming presidential election, the plan was never implemented, even though Congress had approved the funds.[10]

Lacking such an appraisal, the best that anyone could come up with was a report by J. A. Phelan, an investigator for the United States Shipping Board who had spent four months during the fall of 1920 evaluating the Gulf Coast oil supply in the United States and Mexico. As one of the largest consumers of Mexican oil, the Shipping Board found itself squeezed out of the fuel oil picture after the major oil companies signed long-term commitments to other organizations. As an alternative, the Shipping Board hoped to negotiate a deal for royalty oil from the Mexican government based on Phelan's information. While Phelan substantiated the stories that the existing Mexican fields were "fast going into salt water," he went on to emphasize that "there [were] oil indications in practically every county in Mexico, and the possibilities in the state of Vera Cruz [were] almost beyond conjecture." On the whole, Phelan gave a fairly accurate and encouraging assessment of the situation, concluding that Mexico had "the most promising oil output of any country in the world."[11]

In almost every respect, then, Phelan's confidential report paralleled Doheny's efforts to bolster confidence in the future of the Mexican oil supply. Contrary to the "dire predictions of the ill-informed" oil experts and the "doubting Thomas" geologists, Doheny insisted that the undeveloped regions of Mexico were full of "hidden pools" of oil. When the time was right, Doheny concluded, the "genius, courage, faith and industry of the oil pioneer will put [them] at the service of mankind." The only thing standing in the way was President Carranza and his criminal attacks on the industry.[12]

In the meantime, the Mexican Petroleum Company seemed to be doing quite well. Since 1916, the company had averaged about 1.5 million barrels of production a year and exported anywhere from 1 million barrels a year during the war to over 3 million by the end of 1920. Recent net earnings had gone from less than $7 million in 1918 to $12.5 million in 1921. As a reflection of this process, the price of the common stock moved up dramatically, from an average of $90 a share during the war years to over $250 in the fall of 1919, and then dropping only to around $180 for most of the next year. Yet, during the spring and summer of 1921, the salt water scare drove the price below $90 almost overnight and brought the vitality of the company into question.[13]

Rumors that various investigators thought the Mexican oilfields would "soon be a matter of history" started circulating in April 1921, including a story that new Secretary of Commerce Herbert Hoover believed that Mexico would exhaust its oil within eighteen months. Hoover denied it, but the effect remained.[14] Much more damaging was an article published at the same time by Ralph Arnold, a "doubting Thomas" of long standing when it came to Mexico, which directly compared the oil resources of the United States and its southern neighbor. In particular, Arnold emphasized the physical differences between the respective oilfields which accounted for the astonishing productivity of the Mexican gushers: proven oil territory in the United States was 4,500 square miles as compared to 25 square miles in Mexico; oil production for the United States in 1920 was 443,402,000 barrels versus 185 million barrels for Mexico; the United States had 258,000 producing wells, while Mexico had just 200; the average daily production of an American well was 4.9 barrels, while in Mexico it was 2,600 barrels; and, finally, the estimated proven oil reserves in the United States were 5 to 6 billion barrels, and those in Mexico were 300 to 400 million barrels. Under these conditions, Arnold believed, the American fields would last for at least twenty years. The Mexican supply, on the other hand, was entirely at the mercy of its exploiters and "may be exhausted in a few months, or at most in one or two years at the promised rate of development."[15]

By presenting this information in the way he did, Arnold hoped to convince domestic producers that their oil was a valuable commodity not to be wasted. For him, the worsening situation in Mexico was the best argument for conservation at home. What he did instead, however, was to provide ammunition for another round of attacks on the Mexican Petroleum Company. Stock manipulators, in particular, took advantage of the situation through well-timed, rumor-fed raids on Mexpet shares, which affected the whole market. In the weeks that followed Arnold's story, the financial situation worsened as the press hunted for information to corroborate the Mexican situation. In response to repeated requests from reporters for an authoritative statement from the government, Stephen Porter, chairman of the House Foreign Affairs Committee, promised to release an official report on the expected depletion of the Mexican oilfields. But in his haste to placate the media, Porter never checked to see whether such a report existed. When he went looking for it, all he found was Phelan's earlier material written for the Shipping Board.[16]

Initially, Porter refused to use the Shipping Board report, after one analyst from the Foreign Trade Office, W. W. Cumberland, formerly of the Doheny Research Foundation, characterized Phelan's work as "loosely prepared, inaccurate and misleading." In fact, because of the explosive nature of the topic, Phelan had been under government investigation since February 1921. Incredibly, the special agent in charge believed that certain "English-Jewish" financiers were working through Phelan to undercut the price of Mexican Petroleum Company stock. But Porter was under the gun to live up to his promise, and he ended up delivering an abstracted version of Phelan's report to the Associated Press. Not surprisingly, newspapers around the country ran a story the next day stating that Mexico had but one large pool of oil, which could be exhausted overnight. Phelan's observation that Mexico actually had an enormous untapped potential for oil appeared in a follow-up story several days later—too late to undo the damage. The price of Mexpet common dropped immediately from $130 to $101 and continued going down.[17]

Overall, for the preceding year, a reduction in the industrial demand for oil products since January 1921 and a steady erosion of fuel oil prices to their lowest levels in five years had combined with the Mexican crisis to depress the value of all the oil shares on the market by about 40 percent. But given the special circumstances, the Doheny companies suffered the most: Pan American was off by 55 percent and Mexican Petroleum was down by 49 percent. Of the remaining petroleum stocks, Sinclair Oil dropped 48 percent, Royal Dutch-Shell 39 percent, and Texaco 24 percent.

But where Mexpet previously had moved in conjunction with the market, it now appeared to be dragging everything else down with it. Just one raid in mid-June, for instance, that forced Mexpet down another five points supposedly accounted for a paper loss of $40 million on the general list.[18]

The big question on Wall Street was how a stock like Mexican Petroleum, with just over 100,000 shares outstanding, could trade at a volume as high as 90,000 shares a day. With Pan American Petroleum moving with it, at about the same level of activity, the two stocks were the most active issues for several weeks and accounted for as much as 10 to 15 percent of the overall market volume. Suspicion fell on Doheny first, and he was accused of loaning out treasury stock for speculation. The situation was so tense that Clarence Barron, who had been waging a daily battle to prop up Mexpet with positive stories in the *Wall Street Journal*, suggested that Doheny take an auditor into the vault at Pan American Petroleum's headquarters in New York to count the number of shares held by the company. Clearing himself in this way, though not to everyone's satisfaction, Doheny then petitioned the New York Stock Exchange to conduct its own investigation of the case. Despite their best efforts, officials of the exchange never discovered who had been using Mexican Petroleum shares for what they described as "pure unadulterated market manipulation."[19]

There were some likely suspects, however. One of them, who accused Doheny of putting out the stock himself, was Jesse L. Livermore, probably the most notorious stock raider of his day. Livermore was known as the "Boy Plunger of Wall Street" for some immensely profitable and daring short sales in railroad and copper stocks which had made him a millionaire at a very young age. In 1921, Livermore told Barron that he had become interested in Doheny's company as a result of some privileged information he had received about the supply of Mexican oil. After asking him a few direct questions, however, Barron was convinced that Livermore "had never talked with an intelligent person from Mexico familiar with the Mexican oil field." Nevertheless, Livermore acted on the information and apparently sold Mexican Petroleum short several times when it was trading above 160 and bought it back when it bottomed out below 90. The unconfirmed estimates of his profits on these transactions ranged as high as $15 million.[20]

A more pernicious source of trouble was W. C. Moore, the owner of a monthly Wall Street investment guide. Beginning in the spring of 1921, Moore began publicizing the salt water stories about Mexican Petroleum and telling his subscribers to sell the stock short whenever they could. Later, Moore bragged that his customers had "made a killing" on the trades. But along with his advice to sell the stock, Moore went on to accuse Doheny of "lying about the oil situation" and said that information from Mexican Petroleum could not be trusted because there was "a large corps of liars on 'Dough-eney's' staff." As it turned out, Moore was interested in the company only as a way to prevent Doheny from using his profits to support the movement for Irish freedom. As a self-proclaimed "100 per cent American," Moore was "dead set against Sinn Fein." His attack on Doheny even went so far as to include a letter to Obregón, asking him to stick to his plan to increase the export tax on oil. Once Moore's activities were discovered, he was indicted for criminal libel by a New York Grand Jury. Two years later, after a series of legal confrontations, Moore made a public apology in court that the statements in his market letter had been "unfounded and untrue," and the judge ultimately dismissed the incident, to Doheny's satisfaction.[21]

But Mexican Pete's saga on Wall Street made a dramatic turnaround in 1922, when Doheny decided to end the trouble by having Pan American Petroleum buy back shares of Mexican Petroleum to get the stock off the market. That tactic, and a continued rise in corporate earnings, sent the short traders scrambling to cover their losses when the stock price soared as high as $322 by the end of the year. Things got so tight that one desperate trader even attempted suicide in the Mexpet offices in New York. Ultimately, the stock dropped off the market in 1923, with only about 28,000 shares left in the hands of the public. Afterward, Doheny noted with satisfaction that "we made the bears get down on their knees and beg for mercy."[22]

Underlying all of these problems in the early 1920s were the continued political attacks launched by the Mexican government against the American oil companies. Aside from the constant battles over drilling rights and land titles, oil taxation, as Moore had suggested, became the weapon of choice. The new government, under Alvaro Obregón, not only increased the rate of taxation but based its new export tax on the value of oil products in the United States instead of at the port in Tampico. Adding this export tax to the production tax, stamp tax, bar dues, and the license and inspection fees already collected more than doubled the amount exacted by the Mexican government. To make matters worse, Obregón announced these new tax regulations at the same time as the Phelan and Arnold reports on Mexican oil hit the press. Because he was also worried about overproduction, Obregón wanted to launch a preemptive strike to keep foreign governments from raising tariff duties against cheap Mexican oil and to stop the oil companies from operating in a manner that was "contrary to a policy of moderate exploitation." Of course, higher taxes were also a strategy for chipping away at the "big profits" that Obregón saw leaving Mexico.[23]

As before, Doheny objected to these provisions because they were presidential decrees that had not been submitted to, or approved by, the Mexican Congress. The existing export tax of over fifteen cents a barrel was, he said, uncomfortable but legal. On the other hand, the combined tax rate under Obregón's decree, which increased the amount to thirty cents, was "so excessive as to be confiscatory." Carranza had tried the same tactic earlier, and the oil companies had successfully challenged the constitutionality of his decrees in court. They would have to do the same thing with Obregón. Looking for the motive behind that pattern, Doheny stated that "the whole thing appears to me to be a monumental bluff on the part of the Mexican government and I don't believe they feel they can get away with it. . . . Apparently, Obregón is trying to do indirectly, by means of increasing taxes, what they have been trying to do directly for years—confiscate American property."[24]

Doheny also protested the charge that the oil companies made excessive profits from their Mexican operations. Obregón justified the new exactions because he claimed that, in 1920 alone, the Mexican Petroleum Company had sucked $28 million of pure profit out of the Mexican oilfields. In response, Doheny cited the published annual report of the company: Mexican Petroleum had made $17,410,000 in profits from operations, out of which they had paid $5,695,000 in cash dividends to the stockholders, $5,744,000 in taxes to the Mexican government, and $1,898,700 into a reserve fund for United States taxes. It was obvious, Doheny asserted, that Obregón arrived at his number "by merely juggling the figures and adding and overlapping dividends in a way that an American school boy would not be guilty." Furthermore, 1920 was also a year in which the company expended $7,800,000 in Mexico to construct the largest topping plant in the world, including all the roads, pipelines, and support facilities necessary to keep it operating. In conclusion, Doheny chided Obregón for his ingratitude as well as his math: "Without the progress that the development of petroleum is responsible for, the condition of Mexico would indeed be that of vast plains without cattle, of valleys without farms, of mountains without operating mines."[25]

In this sense, Doheny was right to see the tax hike as a political bluff. The Mexican government could not afford to choke off the sale of oil when petroleum taxes were the only means of staying afloat and paying off its foreign debt. Still, Washington was worried enough about the situation to send American gunboats back to Tampico in early July in case of trouble. And sure enough, a military revolt by one of Manuel Pelaez's lieutenants on July 12 added another twist to a thoroughly confusing situation. Fortunately, this was not a major upheaval, and Obregón's troops put down the rebellion in just four days. The question of its origin, however, was harder to solve. Pelaez, of course, was the immediate suspect, although he had been traveling in the United States as an agent of the Obregón government at the time. And although his complicity in the revolt was never proven, it signaled the end of his political career when he was hauled back to Mexico City to answer questions. Suspicions also fell onto Doheny and the oil crowd, as well. On the day the revolt ended, Doheny wrote to Albert Fall: "I note by the morning papers that Green and I are responsible for the latest revolt in Mexico. They have not even paid me the compliment of associating me with your good self this time, and I am sore about it. It is however just as false as if they had said that the U.S. Government was behind it all. What won't those fellows charge up to the Huasteca Company and its officials?"[26]

As the self-appointed expert on Mexican political affairs in Washington, however, Fall received reports from agents of the Justice Department, private investigators, and numerous individuals operating along the political fringes in Mexico, and, without a doubt, he knew as much about the plots swirling around as anybody. Among the materials in his possession were surveillance reports from Los Angeles for the first two weeks of July, stating that Pelaez had been seen visiting Doheny's office and meeting with Esteban Cantu, the former Governor of Lower California, and a well-known opponent of the central government. Many of the reports suggested that a conspiracy to overthrow the Mexican government was in the offing. But part of Pelaez's unofficial mission was also to discuss Obregón's diplomatic recognition with American officials and businessmen, especially the executives of the oil companies.

One frequent informant, William F. Buckley, an attorney and independent oilman who spoke for the small producers in Mexico, received a letter from Pelaez two weeks before the rebellion, stating that he suspected one of his men of plotting a coup—"aided he thought by the Doheny crowd." Pelaez did not know whether to return to Mexico and warn Obregón or to wait and see what happened. Then, as soon as he learned that he was under suspicion in Mexico City, Pelaez went back with information that the recent rebellion had been engineered by William Green. The charge implied Doheny's approval, if not his active participation.[27]

If Doheny wanted to make a decisive show of force, however, he had better and more intelligent ways to do it. And he seemed to be exercising one of those options when he decided to virtually shut down his oil business in Mexico during July and August, cutting shipments from 2.5 million barrels a month to less than 1 million barrels in July and 300,000 in August. For these months, Doheny shipped out the minimum amount of gasoline needed to fill his contract with Standard Oil of New York and put everything else on hold. Citing the adverse market conditions, aggravated by the announcement of new taxes, Standard Oil New Jersey also stopped shipping Mexican crude oil in July and withdrew its fleet of tankers from the trade. Overall, the four largest American companies—Huasteca, Transcontinental (Standard), Texaco, and Gulf—reduced their combined exports from 8.7 million barrels in June to just over 1 million in both July and August. Thus, despite the increased rate of taxation, the total receipts generated by the Mexican government declined from 5.4 million pesos in June to 1.7 million in July and 1.4 million in August.

Official reports were careful to cite the political turmoil in Tampico, a major fire in the Amatlán oil district, and the general depression in the oil market—not the tax problem—for the decline. The American vice-consul in Tampico was explicit: "Their action in suspending shipments was the result of business judgment rather than a desire for retaliation." From Doheny's perspective, however, there was no difference. By the end of August, both sides wanted the standoff to end and were ready to sit down together and hash out their problems. And since Doheny's oil shipments immediately jumped back to 3,179,163 barrels in September and 3,743,011 for October to make up for the previous deficit, retaliation seems to have paid off. The combined shipments for the four big American companies returned to 8.5 million barrels in September. Clearly, when 86 percent of the government's total tax revenue came from the petroleum industry in 1921, the shutdown was designed to get Obregón's attention.[28]

However, there were problems with this strategy from the beginning, due to the difference between the financial wherewithal of the largest companies and that of the small independents, who had only recently entered the market. As Harold Walker explained to an American official, the shutdown had been only partially successful because the British companies, and several other American operators, either refused to cooperate or could not hold out long enough to make the effort worthwhile. "The whole situation," Walker admitted, "was one which certain of the companies could endure no longer. . . . It became necessary for the companies to do something to help themselves down easy. The Mexican Government was winning and the Companies losing."[29]

That is probably why, as the two sides jockeyed for position, the State Department arranged for a committee of the Big Five oil company presidents to go to Mexico at Obregón's invitation. The committee consisted of Doheny, Walter Teagle of Standard Oil New Jersey, J. W. Van Dyke of the Atlantic Refining Company, H. F. Sinclair of Sinclair Oil, and Amos Beatty of the Texas Company. Supposedly, this was to be a chance to solve the oil conflict for good, and the only subject forbidden to the committee was an official loan from the United States government. Short of that, they were on their own. To begin, the oilmen laid out their position in a memo to their Mexican hosts on the opening day of the talks: "We are not unmindful of the fact that misunderstandings have arisen and even prejudices have been aroused, which thus far have raised a barrier to complete accord. . . . Our true interests do not conflict. Nay, they complement each other . . . first, to assure the Mexican Government a reasonable yield from the development of Mexico's oil resources . . . second . . . to afford the companies a return commensurate with the large investments made and the great hazards faced."[30]

Given the exhaustion of the existing properties, however, this plan required the government to give the companies access to new fields. Furthermore, to ensure the health of the industry, the committee did not believe that "taxes should go upward as the prices go down." With these demands clearly stated, the committee turned to the consequences for Mexico: "We try to place ourselves in your place. . . . We at once think of two theories, where a commercial or political power is seeking revenue. One is to exact all the traffic will stand. The other is a policy of frankness. The trouble with the former is that it too often kills the goose that lays the golden eggs. The companies have no desire to further curtail their operations in Mexico, but with them the rules of economics must prevail."

Finally, in a complete reversal of earlier arguments made to the American government, the committee explained that most of the companies had their own production in the United States and held land in proven reserves that could be brought into production at a moment's notice. Thus, if pushed too hard, they would abandon Mexico and let the government strangle the industry on its own. Already, with the prevailing surplus of low-priced oil, they could meet their present contracts by purchasing oil in the market and still make money. "You have doubtless seen results in this direction since the first of July," the committee observed. But a continuous shutdown almost guaranteed that the companies would lose the remaining oil in fields already threatened by salt water. In this way, at least, the producers had their backs against the wall as much as Obregón.[31]

After a half-dozen meetings to work out the details of a compromise, the two sides agreed that the oil companies would pay the full production tax imposed by the decree of May 24, 1921, in return for which the Mexican government would suspend the export tax stipulated in the decree of June 7, at least until the end of the year and possibly longer. The producers also agreed to "use their best efforts" to put together a banking syndicate that would underwrite a sale of bonds to settle the nation's debts.

These actions suggested that, for the first time in years, the oil companies were adopting a new way to conduct their business in Mexico. Despite the implied threats by the company presidents that they would pull out if they did not get what they wanted, the 1921 meeting inspired a second round of talks to reach a workable arrangement. More than anything else, the oilmen wanted a firm decision about the legality of property rights as contained in Article 27 of the constitution. When they met again the following year, the oil committee cited the massive investment of over $500 million in the petroleum industry, not counting the tanker fleets and terminal facilities, and lamented that without some way to expand their operations they faced "a loss of not less than one half of their original investment." It was no exaggeration, they claimed, that if the companies had foreseen the present conditions in Mexico they would never have invested the capital in the first place.[32]

The alternative to the current adversarial relationship was to bring the Mexican government into the fold as a full-fledged partner in the oil business. To do that, the committee offered to organize a completely new company, the Petroleum Development Company (Doheny's influence was obvious just from the name), under the laws of Mexico to which the existing companies would pledge their "resources and experience." They would start by transferring to the new company the petroleum rights to about 700,000 acres of oil lands outside the present producing field. Thereafter, new lands would be acquired as necessary. Once the company was organized in this way, the citizens of Mexico would have the opportunity to invest in its stock, with a guaranteed holding of at least 10 percent of the initial capitalization. The company would also be obligated to pay a fixed tax on oil to the government—as they sold it, not when it was produced. In addition, the company would pay the government 25 percent of all annual profits in excess of total investment and expenditures. Finally, in exchange for the exclusive right to exploit the national lands of Mexico, which had been used by the government as a weapon against American producers in the past, the Petroleum Development Company would pay a fixed royalty on related production.

Of course, the committee wanted certain guarantees in return. First, "all decrees issued by the Carranza administration with regard to the petroleum industry . . . shall be canceled and annulled." A corollary to that provision stipulated that the new company would receive full and exclusive rights on existing lands owned by the partners and on all future acquisitions. Second, they wanted the government to grant the Petroleum Development Company the right to drill at least 100 wells and to agree to additional drilling permits, as requested.[33]

For their part, government officials accepted the drilling concessions but wanted an expanded range of stock options for Mexican nationals, and they absolutely refused to back away from the issue of land titles and subsoil rights. In fact, they went so far as to demand that the companies transfer to the new "association" title to all rights and claims on the land in return for a government concession to explore those same properties. The oilmen responded in kind: "The case in a nutshell is this: Our plan is based upon an interpretation of Article 27 . . . which renders it inapplicable to the lands we have acquired through private contracts with the private owners thereof, and contemplates the Government shall support this position. The Government's counter proposal, on the other hand, is, we regret to find, based upon an interpretation of said Article which renders it completely applicable to our lands. . . . These basic conceptions are diametrically opposed."[34] In other words, despite all of the apparent improvement in relations between the two parties over the past year, nothing had really changed. Article 27, as one Mexican newspaper aptly stated, remained the "Gordian knot."[35]

Still, the two sides had at least become comfortable talking to each other, and they met several more times. But these subsequent discussions began where they had taken up the year before, with tax relief in return for some sort of financial assistance for Mexico, although there was still some lingering hope that the Petroleum Development Company could be salvaged for the right price. If nothing else, Mexico wanted to use the promise to continue the 1921 export tax rate reduction, with an additional 20 percent off each month, in exchange for a $25 million advance from the oil companies on their future tax bill. The State Department advised that, since formal recognition of Obregón's government would not occur until they were certain that Article 27 would not be used to divest Americans of their property, the United States could not approve a loan. But, according to the secretary of state, "if the petroleum companies wished to make a loan to the unrecognized Obregón regime, for the purpose of arriving at a settlement, they were at liberty to do so."[36]

Ultimately, Doheny did just that. In particular, he made loans in return for drilling rights at Juan Felipe, a hacienda adjoining his famous Cerro Azul property. This land had been leased since 1906, but Doheny had been unable to acquire permission to develop the field. Then, in September 1922, he obtained exclusive rights to the new area when other companies were scrambling for production. Earlier, he had offered to make a $3 million personal loan to the Mexican government in return for clear title and drilling rights on some of his oil properties. Instead, he ended up putting $1.5 million on deposit with the government to win a positive decision about Juan Felipe. The following year, he loaned the government $5 million as part of a larger deal to secure $15 million from his banking connections in New York.[37]

At the same time, in 1923, the United States government negotiated a compromise with Obregón that led to formal recognition. Basically, the Mexican government agreed that the expropriation provisions of Article 27 would not be retroactively applied to property acquired before 1917, if some "positive act" of development had been undertaken. While this was obviously open to interpretation, it did away with the most pernicious aspect of the Mexican policy as far as the oil companies were concerned. Ironically, Obregón's enemies in Mexico used this supposed capitulation to the United States as the pretext for a successful rebellion against him.[38]

The important thing to understand about these confusing events, from Doheny's perspective, is that they fit into a larger pattern of activity. Since the end of the World War, Doheny had been conducting private diplomacy simultaneously on a number of fronts. Clearly, his efforts to solve the Irish problem and his decision to get involved in the Pearl Harbor project to protect America against Japan supported his initiatives in Mexico. Oil played a part in each of these decisions, but it was never the sole issue. Idealism, patriotism, and nationalism were all intertwined with Doheny's worldwide petroleum business by this time, whether his detractors believed it or not. Doubtless, Doheny considered the fortunes of his oil companies at every turn, but his motivation was not easily discerned—then or now. Suffice it to say that Doheny did not doubt his own ability to influence events at the highest level and believed that his actions should be immune to criticism.

11 THE BARK OF POLITICAL WOLVES: DOHENY AND THE OIL SCANDAL

If Doheny was worried about the exhaustion of his Mexican oil supply in the early 1920s, he never betrayed his feelings. Even under the most trying political circumstances, he did not express any doubts about Mexico's petroleum reserves, and he continued to develop new fields as the government permitted. Commenting on the new Juan Felipe district, for example, Doheny maintained that "before this field is exhausted a lot of us will be dead and a lot of others will be broke as a result of bearing the prospects of the field." By the end of 1922, however, other companies began to pull out of Mexico as their confidence, along with their production, steadily dropped off.[1]

Among the large companies, the Mexican Eagle fared the worst, suffering a drastic reduction in operations because of the invasion of salt water into their primary fields. La Corona, the other Royal Dutch affiliate, shut down its Mexican refinery after spending almost $100 million developing its properties in the preceding eighteen months—and considered the investment irretrievable. Likewise, Standard Oil closed its Tampico refinery and claimed that recent losses in Mexico had amounted to about $50 million. The remaining American operators, except for Doheny, also started scaling back their Mexican business in the latter part of 1922 for the same reasons. Ironically, La Corona and Transcontinental (Standard Oil) reached peak production in 1923 at 30.5 million barrels and 24 million barrels, respectively. Huasteca Petroleum still led with 36 million barrels, and the Mexican Eagle came in at 10 million. These four companies accounted for almost 70 percent of the production that year.[2]

Looking over the wreckage of his operation in March 1923, A. C. Bedford, the chairman of Standard Oil, contended that the oil industry in Mexico had been brought down because of the opposition of the Mexican government. Without a doubt, Doheny agreed, the confiscatory laws of recent years had impeded oil development in Mexico, but he added that Pan American Petroleum's investments "are and have been satisfactory, having yielded and are still yielding excellent returns." Moreover, Doheny was sure that at some point the Mexican government would "see the light," and until such time the company was "content to continue [its] activities in the undeveloped portions of our great Mexican holdings, with faith in the eventual prevalence of justice and good understanding in Mexico." Doheny also noted that numerous "pencil experts" had been proclaiming the demise of the California oil industry for years, yet the state was producing at twice the 1921 rate, with a future that looked "as bright or brighter than it ever did." And he was willing to gamble that Mexico would do the same.[3]

In the meantime, he was shrewd enough to hedge his bet. As early as March 1921, Doheny tried to diversify his holdings with a bid to buy the Atlantic, Gulf, and West Indies Company. Atlantic Gulf held oil lands in Colombia, operated in Mexico, and had a growing fleet of oil tankers. A major problem, however, was that Joseph F. Guffy, the president of Atlantic Gulf, did not get along with Doheny. Guffy had been a major critic of the conduct of the older companies, and he characterized Doheny as Mexico's "implacable enemy." Guffy's strategy had been to accept the government's tax and land decrees in order to win concessions on federal lands that ran through the developed territory of his rivals. Given their differences, Doheny and Guffy negotiated through a third party for three weeks straight without being able to strike a deal.[4]

Venezuela was another possibility, and it became the destination of choice for the major oil companies abandoning Mexico. Gulf Oil and Standard Oil New Jersey, for instance, had already been there for several years by the time Doheny became interested in 1923. Even then, Doheny moved cautiously by acquiring a concession from the Maracaibo Oil Company and sending Harold Walker and a team of company geologists to scout for further prospects.[5]

At the same time in the United States, Doheny made a tentative move into the Smackover oilfield in Arkansas, where, after spending $3 million, he had about 750 acres of developed land and at least one well producing 20,000 barrels per day, which had been capped off pending construction of a 1.7-million-barrel storage tank and a railroad spur onto the property. Despite continuing to drill for light oil in Smackover, Doheny concentrated his efforts in Southern California. In particular, the new fields in the Los

Angeles basin—including Long Beach, Torrance, and Signal Hill—were
the focus of another oil boom, which flooded the market with low-priced
oil in 1922. Under those conditions, Doheny's first act was to move in, buy
up the surplus, and ship it to the Mexican Petroleum refinery at Destrehan,
Louisiana. And by early 1923, Pan American Petroleum was taking as much
as 130,000 barrels of oil a day out of Los Angeles, which reduced the demand on Mexican crude and helped stabilize the local market.[6]

Because much of the excess California production was light-gravity oil
that yielded over 30 percent gasoline, the large companies also began in-
vesting heavily in new service stations in the region as a way to expand the
market. In this way, local conditions fed into a national movement to reori-
ent the industry to supply the automotive trade in the early 1920s. While
other companies had been headed in this direction for years, this was new
territory for Doheny, who had carved out his niche in the fuel oil business.
But he was prepared to move quickly in response to the market. In the
summer of 1923, he constructed a large refinery in Los Angeles and began
scouting the city for desirable sites for "Pan Gas" stations. To buttress this
development, the company triumphed in a contest with more than a dozen
steamship lines to acquire the property of an old submarine base in Los
Angeles Harbor, which gave Doheny what was expected to be the "finest
oil-loading station on the Pacific coast."[7]

Although the flush-field production around the city afforded him a
ready supply of low-priced oil, he still needed the long-term security of a
stable reserve. Unfortunately, the political climate in Mexico was far from
certain. And even under the best of circumstances, light Mexican crude
yielded only about 11 percent gasoline, and the heavy oil from Ebano and
Pánuco yielded almost none. Besides, Doheny already contracted most of
the product from his topping plant in Tampico to Standard Oil for its retail
outlets on the East Coast.[8]

Consequently, there was no way to get past the need for an assured
supply of better-grade oil, although Doheny had several options available
to him. The simplest solution was to regain working control of the California Petroleum Company. As noted previously, Doheny had pulled back
from the company in 1916 after his failed attempt to consolidate the California independents. Six years later, California Petroleum was one of the
nation's strongest independents, based on policies established under Doheny's leadership in its early years. With gross assets of $46 million, Calpet
was expanding rapidly, and its daily production of 50,000 barrels put it
among the top half-dozen oil companies in the state. In addition, Calpet
had storage capacity for almost 7 million barrels and substantial proven

reserves. Calpet was also doing very well on the stock market. In fact, a surge of activity at the end of 1922 suggested that someone was trying to get control of the company. Most analysts assumed it was Doheny.[9]

Because Calpet was still being run by a group of officers closely associated with Doheny, including his longtime associate T. A. O'Donnell, who was the chairman, there is little doubt that he could have moved back into control. In any case, with about 150,000 shares of common stock outstanding, selling at around $65 a share on the New York Stock Exchange, Doheny could have bought his way back in for no more than $5 to $10 million—a relatively cheap and easy solution if he was really pressed to compensate for Mexico and supply his West Coast business with fresh oil.[10]

Instead, on December 15, 1922, the secretary of the navy announced that the department had just extended its arrangements with the Pan American Petroleum Company, based on the original Pearl Harbor contract of April 1922, to include a lease on the eastern half of Elk Hills Naval Petroleum Reserve No. 1, consisting of about 16,000 acres of proven oil territory. At the time, Doheny's existing California properties totaled about 25,000 acres. With respect to Elk Hills, the government retained control of the western half of the reserve but had the option to have Doheny drill offset wells on those lands at its discretion. According to Secretary Denby, this additional lease was necessary because of the increasing fuel oil demand of the navy and the continued drainage of government oil into private holdings within and alongside the reserve. A report filed in March 1922 stated that at least 22 million barrels of oil had been lost from the reserve because the previous administration had failed to drill offset wells when they were needed. At a standard 30 percent royalty, the government had lost almost 7 million barrels of oil, or about $9 million at current prices.[11]

Just as important as the navy's justification was Albert Fall's determination to open government-held property to commercial development at every opportunity, contrary to the strict conservation policies in place at the time. Because his appointment to the post of interior secretary promised a fundamental shift in this policy, his opponents were ready to take action against him. But Fall made no effort to hide his intentions. In fact, in June 1922, he published an article in the *Magazine of Wall Street* that summarized his philosophy. "Our unused mineral resources are enormous," Fall noted, out of which "we can go for generations turning nature's stored wealth into consumable wealth and enjoying sources of prosperity unknown to older countries." And he believed that "$150,000,000,000 of wealth can be extracted from the coal, oil, oil shale, potash and phosphate

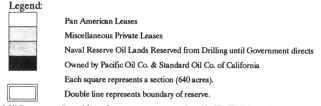

Legend:

Pan American Leases

Miscellaneous Private Leases

Naval Reserve Oil Lands Reserved from Drilling until Government directs

Owned by Pacific Oil Co. & Standard Oil Co. of California

Each square represents a section (640 acres).

Double line represents boundary of reserve.

Map of Oil Reserves replicated from Government map reproduced in The Wall Street Journal, March 15, 1924

Naval Reserve No. 1. *Wall Street Journal,* March 15, 1924.

deposits of the public lands," which "should pour billions of dollars into the public treasuries." With the right policy in place, "there are golden years of development ahead of us."[12]

In pursuing this strategy, Fall was determined to manage the public lands as a business rather than as a conservationist fiefdom, leaving himself free to make arrangements for the government as the opportunities arose. The public would have to trust him to act independently to make the best deal. Thus, when the navy wanted additional storage facilities at Pearl Harbor, Fall did not hesitate to favor Pan American Petroleum. Both Standard Oil and the Associated Oil Company bid on the work, but Doheny submitted two bids: one met the requirements as advertised; the other went much further in offering his services to the navy. The alternative proposal, as explained below, ultimately won the award, and the other companies cried foul, complaining that if they had been aware of Doheny's second offer they would have readjusted their own bids as well. Fall disagreed and characterized these complaints as the "machinations" of individuals "desirous of causing [Doheny] to lose money by making larger bids . . . which they would never have considered making at all."[13]

And so, Doheny's lease for the Elk Hills Naval Petroleum Reserve fulfilled Fall's ideal. In return, Doheny assumed what he justifiably characterized as "a serious and substantial obligation." First, he would construct additional storage facilities at Pearl Harbor for up to 2.7 million barrels of oil. Next, in conjunction with plans for a new Los Angeles refinery and oil depot, he would provide free storage for 1 million barrels of fuel oil at the Los Angeles harbor; he agreed to bunker government ships out of that supply at cost and to deliver the navy's royalty oil from the petroleum reserve to the refinery at tidewater free of any pipeline charges; he would maintain 3 million barrels of fuel oil in storage depots on the Atlantic Coast; and he would furnish, at the government's command, a "reasonable amount" of crude oil products in storage facilities at locations to be determined in the future. Finally, he would give the navy a 10 percent discount off the market price of any additional fuel oil and refined products coming from the reserve. The contract would run for twenty years and "so long thereafter as oil and gas is produced in paying quantities." Government royalties ranged from 12½ to 35 percent, depending on the size of the wells.[14]

Initially, Doheny expected to have to advance the government $12 to $15 million to complete the facilities at Pearl Harbor and estimated the cost of the remaining obligations at $50 million. Although he would eventually recover the entire amount, he admitted that it would be many years before the company was "on velvet" with respect to the contract. But, beyond his own concerns, Doheny saw immediate benefits for the California industry, as a whole: "It will mean the systematic development, when and as the market situation justifies, of an extensive scope of country and the development of a whole additional system of facilities for handling the oil." As Doheny envisioned it, therefore, his leasing of the Elk Hills reserve would help everybody—the navy, the country, and his own company. And despite the grumbling of his competitors, many others agreed with his assessment. The *Wall Street Journal,* for instance, hailed the lease as "one of the most important oil contracts ever closed by any company." Local observers were not willing to go that far but thought that it was at least one of the most spectacular deals ever made in California.[15]

Was this the best way for Doheny to diversify Pan American Petroleum's supply and market activities? Far from being a government handout, this was clearly a risky and expensive proposition. It provided access to a potentially large supply of oil, more than 30,000 acres for the whole reserve, but it put half of the oil under the supervision of the navy and interior departments for decades to come. Although some analysts saw this as a positive step away from a dependence on Mexico, any plan designed to drain one of the navy's oil reserves merely put Pan American Petroleum into the hands of another set of politicians. Unless he had some other motive in mind, Doheny's talent for smart business decisions seems to have failed him.[16]

According to sources close to the company, Doheny faced a good deal of internal opposition to the terms of the deal. In a letter to Admiral Robison, newly appointed head of the Naval Oil Reserve, one attorney noted that "no one of importance in the Pan American organization favors the agreement except Mr. E. L. Doheny. Mr. Doheny told me that the president of the corporation [J. C. Anderson] refused to sign the agreement; and I will say in passing other of the officials of the corporation stated to me that they wished the agreement could be avoided as you had out traded Doheny!" The point the attorney was trying to make was that "some day when the influence of Mr. Doheny is not dominant an escape may be sought by those who succeed him." Doheny conceded that the royalty structure of the contract might be attacked in the future, but he was certain that the lease itself would stand. In his mind, the government could not lose. But, as the attorney warned, there was always the possibility that a disgruntled shareholder might challenge the deal in court.[17]

Notwithstanding these disagreements, Doheny moved ahead with his plans. Before the December contract on Elk Hills, the Pan American Petroleum Company of California had invested almost $21 million in the shipping port, refinery, and associated property. Because all of the funding to that point had been on loan from the parent company, Doheny recapitalized the operation by creating a new subsidiary, called Pan American Western Petroleum, with a capital stock of $20 million and $15 million in new bonds. Then, he launched a major assault on the retail gasoline trade in both the United States and Mexico to set up the next phase of his operation.

Despite owning locations for service stations in Los Angeles, he moved first to the East Coast, where he purchased a 50 percent share in the American Oil Company, which operated the Lord Baltimore filling stations in Maryland, Pennsylvania, and the District of Columbia. Working from this base, Doheny hoped to expand American Oil's marketing area throughout the eastern states and to make it the sole distributor of Pan-Am products. All of this centered on a distribution network radiating out from the Mexican Petroleum Company's refinery at Destrehan. With ocean shipments of California crude oil and distillates from Tampico, Doheny hoped to dominate the gasoline sales market in the southern Gulf and Atlantic states. And from another outpost in Memphis, taking advantage of Pan American Petroleum's ability to ship gasoline by barge, the company could use the upper Mississippi and Ohio rivers, coupled with short rail lines, to move into the Ohio Valley and as far north as Buffalo, in direct competition with Standard Oil Indiana.[18]

Using Doheny's traditional shamrock logo, already familiar to purchasers of Mexpet fuel oil, the recently formed Pan American Southern began selling Panamco gasoline and Panolene motor oil in New Orleans and Atlanta in the winter of 1924. To capture the public's attention, the company's stations were designed in California mission style, with green tile roofs and natural stucco exteriors. Doheny also hired a marketing expert, T. A. LaBelle, who helped Pan American Petroleum's chemists develop a specialized grade of gasoline and laid out the stations using the latest conveniences and time-saving devices so that they could offer "superservice to the motoring public." As the number of these stations spread throughout the Southeast and northern Atlantic Coast, Pan American Petroleum began a major advertising campaign to introduce its line of products to the public, announce Pan Am's commitment to service, and teach some basic lessons in auto maintenance. Such an aggressive and sophisticated promotion enabled Doheny to capture a significant segment of the market almost overnight.[19]

This marketing campaign had actually been inspired by the company's recent experiences in Mexico City, where it operated the first service stations ever seen in that country. While the Pierce Oil Company, the Mexican Eagle, and La Corona (Royal Dutch) were still selling gasoline in bulk, Mexican Petroleum established retail stations in Mexico City, Tampico, and at least a dozen other metropolitan areas. Its most elaborate outlet sat at the foot of an exclusive residential area near Chapultepec Park in the capital and was styled like a palatial arch with hand-carved natural pink stone and a canopy of art glass panes over the service bays. All of the working parts were hidden behind the walls, with only the solid brass handles and dispensers exposed to the public; air and water came from eight solid brass lion heads. While nothing in the United States matched this opulent display, all of the stations reflected the same obsession with distinctive detail.[20]

In Los Angeles, Pan American Petroleum ranked fifth among the major companies, with twenty-three stations by the summer of 1924; Standard Oil California led with 127 stations, Shell had 97, Richfield had 45, and

Los Angeles Service Station, Pan American Petroleum Company, 1927.

Union had 40. As yet, Doheny's operations were only partially based on the Naval Petroleum Reserve, although the production from government leases doubled over the year, from 3.5 million barrels to just over 7 million—at this point, less than 20 percent of Pan American Petroleum's total output. Taking Doheny's California production by itself, 24 percent of 2,061,565 barrels came from Elk Hills in 1921; 71 percent of 4,557,719 in 1922; 55 percent of 3,502,836 in 1923; 47 percent of 7,172,024 in 1924; and 59 percent of 6,236,202 in 1925. The total for Pan American Petroleum and Transport was 31 million barrels in 1921, 57 million in 1922, 40 million in 1923, 36 million in 1924, and 38.6 million in 1925. For the most part, then, Doheny was just getting started in California, and Elk Hills was as yet a small part of his business. Looking into the future, he now believed it would take a $150 million investment, or 3,000 wells at $50,000 apiece, to efficiently develop the reserve.[21]

By the end of 1923, however, there was some doubt that he would get to carry out this plan, when Albert Fall's federal leasing program came under political attack. The year before, Robert La Follette, the progressive senator from Wisconsin, asked for a congressional investigation of the leases made between Fall and Harry Sinclair for Naval Reserve No. 3 at Teapot Dome, Wyoming. Now, Doheny's arrangements at Elk Hills were in for the same treatment. Initially, the investigation revolved around arguments over the severity of the drainage from outside wells as a justification for opening up the reserves, but it turned out that expert opinion about the viability of underground reserves was more guesswork than fact. Rumors of bribery and corruption were also being investigated but had not yet become the focus of the opposition.

Nevertheless, there was cause for alarm. In fact, because Congress had just concluded hearings into rising gasoline prices, at La Follette's urging, many observers feared that the investigation of the reserves was the beginning of an all-out assault on the industry. A former editor of the *Oil Investors' Journal* attributed all the negative attention to faulty leadership by the big oilmen, who were leading the industry astray by their conduct in the United States and their fight with the Mexican government. The sort of wide-ranging activity that Doheny and others were engaged in, the author contended, "will take us just where we do not want to go—into politics; it will excite public condemnation and bring the oil industry into serious disrepute."[22]

Doubtless, industry representatives were right to fear the consequences of the impending investigations when the Senate Committee on Public Lands and Surveys began public hearings on the oil leases in October 1923. Led by Senator Thomas J. Walsh of Montana, an Irish-American associate of Doheny's, the committee heard testimony from almost everyone involved in the leases over the next few months. At the conclusion of the hearings, Walsh believed that they had "produced a new sensation and [gave] the nation another dismaying and disquieting shock almost daily."[23]

Initially, Walsh focused on the intent of Congress in opening the reserve to private development in 1920. At that time, concessions had been granted for certain tracts within the reserve where legitimate private claims had existed before the land was withdrawn by the government. In addition, Congress had authorized some contracts for offset wells to be drilled along the inside perimeter of the reserve to stop private companies from draining the pool from the other side. A subsequent extension of that plan, intended purely as a conservation effort, gave the Navy Department the right to "conserve and develop the reserves by lease, contract, or otherwise, and to use, store, exchange, or sell the oil." Supposedly, to safeguard the navy's oil supply, Congress deliberately intended "to exclude the Interior Department from any general control over the Naval reserves." Nevertheless, President Harding issued an executive order some months later that turned the administration of the reserves over to the Interior Department anyway.

According to Walsh, the president and the secretary of the navy, Edwin Denby, had been duped into this assault on the "sacred Naval oil reserve" by Albert Fall.

Walsh also claimed to have been surprised and shocked when he learned that all of Elk Hills "had been secretly leased, or promised, to the Pan American Petroleum Company" in exchange for the construction of $102 million worth of harbor improvements and oil storage depots in the Pacific. Those contracts, Walsh contended, had been set up to allow the navy to evade congressional approval, and they left the government "powerless to take oil out of this reserve except through request to Doheny to do so." Fall and Denby, on the other hand, claimed that the exchange provisions of the preceding congressional directive gave them full authority to proceed as they had. Admiral Robison, whose role was described earlier, claimed full responsibility for "the idea of converting oil in the ground into tankage and stored fuel oil," but Walsh thought that there was more to it. In fact, Walsh was "convinced that [Robison] caught the idea from Doheny," who was working under the "presiding genius" of Albert Fall.

Furthermore, Walsh thought he knew the purpose behind Fall's actions when he learned that someone had loaned the secretary $100,000 during his negotiations for the Pan American lease. Fall had used the money to buy a small property, the Harris ranch, to fill out his larger holdings in southern New Mexico. This information, which came through various informants, sent Walsh in search of the benefactor. Initially, when confronted with the loan, Fall stated that the money had come from Ned McLean, the wealthy owner of the *Washington Post*, who had, in fact, offered to loan Fall money in the past. Walsh was skeptical, if not unbelieving, and followed McLean to Florida during the Christmas recess to ask him point-blank whether the money was his. McLean confirmed the story but was not convincing. Finally, when it became clear that Walsh was not going to give up, the truth came out.[24]

And so, on January 24, 1924, Doheny asked to appear before the committee and admitted that he was the one who had loaned Fall the money. He then made one of the biggest understatements in the history of American politics when he confessed that Fall had been "making an effort to keep my name out of the discussion for the reason that a full statement might be misunderstood." As Doheny explained it, Fall had been doing legal work for him since resigning from the Interior Department in October 1923. In particular, Fall was helping negotiate with the Obregón government in Mexico as well as organizing the Pan American Western Company. Fall was also planning to accept Doheny's offer of a permanent

A MISUNDERSTOOD PATRIOT
—Fitzpatrick in the New York *World.*

A Misunderstood Patriot. *The Literary Digest,* July 18, 1925.

position with the company. Needless to say, with all those deals in the works, neither Fall nor Doheny wanted to publicly acknowledge the loan. Instead, they laid out the McLean story as a false trail, hoping it would satisfy Walsh's curiosity. Unfortunately, when that ruse failed, it was too late for the truth to do any good.[25]

Apparently, the Harris ranch, which controlled some strategic water resources, had been part of Fall's plans for many years, but he had been unable to negotiate a sale with the current owner. And Fall was afraid that when the property finally came on the market, he would not have the money to pay for it. As it was, his existing holdings made up one of the largest ranches in the state, but they were not producing as he had hoped.

In the meantime, the meager profits from operations and all of Fall's government salary were plowed back into the ranch to try and keep things going. For all the years he had been in Washington, Fall had left the care of the ranch to his wife and son-in-law, and it had been a constant source of aggravation. He knew he was going to have to lease it out, sell it, or retire from the Senate and run it full time. In May 1920, Fall wrote to his wife Emma that he was sick of politics and was "determined to get out of it as soon as my sense of duty will permit me to do so." Unexpectedly, however, President Harding chose him for the interior post nine months later: "He [Harding] thinks that the Interior Department, is second only to the State Department in importance and that there is more opportunity for graft and scandal connected with the disposition of public lands &c than there could be in any other Department and he wants a man who is thoroughly familiar with the business and one he can rely upon as thoroughly honest."[26]

By the summer of 1921, however, things were not going as planned. In particular, Fall worried about Harding's weaknesses as a leader and his own inability to advise the president from within the administration. "I would have very much more influence with him," Fall believed, "if I were not in the Cabinet at all and he certainly needs good, independent and straight from the shoulder advice if ever a man did." Emma was visiting the Dohenys in Los Angeles when Fall wrote to her in July, "Thank God, I am in a way to get out of politics and I shall do it at the earliest possible moment. If the matter comes up in any of your discussions while there, you may truthfully say that you know my mind is definitely and absolutely made up." Fall did not elaborate, but if his plan revolved around dealings with Doheny one wonders why she would have to say anything at all.[27]

Perhaps it was just the knowledge that Doheny and McLean both assured him that he could count on a loan at any time. At any rate, during a drought and depression in the cattle market in the fall of 1921, the owners of the Harris ranch decided to sell out, giving Fall his chance to fortify his own holdings, at the same time that the Interior Department was negotiating the additional Elk Hills leases to Pan American Petroleum. Almost a year later, in August 1922, Fall complained once again to Emma that it was almost impossible to get anything done in Washington, that no one knew what was happening, and that his plans for the naval reserve were bogged down by indecision: "I have been worrying for two or three weeks about trades for royalty oil production from our public land, so that we can let the Shipping Board, or the Navy, have the amount, by exchange, and at the same time so that I can get better prices than have been gotten by my predecessors, but I have to educate the Shipping Board officials, or Naval officials, and as yet have got no where [*sic*]. The President promised this morning that he would join me in settling the matter [within] the next day or two."[28]

Throughout this period, if Fall wanted out of government service, Doheny was prepared to hire him. Already, Doheny had employed Franklin K. Lane and a number of other officials retiring from the Wilson Administration, including Attorney General Thomas W. Gregory, Secretary of War Lindley Garrison, and former Treasury Secretary (and Woodrow Wilson's son-in-law) William Gibbs McAdoo. All of these individuals either left Washington to take positions at Pan American Petroleum with sizable salaries or accepted large retainers from Doheny to help solve his legal problems with the Mexican government.[29]

So what about the loan to Fall? First, as Doheny told Walsh, the amount involved was inconsequential. His oft-repeated comment that it was a mere "bagatelle" worth "no more than $25 or $50 perhaps to the ordinary individual," was pure braggadocio, but it was also true. If it was a bribe, as Walsh had implied, he could have "loaned" Fall a million. Certainly, $100,000 would have been an insult to a crook holding the keys to an oilfield reputed to be worth a thousand times that much. Second, the lease and the loan were coincidental; one did not depend on the other. Fall went into the Interior Department with a deliberate plan to lease out public lands wherever possible and wasted no time putting this plan into effect. He was also determined to leave office as soon as he thought his reforms were secure. And when he got a chance to fill out his New Mexico properties, he asked Doheny for the money as an advance, intending to pay it off from future legal work. Fall's mistake was in the simultaneous pursuit of public and private initiatives that, if not patently illegal, were guaranteed to catch someone's attention.[30]

The most notable thing about the loan, therefore, was the utter stupidity with which it was executed. Surely, two experienced men could have come up with a dozen different ways of handling it. Instead, the public was treated to stories of $100,000 in cash being carried to New Mexico in a "little black satchel," which became the centerpiece of innumerable political cartoons about the oil scandal. Since Doheny still held mining properties in New Mexico that he had acquired back in the 1880s, and had recently invested in a Silver City bank, he could also have easily purchased a ranch next to Fall's in his own name—and with no public comment. As it was, Fall supposedly acted in haste, telephoned Doheny to tell him that the ranch was available, and asked for the money outright. Or, did he?

WHAT WE REALLY EXPECTED TO FIND

—Reid for the Bell Syndicate.

What We Really Expected to Find. *The Literary Digest,* March 1, 1924.

Another interpretation, based upon a close reading of Fall's correspondence, suggests a slightly different possibility. In 1925, Fall wrote to his attorney about the decision to deceive Walsh with the McLean story and recalled an interesting conversation he had had with Doheny. Apparently, as Doheny was about to testify for the first time in December 1923, Fall asked him what he intended to say if the committee asked him about the loan. Without hesitation, Doheny said he would deny it, but he reminded Fall that "as a matter of fact, Ned [Edward Jr.'s nickname] let you have that money and rested under a cloud with the bankers of having drawn that amount of money because of some 'woman scrape.'" Fall gave no indication that Doheny's assertion was either incorrect or in any way mistaken. In fact, one of the more inexplicable elements of the case was the revelation that the younger Doheny had withdrawn the $100,000 from his bank account and delivered it to Fall at his Washington hotel. Doheny senior explained it away during his testimony, claiming that, when Fall asked him for the loan, he did not have that much in his personal account and that his son covered it for him until they could transfer the funds. But from what Fall stated above, he may have asked Ned for the money before his father knew about it. According to a later comment from Estelle Doheny's secretary, Ned suffered from alcoholism and was not completely reliable. Putting these two pieces of information together suggests that Ned might have given Fall the money ill-advisedly and that his father was left to cover it up. In any event, the speed of the transaction belies any conspiracy to defraud the government.[31]

Doheny's long-standing views on the need to open the oil reserves to private drilling demonstrated further the incongruity of a conspiracy theory. Like Fall, Doheny had been outspoken in his criticism of public land policy. To substantiate those views with the Walsh committee, he had his testimony from the first congressional debate over the Elk Hills reserve in 1917 read into the record. The navy's oil reserves, Doheny argued, had always been subject to drainage along the borders, and, contrary to the claims of the conservationists, the oil could not be held in the ground indefinitely. When Walsh asked him to explain why so many of his calculations differed from those of the Bureau of Mines, Doheny replied that the government's conclusions were often predetermined by political considerations. "Policy is not a fact," Doheny contended, whereas his own views were based on solid, practical experience: "No man on earth has access to the same information I have, because my information comes from 29 years of close study of the proposition, such as no other living man has given to the business. That sounds egotistical, I grant you, but that is absolutely the truth, since you have asked the question."[32]

Doheny was equally certain about his work at Pearl Harbor, where Pan American Petroleum rigorously monitored construction bids, took no profit from the subcontracted work, and ultimately saved the government $1 million over what he might have charged had he done it "on a cold-blooded basis." At Elk Hills the company's drilling campaign would require about thirty years of steady development, with the government receiving more than a 50 percent royalty on some leases. "While we didn't squeal" about the terms, Doheny added, "we felt like squealing." Yet, he also admitted that the company would "be in bad luck if we do not get $100 million profit," depending on the future price of gasoline. And with a total investment of $100 to $150 million, Doheny needed to sell at least 250 million barrels of oil to meet his goal. While $3.3 million a year profit over three decades of work would hardly be seen as extraordinary or excessive, Doheny's comment about making $100 million off the deal was misinterpreted and did more to convict him in many people's eyes than almost anything else about the case.[33]

If Doheny miscalculated about the effect of that statement, however, he was being deliberately assertive when he boasted of his ability to lure government officials into his employ. In particular, Doheny singled out William McAdoo, stating that McAdoo had been on retainer for the Mexican Petroleum Company since 1919 and had collected $250,000 in fees. This comment, which portrayed the latter as a paid lackey of the oil company, had a devastating effect on McAdoo's position as the leading Democratic presidential candidate in 1924. Although McAdoo rushed to the committee to clear his name, he could correct Doheny's numbers only by noting that his retainer had actually been $25,000 a year instead of $50,000. It hardly mattered, and McAdoo's campaign suffered accordingly.[34]

Editorial writers and Republican politicians, especially, fearful that the oil scandal would hurt their own chances, gave free rein to their accusations. The *Magazine of Wall Street* criticized McAdoo's "success in pocketing the fat retainers of predatory wealth." The *Wall Street Journal*, which upheld the $100,000 check to Secretary Fall while he was in office as a "genuine loan," accused McAdoo of selling political secrets to the highest bidder in private practice. Later, the *Journal* reconsidered its position but still maintained that while "there may have been a far more compromising moral aspect in Secretary Fall's relations with Mr. Doheny, it is a matter for temperate, judicial . . . decision." McAdoo's acceptance of Doheny's retainer, on the other hand, "completely unfitted him for the presidential office."[35]

But McAdoo's dilemma was as much personal as it was political, and, several days before Doheny made his statement, McAdoo confessed that he was "deeply grieved that Mr. Doheny has become involved in this unpleasant situation, not only because he is a client of mine, but more because he is a friend whom I really like." McAdoo had actually been warned to stay away from Doheny at the time he left the cabinet in 1919 when Wilson's secretary, Joseph Tumulty, gave him a prophetic piece of advice. "I have the highest opinion of Mr. Doheny," Tumulty stated, "but if you intend to be a candidate for the presidency, the Mexican question . . . and your acceptance of a retainer from Mexican interests is sure to come up and embarrass you." McAdoo, known to be above political cant and thoroughly practical, reassured Tumulty that he had accepted the position because he was convinced that Doheny had lawfully acquired rights in Mexico and that he was under no bond "to advocate any particular governmental policy." In the end, after McAdoo's bid for the presidential nomination went down amid shouts of "Oil! Oil! Oil!" at the Democratic convention, he told Walsh that Doheny intentionally tried to hurt him because he had refused to intercede on his behalf to stop the the Elk Hills investigation.[36]

If McAdoo felt that his former friends were out to ruin his chances for public office, though, Doheny was equally dismayed by the conduct of his political associates and its effect on his pending business arrangements. A few weeks after his final appearance before the Walsh committee, Doheny had this to say about the experience: "It reminded me of old times in the West when one of our dogs at the mating season joined the wolves. The wolves would surround our camp at night and I could hear my own dog barking among those wolves as they howled around us. It seemed to me when I was on the stand in Washington that I could hear the bark of my own friends in the pack of political wolves."[37]

Doheny's friends in the oil industry were not as quick to change sides, but they reacted to the howls of the politicians just the same. Warren Platt, the editor of the *National Petroleum News,* characterized the capital as "a mean, sordid, contemptible, un-American town," where the petroleum industry "will be tossed to the dogs without a qualm." Platt was not willing to pass judgment on Doheny's guilt, but he recognized that the loan to a cabinet officer created a serious situation "regardless of how innocent he may really be." Thomas O'Donnell, as one of Doheny's oldest California partners, was also unwilling to condemn him on the spot. But as the first president of the recently established American Petroleum Institute— where Doheny was also a director—O'Donnell wanted to make it absolutely clear to the public that "the integrity of the American petroleum industry was beyond question."[38]

Lost in the headlines over Doheny's personal relationship with Fall was the general opinion among industry analysts that the Elk Hills leases had been too favorable to the government and should have never been undertaken in the first place. In March 1924, with the Walsh investigation finding every reason to question the validity of those leases, the case was turned over to Judge Paul J. McCormick of the Federal District Court in Southern California. In the meantime, Pan American Petroleum's operations on the oil reserve were placed in receivership. With the court's permission, however, the company was permitted to continue drilling on undeveloped land to offset private wells across the border. Nevertheless, the navy made plans to put the administration of the reserve in the hands of officers who were avowed "oil in the ground conservationists," including individuals who believed that the nation's oil supply would be completely exhausted in less than twenty years and who recommended that the onshore use of oil ought to be legally restricted whenever it could be replaced by coal.[39]

Facing this sort of strident opposition, Doheny took comfort in the fact that the issue would be decided in court instead of in Congress: "We have no apprehension as to the final outcome of the litigation, because there has been no conspiracy and no fraud connected with either the Executive Order of President Harding providing administrative machinery for handling the navy's oil, or with our contracts. We have an abiding confidence in the result of the litigation started to-day. The case is now taken out of the forum of partisan politics into the United States Courts, where every citizen is assured of a square deal."[40]

Unfortunately, the controversy had already taken a toll on his business; as Fall put it, the plans for the Pan American Western Petroleum Company "went up in smoke" the moment Doheny confessed to the loan. In light of the circumstances, Doheny canceled the new bond issue and withdrew the stock offer for the company. Nevertheless, with Clarence Barron running interference for him, this announcement did not set off a panic on Wall Street. In the days that followed, Barron gave what he described as "splendid support" in the Wall Street Journal to head off any short sellers trying to capitalize on the situation. In particular, the paper emphasized that, even if the company lost the government lease and could not develop the reserve, it still had an enormous daily production, large stocks of crude oil and gasoline, and growing cash reserves. For his part, Doheny was not willing to concede the leases under any circumstances, because, as he told the stockholders, they not only protected the oil reserve from competitive drainage but "[made] possible the defense of the Pacific Coast and our island possessions against hostile attack."[41]

Meanwhile, except for canceling the Pan American Western bonds, Doheny maintained the construction schedule on his Los Angeles shipping depot, the big refinery, and the 140-mile pipeline from Elk Hills. From everything that could be seen, Doheny's plans for a major assault on the retail gasoline market continued unabated during the remainder of 1924. While market analysts celebrated the future prospects for Pan American Petroleum, the ongoing litigation over the naval oil reserve was still a cause for concern. But the Elk Hills situation was also offset by a turnaround in the fuel oil business, where Doheny enjoyed a solid and comfortable lead. Whereas fuel oil prices had been below a dollar a barrel in the early twenties, they had almost doubled—to $1.85 a barrel—by the winter of 1924–1925. "Every tick of the clock," according to one writer, "registers ten and one-half barrels of fuel oil [a million barrels a day] consumed in the United States." With the second largest tanker fleet in the country and a total oil production ranked first or second in the world alongside the Royal Dutch interests, Doheny would, without a doubt, capture the lion's share of the business. And that was more than enough, wrote another commentator, "for those who believe in the financial genius of E. L. Doheny, and also in his reputation as being one of the best if not the best oil man of his generation."[42]

At the same time, by the summer of 1924, there were rumors that Doheny was ready to sell out and retire. Doheny categorically denied every report, especially those dealing with a rumored sale to Standard Oil Indiana: "There never has been a time since I have been in business that I have not had some individual or organization seeking an option on my stock and there never has been a time when I would not have sold if the price had been right." This time, however, the talk was more than idle gossip, since the Indiana company had been hunting for a producing partner for several years. Standard's chairman, Robert W. Stewart, had two possibilities in mind for a merger: Gulf Oil and Pan American Petroleum.[43]

In fact, Stewart's interest in Doheny's company began around 1921 or 1922 and may have been one more reason that Doheny was willing to encumber Pan American—to make it a less attractive target—with a long-term obligation to the federal government against the advice of his directors. Regardless, by 1924, Stewart had failed in his bid to capture Gulf and was even more determined to make, or force, a deal with somebody else: "I am ambitious to get into a bigger field of operations for the Standard of Indiana." With its large reserve holdings in South America and Mexico, not to mention Doheny's recent invasion of Stewart's marketing area, Pan American Petroleum was the logical choice.[44]

Negotiations along these lines took place through Blair & Company, a successor to William Salomon & Company, which handled all of the financing and stock issues for Doheny's corporate interests. Blair operated as a small firm specializing in oil company mergers, and it handled several large consolidations featuring former California independents, including Associated Oil's merger with Tidewater Oil, General Petroleum's purchase by Standard Oil New York, and Pacific Oil's absorption by Standard Oil California. Blair's managing partner, Elisha Walker, was a former partner with William Salomon and had been on the board of Pan American Petroleum & Transport since 1916. So it was, in January 1925, that Walker,

Stewart, and E. R. Tinker Jr., a Pan American Petroleum director from Chase National Bank, negotiated an "unexpected" sixty-nine-day option to purchase all of Doheny's personal stock in the company.[45]

According to the most recent government audit of Pan American Petroleum & Transport for June 1922, there were 1,265,152 shares ($50 par) of stock outstanding. Doheny held 485,977 (38 percent) shares through his family-owned Petroleum Securities Company. Eight other shareholders each had 1 percent or more of the stock. Herbert Wylie, Norman Bridge, Florence Whitney (Charles Canfield's daughter), and S. M. Spalding held a combined total of 92,845 (7 percent) shares. Another 59,812 (5 percent) shares were held by five New York brokerage houses, leaving 626,518 shares in the hands of some 3,300 shareholders, at an average of 190 shares apiece.[46]

Because of this tight financial control, the final negotiations took everyone by surprise. The *Wall Street Journal* reported in February that Doheny would most likely repurchase the California Petroleum Company. Two weeks later, the *Journal* wrote that Doheny was planning to split Pan American Petroleum & Transport into two companies, an eastern and a western division, in a move similar to his earlier proposal for a western subsidiary. A subsequent Pan American Petroleum press release called this a reorganization, not a sale, and failed to mention Stewart in any way. "There may be changes in the personnel of the two companies," the report noted, "but Mr. Doheny will always remain interested and active in the Pan American affairs, and he will give special attention to the California end of the business." A week after that, the *Journal* reported that interests related to Standard Oil of Indiana had been heavy investors in Doheny stock but still did not say that they were attempting to buy Pan American. Finally, on April 2, almost three weeks after the initial report, Doheny announced his resignation from the eastern half of the business, with Stewart taking over "at a time of the greatest prosperity thus enjoyed."[47]

"This deal," according to the *National Petroleum News*, "will be, by far, the most important event in the oil world since the dissolution of the Standard Oil Company of New Jersey more than 13 years ago." The Pan American stock included in the sale had a book value of $193 million and a market value of $220 million and, in combination with Standard Indiana, created an international oil titan big enough rival Standard Oil New Jersey and Royal Dutch-Shell as one of the industry's three largest organizations. The benefits for Robert Stewart were obvious, since he acquired Pan American Petroleum's Mexican and Latin American properties, the Destrehan refinery, Gulf Coast and south Atlantic Coast service stations, East Coast distribution outlets, British and European interests, and the tanker fleet. The advantages for Doheny, who retained control of Pan American's West Coast properties, including full liability for the oil reserve contracts, were not so clear.[48]

Perhaps, as many people have suggested, Doheny was just getting too old at the age of sixty-nine to keep up the pace after thirty years in the business. But keeping Pan American Petroleum intact would have been the best way to absorb a potential loss of the Elk Hills production. On the other hand, if Doheny had any hopes of maintaining a family dynasty in the fuel oil industry, which he had mentioned years before, he must have given up on them by this time. Perhaps, as suggested earlier, he had too little confidence in his son's ability to handle a major corporation, and it would be many years before any of his three grandsons was old enough to assume the role.[49]

Family considerations notwithstanding, it seems apparent that, once Doheny got a taste of the government's intentions for litigating the case in the civil trial, he knew he was in for the fight of his life. And looking into the future, he may have anticipated that it would take most of his energy and resources just to save his name let alone his business. Writing to Albert Fall in July 1925, Doheny suggested as much:

> I have come, however, at this late date in my life, to that period when substantial returns which nature has so bounteously given do not supply that which I seem to want most, the good opinion of the public, or, in other words, recognition on its part of real effort made to serve. If there is one thing more than another that a man possesses who has followed the life of a prospector, it is hope, and I have not yet given up hope that public opinion may be greatly changed with regard to both you and I, and those who have been reviled with us because of our efforts to serve the Government.[50]

Doheny was responding, in particular, to the adverse decision in the civil trial, handed down two months earlier, in which Judge McCormick had found "elements of a criminal conspiracy" behind the Elk Hills contract. Although the government did not have to prove a conspiracy between Fall and Doheny, McCormick concluded that the intention of the defendants was "injurious and pernicious to the public welfare and governmental integrity" and "inimical" to the stated purposes of the naval oil reserves. With respect to the $100,000 loan, McCormick thought it was possible that Fall might not have been influenced by the money—but not probable. At the very least, the attempt to keep it a secret suggested a "consciousness of wrongdoing." In the judge's opinion, therefore, Doheny's contract for the Elk Hills reserve was illegal and unenforceable. Nevertheless, because McCormick conceded that the work already completed for the government at Pearl Harbor was of superior quality and obviously beneficial to the navy, Doheny was entitled to have the $10 million invested in the project up to that point refunded by the government.[51]

For Doheny, who had just reincorporated the Pan American Western company a week earlier, McCormick's decision was disheartening but not catastrophic. He could accept the loss of the government leases so long as he was not punished financially for reinforcing the nation's petroleum defenses. Without oil from Elk Hills, Doheny was still producing about 11,500 barrels a month from his other properties and could easily purchase the remaining 30,000 to 40,000 barrels required to run the Los Angeles refinery at capacity. But he was going to need a new source of oil fairly soon, since the California company now had sixty-seven gasoline/oil lubricating stations operating throughout the state and was committed to a "progressive policy of refining and marketing."[52]

In the meantime, he continued to fight McCormick's decision through the legal system. On January 4, 1926, the Circuit Court of Appeals not only upheld the negative decision on the leases but reversed the ruling on the money. The Appeals court decided that, once the contracts for the Elk Hills project were declared fraudulent, the company was no longer entitled to any equity from the government, regardless of the utility of its work. Doheny appealed that decision to the Supreme Court. But Pan American Petroleum lost all hope for legal redress in February 1927, when the high court agreed that the company should lose its contract on Naval Reserve No. 1 and should not be recompensed for construction costs and improvements made to government property. In addition, the court ruled that Doheny should have to pay for all of the oil taken from the reserve since 1921. In the opinion of Justice Butler, "It was the purpose of those making the contracts and leases to circumvent the laws and defeat the policy of the United States established for the conservation of the naval petroleum reserves." On the civil side, then, Doheny had gone to the limit of the law but was unable to recover the money invested in the reserves and the storage depot at Pearl Harbor; furthermore, he owed the government an additional $9.5 million for all of the royalties, profit, and interest on the oil taken out of Elk Hills.[53]

One final point about the oil reserve is that recent investigations have shown that it was actually the government's subsequent policy of leasing out small portions of the reserve to different companies for offset wells that cost the most oil. Fall's idea of giving the whole reserve to one large company for systematic development was actually the best thing that could have happened to the field.[54]

Fortunately for Doheny at least, the criminal cases went much better. In December 1926, Fall and Doheny went to trial together in Washington, D.C., on the charge of conspiring to defraud the government. As yet, except for his appearance before Walsh's committee, Doheny had not taken the stand in his own defense. Anticipating a criminal trial, his attorneys had advised him to wait before opening himself up to cross-examination. They also believed—correctly—that Doheny's testimony would not do him any good before a judge but would be a marvelous antidote to the government's personal attacks in front of a jury. In particular, Doheny and his counsel counted on the public's reverence for the pioneer West as their best defense. In addition to playing up Doheny's own frontier days, defense counsel called several of his old acquaintances from the mountains of New Mexico as character witnesses to testify about his friendship and generosity over the years. And it was true that Doheny had kept some of them prospecting for decades and had doled out grubstakes whenever they asked. The loan to Fall, his attorneys argued, was just the same, and the jury had no trouble acquitting them both.[55]

Failing to convict them of conspiracy, the government next tried Fall and Doheny on the bribery charge, with an even more controversial result. In these cases, because the guilt or innocence of each defendant depended on his state of mind, the two men were tried individually. And in October 1929, just a few days before the stock market crash, Albert Fall was found guilty of having accepted a bribe from Doheny. Five months later, however, Doheny was acquitted of having ever offered one to Fall. The split verdicts, from separate juries, convinced many people that the legal system in America was completely worthless. For others, it suggested that it was impossible to convict a millionaire of anything. After Doheny's acquittal, Fall summed up the opposing decisions as a "puzzle," and they have seemed so ever since.[56]

It was apparent at the time, however, that the juries had responded to the men themselves rather than to the confusing, and often disputed, details of the case. In that respect, Fall, who was sick during his trial, and bound to a wheelchair, appeared old, haggard, and mean-spirited, like someone who could accept a bribe. Doheny, on the other hand, with his grandfatherly white hair and a hint of a sparkle in his eyes, was an altogether sympathetic witness, someone who always loaned money to his friends regardless of their circumstances.

Doheny at an anniversary celebration of his first oil strike in Los Angeles, 1929. Security Pacific National Bank Photograph Collection, Los Angeles Public Library.

In the meantime, as the legal history of the oil scandal wound down, Doheny's business career also came to an end. But not before he made the last, and perhaps shrewdest, deal of his career by selling his interest in Pan American Western to Richfield Petroleum in May 1928. When he lost the California Appeals Court decision in 1926, there were unsubstantiated rumors that Doheny was still trying to put together another big merger with either California Petroleum or Associated Oil, in conjunction with Blair & Company. In the end, Blair eventually negotiated mergers with Texaco and Tidewater Oil, respectively. In Doheny's case, a former Blair partner was apparently in control of California Petroleum and resented his competition or interference. More to the point, however, assuming Doheny was truly interested in such a merger, was that he no longer had enough financial leverage to be effective.[57]

Instead, he negotiated the best deal he could to sell the company. None of the details of the transaction, handled again by Blair & Company, were made public, but the consensus has been that it was Richfield's greatest mistake. Supposedly, Richfield paid Doheny somewhere around $10 million to secure 80 percent of Pan American Western stock, $7.5 million of this in cash. In return, Richfield received the unfinished marine terminal at Los Angeles harbor, the refinery and pipeline to the Midway oilfields, a large inventory of refined products, and a varied portfolio of oil properties mortgaged by a $10 million bond issue. Richfield thought it was buying a path into the ranks of the major oil companies. Instead, by replicating many of its own holdings, the Pan American acquisition sent it into receivership two years later. Before that happened, though, Doheny made a second deal with Richfield to turn over two issues of Pan American bonds totaling $24 million and a contract for Richfield to buy the production of the Petroleum Securities Company, Doheny's small family-owned producing company. In the end, Doheny supposedly walked away with $25.6 million in cash, proving that he had not yet lost his touch.[58]

After his acquittal on the bribery charge, however, Doheny was in his mid-seventies, obviously still mentally sharp but physically frail and often relegated to a wheelchair. Supposedly, he was still conducting business through a number of small operations, but his health was failing fast, and the government was refusing to give up its efforts to secure a financial judgment against him. By this time, several suits had been filed on behalf of Pan American shareholders and the Richfield Petroleum Corporation claiming that Doheny's actions in making the naval reserve leases violated his fiduciary responsibility to the company and made him personally liable for the penalties.

In the end, attorneys for the federal government fought on for three years after Doheny's death on December 8, 1935, before they finally settled the case, receiving a total of $8.5 million from the Doheny estate. Former senator Atlee Pomerene, a Democrat from Ohio, was particularly hostile to Doheny after failing to convict him on two occasions and imputed the worst motives to everything he did. For Pomerene and his associates, Doheny's acquittal was a travesty of justice that could be explained only by a pool of stupid, and easily impressed, jurors.[59]

It was little wonder, then, that after Doheny died, Estelle followed through with his request to destroy his correspondence and business records, and subsequently refused to discuss the case with anyone. But, as has been shown throughout this book, the loss of that information did irreparable damage to a full understanding of the details of Doheny's extraordinary life and career.

CONCLUSION

This study of Doheny's business career began with a statement describing how the indelible effects of the oil scandal have colored perceptions of his life. Doheny knew this was going to happen, and after exhibiting faith and optimism in the face of innumerable obstacles, he spent his last years a bitter and dispirited man, the victim of political forces that he could not control. Had he died before 1924, Doheny would have left a large void in the front ranks of the oil industry, and his accomplishments would have been duly celebrated. Instead, the oil scandal became the motif for his whole career. To his critics, both then and now, Doheny was one of the last of a generation of oil buccaneers who symbolized everything that was wrong with the industry.

The details of his business conduct, however, do not bear out this negative assessment. Doheny was not a ruthless plutocrat scheming to rob the world of its oil, nor was he a simple prospector who lived by the code of the West and struck it rich by luck. In reality, Doheny built an oil empire at a time when he was forced to bridge the gap between the individual wildcatter and the Wall Street industrialist—and he tended toward the latter almost from the beginning. But along the way, he also stood out as a pioneer in almost everything he did. This was especially true with respect to his activities in Mexico, where Doheny set the pattern for the expansion of the American oil industry abroad. Over the years, he assembled a massive corporate structure to support the exploration of Mexican oil in an era of rapid economic change. In pursuing his objectives, Doheny paved the way, and paid the price, for much of the modern oil industry.

Although part of Doheny's success came from hard work and perseverance, he complemented these prosaic virtues with a vision of the future of the oil industry that enabled him to press forward when others hesitated or failed to see. In this way, Doheny's career can be seen as an example of the entrepreneurial spirit at its best. As a usable concept, the nature of entrepreneurial behavior has escaped concise description but encompasses what one economic historian calls an "alertness" to heretofore undiscovered, or overlooked, possibilities in the market.[1] After having reviewed Doheny's business dealings in detail, I find that nothing describes his role better than this emphasis on being alert to the opportunities around him. As we have seen, Doheny never actually discovered anything that had not been known and explored by someone before him. But what he recognized, both in California and in Mexico, was the possibility of marketing fuel oil to the railroads, industry, and maritime companies as a cost-efficient replacement for coal. Doheny was only slightly ahead of his competition in most of his endeavors, but he always proved to be more strong-willed and determined than his rivals.

When Doheny "discovered" oil in Los Angeles in 1892, his desire to succeed had been fortified by twenty years of frustration, near misses, and repeated failure as a mining prospector, but he came away from his years in New Mexico with an invaluable education. On the most basic level, he had learned the rudiments of practical geology, which were readily transferable from mineral treasure to oil. More important were the hard lessons learned about building a business in a volatile environment. After working in isolated places like Kingston or Silver City, Doheny understood the value of infrastructure and integration when his lead or silver ore proved to be as worthless as the dirt around it without the smelters and railway links required to deliver the product to market. And like most prospectors, Doheny soon discovered the necessity for external financial support. But, from his own experience, he also knew that viable opportunities were often wasted through the machinations of stock promoters who cared little for the mining business and devoted themselves to quick profits at someone else's expense. Outside investors played a crucial role in the early success of Doheny's oil companies, but he made certain that they were dependable, close relationships that could stand the strain of long-term development.

Similarly, one of Doheny's greatest assets was his ability to cultivate advantageous friendships with influential individuals, from corporate heads to Washington officials. Nowhere was his promotional ability more impressive than in his initial success in winning the business and financial support of the Santa Fe Railway in Los Angeles. Whether Doheny sought out the local officials of the Southern California Railroad, whether they

approached him, or whether he and the railroad met by accident is unknown, but he did not hesitate to couple his fledgling oil business to the
railway. To his good fortune, the Santa Fe wanted to have a secure supply
of oil, immune from market fluctuations, and it paid Doheny a premium
for his Los Angeles product. Later, the railroad gave him a free hand to
expand its oil operations whenever, and wherever, he saw the chance. Thus,
when he became the railroad's exclusive oil agent in 1897, Doheny held the
unique position of being a wildcatter with a safety net. Over the next five
years, Doheny provided the Santa Fe with the oil expertise it required, and
he gained a first-hand education in how to successfully build and operate
a large business. The railroad also supplied a core set of investors who
stayed with him through the first crucial decade in Mexico.

However, Doheny never intended to rely solely upon the railroad for
business, and because he had to scour Los Angeles for every conceivable
customer in the early 1890s, he developed a broad conception of the fuel-
oil market. In particular, he believed that the conversion to fuel oil would
have its greatest impact on the shipping lines engaged in mass long-
distance distribution. And once the shipping industry adopted oil, Doheny
knew he would reap the rewards of industrial expansion on an international scale. Although this was not a plan he could put into effect immediately, it was another instance of his alertness to the potential for his
product. When the opportunity to push the use of oil came during the
First World War, Doheny was in position to monopolize the business by
virtue of his large holdings in Mexico. In fact, as we have seen in detail,
Doheny waged a sales campaign during the war which, in the opinion of
one analyst, literally created the fuel-oil age.[2]

Thus, when Doheny accepted the Mexican Central Railway's offer to
hunt for oil near Tampico in 1900, he was already aware of the many possibilities for the heavy crude he would find at Ebano. Furthermore, despite
his putative contract with the railroad, Doheny went to Mexico not simply
to locate oil but to establish an industry based on domestic consumption.
After transforming the industrial capacity of Mexico with the use of fuel
oil, he knew he could move on to a larger international market. In the
beginning, except for the fear of excessive American control, Doheny's
plans fit into the economic modernization program undertaken by Porfirio
Díaz. But after 1911, the foreign-owned petroleum sector, with Doheny in
the lead, entered a protracted conflict with Mexico's revolutionary government over the control of natural resources. Doheny's attempt to build an
internal market for fuel oil was one of the first casualties of Mexico's civil
war. Thereafter, the demands of the European war siphoned an increasing

amount of Mexican oil into the United States, as the Mexican oil business came to resemble other extractive industries. Consequently, as the only profitable sector in an economy otherwise devastated by revolution, the petroleum industry garnered an unprecedented degree of attention and criticism from the Mexican government.

Nevertheless, because of the political conflict in Mexico and the accompanying fight with the Wilson administration over American policy, Doheny emerged as a national leader of the oil industry in the late 1910s. Throughout this period, his companies accounted for the largest production of fuel oil in the world. However, Doheny's success in Mexico and his total dominance of one phase of the industry cost him a larger role in other areas. In particular, he did not see that it was gasoline, rather than fuel oil, which would ultimately revolutionize the transportation industry. For several years, therefore, Doheny lagged behind as the other major firms expanded rapidly to capture the American gasoline market. Part of his interest in the Elk Hills Naval Reserve in 1921, aside from the issues of security in the Pacific, stemmed from the need to jump into the gasoline trade in mid-stream.

Another miscalculation was his abandonment of the California Petroleum Company after he failed to consolidate the West Coast independents into Pan American Petroleum in 1916. Had he at least maintained some financial control over California Petroleum, he might not have taken any interest in the Naval Petroleum Reserve as a business proposition in 1921. Doheny realized this mistake in the mid-1920s and tried to reacquire the company, but he was unsuccessful. Ultimately, California Petroleum, with its large production and growing network of distributing stations, became a crucial component in the Texas Company's strategy to diversify its operations in 1928.[3]

Thus, by 1925 Pan American Petroleum, with its vast holdings in Mexico, was still the preeminent company in the fuel-oil market, but it was only beginning to develop its gasoline business in the United States through the purchase of several retail outlets east of the Mississippi. Unfortunately, this lopsided development made it an ideal target for an established retail company seeking crude oil reserves, and it did not take long before Standard Oil of Indiana set its sights on Pan American. At that point, although Doheny was fully engaged in making up ground in the hunt for marketing areas on both coasts, he was growing weary of the Mexican headache he had been battling for almost fifteen years. Surveying his predicament in the early months of 1925, Doheny decided to retain the western segment of the company, represented by his investments in Elk

Hills, and let Standard Oil have the remainder. In the end, by absorbing the bulk of the assets of Pan American Petroleum, which had been the nation's ninth-largest oil company for the preceding decade, the Indiana corporation vaulted into permanent position as an oil giant. Doheny, on the other hand, staked the future of his California operations on the sanctity of his government leases, and he lost.

An argument can be made that, under different circumstances, events could have gone in another direction. Despite its concentration in Mexican production, Pan American Petroleum was never in a vulnerable financial position and did not have any fatal weakness. In the United States, Doheny proved to be an effective competitor in the retail market and was even challenging Standard Oil Indiana in its own territory. But in 1925, Doheny was also nearing retirement, and the Elk Hills project had become a legal and political nightmare. While there was no overwhelming reason to sell the company, there was no compelling justification for continuing the business along its present lines.

Despite occasional comments in the press about creating a family dynasty in the fuel-oil trade, Doheny seems to have abandoned any idea of maintaining the company for the sake of posterity. The most likely reason was that his son had not have proven to be a viable successor. After several years as a vice-president, Ned Doheny had not made his role in the company obvious, and if the information about his alcoholism is correct, he was in no shape to assume control of an international oil business. Doheny's grandsons were, at the time, just young boys; Doheny may have assumed that they would do better inheriting a fortune than a demanding corporate obligation. Despite the presence of numerous outside directors and a large managerial staff, Doheny retained a controlling financial interest in the company as its founder and chief executive officer, and his decision to sell out determined its fate.

In the absence of the litigation surrounding the Elk Hills lease, Doheny might have had the energy and the determination to keep the company intact and to ensure its future. From a financial standpoint, even the problems at the Naval Petroleum Reserve were not great enough to force the sale to Standard Oil, and the loss of the government leases could have been made up without crippling the business. But the oil scandal took such a personal toll that it soured Doheny on everything else and made him a victim of his own ego. On one level, his proposal to privately develop the oil reserve offered genuine cost advantages to the government and guaranteed his company a field of expansion far into the future. For all his astuteness, though, Doheny seemed to disregard the political consequences of his actions. Against the better judgment of his business associates, he went ahead with his plans, believing that he alone could save the country from Japanese aggression. When the details of the Elk Hills arrangement became public knowledge, Doheny expected Washington's gratitude, not suspicion and hostility. Having succumbed to the blandishments of naval officers and government officials, Doheny truly believed that he could ensure the nation's military preparedness in the Pacific. And he was not pretending when he appeared genuinely wounded during the oil investigation, as critics interpreted his actions in a sinister and self-serving light. He never understood why so many of his friends in both political parties abandoned him as a liability during the 1924 campaign and thereafter. In the end, disillusionment and frustration consumed all other concerns in his fight to save his name. Unfortunately, the criminal trials were not concluded until 1930, when Doheny's declining health left him a reclusive invalid. And what remained of his public image was inextricably tied to the scandal.

Eventually, it took Doheny's death and Estelle's subsequent rise to prominence in her own right to begin to resurrect the family's reputation. That process started the day Estelle burned her husband's private papers in the basement incinerator of their Chester Place mansion. Over the years, Estelle Doheny had given Edward every assistance in his business, accompanying him on dozens of shared trips to the Mexican oilfields during the revolution. She sat on the board of Pan American Petroleum as one of the first female directors of a major oil company. Knowing how much of her life had been tied up in the fortunes of the company makes it hard to believe that she would willingly destroy the only record of their accomplishments. But during his final years, when Edward could no longer talk and was confined to a wheelchair, Estelle stood as his protector. The destruction of his papers was the final defense of her husband's reputation. Still, even though she was only acceding to Edward's wishes, Estelle must have come to regret this decision many times during the remainder of her life. Her friend and personal assistant, who reluctantly helped burn the documents, stated that it was Mrs. Doheny's greatest mistake.[4]

In the twenty-three years between Edward's death and her own in 1958, Estelle Doheny earned a different reputation than her husband's through her philanthropic work in Southern California, large benefactions to the Catholic Church, and a late career as a rare book collector with a national reputation. And she intended her collection and the Doheny Memorial Library she commissioned to house it as a lasting tribute to Edward, hoping that it would grow in value and scholarly importance over time.

But in a region which included such institutions as the Huntington Library and the Getty Museum, the Doheny collection at St. John's Seminary in Camarillo proved to be too isolated and esoteric to attract much attention. Ultimately, the Church sold it for over $37 million, a record amount for a private library sold at auction.[5]

What proved more lasting was Estelle's creation and funding of the Doheny Eye Foundation and Eye Bank in Los Angeles. When she discovered in 1944 that she was suffering from glaucoma, Estelle learned that the region had no facility to study and treat the disease, and her efforts to rectify that situation did as much as anything else to rehabilitate the Doheny name. But for Estelle to succeed, Edward and the legacy of the oil scandal had to be left behind. The success of her efforts was recently made clear when, in December 1991, *Town & Country* magazine featured a picture of Mrs. William H. Doheny Jr. on its cover. Inside, the young Mrs. Doheny was noted for being the granddaughter of Loren Berry, a pioneer of the telephone industry. Her husband, William Doheny, was identified as the great-grandson of Carrie Estelle Doheny, known for her endowment of the Doheny Eye Institute. Edward L. Doheny, pioneer of the American oil industry, was not mentioned at all.[6]

APPENDIX A

Oil Production and Sales (in barrels) of the Mexican and Huasteca Petroleum Companies, 1901–1914

YEAR	PRODUCTION	SALES (EXPORT/DOMESTIC)
1901	18,000	0/0
1902	40,000	0/0
1903	40,000	0/16,686
1904	324,000	0/81,314
1905	423,059	0/166,313
1906	1,097,264	0/781,307
1907	1,717,690	0/1,776,614
1908	1,847,024	0/2,423,948
1909	2,398,811	0/2,028,199
1910	3,435,037	0/3,871,522
1911	9,202,117	841,648/5,360,952
1912	9,825,316	4,453,775/4,397,948
1913	9,624,764	8,078,019/4,083,268
1914	9,173,618	6,199,797/2,180,166

Source: Company records as given in the *Fuel Oil Journal,* Mar. 1915.

APPENDIX B

Oil Production and Exports (in barrels) for the Mexican Petroleum Industry, 1916–1924

COMPANY	PRODUCTION*	EXPORTS*
	1916	
El Aguila	16,376,293 (40)	9,519,970 (35)
Mexican Petroleum	12,932,114 (32)	5,279,714 (19)
Penn Mex Fuel Co.	3,444,490 (8)	3,353,489 (12)
Brooks	1,728,079 (4)	na
Freeport & Mexican (Sinclair)	1,640,202 (4)	na
East Coast Oil Co. (S. Pac)	1,110,062 (3)	na
Mexican Gulf (Gulf Oil)	886,180 (2)	na
International	644,204 (2)	na
La Corona (Royal Dutch)	557,792 (1)	na
Panuco Boston Oil (Atlantic Ref.)	246,286 (1)	na
Other Companies	981,213 (2)	na
Total	40,546,915	27,268,749
	1917	
Mexican Petroleum	18,450,874 (33)	na
El Aguila	16,922,323 (31)	na
Penn Mex Fuel Co.	4,129,297 (7)	na
Freeport & Mexican	4,076,982 (7)	na
East Coast Oil Co.	3,143,221 (6)	na
Texas Co. (Brooks)	2,315,433 (4)	na
Mexican Gulf	1,160,794 (2)	na
Cia. Petrolera Tal Vez	989,562 (2)	na
Panuco Boston	828,067 (1)	na
National Oil Co.	753,590 (1)	na
La Corona	740,576 (1)	na
International	619,828 (1)	na
Veracruz Mex. Oil Syn. (SONJ)	360,259 (1)	na
Other Companies	801,964 (1)	na
Total	55,292,770	45,256,077
	1918	
Mexican Petroleum	21,632,436 (34)	11,708,539 (23)
El Aguila	16,910,646 (26)	8,583,573 (17)
Penn Mex Fuel Co.	6,854,081 (11)	7,008,092 (14)
Freeport & Mexican	4,119,654 (6)	3,939,899 (8)
East Coast	3,457,236 (5)	3,398,581 (7)

COMPANY	PRODUCTION*		EXPORTS*	
Cortez Oil Corp.	2,161,757	(3)	1,935,433	(4)
Mexican Gulf	1,728,190	(3)	1,734,254	(3)
Island Oil	1,550,869	(2)	1,604,579	(3)
Texas Co.	1,279,747	(2)	1,256,176	(2)
Cia. Petrol. Tal Vez	1,152,064	(2)	98,898	(0.2)
International	609,734	(1)	0	
Tampascas Oil Co.	578,479	(1)	0	
Panuco Boston	531,511	(1)	0	
Transcontinental (SONJ)	382,029	(1)	4,346,837	(8)
La Corona	337,603	(1)	0	
Other Companies	542,290	(0.9)	6,153,147	(12)
Total	63,828,326		51,768,008	

1919				
El Aguila	18,798,307	(22)	12,665,824	(16)
Mexican Petroleum	16,845,139	(19)	15,574,083	(19)
Penn Mex	8,703,169	(10)	8,390,205	(10)
Transcontinental	7,172,099	(8)	4,536,543	(6)
Texas Co.	5,769,507	(7)	6,807,003	(8)
Mexican Gulf	5,250,890	(6)	4,504,459	(6)
Freeport & Mexican	4,986,705	(6)	4,752,776	(6)
Nayarit Pet. Co., S.A.	4,318,813	(5)	0	
East Coast	4,108,200	(5)	2,677,845	(3)
Cortez Oil Corp.	4,035,279	(5)	0	
Tal Vez	1,632,129	(2)	0	
La Libertad	898,541	(1)	0	
Panuco Boston	836,525	(1)	0	
La Corona	822,648	(1)	0	
International	496,181	(1)	0	
Other Companies	2,271,824	(3)	20,275,682	(25)
Total	87,045,956		80,184,420	

1920				
El Aguila	32,381,547	(21)	16,166,489	(11)
Transcontinental	14,411,455	(9)	23,059,630	(16)
Texas Co.	12,563,918	(8)	11,441,026	(8)
Mexican Petroleum	12,500,149	(8)	25,433,879	(17)
International	10,572,682	(7)	0	
Mexican Gulf	9,161,272	(6)	10,279,508	(7)
Penn Mex Fuel Co.	7,234,718	(5)	6,348,440	(4)
Atlantic Gulf	6,805,679	(4)	6,549,293	(5)
Mexican Sinclair	6,669,340	(4)	0	
Nayarit Pet. Co., S.A.	6,350,403	(4)	0	
Freeport & Mexican	4,457,269	(3)	7,750,966	(5)
La Corona	4,267,377	(3)	3,027,484	(2)
East Coast	3,020,398	(2)	5,616,177	(4)
New England Fuel (SONY)	2,977,975	(2)	1,150,504	(1)
Panuco Boston	1,581,344	(1)	715,072	(0.5)
Other Companies	22,113,152	(14)	27,970,479	(19)
Total	157,068,678		145,508,948	

COMPANY	PRODUCTION*	EXPORTS*
	1921	
El Aguila	32,434,576 (17)	20,772,889 (12)
Mexican Petroleum	31,221,119 (16)	27,384,446 (16)
Mexican Gulf	19,057,763 (10)	12,845,903 (7)
Transcontinental	13,709,363 (7)	25,903,264 (15)
La Corona	12,833,192 (7)	7,761,407 (5)
International	12,438,859 (6)	9,890,767 (6)
Atlantic Gulf	8,673,621 (4)	11,042,900 (6)
Texas Co.	6,416,964 (3)	10,965,055 (6)
Freeport & Mexican	6,150,356 (3)	7,195,880 (4)
Penn Mex Fuel Co.	5,184,589 (3)	3,567,688 (2)
Mexican Sinclair	4,309,656 (2)	0
New England Fuel Co.	3,882,724 (2)	3,005,714 (2)
East Coast	2,131,304 (1)	5,742,154 (3)
Other Companies	36,311,626 (19)	26,223,274 (15)
Total	194,755,712	172,304,341
	1922	
Mexican Petroleum	57,438,425 (31)	39,508,880 (22)
Mexican Gulf	28,240,232 (15)	19,791,441 (11)
International	19,923,953 (11)	13,759,671 (8)
La Corona	17,658,244 (10)	20,262,134 (11)
El Aguila	13,840,397 (7)	16,018,328 (9)
Transcontinental	5,392,141 (3)	19,854,433 (11)
Atlantic Gulf	4,713,487 (3)	7,250,213 (4)
New England Fuel Co.	4,441,338 (2)	3,544,038 (2)
Texas Co.	3,999,981 (2)	9,793,956 (5)
Penn Mex Fuel Co.	2,886,072 (2)	3,018,068 (2)
East Coast	1,918,651 (1)	4,675,502 (3)
Other Companies	24,604,328 (21)	23,385,575 (22)
Total	185,057,249	180,862,239
	1923	
Mexican Petroleum	35,188,777 (24)	32,152,116 (24)
La Corona	30,543,711 (20)	21,632,708 (16)
Transcontinental	23,971,932 (16)	16,784,299 (12)
El Aguila	10,120,081 (7)	13,212,082 (10)
Mexican Gulf	7,863,069 (5)	7,852,919 (6)
International	6,233,817 (4)	3,369,214 (2)
Imperio, S.A.	5,643,918 (4)	1,959,240 (1)
New England Fuel Co.	4,981,110 (3)	3,599,465 (3)
East Coast	3,402,418 (2)	8,401,509 (6)
Texas Co.	2,618,099 (2)	9,053,614 (7)
Atlantic Gulf	1,892,465 (1)	2,444,394 (2)
Other Companies	17,122,035 (11)	15,144,965 (11)
Total	149,581,432	135,606,525
	1924	
Mexican Petroleum	29,170,596 (21)	28,302,207 (22)
Transcontinental	20,406,320 (15)	30,542,711 (24)

COMPANY	*PRODUCTION*	EXPORTS*
International	15,328,390 (11)	1,843,442 (1)
La Corona	13,516,053 (10)	15,184,205 (12)
Mexican Gulf	10,786,865 (8)	9,915,650 (8)
Imperio, S.A.	7,871,195 (6)	0
El Aguila	5,793,832 (4)	12,345,609 (10)
Mexican Sinclair	5,194,037 (4)	12,499,897 (10)
East Coast	3,738,172 (3)	5,069,476 (4)
New England Fuel Co.	2,474,889 (2)	0
Texas Company	1,568,650 (1)	3,180,526 (2)
Penn Mex Fuel Co.	1,486,314 (1)	312,009 (0.2)
Atlantic Gulf	840,476 (0.6)	746,812 (1)
Other Companies	21,502,505 (15)	9,757,244 (8)
Total	139,678,294	129,699,788

Source: Figures compiled from annual reports of the *Boletin del Petroleo* and *Oil Trade Journal.*

*Percentage of total production/exports given in parentheses.

APPENDIX C

Companies Owned and Controlled by the Pan American Petroleum & Transport Company at Its Incorporation, 1916 (incorporation dates in parentheses).

Mexican Petroleum Company, Delaware (1907)

> Mexican Petroleum Company, California (1900, original company based at Ebano, Mexico)

> Huasteca Petroleum Company (1907, producing company with its main properties at Casiano and Cerro Azul, Mexico)

> Compania Naviera Transportadora de Petroleo, S.A. (1912, transportation company that owned the small boats and barges used in Mexico)

> Tuxpan Petroleum Company (1912, producing company, Mexico)

> Tamiahua Petroleum Company (1912, producing company, Mexico)

> Mexican Petroleum Corporation (1912, refining and distribution company for the United States, with a major refinery at Destrehan, Louisiana, and oil storage and sales outlets along the eastern seaboard)

Petroleum Transport Company (1912, main transportation company, which controlled the oil tanker fleet)

Caloric Company (1915, distribution company for South America based in Brazil)

Buena Fe Company (1915, producing company, Midway oilfield, California)

Pan American Investment Corporation (1916, holding company for California oil lands, owned 50/50 between Pan American Petroleum & Transport Company and the California Petroleum Corporation, also operated in the Cat Canyon oil district, Santa Maria field, California)

> Pan American Petroleum Company (1916, producing company, Ojai oil district, Ventura-Newhall field, California)

> Doheny Pacific Petroleum Company (1916, producing company, Casmalia, Midway, and Simi Valley, California)

> Fairfield Petroleum Company (1916, producing company, Texas)

California Petroleum Corporation (1912, holding company)

American Petroleum Company (1908, producing company, Midway oil district, California)

> Niles Lease Company (1910, producing company, Salt Lake oilfield, Los Angeles County, California)

American Oilfields Company (1910, producing company, Coalinga oil district, Fresno County, California)

Midland Oilfields Company, Ltd. (1910, producing company, Midway, Sunset, Lost Hills, McKittrick oilfields, Kern County, California)

Midland Oil Company (1910, producing company, Midway oilfield, California)

Petroleum Midway Company, Ltd. (1915, producing company, Midway oilfield, California)

APPENDIX D

Relative Sizes of the Largest American Oil Companies by Total Assets (in $1,000s)

	1917	1921	1925
Standard Oil New Jersey	574,149	1,115,940	1,369,170
Standard Oil New York	204,338	333,242	532,961
The Texas Co.	144,585	335,990	397,638
Gulf Oil Corp.	142,963	272,774	427,610
Standard Oil Indiana	126,935	305,676	406,060
Standard Oil California	126,923	276,733	373,723
Magnolia Petroleum	122,822	190,858	212,828
Prairie Oil & Gas Co.	102,605	130,906	154,424
Sinclair Oil Corp.	93,804	342,424	447,965
Mexican Petroleum Co.	83,034	101,262	122,009
Associated Oil Co.	80,688	100,133	124,857
Union Oil Co.	77,567	104,616	302,454
Vacuum Oil	76,166	109,664	144,492
Atlantic Refining	60,772	111,077	134,017
Pan American Petroleum & Transport Co.	52,015	111,213	189,119
Tide Water Oil Co.	42,712	90,306	111,469

Source: Moody's, *Industrials.*

NOTES

The following abbreviations are used throughout the notes:

CFC	*The Commercial and Financial Chronicle* (New York)
COW	*California Oil World*
DC	*The Daily Californian* (Bakersfield)
DRF	Papers of the Doheny Research Foundation, Occidental College Library, Los Angeles, California
FOJ	*Fuel Oil Journal* (Houston)
IMA	Investigation of Mexican Affairs, U.S. Congress, Senate
IOPA	Independent Oil Producers Agency Records, Taft, California
KWS	*Kingston Weekly Shaft* (Kingston, New Mexico)
LAH	*Los Angeles Herald*
LAMR	*Los Angeles Mining Review*
LAT	*Los Angeles Times*
MH	*Mexican Herald* (Mexico City)
MOB	*Mining and Oil Bulletin* (Los Angeles)
MSP	*Mining and Scientific Press* (San Francisco)
MWS	*Magazine of Wall Street*
NMHR	*New Mexico Historical Review*
NPN	*National Petroleum News* (Cleveland)
NYT	*New York Times*
OA	*The Oil Age* (Los Angeles)
OGJ	*The Oil and Gas Journal* (Tulsa)
OIJ	*Oil Investor's Journal* (Houston)
OTJ	*Oil Trade Journal* (New York)
SCA	*Sierra County Advocate* (Hillsboro, New Mexico)
SCE	*Silver City Enterprise* (Silver City, New Mexico)
SFC	*San Francisco Chronicle*
SFE	*San Francisco Examiner*
WP	*Washington Post*
WSJ	*Wall Street Journal*

INTRODUCTION

1. B. C. Forbes, *Men Who Are Making the West* (New York: B. C. Forbes Publishing Company, 1923), 7.

2. See Lucille V. Miller, "Edward and Estelle Doheny," *Ventura County Historical Society* 6 (Nov. 1960): 3–20. The best description of Mrs. Doheny's collection comes from Msgr. Francis J. Weber, of the Archival Center, who helped arrange the sale of the St. John's material; see *Southern California's First Family: The Dohenys of Los Angeles* (Santa Barbara: Kimberly Press, 1993).

3. For contrasting examples, see Ward Ritchie, *The Dohenys of Los Angeles* (Los Angeles: Dawson's Book Shop, 1974); and Gene Hanrahan, *The Bad Yankee: American Entrepreneurs and Financiers in Mexico* (Chapel Hill: The University of North Carolina Press, 1985).

4. Clarence W. Barron, *The Mexican Problem* (Boston and New York: Houghton Mifflin Company, 1917), 127–29.

5. Wilbur Hall, "How Doheny Did It," *Sunset* 41 (July 1918): 21–23.

6. Forbes, *Men Who Are Making the West,* 101–6.

7. The primary examples are James C. Young, "Doheny's Napoleonic Career in Oil," *NYT* (Feb. 17, 1924); "Doheny's Luck," *Literary Digest* 80 (Mar. 1, 1924): 40–42; "Trailing Doheny over Oil and Quicksands," *Current Opinion* 76 (Mar. 1924): 282–84; Duncan Aikman, "The Rawhider's Verdict," *The Independent* 117 (Dec. 4, 1926): 645–46. A later summary of these items is in W. W. Jennings, *A Dozen Captains of Industry* (New York: Vantage Press, 1954), 201–18.

8. Dan La Botz, *Edward L. Doheny: Petroleum, Power, and Politics in the United States and Mexico* (New York: Prager Press, 1991).

CHAPTER 1

1. Background information is taken from C. W. Butterfield, *The History of Fond du Lac County, Wisconsin* (Chicago: Western Historical Company, 1880); Sister M. Justille McDonald, *History of the Irish in Wisconsin in the Nineteenth Century* (Washington: Catholic University of America Press, 1954); A. D. Brigham, *Fond du Lac City Directory for 1857–58* (Fond du Lac, Wis.: Union Book & Job Printing, 1858); Bureau of the Census, *Records of the Federal Census for Wisconsin from 1860–1880,* Federal Population Census Schedules for Wisconsin, RG29, 1860, 1870, 1880; Stan Gores, "Doheny Gained Riches—and Troubles," *The Fond du Lac Reporter,* June 25, 1986, 36–37.

2. *Fond du Lac Commonwealth,* July 6, 1872.

3. *Fond du Lac Reporter,* Nov. 2, 1871, Nov. 23, 1871, Dec. 14, 1871, Feb. 22, 1872.

4. Forbes, *Men Who Are Making the West,* 107. The following account of Doheny's years in New Mexico is based on Martin R. Ansell, "Such Is Luck: The Mining Career of Edward L. Doheny in New Mexico, 1880–1891," *NMHR* 70 (Jan.

1995): 47–65. I thank the *New Mexico Historical Review* for allowing me to use the material here.

5. Grant County, Mining Locations, book 3, 245–46, Grant County Courthouse, Silver City, N.Mex.; Paige Christiansen, *The Story of Mining in New Mexico* (Socorro, New Mexico Bureau of Mines & Mineral Resources, 1974), 78, 97.

6. Grant County, Mining Record of Deeds, book 8, 399, 513; book 10, 63, 682. Charles W. Greene, *The Mines of Kingston, New Mexico* (Kingston, N.M.: Kingston Tribune, 1883), 32.

7. Dona Ana County, Deed Record, book 6, 20, 240; Mining Claims, book 1, 239, Dona Ana County Courthouse, Las Cruces, N.M.

8. James A. McKenna, *Black Range Tales* (New York: Wilson-Erikson, 1936), 116–19. McKenna's recollections were not taken down until fifty years after the fact, but they accord well with the information available from contemporary newspaper accounts and census material, except for any mention of Doheny's stint as a teacher (McKenna is the only one to note Doheny's teaching job).

9. *KWS,* January 4, 1890, Department of Commerce, *Records of the Bureau of the Census,* Schedules of the New Mexico Territory Census of 1885, RG29; information about Dr. Wilkins comes from Mariah's application for a position as the postmistress of Kingston. See *Territorial Archives of New Mexico* (New Mexico State Records Center and Archives, Santa Fe), microfilm, reel 103, 475–76, 605–6. "Marriage Register, 1872–1899," Grant County Courthouse, Silver City, N.Mex. This should put to rest one of the most lurid and poorly researched aspects of La Botz's treatment of Doheny. Based on a reference from *Who's Who in California,* in which Edward L. Doheny Jr. (born in Los Angeles in 1893) listed his mother as "Louella Wilkins" (Carrie's maiden name having been Wilkins), La Botz presumes that Wilkins was merely another partner in a string of illicit relationships and concludes that the younger Edward's parents were never married. Then, in looking for a reference to any woman named Wilkins in Los Angeles, he located a person who died of a skull fracture, introducing the suggestion of Doheny's involvement in foul play. See La Botz, *Edward L. Doheny,* 11–13, 17 n. 16.

10. *LAT,* Aug. 25, 1896.

11. Caspar Whitney, *Charles Adelbert Canfield* (New York: privately printed, 1930), 51–56.

12. *MSP,* Nov. 18, 1882.

13. Fayette Jones, *New Mexico Mines and Minerals* (Santa Fe: New Mexico Printing Company, 1904), 96; Forbes, *Men Who Are Making the West,* 105–6.

14. *SCE,* Nov. 30, 1883.

15. For an overview of mining strategy, see Richard H. Peterson, *The Bonanza Kings: The Social Origins and Business Behavior of Western Mining Entrepreneurs, 1870–1900* (Norman: University of Oklahoma Press, 1971).

16. *SCA,* Mar. 4, 1887; Kingston paper quoted in the *SCE,* Jan. 18, 1883.

17. *SCA,* Dec. 5, 1885.

18. Keith L. Bryant Jr., *History of the Atchison, Topeka and Santa Fe Railway*

(New York: Macmillan, 1974), 59–63; David F. Myrick, *New Mexico's Railroads: A Historical Survey,* rev. ed. (Albuquerque: University of New Mexico Press, 1990), 193–205.

19. *SCA,* Apr. 22, 1892; *KWS,* Dec. 9, 1893.

20. For the Occidental Hotel, see Quit Claim Deeds, book A, 449–50; for Doheny's mining claims, see Mortgage Deed Records, book A, 328, 429; for Doheny's house in Kingston, see Quit Claim Deeds, book A, 547; Mortgage Deed Records, book A, 692–97, 729; Quit Claim Deeds, book B, 490; all on file with Sierra County Clerk, Truth or Consequences, N.Mex.

21. William Ralston Balch, *The Mines, Miners and Mining Interests of the United States in 1882* (Philadelphia: Mining Industrial Publishing Bureau, 1882), 850; *SCA,* May 9, 1885.

22. *SCA,* Apr. 25, 1885.

23. Edward L. Doheny to William Higgins, July 27, 1886, exhibit B, case 154, Sierra County District Court, Sept. 1886. Case file is in the New Mexico State Records Center and Archives, Santa Fe, N.Mex.

24. Articles of Incorporation, no. 717, Satisfaction Mining Company, January 31, 1887, New Mexico State Corporate Filing Division. The capital stock was listed at $2 million, divided into 200,000 shares at $10 each. An agreement listed in Sierra County, *Miscellaneous Deeds,* Book A, 456, stated that the stock would be divided so that, for every 24 shares, Doheny and two other men received 1 share each, F. A. Urban got 2½ shares, another got 3½ shares, and R. C. Troeger received 15. Doheny's appointment as mining superintendent is also noted in *Miscellaneous Deeds,* Book A, 467.

25. *SCA,* Mar. 4, 25, 1887.

26. *St. Louis Globe-Democrat,* Mar. 11, 15, and Apr. 5, 1887; Incorporation Record of the Satisfaction Mining Company.

27. David H. Stratton, ed., "The Memoirs of Albert B. Fall," *Southwestern Studies* 4, no. 3 (1966): 25–26; *SCA,* July 26, 1889.

28. *KWS,* Dec. 7, 1889. H. L. Pickett was a well-known and respected lawyer whose firm served as counselor for Sierra County. See *SCA,* Apr. 25, 1885.

29. Forbes, *Men Who Are Making the West,* 100; Stratton, "The Memoirs of Albert B. Fall," 31. For Doheny's testimony about these events, see *United States v Doheny and Fall,* Supreme Court of the District of Columbia, Dec. 1926, Records Relating to the Naval Oil Reserve Investigations, 1922–1935, RG 60, no. 411, File of Atlee Pomerene, 1917–1935, box 14, vol. 14, 2977–82, National Archives, Washington, D.C. The 1885 census does list Doheny as "disabled," so the accident may have occurred, but it was much earlier than his stint with Pickett.

30. For a comment on Doheny's consulting work, see *SCE,* Feb. 7, Sept. 12, 1890; Doheny was commissioned on Apr. 5, 1890, and took the "Bond and Oath of Office" on May 7. See Grant County, *Deed Record,* book 28, 18–19.

31. McKenna, *Black Range Tales,* 295. The comment about alcoholism came

from my conversations with Msgr. Francis Weber at the Archival Center in San Fernando.

32. *SCE*, Nov. 21, 1890; Jan. 23, Mar. 6, 1891; *KWS*, Oct. 4, 25, 1890.

33. For a later description of Carrera, see *MH*, May 19, 1904.

34. *SCE*, Sept. 12, Oct. 31, Nov. 14, 28, and Dec. 5, 1890; quotation from Jan. 2, 1891.

35. Marvin D. Bernstein, *The Mexican Mining Industry, 1890–1950* (Albany: State University of New York Press, 1965), 37. A contemporary discussion of the lead tariff can be found in *MSP*, May 18, 1889, and July 21, 1900.

36. *SCE*, February 27, March 6, April 24, July 3, 1891.

37. Ibid., Dec. 5, 1890; *SCA*, May 15, June 19, July 10, 1891.

38. *SCA*, Oct. 30, 1891; *KWS*, Sept. 29, 1891.

39. Edward L. Doheny to A. B. Fall, Nov. 24, 1925, Rio Grande Collection, box 1, folder 1, Fall Papers, Las Cruces, New Mexico State University.

CHAPTER 2

1. Whitney, *Charles Adelbert Canfield*, 106–7; *SCE*, Oct. 2, 30, Nov. 20, Dec. 25, 1891.

2. See *John Boyle v James P. Welch and E. L. Doheny*, case no. 322, Jan. 18, 1892, RG 21, box 53, Civil Case Files, 1887–1912, National Archives, Pacific Southwest Region, Laguna Niguel, Calif.

3. *MSP*, Apr. 23, 1892; Articles of Incorporation, Pacific Gold and Silver Extracting Company, May 12, 1892, California State Archives, Sacramento, Calif. Rentchler, who still owned several large mines in Kingston, put up half the money himself.

4. *MSP*, Jan. 30, 1892. Reprinted from the *LAH*.

5. *Report on Mineral Industries*, Eleventh Census (1890), 487–91; Lionel Redpath, *Petroleum in California* (Los Angeles: Lionel Redpath, 1900), 37; W. A. Goodyear, "Petroleum, Asphaltum, and Natural Gas," California State Mining Bureau, *Seventh Annual Report of the State Mineralogist* (Sacramento, 1888), 76–79. For an overview of the industry within the context of the overall economic development of California, see Mansel G. Blackford, *The Politics of Business in California, 1890–1920* (Columbus: Ohio State University Press, 1977), chap. 3.

6. Pan American Petroleum & Transport Company, *Mexican Petroleum*, edited by W. J. Archer (New York, 1922), 23.

7. Ward Ritchie, *The Dohenys of Los Angeles*, 15.

8. *LAH*, Nov. 2, 1893; *MSP*, Nov. 14, 1891, 310.

9. The observer was William M. Bohen, who remembered watching them work when he was a boy. See Oil Producers Agency of California, *The Agency Date Book: 100 Years of Events in the California Oil Industry* (Los Angeles: Oil Producers Agency of California, 1946), 87; Whitney, *Charles Adelbert Canfield*, 111. Doheny's

comments are in "Trailing Doheny over Oil and Quicksands," *Current Opinion* 76: 283–84.

10. Whitney, *Charles Adelbert Canfield,* 112–13; Henry B. Ailman, scrapbook, "My Memoirs," 43–45, Silver City Museum, Silver City, N.Mex. An edited version of Ailman's memoirs, including some of his notes about Doheny, is in Helen J. Lundwall, ed., *Pioneering in Territorial Silver City* (Albuquerque: University of New Mexico Press, 1983). Subsequent references to Ailman and Doheny are from Ailman's manuscript.

11. From a reference in the *LAH* for Nov. 2, 1893, this episode took place sometime in Apr. 1893. Doheny bought at least one lot from a Moses W. Bishop for $500; he paid Bishop $70 cash and agreed to pay off the balance at $15 a month until 1894 and $30 a month thereafter. See Deed Book, no. 860, 192, Apr. 6, 1893, Los Angeles County Courthouse. Carrie Doheny later purchased another lot in her own name for $500. See Deed Book, no. 892, 227, Sept. 30, 1893. By 1894, prices for lots in the oil zone had risen to more than $1,000, and, in May 1895, Doheny paid $7,500 for a one-third and a one-sixth interest in two lots on proven oil land. See Deed Book, no. 962, 222; no. 982, 17; no.1005, 174.

12. *LAH,* Nov. 2, 1893.

13. One author stated that, within a year after Doheny put down his discovery well, he had eighty producing wells, with 2,000 more going in around him. See Walter V. Woehlke, "California's Black Gold: The Romance of the Oil Gushers," *Sunset* 25 (Aug. 1910): 180–81. A modern account, which still has "wildcatters [swarming] into Los Angeles" at the first sign of Doheny's work, is in Charles Lockwood, "In the Los Angeles Oil Boom, Derricks Sprouted Like Trees," *Smithsonian* 11 (Oct. 1980): 190. The best treatment of the 1890s is Lionel Redpath, *Petroleum In California* (Los Angeles: Lionel V. Redpath, 1900). For the look of the oil region, itself, see Kenny A. Franks and Paul F. Lambert, *Early California Oil: A Photographic History, 1865–1940* (College Station: Texas A & M University Press, 1985); *LAT,* Oct. 6, 1894.

14. *LAH,* Dec. 25, 1894.

15. See Articles of Incorporation, Metropolitan Oil Company, Oct. 23, 1894. The actual subscribed stock of the company was $100,000, divided among five shareholders.

16. *LAT,* Oct. 6, 20, 9, 1894; *LAH,* Dec. 25, 1894.

17. For examples, see Los Angeles City Records and Archives, City Council, Minutes of Meetings, vol. 40, pp. 545, 546, 568, 594, 644, 691, and vol. 41, pp. 384, 397, 473; quotations are from Petitions, no. 520, 525.

18. See *Frederick J. Gillete et al. v Edward L. Doheny et al.,* case no. 621, Civil Case Files, 1887–1912, RG 21, box 90, Records of the District Courts of the United States, National Archives, Pacific Southwest Region, Laguna Niguel, Calif.

19. *LAT,* Nov. 24, 1894.

20. Ibid., Jan. 4, Apr. 20, 1895.

21. Ibid., July 2, 13, 1895.

22. See Los Angeles City Council, Petition no. 310, Mar. 25, 1895; *LAH*, Sept. 7, 14, 1895. The unspecified difficulty that Doheny encountered using electric motors for drilling oil wells was apparently not solved for many years. See H. Cowan, "Problems Confronting Introduction of Electric Power in the Oil Industry and Its Growth in Use," *OA*, Mar. 1928, 24.

23. Often misspelled as "McGinnis," he might have been the same McGinnis mentioned in W. A. Goodyear's report as an experienced driller in the Los Angeles area in the 1880s. Goodyear, "Petroleum, Asphaltum, and Natural Gas," 78. For a brief note on his later activities with Doheny, see *LAMR* 27 (Mar. 19, 1910): 22–23; for his railroad work, see General Report: "Pacific Land Improvement Company," June 30, 1895, p. 3, file RR 528.7, no. 630, box RR 528, New York Executive Files. "Splinters," vol. 29, 185–87, Santa Fe Railway Archives, Kansas State Historical Society, Topeka, Kans.; *LAH*, Dec. 25, 1895.

24. W. H. Hutchinson, *Oil, Land, and Politics: The California Career of Thomas Robert Bard*, 2 vols. (Norman: University of Oklahoma Press, 1965), 2:75–76; Gerald T. White, *Formative Years in the Far West* (New York: Appleton-Century-Crofts, 1962), 149–50; Glenn D. Bradley, "The Santa Fe's Great California Oil Fields," *Santa Fe Magazine* 10 (Nov. 1916): 23–24. Bradley detailed some of Wade's efforts but did not mention the Union Oil Company at all, stating instead that Wade had been "largely assisted by E. L. Doheny" in procuring a sufficient supply of fuel oil at a competitive price. Another source for Doheny's role in these tests is from an interview with E. O. Faulker, a later vice-president of the Santa Fe's oil company; see *MOB*, July 1923, 560. Gerald White, on the other hand, substantiates a discussion of the Union Oil deal with the Santa Fe through specific letters from Wade to Lyman Stewart, the head of Union Oil; see White, *Formative Years in the Far West*, 616 n. 58. Wade sent reports on his work converting passenger engines to the *Railroad Gazette;* see Jan. 18, 1895. But the whole question of "firsts" with respect to railroads and oil in California is muddled beyond clarification. Caspar Whitney, for example, stated that the earliest known experiment occurred in 1897—which is at least three years too late—and that it was Canfield and his partner, J. A. Chanslor, "who assisted in equipping the locomotive and served as firemen on its trial run." See Whitney, *Charles Adelbert Canfield*, 128–30. The records in the Santa Fe Archives at Topeka have almost no information on any oil activity prior to 1900, and nothing about Wade's early experiments using fuel oil, which suggests that they were not officially sanctioned.

25. *Los Angeles Daily Journal*, Oct. 17, 1894. This article also mentioned a new development undertaken by Maginnis and several other men to lease 115 city lots in the Los Angeles Heights, a half mile above the original oil district, as wildcat properties.

26. *LAT*, May 21, June 10, 1895.

27. Ibid., Dec. 15, 1895.

28. Ibid., Dec. 28, 1895.

29. Ibid., Jan. 14, 1896. Articles of Incorporation, Asphaltum and Oil Refining

Company, Mar. 25, 1896, California State Archives. The company operated independently until it was voluntarily dissolved on Oct. 3, 1922. A full-page advertisement for the company from 1900 is shown in Redpath, *Petroleum in California*, 153. The official 1896 oil report listed the five refineries in the Los Angeles district and their output: Union Oil Co. (400 bbls/day), Asphaltum and Oil Refining Co. (330 bbls), Oil Burning Supply Co. (300 bbls), Puente Oil Co. (200 bbls), and Clark, Johns and Co. (60 bbls). See W. L. Watts, "Oil and Gas Yielding Formations of Los Angeles, Ventura, and Santa Barbara Counties," California State Mining Bureau, Bulletin No. 11 (Dec. 1896), 61.

30. *LAT,* Mar. 14, 1895.

31. *LAH,* Dec. 25, 1894.

32. See Articles of Incorporation, the Producers' Oil Company, Jan. 3, 1895. Seven of the ten largest shareholders were part of the Doheny organization, although several other companies were represented, along with a dozen or so other individual producers.

33. White, *Formative Years in the Far West*, 153–54; "Proposition of the Union Oil Company of California, to the Fuel Oil Producers of Los Angeles," Papers of Thomas Bard, box 5 (first section), Henry E. Huntington Library, San Marino, Calif.; quotation is from the *LAH,* Dec. 25, 1894.

34. *LAH,* June 7, 22, Aug. 31, 1895.

35. Robert E. Hardwicke, "The Rule of Capture and Its Implications as Applied to Oil and Gas," *The Texas Law Review,* vol. 13, no. 4 (1935): 6; *LAT,* Oct. 4, 1895.

36. *LAT,* Oct. 5, 10, 1895.

37. See Articles of Incorporation, Los Angeles Oil Exchange, Aug. 16, 1895, Secretary of State, Sacramento, Calif. A brief biographical sketch of Herron is found in Redpath, *Petroleum in California,* 112. Harold F. Williamson and Arnold R. Daum, *The American Petroleum Industry: The Age of Illumination, 1859–1899* (Evanston: Northwestern University Press, 1959), 564–68.

38. *LAT,* Oct. 3, Dec. 8, 1895.

39. Ibid., Dec. 17, 1895.

40. Ibid., Jan. 21, Feb. 20, July 10, July 13, 1896. White, *Formative Years in the Far West,* 156. The Oil Exchange bought their own 7,000-barrel tank steamer to transport oil up the coast but lost it in a storm after only a few trips. This disaster and internal dissention caused the Exchange to self-destruct in July 1896.

41. *Los Angeles Evening Express,* July 30, 1894.

42. *LAT,* Apr. 13, 1896, p. 5; *LAH,* May 26, Aug. 1, 1896. The furious pace of Doheny's operations is evident from a tangential source, a legal suit filed against him by George Allen, the Pennsylvania oilman who developed a "pumping jack," which allowed up to twenty wells to be pumped simultaneously from one engine. Most local producers replicated Allen's device without acknowledging his patent. When Allen went to Los Angeles to investigate in December 1895, he went after

Doheny as the most conspicuous violator in the field. See *George Allen v E. L. Doheny and S. Connon*, case no. 700, May 23, 1896, RG 21, box 108, Records of the District Courts of the United States, National Archives, Pacific Southwest Region, Laguna Niguel, Calif. For a description and illustration of the process, see California State Mining Bureau, Bulletin No. 11, 62–63.

43. *LAT,* Apr. 13, 1896, Aug. 1, 2, 1896. Doheny and Connon made the agreement on July 28, 1896, and assigned their assets to Morgan for $10. See Deed Book, no. 1109, p. 255, Los Angeles County.

44. "Statement of Edward L. Doheney [*sic*] of the Mexican Oil Co.," Los Angeles, Calif., June 24, 1905, RG 122, Records of the Federal Trade Commission, box 17, General File, 1903–1914, file no. 3220, pt. 4, "Oil Investigation," 2–4. There was a new vice-president of the bank in Apr. 1896, Jackson A. Graves, who was involved in the oil business in the late 1890s, but there is no indication that he opposed Doheny for political or business motives. See Ira B. Cross, *Financing an Empire: History of Banking in California* (Chicago-San Francisco-Los Angeles: S. J. Clarke Publishing Co., 1927), 384–87.

45. Harold F. Taggart, "The Silver Republican Club of Los Angeles," *The Quarterly Historical Society of Southern California* 25 (Sept. 1943): 105–9; *LAH,* July 5, Sept. 10, 1897.

46. *LAT,* Nov. 16, Dec. 7, 14, 1896, Mar. 1, June 14, 1897.

47. Ibid., Mar. 15, 22, Oct. 25, 1897. Deed Book, no. 1215, p. 25, Dec. 21, 1897, Los Angeles County. A later reference from Forbes indicating that Doheny got his company back after two years was obviously mistaken; see Forbes, *Men Who Are Making the West,* 113.

48. See Book of Deeds, no. 1, 163, Orange County Courthouse, Santa Ana, Calif. If they failed to find oil in paying quantities, defined as ten barrels a day, they had to put a minimum of $2,500 on each lease to keep the purchase option alive. The lease required a monthly royalty of at least $50, or one-eighth of the gross product of the wells for each property.

49. Contract between K. H. Wade and Edward L. Doheny, February 12, 1897, RR 258, Contracts, file 466, Archives of the Atchison, Topeka, and Santa Fe Railroad, Kansas State Historical Society, Topeka, Kans. (hereafter cited as ATSF).

50. *LAT,* July 15, Aug. 16; Oct. 25, 1897; *Railroad Gazette,* Mar. 19, 26, 1897.

51. *LAT,* Aug. 15, Sept. 19, 1898, Feb. 20, 1899. W. L. Watts, "Oil and Gas Yielding Formations of California," California State Mining Bureau, Bulletin No. 19 (Nov. 1900), 79–81.

52. See Articles of Incorporation, Brea Cañon Oil Company, July 17, 1899, Secretary of State, Sacramento, Calif.; Redpath, *Petroleum in California,* 84; Watts, "Oil and Gas Yielding Formations in California," Bulletin No. 19, 79.

53. Alfred Howe Davis, "The Romance of California Oil," part 1, *Overland Monthly* 61 (Feb. 1913): 132–34. William Rintoul, *Spudding In: Recollections of Pioneer Days in the California Oil Fields* (San Francisco: California State Historical

Society, 1976), 10–15. The Elwoods actually hired someone to drill the well for them; see F. F. Latta, *Black Gold in the Joaquin* (Caldwell, Idaho: Caxton Printers, 1949), 165–77.

54. See Articles of Incorporation, Petroleum Development Company, May 26, 1899. H. A. Crafts, "California's Newest Oil Fields," *Overland Monthly,* 44 (Nov. 1904): 2. Watts, "Oil and Gas Yielding Formations in California," Bulletin No, 19, 114–15.

55. *DC,* Feb. 9, 1900.

56. See Book of Deeds, no. 25, 336; Book of Deeds, no. 31, 194–95, Orange County Courthouse, Santa Ana, Calif. See, W. B. Jansen to Walker D. Hines, Acting Chairman, April 26, 1909, "Fuel Oil Properties, Oil, California, 1900–1925," RR 36:11, file 19–3a, New York Executive Department Files, ATSF.

57. Ripley to A. F. Walker, Chairman of the Board, "Fullerton Oil Wells—Agreement with E. L. Doheny," Oct. 15, 1900, RR 36:11, file 19–3a, ATSF.

58. Doheny to W. G. Nevin, Oct. 24, 1901, Edward and Estelle Doheny Collection, Archdiocese of Los Angeles, Archival Center, Mission Hills, Calif. (hereafter cited as AALA). Doheny received a cash payment of $261,721.60 at the time of the sale and collected the balance, $577,764.40, in four annual installments through 1906. A copy of the final sales agreement dated April 2, 1902, is in "Petroleum Development Company," RR 116:1, file 647, New York Executive Files, ATSF.

59. *Fond du Lac Daily Commonwealth,* Aug. 19, 25, 1896; *Chicago Daily Tribune,* Aug. 25, 1896; *LAT,* Aug. 25, 1896. For a short description of Barber's career, see *MOB,* July 1923, 566, 626.

60. For a discussion of Los Angeles divorces in this era, see the first few chapters and the appendix of Elaine Tyler May, *Great Expectations: Marriage and Divorce in Post-Victorian America* (Chicago: University of Chicago Press, 1980). A brief report of the wedding appeared in *The Albuquerque Daily Citizen,* Aug. 22, 1900, under the headline "Millionaire Married."

61. For Carrie's death, see "Inquest on the Body of Carrie Doheny," Sept. 27, 1900, Alameda County Coroner's Office, Oakland, California. The official verdict was that her death was caused by "aromatic coma, due to taking poisonous battery fluid, in mistake for medicine, for a cold." The interview with Morgan is from *The San Francisco Call,* Sept. 28, 1900. Another report on the same day in the *Oakland Enquirer* noted that Carrie's nurse, a Miss Rose Ridley, told substantially the same story as Morgan, adding that Carrie's condition was not something that required constant attention. The material she consumed was salammoniac, or ammonium chloride, which was used in galvanizing metal, as a soldering flux, and in dry-cell batteries. It also had some medicinal applications and was sometimes mixed with licorice as a lozenge; see *The New Dictionary of Chemistry* (London: Longmans, Green & Co., 1940), 32–33.

62. The existing letters written between Edward and Estelle are from the early years of their marriage and reveal a lonely and stressful period of adjustment. As Estelle stated on one occasion, she was more than willing to trade in her "jewels-

horses-gowns-home" if she could have Edward come home from Mexico to keep her company; see C. F. Doheny to E. L. Doheny, Oct. 28, 1903, AALA.

CHAPTER 3

1. Mira Wilkins, *The Emergence of Multinational Enterprise: American Business Abroad from the Colonial Era to 1914* (Cambridge: Harvard University Press, 1970), 72, 122–25, 169–72.

2. *San Francisco Daily Morning Call,* May 11, 1865. *American Journal of Science and Arts* 136 (July 1868): 147–48. Niagara quotation cited in "Prospectus of the Boston and Mexican Oil Company (1882)," Papers of Robert G. Cleland, box 2, Huntington Library. Arthur W. Ferguson, "Mexico," *Bureau of the American Republics* 9 (July 1891): 82–83.

3. Frederick Upham Adams, *The Waters Pierce Case in Texas* (St. Louis: Skinner and Kennedy, 1908), 12–13. The details and consequences of Pierce's association with Standard Oil have been outlined in detail in Jonathan C. Brown, *Oil and Revolution in Mexico* (Berkeley and Los Angeles: University of California Press, 1993), 13–25.

4. *MH,* Jan. 28, Mar. 9, 18, 1900.

5. *OGJ,* Oct. 29, 1914, 27. For Robinson's career, see Glenn D. Bradley, "Albert A. Robinson: The Greatest Builder of Them All," *Splinters* 19, 254–73, ATSF. Reprint from the *Santa Fe Magazine* 11 (January 1917).

6. Contract quotation is from an interview with Edward L. Doheny, Jan. 25, 1918, interview no. 45, box K, 1001–3807, DRF. The story of Doheny's first trip in Mexico has been variously retold in a number of places: *Annual Report of the Mexican Petroleum Company* (1912); testimony of Edward L. Doheny, Sept. 1919, IMA, S. Doc 285, 66th Cong., 2nd Sess., 1920, 1: 209–94. The single best work based on these sources and interviews with Herbert G. Wylie is Fritz L. Hoffmann, "Edward L. Doheny and the Beginnings of Petroleum Development in Mexico," *Mid-America* 24 (Apr. 1942): 94–108.

7. Doheny interviews no. 401, Apr. 16, 1918, box K, 101–1000, and no. 503, May 20, 1918, box K, 1001–3807, DRF. *MH,* June 16, 1900.

8. Mexican Petroleum Company, *Annual Report* (1915), 13.

9. Articles of Incorporation, Mexican Petroleum Company, California State Archives. For information on Nevin and Kenna, see *The National Cyclopedia of American Biography,* vol. 14, 279, and vol. 6, 144, respectively. For Waters, see *The Biographical Dictionary of the American Congress, 1774–1971* (Washington, D.C.: Government Printing Office, 1971), 1886–87.

10. *MH,* May 6, 15, Sept. 13, 1901.

11. The company had to begin work within six months, drill at least twenty wells within two years' time, build transportation facilities to get the oil to market, spend at least $200,000 in the general expenses of the business, and invest at least $50,000 a year operating the business and a total of $600,000 over the life of the

concession. See *MH,* May 19, 1901; Mexican Petroleum Company, *Annual Report* (1912), 3; Doheny interview no. 503, 5, DRF.

12. Doheny interview no. 503, 5–7, DRF.

13. *NYT,* Mar. 29, Apr. 1, 16, May 2, 1901.

14. The observation about Pierce is in Allan Nevins, *Study in Power: John D. Rockefeller, Industrialist and Philanthropist* (New York, Charles Scribner's Sons, 1953), 41–42. *NYT,* Nov. 17, 1901.

15. *MH,* Aug. 10, 1901.

16. Ibid., Aug. 28, 1901.

17. Ibid., Oct. 6, Dec. 7, 1901.

18. Ibid., Dec. 9, 1901.

19. IMA, 1: 225.

20. R. C. Kerens to Doheny, July 20, 1902, AALA.

21. For Kerens' New Mexico properties, see *MSP,* Feb. 9, 1889, Aug. 23, 1890. Biographical information is from *National Cyclopedia of Biography,* vol. 31, 408. *MH,* May 25, 1901; Kerens to Doheny, July 20, 1902, AALA.

22. *MH,* Feb. 9, 16, 20, Apr. 11, 1900.

23. Ibid., Feb. 19, Apr. 11, 1900.

24. Ibid., May 15, 1902.

25. *NYT,* Dec. 29, 30, 31, 1901, Jan. 3, 1902. *MH,* Jan. 7, 1902. The promotional schemes behind the formation of the Asphalt Trust of America in 1899 have also been interpreted as being among the most fraudulent investment deals of the era. See Lewis W. Haney, *Business Organization and Combination* (New York: Macmillan, 1934), 333–35.

26. Articles of Incorporation, Mexican Asphalt Paving and Construction Company, California State Archives. With a dozen shareholders, the company started work with $48,000 of initial capital.

27. Fairchild and Gilmore to E. L. Doheny, July 1, 1902; Ezequiel Ordonez to Doheny, October 6, 1902, AALA. E. W. Gilmore was the president of the Mexican Asphalt and Paving Company at the time. See *MH,* Oct. 16, 1902.

28. *MH,* Aug. 3, 1902.

29. Ibid., Oct. 16, 17, 1902.

30. Wylie to Charles E. Harwood, January 23, 1903, AALA.

31. Wylie to Doheny, January 13, 22, 1903, AALA.

32. *MH,* Apr. 12, 1903.

33. Ibid., Sept. 3, Oct. 25, Nov. 2, 1901, Mar. 30, 1903.

34. Ibid., Sept. 22, 23, 1901. "Interview with Mr. S. W. Smith," no. 596, box I: 2000–2701, file 2498–2603, DRF.

35. Ibid., Jan. 13, 1902.

36. Interview with Edward L. Doheny, no. 45, DRF; IMA, 1: 213.

37. Robert Freeman Smith, *The United States and Revolutionary Nationalism in Mexico, 1916–1932* (Chicago: University of Chicago Press, 1972), 5–6; Friedrich

Katz, *The Secret War in Mexico* (Chicago: University of Chicago Press, 1981), 27–29. Doheny quotation from interview no. 503, DRF.

38. *MH*, Dec. 4, 1902. To modern critics of America's role in Mexico, Doheny's dominance of the oil industry has been singled out for special retribution. See Gabriel Antonio Menendez, *Doheny el Cruel: Episodios de la sangrienta lucha por el petroleo mexicano* (Mexico City: Ediciones "Bolsa Mexicana del Libro," 1958); Gene Hanrahan, *The Bad Yankee: American Entrepreneurs and Financiers in Mexico* (Chapel Hill, University of North Carolina Press, 1985); Dan La Botz, *Edward L. Doheny: Petroleum, Power, and Politics in the United States and Mexico* (New York: Praeger Press, 1991).

39. *MH*, March 7, 1904. Moran was a federal deputy for District 7 in Jalisco from 1898–1906. Also see Roderic A. Camp, *Mexican Political Biographies, 1884–1935* (Austin: University of Texas Press, 1991), 317, 332.

40. *MH*, Feb. 9, 1904, Oct. 5, 1906; Doheny interview no. 503, DRF.

41. *MH*, June 23, 1903, December 25, 1904; Doheny interview no. 45, January 25, 1918, box K, 1001–3807, DRF.

42. *MH*, Feb. 28, May 3, Aug. 10, 1904, Nov. 3, 1905, Nov. 19, 1906, Jan. 22, 1908.

43. Ibid., Feb. 21, 1904.

44. Ibid., Dec. 25, 1904, June 5, 1908.

45. *NYT*, Aug. 10, Nov. 30, 1902, Aug. 23, 1903, May 15, 1904; *Poor's Manual of Railroads*, 1900–1905 (New York: H. V. & H. W. Poor).

46. *NYT*, Sept. 4, 1904.

47. Desmond Young, *Member for Mexico* (London: Cassell & Co., 1966), 119–22. Pearson even hired Anthony F. Lucas, the man who drilled in the Spindletop well, to investigate his oil properties for him. See *MH*, Feb. 25, Mar. 30, Oct, 3, 1904.

48. *MH*, Mar. 30, 1904, Feb. 28, 1905.

49. M. Martinez del Rio to Doheny, October 23, 1902; F. B. McKercher to Doheny, June 5, 1903, AALA.

50. *MH*, Oct. 11, 21, 1904.

51. Marvin D. Bernstein, *The Mexican Mining Industry: 1890–1950* (Albany: State University of New York Press, 1964), 35–36; *MH*, June 2, 1905, Oct. 16, 1907.

52. *MH*, June 14, 1904.

53. Ibid., Apr. 20, 1904. The board of directors' certificate authorizing the issue of bonds on June 10, 1904, is filed with the Articles of Incorporation for the Mexican Petroleum Company.

54. *MH*, June 26, 1904.

55. Ibid., Jan. 6, 1905. Topping is the process of taking off successive layers of vapor when crude oil is heated in a still.

56. Ibid., Jan. 24, Feb. 15, Mar. 6, 29, 30, Apr. 25, 1905.

57. Ibid., May 5, 1905.

58. Ibid., June 11, July 10, 1905.

59. Ibid., Sept. 13, Oct. 1, Oct. 14, 1906.

60. According to company history, Doheny signed the initial contract with the Mexican Central on May 10, 1905, for 6,000 bbls/day. See Pan American Petroleum & Transport Company, *Mexican Petroleum*, 52. But as reported in the railway press at the time, the Mexican Central did not commit to using oil until November 1905, when it contracted for the full amount. See *Railroad Gazette*, Nov. 24, 1905; *COW*, Apr. 29, 1909; H. L. Wood, "Oil Fields of Mexico," *OA*, Apr. 21, 1911, p. 3.

61. *Railroad Gazette*, Dec. 21, 1906. The *WSJ* information was recorded in the *MH*, Nov. 7, 1907.

62. T. W. Osterheld, "History of the Nationalization of the Railroads of Mexico," *Journal of the American Bankers Association* (May 1916): 3. Fred Wilbur Powell, *The Railroads of Mexico* (Boston: Stratford Co., 1921), 4–6, 131.

63. Mexican Petroleum Company, *Annual Report* (1913), 5; IMA, 1:236.

64. *MH*, Aug. 4, 1905.

65. Ibid., Dec. 23, 1905.

66. Joseph E. Pogue, *The Economics of Petroleum* (New York: John Wiley & Sons, 1921), 300–303, 326–27. I. C. White, "Report and Appraisal: Properties of the Mexican Petroleum Co., Ltd.," Dec. 21, 1911, 10–11 (copy located in the Science Library at Southern Methodist University, Dallas, Tex.). The officers of the gas company were as follows: E. L. Doheny, president; C. A. Canfield, first vice-president; H. C. Miner of Los Angeles, secretary and treasurer. The remaining directors included E. P. Ripley, president of the Santa Fe Railroad; E. C. Bradley, manager of the Pacific Telegraph and Telephone Company; W. L. Hardin of Los Angeles; and Harold Walker. See *MH*, Nov. 24, 1906, Nov. 25, 1907, Apr. 2, 1909.

67. *MH*, June 23, July 16, Aug. 31, Dec. 25, 1909, May 6, May 13, 1910.

68. Ezequiel Ordonez, "The Oil Fields of Mexico," *Transactions of the American Institute of Mining Engineers* 50 (1915): 865–67; *OGJ*, Oct. 29, 1914.

69. Pan American Petroleum & Transport Company, *Mexican Petroleum*, 28–29; Mexican Petroleum Company, *Annual Report* (1912).

70. *MH*, June 12, 16, 1908.

71. Ibid., Aug. 23, 1909, Sept. 20, 1910; *OA*, Dec. 30, 1910. When the Mexican government tabulated its grievances against the oil companies in the late 1930s, it cited the abandonment of the Mexico City pipeline as one example of bad faith. See *Mexico's Oil* (Mexico City: Government of Mexico, 1940), xxxi–xxxii, 93.

72. *MH*, July 26, Sept. 20, 1908.

73. Ibid., Jan. 12, Dec. 12, 1909.

74. Ibid, Aug. 27, Sept. 20, 1910; Pan American Petroleum & Transport Company, *Mexican Petroleum*, 31; White, "Report and Appraisal," 8–12; Mexican Petroleum Company, *Annual Report* (1912), 4–5. A well is shut in when the control valves are closed to stop or reduce the flow of oil.

75. *OGJ*, Oct. 20, 1910, p. 20.

76. *OIJ*, Feb. 20, 1909, p. 18; *MH*, Mar. 16, Apr. 18, 1909.

77. *OIJ*, Oct. 20, 1909, p. 18. Doheny quotation from *COW*, Apr. 29, 1909.

78. *NYT*, June 6, 26, 1909; *COW*, June 10, 1909.

79. Statistics compiled from *Mexico's Oil*, 18; White, "Report and Appraisal," 11.

80. *MH*, Mar. 27, 1910.

81. Ibid., June 11, 1908, Aug. 15, 1909.

82. *OIJ*, Dec. 6, 1909, p. 28; *The Petroleum Review*, July 17, 1909, p. 37; *MH*, Mar. 27, June 17, 1909. The remaining oil lands and refining south of Veracruz remained under the name of S. Pearson & Son but would henceforth be devoted to the export trade to Europe and would have no connection to the Mexican retail market except through the refinery and as a stockholder in the new company.

83. *MH*, Apr. 23, 1904, June 11, 1908.

84. Ibid., Nov. 25, 1909.

85. Everette Lee DeGolyer, "The Oil Fields of Mexico: With Particular Reference to the Tampico-Tuxpan Region" (chief geologist's report for the Mexican Eagle Oil Co., July 1, 1916), 19–20. (A bound copy is in the Science Library at SMU.) White, "Report and Appraisal," 11.

86. *OGJ*, Oct. 29, 1914, p. 27.

87. *OA*, May 5, 1911, p. 17.

88. *COW*, June 15, 1911.

CHAPTER 4

1. Keith L. Bryant Jr., ed., *Encyclopedia of American Business History and Biography: Railroads in the Age of Regulation, 1900–1980* (New York: Bruccoli Clark Layman, 1988), 371; Bryant, *History of the Atchison, Topeka and Santa Fe Railway*, 200–205. For a recent analysis of the railroad business, which is highly critical of the management decisions made by Ripley and other leading executives, see Gregory Thompson, *The Passenger Train in the Motor Age: California's Rail and Bus Industries, 1910–1941* (Columbus: Ohio State University Press, 1993), 58–62.

2. "Statement of Edward L. Doheny [sic] of the Mexican Oil Co., Los Angeles, Calif., June 24, 1905," RG 122, box 17 (1903–1914), file no. 3220, pt. 4, "Oil Investigation," p. 4, Bureau of Corporations, Records of the Federal Trade Commission, National Archives, Washington, D.C.

3. Ibid.; Earl M. Welty and Frank J. Taylor, *The 76 Bonanza: The Fabulous Life and Times of the Union Oil Company of California* (Menlo Park, Calif.: Lane Magazine & Book Co., 1966), 135, 138.

4. *DC*, July 23, 1900.

5. Ibid., Sept. 4, 1900.

6. Ibid., Aug. 11, Sept. 3, 1900.

7. Arthur M. Johnson, "California and the National Oil Industry," *Pacific Historical Review* 39 (May 1970): 157–58. In the same issue, devoted to oil in the western United States, see Ralph Andreano, "The Structure of the California Petro-

leum Industry, 1895–1911," 171–92; for more detail, see Andreano's "The Emergence of New Competition in the American Petroleum Industry Before 1911" (Ph.D. diss., Northwestern University, 1960), chap. 5. In a section on the early development of the Kern River oilfield, Gerald White discusses his belief that, at least for the early 1900s, Standard's actions "[did] not reveal a determination to force a dictatorship upon the industry. If it did entertain such an ambition, it was doomed to disappointment." See Gerald T. White, *Formative Years in the Far West* (New York: Meredith Publishing Co., 1962), 238.

8. "Statement of C. A. Canfield, Los Angeles, Calif., June 23, 1905," RG 122, box 17 (1903–1914), file no. 3220, pt. 4, p. 7, Bureau of Corporations, Records of the Federal Trade Commission, National Archives, Washington, D.C.

9. *DC,* Sept. 7, 20, 24, 1900. Articles of Incorporation, Producers' Oil, Storage, and Transportation Company, Secretary of State, California State Archives.

10. *LAT,* Oct. 31, 1901; White, *Formative Years in the Far West,* 229–33; *DC,* May 7, 1901; Federal Trade Commission, *Report on the Pacific Coast Petroleum Industry,* pt. 1 (Washington: Government Printing Office, 1921), 101–2; Andreano, "The Emergence of New Competition," 273–76.

11. E. P. Ripley to Victor Morawetz, May 6, 1904, RR 36:11, file 19–3a, "Fuel Oil Properties, California, 1900–1925," New York Executive Department Files, ATSF.

12. Ripley to Morawetz, Nov. 23, 1904, RR 50:2, file 513–4, ATSF. Harriman paid 37½ cents a share when the market price was 18 cents. Supposedly, according to Ripley, the oil stock was structured so that Harriman could not achieve working control of the company.

13. Don L. Hofsommer, *The Southern Pacific, 1901–1985* (College Station, Texas A & M University Press, 1986), 113–14. During the 1910s, the federal government tried to regain control of much of this undeveloped property in its bid to secure a strategic oil reserve in California, plunging the company into a decade-long legal battle over the issue.

14. Maury Klein, *Union Pacific: The Rebirth, 1894–1969* (New York, Doubleday, 1989), 91, 119–22; Bryant, *History of the Atchison, Topeka, and Santa Fe Railway,* 186. In 1906, Harriman made some heavy investments in competitors' stock, which included a $10.4 million (7.61%) purchase of Santa Fe preferred stock. See Klein, *Union Pacific,* 167.

15. E. P. Ripley to Victor Morawetz (Chairman of the Executive Committee), Nov. 21, 1903, Feb. 15, 1904, Mar. 2, 1904, RR 36:11, file 19–3a, ATSF.

16. Ibid., Feb. 15, 1904.

17. Ibid., Nov. 21, 28, 1904; Victor Morawetz to E. P. Ripley, Apr. 13, 1905, RR 50.2, file 513–4, ATSF.

18. E. P. Ripley to D. L. Gallup, July 29, 1905, RR 50.2, file 513–4, ATSF.

19. Ibid. The principal stockholders of the Midway Oil Company were also officers and stockholders of the Mexican Petroleum Company. When the first half of the company changed hands, Canfield and his California partner, J. A. Chanslor,

received $195,140, H. M. McIntosh received $77,575, and E. T. Stimson received $26,807. McIntosh and Stimson were also original directors of Mexican Petroleum. See contract between H. M. McIntosh and C. A. Canfield and the Atchison, Topeka, and Santa Fe Railway, Feb. 24, 1905, RR 270, file 830, New York Executive Department Files, ATSF. *OGJ,* Aug. 11, 1910, p. 10.

20. *Report of the Commissioner of Corporations on the Transportation of Petroleum* (Washington: Government Printing Office, 1906), 396.

21. E. P. Ripley to Victor Morawetz, May 6, 1904, RR 36:11, file 19–3a, ATSF. Bryant, *History of the Atchison, Topeka, and Santa Fe,* 210–11.

22. *Report of the Federal Trade Commission on the Pacific Coast Petroleum Industry,* Production, Ownership, and Profits, pt. 1 (Washington: Government Printing Office, 1921), 52.

23. White, *Formative Years in the Far West,* 262. "Minutes of the Board of Directors," Sept. 2, 1907; February 12, 1908; February 20, 1908, IOPA.

24. Whitney, *Charles Adelbert Canfield,* 144, 200.

25. For a brief biographical sketch, see *LAMR,* Mar. 5, 1910. O'Donnell's early experiences in Los Angeles are mentioned in Guy W. Finney, *Mericos H. Whittier* (n.p., 1940), 46–56.

26. John S. McGroarty, ed., *History of Los Angeles County* (Chicago and New York: American Historical Society, 1923), 3–4. Frederic Cople Jaher, *The Urban Establishment: Upper Strata in Boston, New York, Charleston, Chicago, and Los Angeles* (Urbana: University of Illinois Press, 1982), 636. *LAMR,* Mar. 19, 1910.

27. Norman Bridge, *The Marching Years* (New York: Duffield & Co., 1920), 206–15.

28. *MOB,* Feb. 1923, pp. 104, 106.

29. Incorporation dates were as follows: American Petroleum Company, Feb. 5, 1908; Niles Lease Oil Company, Feb. 6, 1908; American Oilfields Company, Jan. 6, 1910; Midland Oilfields Company, originally incorporated in Delaware on Feb. 9, 1910, and registered in California on Apr. 12, 1910, with Norman Bridge as the designated attorney for the company. The American Petroleum Company was capitalized for $10 million dollars with five directors: E. L. Doheny, C. Estelle Doheny, Norman Bridge, Charles Wellborn, and I. C. Rolph. The stated capital stock of the company was $500, or one share apiece for each director. The American Oilfields Company had a capitalization of $25 million, with $700 of capital stock divided equally between seven directors: E. L. Doheny, C. A. Canfield, J. C. Anderson, T. A. O'Donnell, J. M. Danzinger, Norman Bridge, and L. A. McCray. The smaller companies were capitalized at $1 million, with as little as $5 of capital stock. The officers were the same for all of these companies, with O'Donnell as the president and Bridge as the secretary-treasurer.

30. *COW,* Apr. 8, 1909.

31. Ibid., Oct. 20, 1908. Specifically, Doheny's contract called for the delivery of 2,000 barrels per day in 1909, 4,000 in 1910, and 5,000 for 1911–13.

32. For production and consumption figures, see California State Council of

Defense, *Report of the Committee on Petroleum* (Sacramento: California State Print-ing Office, 1917), 80. Crude oil prices are from *Mineral Resources,* 1913, pt. 2, p. 1067. *Report of the Federal Trade Commission on the Pacific Coast Petroleum In-dustry,* pt. 2, p. 236.

33. *COW,* June 17, 1909; *OA,* Feb. 4, 1910.

34. IOPA Minutes, June 23, 25, 1909, Apr. 14, 1910. California State Mining Bureau, *Petroleum Industry of California* 69 (Oct. 1914): 83.

35. *COW,* June 17, 24, 1909.

36. *Mineral Resources,* 1910, pt. 2, pp. 415–16; *COW,* June 16, 1910; *OGJ,* June 23, 1910.

37. William Rintoul, *Spudding In,* 109–13. Bridge's statement appeared in a reprint of his treasurer's report for Sept. 7, 1910. See *OA,* Sept. 16, 1910. The pro-duction figures for the American Oilfields Company have been extrapolated from the information contained in this same report.

38. *Mineral Resources,* 1910, pt. 2, pp. 419–20.

39. IOPA, Minutes of Directors' Meeting, Apr. 15, 1910, p. 100; *Book of Assign-ments,* book 22, pp. 98–101, Kern County Recorder, Bakersfield, Calif.; *COW,* May 26, 1910.

40. Agency quote from *COW,* Mar. 31, 1910. Articles of Incorporation, California-Arizona Pipe-Line Company, California State Archives. The company was capitalized at $25 million and had eleven directors who invested $1,000 apiece in the initial enterprise. The Doheny interests took up six of those positions: Do-heny, Norman Bridge, Charles Canfield, T. A. O'Donnell, J. M. Danzinger, and Charles Wellborn.

41. IOPA, Minutes of the Executive Committee, Feb. 28, May 9, 1912.

42. Ibid., June 14, 1911.

43. Ibid., Dec. 28, 1910. For example, in April 1911, Doheny secured an inter-est in a pipeline being constructed from the Midway field to the coast by the Guar-anty Oil Company, intending to market oil from the two subsidiaries, which were technically free to sell their production outside the Agency. This line would have been a direct competitor with the pipeline of the Producers Transportation Com-pany, a joint effort between the Agency and Union Oil. See Welty, *The 76 Bo-nanza,* 147–48.

CHAPTER 5

1. *OA,* Apr. 7, 1911.

2. *FOJ,* Nov. 1911, pp. 12–17, Dec. 1911, pp. 13–21.

3. E. DeGolyer, "Production of Petroleum in Mexico in 1912," *Mineral Re-sources,* 1912, pt. 2 (Washington, D.C.: Government Printing Office, 1913), 468–72. DeGolyer's experiences in Mexico, including locating the famous Potrero gusher, are detailed in Lon Tinkle, *Mr. De: A Biography of Everette Lee DeGolyer* (Boston: Little, Brown & Co., 1970).

4. Compiled from *The Mexico Year Book* (London: McCorquodale & Co., 1914), 82–90.

5. *OA,* June 9, 1911, p. 7; *OGJ,* July 6, 1911, p. 1, Mar. 21, 1912, p. 1.

6. White, *Report and Appraisal of the Properties of the Mexican Petroleum Company,* 15–16. The National Railways of Mexico took 10,000 bbls/day; Standard Oil, 6,000 bbls/day; Waters-Pierce Refinery, 3,900 bbls/day; Santa Fe Railway, 2,500 bbls/day; Gulf Refining Company, 2,000 bbls/day; Mexican Asphalt Paving and Construction Company, 2,000 bbls/day; and Mexican National Gas Company, 250 bbls/day. See Herbert Wylie, "Contract of Mexican and Huasteca Petroleum Companies," Cleland Papers, box 201; Mexican Petroleum Company, *Annual Report* (1915), 19.

7. See "Certificate as to Increase of Bonded Indebtedness of the Mexican Petroleum Company," Oct. 18, 1910, California State Archives; *FOJ,* Jan.–Feb. 1912, pp. 11–12.

8. Ruth Sheldon Knowles, *The Greatest Gamblers: The Epic of American Oil Exploration* (Norman: University of Oklahoma Press, 1978), 44–104 passim.

9. Sam T. Mallison, *The Great Wildcatter* (Charleston: Education Foundation of West Virginia, Inc., 1953), 102, 233. Mallison's biography of Mike Benedum was based on extensive interviews with the subject in the 1950s, some of which are contained in *The Reminiscences of Michael L. Benedum* (1951), in the Oral History Collection of Columbia University. Mallison's account is interesting, but the information is unreliable without corroboration.

10. *The Reminiscences of Michael L. Benedum,* 55–56; Mallison, *The Great Wildcatter,* 233, 235; Moody, *Moody's Mining and Oil Companies: 1911* (New York: Moody Manual Company), 3712.

11. Mexican Petroleum Company, *Annual Report* (1912), 5; *Reminiscences of Michael L. Benedum,* 56–57.

12. Mexican Petroleum Company, *Annual Report* (1912), 6.

13. Wylie, "Contract of Mexican and Huasteca Petroleum Companies"; *OA,* Oct. 21, 1910, 15.

14. E. P. Ripley to Walker D. Hines, May 23, 1911, RR 36:10, file 19–3, "Fuel Properties, Oil, General: 1906–1924," New York Executive Department Files, ATSF. Previously, in 1903, the Santa Fe tried to get a permanent source of oil for the Gulf Coast railway by purchasing oil land in Texas and Oklahoma. After spending almost a million dollars by 1908 to develop the properties, the company had yet see any appreciable oil. See RR 36:10, file 19–3, "Oil Properties," unsigned report, Jan. 20, 1909; and W. B. Jansen to W. D. Hines, April 1909, 8–10.

15. *Reminiscences of Michael L. Benedum,* 57; *Moody's Analyses of Investments* (New York: Moody's Investors Service, 1919), 1676.

16. A small amount of Mexpet stock had been circulating in Los Angeles for years and was traded at about $29 a share on the regional exchange; the company sold 26,357 shares in 1910. Since Benedum and Trees received 5,000 shares of common stock as a bonus with their preferred stock, there would have been at least

21,357 shares sold that year, worth about $600,000. See *Moody's Mining and Oil Companies*, 1909, 3712, and 1910, 3343; Mallison, *The Great Wildcatter*, 237; *OGJ*, Oct. 20, 1910, p. 20; *OA*, Mar. 31, 1911, p. 16; *COW*, Apr. 6, 1911, p. 7; *Moody's Mining and Oil Companies*, 1911, 3712; Mexican Petroleum Company, *Annual Report* (1912), 6.

17. Ralph Arnold, "Appraisal of the Physical Properties of the Mexican Petroleum Co. Ltd. of Delaware," Aug. 26, 1911, box 201, Arnold Papers, Huntington Library. Doheny's letter to William Salomon & Co., dated September 7, 1911, is appended to the copy of Arnold's report.

18. For a comment on White's career, see Samuel W. Tait Jr., *The Wildcatters: An Informal History of Oil Hunting in America* (Princeton: Princeton University Press, 1946), 79–83. White, "Report and Appraisal," 14–18; *Mexican Petroleum*, 36.

19. *Pan American Record*, vol. 2 (Sept. 1917), 7; *Mexican Petroleum*, 35; Vincent Carosso, *Investment Banking in America* (Cambridge: Harvard University Press, 1970), 140–41; *NYT*, July 6, 1917.

20. *WSJ*, Apr. 22, 29, 1912.

21. A classic study of this period is Charles C. Cumberland, *Mexican Revolution: Genesis under Madero* (Austin: University of Texas Press, 1952). The most comprehensive recent discussion is in Alan Knight, *The Mexican Revolution: Porfirians, Liberals, and Peasants*, vol. 1 (Cambridge, Cambridge University Press, 1986). For one of the first attacks on Standard Oil, see Alfred Henry Lewis, "The Maligners of Mexico," *Cosmopolitan Magazine* 48 (March 1910): 432d-e.

22. P. De Medici, "Mexican Pete in Wall Street," *United States Investor*, May 11, 1912, reprinted in *FOJ*, June 1912, p. 19.

23. *OA*, June 9, 1911, p. 13; Jan. 5, 1912, p. 11; Apr. 5, 1912, p. 11.

24. Ibid., May 24, 1912, p. 2.

25. Ibid., May 24, 1912, p. 11; June 7, 1912, p. 9.

26. Ibid., Sept. 6, 1912, p. 11; Sept. 20, 1912, pp. 11–12.

27. Knight, *The Mexican Revolution*, vol. 1, 480–90.

28. Annual tax rates, as a percentage of total oil sales of the Mexican Petroleum Company, reveal this escalating process during the early years of the revolution: 3.7% (1912), 9.9% (1913), 19% (1914), 30.8% (1915), 25.8% (1916), 15.8% (1917). See Mexican Petroleum Company, *Annual Report* (1913–1917); Moody, *Industrials*, 1912–1917; *FOJ*, June 1913, pp. 6, 40.

29. *FOJ*, Oct. 1912, p. 8; *NYT*, Nov., 4, 7, 13, 1913; *OA*, May 1, 1914, p. 8.

30. *FOJ*, June 1913, 1, p. 6; Apr. 1914, p. 6.

31. Arthur S. Link, *Woodrow Wilson and the Progressive Era, 1910–1917* (New York: Harper and Row, 1954), 109.

32. Douglas W. Richmond, "Carranza: The Authoritarian Populist as Nationalist President," in George Wolfskill and Douglas W. Richmond, eds., *Essays on the Mexican Revolution* (Austin: University of Texas Press, 1979), 48–52.

33. S. G. Blythe, "Mexico: The Record of a Conversation with President Wilson," *Saturday Evening Post* 186 (May 23, 1914): 2–4; Robert E. Quirk, *An Affair of*

Honor: Woodrow Wilson and the Occupation of Veracruz (Lexington: University Press of Kentucky, 1962), 46–112 passim; Brown, *Oil and Revolution in Mexico,* 190–99.

34. "Statement of John I. Newell," *Congressional Record,* 63d Cong., 2d sess., 1914, 51, pt. 9:8965–66; another statement signed by 372 refugees quarantined in Galveston is pt. 8:8232–33.

35. *FOJ,* July 1914, p. 8.

36. Quirk, *An Affair of Honor,* 156–71; Knight, *The Mexican Revolution,* vol. 2, 152–62.

37. Blythe, "Mexico," 4.

38. Mexican Petroleum Company, *Annual Report* (1913), 13–14. For a recent reappraisal of the impact of foreign business in Latin America, which confirms Doheny's assertion that the foreign investor was often at the mercy of the native landowner, see Stanley Lebergott, "The Return to U.S. Imperialism, 1890–1929," *The Journal of Economic History* 15 (June 1980): 245–46.

39. Bernstein, *The Mexican Mining Industry,* 84–91; Mexican Petroleum Company, *Annual Report* (1913), 14; *OA,* Sept. 20, 1912, p. 6.

40. For a recent discussion that attempts to balance the extremes of labor theory, revolutionary ideology, and objective reality, see Brown, *Oil and Revolution in Mexico,* 323–36. Another account, which idealizes the social condition of the agricultural workers before they went to work for the oil companies but provides a clear description of the culture shock encountered on the job, is Lief Adelson, "The Cultural Roots of the Oil Workers' Unions in Tampico, 1910–1925," in *The Mexican Petroleum Industry in the Twentieth Century,* eds. Jonathan C. Brown and Alan Knight (Austin: University of Texas Press, 1992), 36–57.

41. Porfirio Díaz, Jr., to E. L. Doheny, undated letter, AALA. At the time, in late 1914 or early 1915, Díaz's 508 shares of Mexpet preferred, at around $80 a share, were worth at least $40,000.

42. All figures here and below are from the 1912–1915 annual reports, except for the export totals for 1915, which are compiled from the monthly reports of the *FOJ.*

43. Mexican Petroleum Company, *Annual Report* (1914), 17; *FOJ,* Apr. 1915, p. 28.

44. The large mining companies followed a similar pattern over this same period, as they experienced at least a 50 percent reduction in mineral production in 1914 and 1915. But they did not have the same opportunity as the oil companies to continue exporting from stocks on hand. Thus, after failing to make any earnings and eliminating their stock dividends, only those enterprises with the largest cash reserves were able to ride out the storm until 1917. See Bernstein, *The Mexican Mining Industry,* 100–105.

45. *COW,* Feb. 5, 1915, p. 2.

46. *FOJ,* Jan.–Feb. 1912, p. 12.

47. Ibid., Mar. 1912, pp. 7, 23.

48. Ibid., May 1912, p. 19; Mexican Petroleum Company, *Annual Report* (1914), 21; *Mexpet Record* 1 (Nov. 1915): 7.

49. *Mexpet Record* 1 (Nov. 1915): 3–13.

50. Mexican Petroleum Company, *Annual Report* (1914), 27; *FOJ*, June 1915, p. 3.

51. *FOJ*, June 1915, p. 5.

52. Mexican Petroleum Company, *Annual Report* (1914), 29–30.

53. Ibid., 33.

54. Pogue, *The Economics of Petroleum*, 153–57. According to Pogue, the U.S. merchant marine was substantially an oil-burning fleet by 1920. John Ise, *United States Oil Policy* (New Haven: Yale University Press, 1926), 157–60. Williamson and Daum, *The American Petroleum Industry*, 181–85.

55. U.S. Department of the Navy, *Report of the U.S. Naval Liquid Fuel Board* (Washington: Government Printing Office, 1904), 389–435. Also see "Fuel Oil in the Navy: Its Present Use and Future Possibilities," *OGJ*, Nov. 24, 1910, pp. 9–11; *FOJ*, Nov. 1913, p. 9. For an overview of official policy regarding the conversion to fuel oil, see John A. DeNovo, "Petroleum and the United States Navy before World War I," *Mississippi Valley Historical Review* 41 (June 1954–Mar. 1955): 641–56.

56. To promote the use of fuel oil for all types of ships, Cowdray published an article compiling the performance advantages of oil over coal. See Lord Cowdray, "Mexican Fuel Oil and Its Application to Marine Propulsion," *The Petroleum Review* (London), Oct. 30, 1915, 357–58. *FOJ*, Apr. 1912, p. 17, Aug. 1912, p. 7.

57. Geoffrey Jones, *The State and the Emergence of the British Oil Industry* (London: Macmillan, 1981), 74–76, 154–155; Friedrich Katz, *The Secret War in Mexico: Europe, the United States, and the Mexican Revolution* (Chicago: University of Chicago Press, 1981), 173–74; *FOJ*, Nov. 1914, p. 4.

58. *United States Naval Institute Proceedings* 40 (Mar.–Apr. 1914): 577–78.

59. For information on the withdrawal suits, see *Report of the Committee on Petroleum*, 38–65.

CHAPTER 6

1. To take advantage of certain tax or business provisions for reasons that are no longer apparent, the company was incorporated in Virginia; see Incorporation Papers, California Petroleum Corporation, California State Archives. Also see *Moody's Analysis of Investments*, 1913, 1058–59. For a discussion of the potential legal, tax, and stockholding advantages of such arrangements, see James C. Bonbright and Gardiner C. Means, *The Holding Company: Its Public Significance and Its Regulation* (New York: McGraw-Hill, 1932), chaps. 2–4.

2. See House Committee on Banking and Currency, "Testimony of Mr. George Henry," vol. 2, *Money Trust Investigation: Investigation of Financial and Monetary Conditions in the United States, under H. R. nos. 429 and 504, before a*

Subcommittee of the Committee on Banking and Currency, 3 vols. (Washington, D.C.: Government Printing Office, 1913), 1253–85 passim.

3. Ralph Arnold, "Report on the Properties of the California Petroleum Corporation," Apr. 9, 1912, box 176, Arnold Papers.

4. *Money Trust Investigation*, "Testimony of Frederick Lewisohn," Vol. 1, 925, 940, "Testimony of Mr. George Henry," 1284; *WSJ*, Oct. 9, 1912; *NYT*, Jan. 8, 1913; John T. Flynn, *Security Speculation: Its Economic Effects* (New York: Harcourt, Brace & Company, 1934), 180–82.

5. For a description of Untermeyer, see Carosso, *Investment Banking in America*, 137–39; Ron Chernow, *The House of Morgan: An American Banking Dynasty and the Rise of Modern Finance* (New York: Simon & Schuster, 1990), 54–55; *Money Trust Investigation*, vol. 2, 1282–87, vol. 3, 42–45, 50–52. For a discussion of Untermeyer's role in the investigation, see James Grant, *Money of the Mind: Borrowing and Lending in America from the Civil War to Michael Milken* (New York: Noonday Press, 1992), 124–35.

6. *Money Trust Investigation*, vol. 2, exhibit 88, 1146.

7. *COW*, "Gossip of the Petroleocrats," Oct. 17, 1914.

8. California State Mining Bureau, *Petroleum Industry of California* 69 (Oct. 1914): 29, 37–39, 41–42.

9. It had been the future value of this strategic mix of properties which most impressed Ralph Arnold when he appraised the company; see "Report on the Properties of the California Petroleum Corporation," 5–6.

10. Mark L. Requa, "Address at Bakersfield," July 1914, box 2, p. 4, Mark L. Requa Papers, American Heritage Center, University of Wyoming, Laramie.

11. Ibid., 5, 10; *OA*, May 15, 1914, p. 8.

12. See *FOJ*, Sept. 1915, p. 99. Appraisement Committee Report, "Method of Valuing Oil Land," July 20, 1915, box 5, Requa Papers; oil conference speech, January 12, 1919, box 2, Requa Papers.

13. M. L. Requa, "Oil Resources of California," delivered before the Mining Association, University of California, Berkeley, n.d. (1911?), box 2, pp. 21–23, Requa Papers.

14. Requa, "Method of Valuing Oil Land," 2–5.

15. *LAT*, Jan. 6, 7, Feb. 5, 1916; Welty and Taylor, *The 76 Bonanza*, 166–69. In writing an official history of Union Oil, Welty and Taylor mentioned Requa's role in this affair but misconstrued the relationship between the principal actors in the merger. In particular, they failed to connect O'Donnell, Doheny, and California Petroleum. Instead, they assumed that Doheny had been allied with the British investors under Weir in competition with Requa for control of the company.

16. *LAT*, Jan. 7, 1916; *SFE*, Feb. 19, 1916; *FOJ*, Apr. 1916, pp. 102–3; June 1916, p. 108.

17. *NYT*, Sept. 18, Nov. 25, 1915.

18. Ibid., Dec. 11, 1915; *SFE*, Jan. 4, 15, 1916; *OA*, Jan. 1916, p. 21; *FOJ*, Jan. 1916, p. 50; *LAT*, Jan. 7, 1916; *CFC*, Jan. 15, 1916.

19. *SFE,* Jan. 4, 1916; *WSJ,* Jan. 10, 1916.

20. *NYT,* Jan. 29, 1916; Sproule quote from "A California View of the Proposed Doheny Merger," *FOJ,* Feb. 1916, p. 124; *OTJ,* Dec. 1920, p. 135.

21. *SFE,* Feb. 16, 1916; *OA,* Feb. 1916, p. 2.

22. *OA,* Jan. 1916, p. 21; *Moody's Industrials,* 1915, 1139–40; *FOJ,* Apr. 1916, pp. 102–3; Nov. 1916, pp. 109–10.

23. *OA,* Apr. 1915, p. 12, Dec. 1916, p. 16; *Report of the Federal Trade Commission on the Pacific Coast Petroleum Industry,* pt. 2 (Washington, D.C.: Government Printing Office, 1922), 236; *WSJ,* Mar. 7, 14, 1916.

24. Asset figures were compiled from *Moody's Industrials* and *Moody's Analysis of Investments.* The case for adding General Petroleum to the merger was problematic, since the company was experiencing severe financial difficulty, which resulted in a complete internal reorganization in the spring of 1916. See *WSJ,* Apr. 4, 1916. Still, without General Petroleum, the combined assets of the remaining three companies would have totaled $153,649,860—putting them comfortably ahead of Standard as the state's largest oil company.

25. Pan American Petroleum and Transport Company, *Annual Report,* 1916.

26. *WSJ,* Mar. 25, 1916.

27. Ibid., Feb. 8, 1916; Mexican Petroleum Company, Ltd., *MexPet Record* 1 (Mar. 1916): 10–11.

28. *FOJ,* Apr. 1916, p. 101; *NYT,* Mar. 22, Apr. 2, 1916. By way of comparison, the overall daily average for California in 1915 was 245,824 barrels, falling to 223,767 for January 1916. See "Statistical Review of 1916," *OA,* Jan. 1917, p. 10. A similar event took place before the Chamber of Mines and Oil in Los Angeles a few months later. See *MOB,* May 1916, pp. 130–35.

29. *MexPet Record* 1 (Mar. 1916): 15–16; *FOJ,* Mar. 1916, p. 44. The dramatic story of bringing the well under control is recounted in Pan American Petroleum & Transport Company, *Mexican Petroleum* (1922), 95–108.

30. *WSJ,* Mar. 17, 1916; *FOJ,* Apr. 1916, pp. 10–11.

31. For a detailed discussion of the plan and Villa's reasoning, see Friedrich Katz, "Pancho Villa and the Attack on Columbus, New Mexico," *American Historical Review* 83 (Feb. 1978): 101–30.

32. *WSJ,* Jan. 14, Mar. 25, 1916. A concise history of the Pershing Expedition can be found in Linda B. Hall and Don M. Coerver, *Revolution on the Border: The United States and Mexico, 1910–1920* (Albuquerque: University of New Mexico Press, 1988), 57–77.

33. *WSJ,* Jan. 1, 4, 1916; *CFC,* Jan. 1, 1916.

34. *OA,* May 1916, p. 2; *FOJ,* June 1916, p. 108.

35. *OA,* Apr. 1916, p. 20; Sept. 1916, pp. 8, 13; Oct. 1916, p. 10. California State Mining Bureau, *Bulletin,* no. 82, p. 384; *FOJ,* Sept. 1916, p. 89; *OTJ* (continues the former), Nov. 1916, p. 108.

36. Federal Trade Commission, "Production Ownership and Profits," pt. 1 of *Report on the Pacific Coast Petroleum Industry* (Washington, D.C.: Government

Printing Office, 1921), 13–14. C. N. Linkroum, "California Petroleum Improves," *MWS* 25 (Dec. 27, 1919): 224–25. All calculations were based on the annual reports of the companies, as found in *Moody's Industrials.*

37. James W. Maxwell, "What is the Outlook for: California Petroleum, Cosden & Co., Houston Oil," *MWS* 32 (June 23, 1923): 338.

38. Federal Trade Commission, "Production Ownership and Profits," 63–65.

CHAPTER 7

1. Wilbur Hall, "How Doheny Did It," 21–23.

2. Barnard Powers, "E. L. Doheny Tells of Great Future for Oil," *MWS* 2 (Nov. 9, 1918): 87.

3. Gregory P. Nowell, *Mercantile States and the World Oil Cartel, 1900–1939* (Ithaca: Cornell University Press, 1994), 89. Nowell focuses on the rivalry between Standard Oil and Royal Dutch-Shell for markets in Europe and Asia during the war. Also see Daniel Yergin, *The Prize: The Epic Quest for Oil, Money, and Power* (New York: Simon & Schuster, 1991), chap. 9.

4. Samuel G. Blythe, "Gasoline and the War," editorial in *OA*, Nov. 1914, p. 13.

5. Pan American Petroleum and Transport Company, *Pan American Record* 1 (Sept. 1916): 12. This publication continued the *MexPet Record* as of this date.

6. Ibid., 1 (Nov. 1916): 2; 1 (Jan. 1917): 14.

7. Advertisement, *MexPet Record* 1 (Mar. 1916): n. p. David M. Kennedy, *Over Here: The First World War and American Society* (New York: Oxford University Press, 1980), 30–44.

8. *Pan American Record* 1 (Mar. 1917): 9. The illustration was included as the frontispiece to this issue.

9. "Who Shall Rule the World," *MexPet Record* 1 (Mar. 1916): 1.

10. *LAT*, Feb. 8, 1917; telegram reprinted in the *NYT*, Feb. 9, 1917. At its incorporation, Pan American's ten oil tankers ranked among the top seven tanker fleets in the world, not counting the eleven tank ships it had under construction. Standard Oil New York and the Eagle Oil Transport Company headed the list of oil shippers with carrying capacities of well over 1 million barrels of oil. Union Oil, Anglo-American Oil Company, and Deutsche-Amerikanische (the German branch of Standard Oil) came in at just under a million barrels. Standard Oil California, Pan American Petroleum, Gulf Refining Company, and Texaco comprised the next rank with total capacities of just under a half-million barrels. See "Ocean Going Oil Carriers of the United States," *OA*, May 1916, pp. 10–11; "The World's Oil-Tankers," *The Petroleum Review* (Feb. 20, 1915): 155–71.

11. *LAT*, Feb. 18, 1917; Kennedy, *Over Here*, 31, 146; *Pan American Record* 1 (Sept. 1916): 13–14.

12. *LAT*, Apr. 11, 1917.

13. H. Walker to Franklin K. Lane, Nov. 14, 1916, box 106, Fall Papers, Huntington.

14. G. F. Weeks (Mexican News Bureau) to Charles A. Douglas (University Club, Mexico City), Subject: U.S. Postal Censorship, Mar. 12, 1918, Records of the War Department, General Staff, Military Intelligence Division, 1917–1941, RG 165, National Archives, Washington, D.C. (hereafter cited as MID).

15. Memo, Office of Naval Intelligence, August 2, 1918, doc. 8231–194/1, MID; *LAT,* Nov. 19, 1916. Cantu quote is from Alan Knight, *The Mexican Revolution,* vol. 2, 210, 217–18. For a general discussion of Cantu's motives, see Joseph R. Werne, "Esteban Cantu y la soberania mexicana en Baja California," *Historia Mexicana* 30 (1980): 25–26.

16. George S. Gibb and Evelyn H. Knowlton, *History of the Standard Oil Company (New Jersey): The Resurgent Years, 1911–1927* (New York: Harper & Brothers, 1956), 237–39. A more detailed discussion of the committee organization can be found in Harold F. Williamson and Ralph L. Andreano, *The American Petroleum Industry: The Age of Energy, 1899–1959* (Evanston: Northwestern University Press, 1963), 268–76.

17. Mark L. Requa, "Mr. Bedford in the War," *The Lamp* [Standard Oil Company Magazine] 8 (Feb. 1926): 17–18; Gibbs and Knowlton, *History of the Standard Oil Company,* 238.

18. *Pan American Record* 1 (May 1917): 3; 1 (July 1917): 3; 2 (Sept. 1917): 14; 2 (Jan. 1918): 14.

19. *LAT,* Jan. 11, 1918.

20. Minutes of the Meetings of the National Petroleum War Service Committee, December 21, 1917, box 6, pp. 2–4, Requa Papers.

21. Minutes of the Petroleum War Service Committee, Dec. 21, 1917, Apr. 30, June 14, June 21, 1918, box 6, Requa Papers.

22. *OTJ,* June 1918, p. 18.

23. *Pan American Record* 2 (Mar. 1918): 4.

24. Ibid. Prior to the spring of 1917, the Union Oil Company had been supplying the Chilean market with California oil through arrangements made with the Independent Oil Producers Agency. But as a conservation measure to ease the oil shortage in California, Union made a deal with Doheny on behalf of the IOPA to use Mexican oil instead of the local product. Thereafter, Union Oil ships were loaded at Tampico by the Mexican Petroleum Company, and they made deliveries to Chile through the Panama Canal. This apparently proved to be a beneficial move for everyone involved, especially for the IOPA, which received an extra 50 cents of profit on every barrel of oil. See *OA,* Apr. 1917, p. 38.

25. Pan American Petroleum and Transport Company, *Annual Report,* 1917, reprinted in *CFC,* August 24, 1918, pp. 809–10. A discussion of the government's shipbuilding policy at this time is in René De La Pedraja, *The Rise and Decline of U.S. Merchant Shipping in the Twentieth Century* (New York: Twayne Publishers, 1992), 47–58.

26. *NYT,* June 28, 29, 1918; *OTJ,* Aug. 1918, p. 76; Mexican Petroleum Company, *Annual Report,* 1917.

27. All figures taken from the official annual reports of the companies for these years.

28. Mexican Petroleum Company, *Annual Report,* 1918.

29. *MWS,* Sept. 28, 1918, p. 1003.

30. For contemporary appraisals of the company's performance, see *MWS,* Aug. 31, 1918, pp. 833–36, and June 7, 1919, pp. 341–44. Financial information was derived from the annual stock market reports found in *CFC.* Dividends during this period were as follows: 1916, no common/ $240,000 (2%) preferred; 1917, $590,132 (1.5%) common/ $240,000 (2%) preferred; 1918, $3,168,008 (8%) common/ $960,000 (8%) preferred; 1919, $3,672,506 (9%) common/ $960,000 (8%) preferred. See Mexican Petroleum Company, *Annual Report,* 1916–1919.

31. Edward L. Doheny, *Letter of Mr. Edward L. Doheny to Hon. Mark L. Requa Concerning the Importance to the United States of the American Owned Petroleum Properties in Mexico* (privately published, Mar. 15, 1918), 2.

32. Mark L. Requa to Frank L. Polk, Aug. 12, 1918, Records of the Department of State Relating to the Internal Affairs of Mexico, 1910–1929, RG 59, decimal file 812.6363/411, Microfilm Publications, microcopy 274, National Archives, Washington, D.C. (hereafter cited as RDS 812). The closest Requa came to rationing was in September 1918, when he instituted a series of "gasless Sundays" on the East Coast to slow down the reduction of gasoline stocks. See Williamson and Andreano, *The American Petroleum Industry,* 284–85; A. C. Bedford, "American Oil and the War," *OA,* June 1919, p. 13. Ironically, it seems that, without a rationing program, the efficient work of the Petroleum Committee went largely unnoticed and unappreciated. See Paul Foley, "Petroleum Problems of the War," *United States Naval Institute Proceedings* 50 (Nov. 1924): 1827–30.

33. Requa to Polk, RDS 812.6363/411.

34. For a self-congratulatory summary of his ideas, especially about California, see Josephus Daniels, *The Wilson Era: Years of War and After, 1917–1923* (Chapel Hill: University of North Carolina Press, 1946), 246–48. A detailed history of the arguments over oil reserves can be found in Aaron Wildavsky and Ellen Tenenbaum, *The Politics of Mistrust: Estimating American Oil and Gas Resources* (Beverly Hills: Sage Publications, 1981). For the range of opinion on this issue during the First World War, see Edgar D. Pouch, "The Other Side of the Oil Question," *MWS,* May 12, 1917, pp. 203–5; John Warren, "War and Oil," *MWS,* Dec. 22, 1917, p. 389.

CHAPTER 8

1. For a through discussion of this program, see Emily S. Rosenberg, *World War I and the Growth of United States Predominance in Latin America* (New York: Garland Publishing, 1987).

2. Wilson's comments are from an unpublished article written in 1907, as quoted in William Diamond, *The Economic Thought of Woodrow Wilson* (Baltimore: Johns Hopkins Press, 1943), 141–45; Rosenberg, 187. For a recent discussion of Wilson's economic policy, see Martin J. Sklar, *The Corporate Reconstruction of American Capitalism, 1890–1916* (Cambridge: Cambridge University Press, 1988), 401–30.

3. Benjamin T. Harrison, *Dollar Diplomat: Chandler Anderson and American Diplomacy in Mexico and Nicaragua, 1913–1928* (Pullman, Wash.: Washington State University Press, 1988), 12–13, 19.

4. Diary of Chandler P. Anderson, Jan. 3, Mar. 8, 1917, Papers of Chandler P. Anderson, Manuscript Division, Library of Congress, Washington, D.C. (hereafter cited as Anderson Papers). The diplomatic dilemmas are discussed in Robert Freeman Smith, *The United States and Revolutionary Nationalism in Mexico, 1916–1932* (Chicago: University of Chicago Press, 1972), 92–117.

5. Merrill Rippy, *Oil and the Mexican Revolution* (Leiden: E. J. Brill, 1972), 9, 11, 22; J. Reuben Clark Jr., "The Oil Settlement with Mexico," *Foreign Affairs* 6 (July 1928): 601; Robert G. Cleland, *The Mexican Yearbook, 1920–1921* (Los Angeles: Mexican Yearbook Publishing Co., 1922), 301.

6. E. V. Niemeyer Jr., *Revolution at Queretaro: The Mexican Constitutional Convention of 1916–1917* (Austin: University of Texas Press, 1974), 165; H. N. Branch, "The Mexican Constitution of 1917 Compared with the Constitution of 1857," *The Annals* (Supp., May 1917): 15–19.

7. Frederic R. Kellogg, "The Mexican Oil Situation," in George H. Blakeslee, ed., *Mexico and the Caribbean: Clark University Addresses* (New York: G. E. Stechert and Co., 1920), 60–61. For a shorter description by Kellogg of the constitutional question and the Carranza oil decrees, see his article "The Mexican Problem," *The Nation* 107 (Oct. 5, 1918): 6–8.

8. Anderson Papers, May 11, 16, 29, 1917; Edgar W. Turlington, *Mexico and Her Foreign Creditors* (New York: Columbia University Press, 1930), 265–80.

9. A positive appraisal of Carranza's performance in comparison with Fidel Castro's later efforts in Cuba is in the concluding chapter of P. Edward Haley, *Revolution and Intervention: The Diplomacy of Taft and Wilson with Mexico, 1910–1917* (Cambridge: MIT Press, 1970). Quotation is from Friedrich Katz, *The Secret War In Mexico*, 524. This is still the best source on foreign intrigue in Mexico.

10. Harold Walker, "Fuel Oil Need and Supply for the War," April 18, 1917, RDS 812.6363/296.

11. L. Richardson (USS *Annapolis*) to Navy Ops, Situation Report, Nov. 5–7, 1917, box 88, doc. 4225–188, General Records of the Navy, Secretary of the Navy General Correspondence, 1916–1926, RG 80, National Archives, Washington, D.C. (hereafter cited as GRN).

12. Clarence W. Barron, *The Mexican Problem* (Boston: Houghton Mifflin, 1917), 80. Situation Report, USS *Annapolis*, Jan. 15, 1918, box 660, Naval Records Collection, Subject File 1911–1927, WE-5, "East Coast of Mexico," RG 45, National

Archives, Washington, D.C. (hereafter cited as WE-5); Situation Report, USS *Annapolis*, Aug. 31, 1917, GRN, box 88, doc. 4225–175. For the investigation of Green, see Director of Naval Intelligence to Leland Harrison, May 29, 1918, box 661, WE-5.

13. Anderson Papers, May 16, 1917, Feb. 4, 11, 1918; Katz, *The Secret War*, 467–73.

14. Anderson Papers, May 29, 1917.

15. Ibid., Sept. 6, 1917.

16. See "An Address to a Party of Mexican Editors," June 7, 1918, reprinted in Lloyd C. Gardner, *Wilson and Revolutions: 1913–1921* (Philadelphia: J. B. Lippincott, 1974), 66–69. As the address was intended as a statement to the Mexican people at large, Wilson withheld press copies in the United States until the text had been published in Mexico and sent to American embassies and legations abroad. See "President Wilson on Attitude of United States toward Mexico," *CFC*, June 15, 1918, p. 2517.

17. See "Don Manuel Pelaez, Dictator in Mexico's Oil Fields," *OTJ*, Dec. 1917, p. 62.

18. Harold Walker to Maj. Gen. Hugh Scott, Chief of Staff, U.S. Army, June 30, 1916, MID; Dawson to Lansing, Aug. 11, 1916, RDS 812.6363/245.

19. For Pelaez's goals, see "Translation of Huasteca Home Defense Movement of May 5, 1917," RDS 812.6363/302; Fred I. Kent, Director, Division of Foreign Exchange, to W. G. Harding, Governor General of the Federal Reserve Board, May 3, 1918, RDS 812.6363/394; Harold Walker, "The Allies' Oil Supplies," June 18, 1917, MID 7708–27. For a list of contending forces, see "Estimate of Situation if Disturbances in the Oil Fields make Intervention Necessary," June 4, 1918, box 660, WE-5.

20. Anderson Papers, Mar. 10, 1917.

21. Walker to Polk, Nov. 5, 1917, box 1 ("1st Outlines"), DRF.

22. Doheny to William Green, Mar. 11, 1918, RDS 812.6363/357. For more communications between Green and his superiors, see RDS 812.6363/373.

23. Walker to Auchincloss, Sept. 9, 1917, RDS 812.6363/312.

24. In the most recent evaluation, Jonathan Brown emphasizes Pelaez's independence from the oil companies, the unique sociology of his political support, and the fact that his bandit activity was far more destructive to oil property than anything done by the federal government. Furthermore, Brown found no evidence to prove the charge of supplying weapons to the rebels. See Brown, *Oil and Revolution*, 253–304.

25. Anderson Papers, Sept. 11, 12, 20, 1917.

26. Doheny letter, Sept. 20, 1917, box 1 ("1st Outlines"), DRF.

27. *SFE*, Nov. 11, 1917. Information on Scott's initial work is contained in a collection of letters from Arthur Young, another early member of the research team. See Young Letters, July 1, 16, Aug. 12, Nov. 11, 1917, DRF.

28. Doheny testimony, vol. 1, 270–72, IMA. For the report, see George B. Win-

ton, *A Study of Educational Conditions in Mexico* (Cincinnati: Committee for the Study of Educational Conditions in Mexico, 1916).

29. Lawrence E. Gelfand, *The Inquiry: American Preparations for Peace, 1917–1919* (New Haven: Yale University Press, 1963), x–xi, 25–30, 73.

30. For a good discussion of this trend among academics during this period, see Donald J. Murphy, "Professors, Publicists, and Pan Americanism, 1905–1917: A Study in the Origins of the Use of 'Experts' in Shaping American Foreign Policy" (Ph.D. diss., University of Wisconsin, 1970). For some specific examples from Inquiry records, see Chester Lloyd Jones to A. A. Young, June 3, 1918; Bailey Willis to Herbert Bolton, Aug. 26, 1918; Bailey Willis to Percy A. Martin, August 26, 1918; entry 1, General Correspondence, American Commission to Negotiate Peace, Records of the Inquiry, RG 256, National Archives, Washington, D. C.

31. See *El Democrata*, Jan. 28, 1918, copy contained in G. W. Scott to Members of the Board of Managers, Doheny Research Foundation, February 15, 1918, Doheny Research Foundation file, Benjamin Ide Wheeler Papers, Records of the Office of the President, Bancroft Library, University of California, Berkeley. Carranza's comments are from *El Democrata*, March 5, 1918, as quoted in Clifford Trow, "Senator Albert B. Fall and Mexican Affairs: 1912–1921" (Ph. D. diss., University of Colorado, 1966), 214. This work also contains a short summary of the Doheny Research Project.

32. "Memorandum of Agreement between the University of California and the Doheny Research Foundation," Wheeler Papers. Wheeler to Doheny, July 21, 1919, Wheeler Papers. A formal announcement of this arrangement can be found in *University of California Chronicle* (Berkeley) 20 (1918): 271–72. "Suggestions and Instructions for the Members of the Doheny Research Foundation," p. 8, box titled "Indexes," folder A, DRF.

33. Taken together, these interviews were the singular achievement of the foundation for modern scholars and provide invaluable information about the attitudes of the period. For example, Doheny, Harold Walker, and Herbert Wylie each gave several interviews about the development of the oil industry in Mexico. Similar material was collected for virtually every industry in the country. Recently, Gene Hanrahan claimed that the oil material was conspicuously absent from the existing collection (*The Bad Yankee: American Entrepreneurs and Financiers in Mexico* [Chapel Hill: University of North Carolina Press, 1985], 10). While the files do not contain the full report, they include copies of the conclusion to Cleland's oil report as well as other editorial discussions concerning his work. All of the interviews with oilmen are also available and have not fallen victim to some sinister plot. See "Conclusions and Suggestions," n.d., box 2 ("Miscellaneous"); "Discussion of Mr. Cleland's Report on Oil," Aug. 24, 1918, box 4 ("Miscellaneous"); "List of Persons Interviewed," box 3 ("Miscellaneous"). Cleland's conclusions are in "Relations of the Oil Companies with the Mexican Authorities," interview no. 683, box J 11,401–11,901, folder 11,801–11,901, DRF.

34. James R. Mock and Cedric Larson, "Activities of the Mexico Section of the Creel Committee, 1917–1918," *Journalism Quarterly* 16 (June 1939): 136–50. One of those who did succeed in getting into Mexico was Walter Cumberland, an economist working on Mexico's domestic commerce, who managed to avoid the Mexican official checking travel documents against the government blacklist. See "The Reminiscences of W. W. Cumberland," 31–36, in the Oral History Collection of Columbia University.

35. G. W. Scott, "Memorandum to the Regents of the University of California," Dec. 19, 1919; Scott to Ralph P. Merritt, comptroller, Dec. 26, 1919, Wheeler Papers. Scott's partially completed manuscript ended up buried in the collection of the Los Angeles Public Library, titled *Mexico: An Impartial Survey*. The subsequent publications were Robert Cleland, *Mexican Yearbook* (Los Angeles: Mexican Yearbook Publishing Company, 1921); Chester Lloyd Jones, *Mexico and its Reconstruction* (New York: D. Appleton and Company, 1921); Walter F. McCaleb, *Present and Past Banking in Mexico* (New York: Harper and Brothers, 1920) and *The Public Finances of Mexico* (New York: Harper and Brothers, 1921); Fred W. Powell, *The Railroads of Mexico* (Boston: Stratford Company, 1921); Wallace Thompson, *The People of Mexico* (New York: Harper and Brothers, 1921).

36. For some examples, see Clifford Trow, "Woodrow Wilson and the Mexican Interventionist Movement of 1919," *Journal of American History* 58 (June 1971): 53–54; Mark Gilderhus, *Diplomacy and Revolution* (Tucson: University of Arizona Press, 1977), 90–91; IMA, vol.1, 290–91; *NYT,* Jan. 30, 1919.

37. Dennis Wingsou Lou, "Fall Committee: An Investigation of Mexican Affairs" (Ph.D diss., Indiana University, 1963), intro. Harold Walker to Chester O. Swain, Feb. 6, 1920, Albert Fall Papers, Special Collections, University of New Mexico, Albuquerque (hereafter cited as Fall Papers Albuquerque). In collecting his material, Fall used his own agents plus a number of holdovers from the Doheny Research Foundation.

38. See Samuel Guy Inman, *Intervention in Mexico* (New York: George H. Doran Co., 1919). A sympathetic but simplistic account of Inman's appearance before the Fall Committee is found in Kenneth F. Woods, "Samuel Guy Inman and Intervention in Mexico," *Southern California Quarterly* 46 (Dec. 1964): 351–70. Woods portrays Inman as a hero whose charges against Doheny and Fall were vindicated during the subsequent oil scandal.

39. Inman, IMA, vol. 1, 3–13, 213.

40. Ibid., 204–8, 233, 248, 274; *OTJ,* Dec. 1917, p. 64. Doheny's testimony covered almost ninety pages of the published report and includes a good review of his early career, although much of it is slanted toward the purposes at hand. And if not intentionally disingenuous, his recollection of events twenty or thirty years earlier is not wholly reliable.

41. Brown, *Revolution and Oil,* 298.

42. NAPARIM, "Plow with Petroleum" (pamphlet), pp. 1, 12.

CHAPTER 9

1. Robert E. Hennings, *James D. Phelan and the Wilson Progressives of Califor-nia* (New York: Garland Publishing, 1985), 51; *COW,* Dec. 19, 1912, p. 10; *California Blue Book, 1913–1915* (Sacramento: California State Printing Office, 1915), 286–87; *California Blue Book, Legislative Manual* (Sacramento: California State Printing Office, 1924), 440; *LAT,* Feb. 6, 1916.

2. *New York Evening Journal,* June 29, 1920.

3. *LAT,* June 7, 1920. A less likely source for this quote was Senator James D. Phelan of San Francisco, once described as "California incarnate in Washington," by Lane. See Anne Wintermute Lane and Louise Herrick Wall, eds., *The Letters of Franklin K. Lane* (Boston: Houghton Mifflin Co., 1922), 359. A check of the Demo-cratic party files among Phelan's papers, held at the Bancroft Library, University of California at Berkeley, turned up no mention of Doheny—a clear indication that former political associates thought it prudent to file such material in a differ-ent receptacle after the oil scandal.

4. F. M. Carroll, *American Opinion and the Irish Question, 1910–23: A Study in Opinion and Policy* (New York: St. Martin's Press, 1978), 155–59; Timothy J. Sar-baugh, "John Byrne: The Life and Times of the Forgotten Irish Republican of Los Angeles," *Southern California Quarterly* 63 (Winter 1981): 379–82; Clarence W. Barron, *They Told Barron* (New York: Harper & Brothers Publishers, 1930), 15.

5. Alan J. Ward, *Ireland and Anglo-American Relations: 1899–1921* (Toronto: University of Toronto Press, 1969), 221–24; Charles C. Tansill, *America and the Fight for Irish Freedom, 1866–1922* (New York: Devin-Adair Co., 1957), 381–82; Earl of Longford and Thomas P. O'Neill, *Eamon De Valera* (Boston: Houghton Mifflin Co., 1971), 109–10.

6. *Official Report of the Proceedings of the Democratic National Convention, 1920* (Indianapolis: Bookwalter-Ball Printing Co., 1920), 205–6; Sinn Fein quote from *The Irish World and American Industrial Liberator,* July 24, 1920, p. 2; *NYT,* July 3, 1920; Carroll, *American Opinion and the Irish Question,* 155; Tansill, *America and the Fight for Irish Freedom,* 382. De Valera finally received a pledge of direct support from the labor party, but this was of no political consequence for gaining the help of the United States government. See, Longford and O'Neill, *Ea-mon De Valera,* 111.

7. *Proceedings of the Democratic National Convention,* 438.

8. For an appraisal of the Cox-Roosevelt ticket, see David Burner, *The Politics of Provincialism: The Democratic Party in Transition, 1918–1932* (W. W. Norton, 1967), 63. Burner noted that Cox's defeat had as much to do with the "dark shadow of Woodrow Wilson" as it did with his uninspired and disorganized campaign, despite Roosevelt's presence (see pp. 68, 72–73).

9. Lane and Wall, *The Letters of Franklin K. Lane,* 335, 338, 362, 416; Keith W. Olson, *Biography of a Progressive: Franklin K. Lane, 1864–1921* (Westport, Con-necticut: Greenwood Press, 1979), 111–19, 170.

10. Lane and Wall, *The Letters of Franklin K. Lane,* 351, 363–64. These were obviously private concerns only, since no trace of these sentiments is evident in Keith Olson's biography of Lane's public career.

11. *NYT,* Nov. 18, 1920; Timothy J. Sarbaugh, "American Recognition and Eamon de Valera: The Heyday of Irish Republicanism in California, 1920–1922," *Southern California Quarterly* 69 (Summer 1987): 135, 141–45. F. M. Carroll gives a particularly unflattering appraisal of Doheny's contribution to the AARIR. For Carroll, Doheny's involvement in the Teapot Dome made it seem that he was "merely another of the corrupt old Irish-American leaders who continued to reflect badly on the national cause." See Carroll, *American Opinion and the Irish Question,* 159–60. If Carrol's attitude is typical, it would account for the fact that there are very few references, good or bad, to Doheny among the works on prominent Irish Americans.

12. Franklin K. Lane to Edward L. Doheny (Dec. 8, n.y.), AALA. Lane died six months later, in May 1921.

13. Carroll, *American Opinion and the Irish Question,* 166–67. Doheny's comments appeared in the *LAT,* March 24, 1921.

14. For details on the talks, see O'Neill, *Eamon De Valera,* chap. 11; Peter Rowland, *Lloyd George* (London: Barrie & Jenkins, 1975), 545–55.

15. Rowland, *Lloyd George,* 549; Carroll, *American Opinion and the Irish Question,* 282 n. 10. Carroll makes no comment on the issue one way or the other.

16. *NYT,* Dec. 7, 1921.

17. Carroll, *American Opinion and the Irish Question,* pp. 176–81; Giovanni Costigan, *A History of Modern Ireland* (New York: Western Publishing Co., 1969), 346–52.

18. A copy of this message, signed by Doheny and the other members of the committee, is attached to a letter from Thomas W. Lyons, Executive Secretary, AARIR, to Senator Thomas J. Walsh, September 24, 1921, Thomas J. Walsh Papers, Manuscript Division, Library of Congress.

19. Matthew Cummings to Charles E. Hughes, Mar. 15, 1921, RDS 812.6363/ 808, 821.

20. Carroll, *American Opinion and the Irish Question,* 169–70. For the larger issues surrounding the arms talks, see Erik Goldstein, "The Evolution of British Diplomatic Strategy for the Washington Conference," in Erik Goldstein and John Maurer, *The Washington Conference, 1921–1922: Naval Rivalry, East Asian Stability and the Road to Pearl Harbor* (Portland: Frank Cass, 1994), 4–34.

21. Edward L. Doheny to Senator A. B. Fall, Nov. 4, 1920, box 1, folder 1, Albert Fall Papers, Rio Grande Historical Collection, New Mexico State University Library, Las Cruces, N.Mex. (hereafter cited as Fall-LC).

22. Francis Russell, *The Shadow of Blooming Grove: Warren Harding in His Times* (New York: McGraw-Hill, 1968), 413–15. See Doheny's testimony in *Leases upon Naval Oil Reserves, Hearing before the Committee on Public Lands and Surveys,* United States Senate, S. Res. 282 and S. Res. 294, Oct. 22, 1923 (Washington, D.C.:

Government Printing Office, 1924), 997–98. This was in addition to the $75,000 he had already given the Democrats before the race tactics became an issue.

23. Doheny to Fall, Nov. 4, 1920, Fall-LC.

24. Thomas H. Buckley, "The Icarus Factor: The American Pursuit of Myth in Naval Arms Control, 1921–36," in Goldstein and Maurer, *The Washington Conference*, 124–34.

25. William Reynolds Braisted, *The United States Navy in the Pacific, 1909–1922* (Austin: University of Texas Press, 1971), 581–87; Edward S. Miller, *War Plan Orange: The U.S. Strategy to Defeat Japan, 1897–1945* (Annapolis: Naval Institute Press, 1991), 113–15.

26. Hector C. Bywater, *Sea Power in the Pacific* (London: Constable and Co., 1921, new edition, 1934), ix; Braisted, *The United States Navy in the Pacific*, 545.

27. Sadao Asada, "From Washington to London: The Imperial Japanese Navy and the Politics of Naval Limitation, 1921–1930," in Goldstein and Maurer, *The Washington Conference*, 151–56.

28. Commander C. C. Gill, "The New Far East Doctrine," *United States Naval Institute Proceedings* 48 (Sept. 1922): 1485.

29. Braisted, *The United States Navy in the Pacific*, 548.

30. Ibid., 544–48; Buckley, "The Icarus Factor," 129.

31. Bywater, *Sea Power in the Pacific*, 88–89; Braisted, *The United States Navy in the Pacific*, 548, 580.

32. Denby cited the official reasons for this exchange in a letter to Harding on May 26, 1921, and outlined the Pearl Harbor plan in a subsequent communication with Albert Fall. See *Leases upon Naval Oil Reserves*, vol. 1, 286–87, 921.

33. See testimony of Edward L. Doheny, Dec. 9, 1926, vol. 14, 3029–3036, file of Atlee Pomerene, Teapot Dome Documents, RG 60, National Archives, Washington, D.C.

34. See "Statement of Rear Admiral John Keeler Robison," *Leases upon Naval Oil Reserves*, 894–905.

35. Doheny testimony, 3037–38. A recent book claiming to have discovered "secret" government documents concerning the Japanese threat is Herman B. Weisner, *The Politics of Justice: A. B. Fall and the Teapot Dome Scandal* (Albuquerque: Creative Designs, 1988). Actually, Weisner's documents are additional copies and compilations of most of the material already included in *Leases upon Naval Oil Reserves*.

36. Doheny testimony, *Leases upon Naval Oil Reserves*, 3038–3040.

37. Ibid.

38. *Congressional Record*, 67th Cong., 2d sess., 1922, 6041–49.

39. Ibid. This line of reasoning from Daniels' perspective is also detailed in J. Leonard Bates (Lieutenant, U.S. Naval Reserve), "Josephus Daniels and the Naval Oil Reserves," *U.S. Naval Institute Proceedings* 79 (Feb. 1953): 171–79. In January 1921, one reporter noted that, after living under Daniels' heel for so long, there were few California oilmen "who will not feel like singing for joy, when he leaves

office on March 4." See *OTJ*, Jan. 1921, p. 36. The comment about La Follette is in *NPN*, June 24, 1925, p. 59.

CHAPTER 10

1. See "Facts and Theories as to Salt Water in Mexico Wells," *OTJ*, May 1919, p. 98; *WSJ*, Feb. 9, 1923.

2. Mexican Petroleum Company, *Annual Report*, 1920.

3. Dennis Jay O'Brien, "The Oil Crisis and the Foreign Policy of the Wilson Administration, 1917–1921" (Ph.D. diss., University of Missouri, 1974), 130–31, 162 n. 7.

4. *NYT*, Jan. 22, 29, 1919.

5. O'Brien, "The Oil Crisis," 131.

6. A. E. Burgess, "British Mexican Petroleum Co. Plans for Future," *OTJ*, Nov. 1920, pp. 26–27; *CFC*, July 26, 1919, p. 377; "Investment Value of Royal Dutch Petroleum," *MWS*, Jan. 4, 1919, pp. 480–83. Mexican figures were taken from the monthly and annual reports of the *OTJ*.

7. Clarence W. Barron, *A World Remaking or Peace Finance* (New York: Harper & Brothers Publishers, 1920), 80–87; Burgess, "British Mexican Petroleum Co.," 26. Barron also claimed that Royal Dutch-Shell had been buying Mexican Petroleum shares on the New York Stock Exchange, although Doheny said that this was impossible because he knew every broker handling the trades (see pp. 85, 87).

8. Copies of this report also went to the secretary of state via the War Department. See Newton D. Baker to the Secretary of State, Feb. 27, 1920, RDS 812.6363/648. A copy of the original report, titled "Petroleum: With Particular Reference to the Mexican Situation," can be found in box 2, Requa Papers.

9. Letter reproduced in the *OTJ*, Feb. 1920, pp. 11–12; Requa to Secretary of State, Jan. 20, 1920, RDS 812.6363/628.

10. RDS 812.6363/630, 650, 831, 836.

11. The report is in J. A. Phelan, Oil Examiner, to M. W. Bowen, Special Assistant to the President, Dec. 21, 1920, RDS 812.6363/994. For an interview with Phelan about the situation, see RDS 812.6363/731, enclosure no. 3.

12. Mexican Petroleum Company, *Annual Report* (1920), 13–14.

13. Production figures were compiled from the monthly reports of the *OTJ* and the *Boletin del Petroleo*. Earnings are from the annual reports of the Mexican Petroleum Company. Monthly stock prices are from the *CFC* and the *WSJ*.

14. *WSJ*, Apr. 30, May 3, 1921.

15. Ralph Arnold, "Mexico's Dwindling Oil Resources," *MWS*, Apr. 2, 1921, pp. 782–83. In an incredible understatement, the editors added a disclaimer noting that "some authorities may find Mr. Arnold unduly pessimistic."

16. *WSJ*, May 3, 16, June 4, 1921.

17. WWC [Cumberland], Office of the Foreign Trade Adviser, to Dr. Mills-

paugh, Under-Secretary of State, May 31, 1921, RDS, 812.6363/996; Report from R. J. Sharp, Special Agent in Charge, to R. C. Bannerman, Chief Special Agent, July 20, 1921, RDS, 812.6363/1085.

18. *WSJ*, June 16, July 23, 1921. Market information is from a statistical review of the industry through 1925, published in the *OTJ*, Mar. 1926, pp. 48–67.

19. *WSJ*, June 16, 21, 24, Aug. 26, 27, 1921; *NYT*, Sept. 8, 1921.

20. For Livermore, see *The National Cyclopedia of American Biography*, vol. 47, 506; Arthur Pound and Samuel Taylor Moore, *They Told Barron* (New York: Harper & Brothers Publishers, 1930), 43–48.

21. *NYT*, July 1, 1921, Sept. 3, 1921, Nov. 25, 1922, June 20, 1923.

22. Ibid., June 23, 24, 1922; *WSJ*, Nov. 11, 1922, Mar. 13, 1924.

23. See "Skeleton History of Petroleum Taxes in Mexico," included in a memo from H. N. Branch, an attorney for the Mexican Petroleum Company, Aug. 24, 1921, RDS 812.6363/1231; *The Mexican Review* (July 1921): 6; *OTJ*, July 1921, p. 13.

24. *WSJ*, June 10, 1921.

25. Ibid., June 28, 1921.

26. Peter S. Linder, "Every Region for Itself: The Manuel Pelaez Movement, 1914–1923" (M.A. thesis, University of New Mexico, 1983), 169–76; Doheny to Fall, July 16, 1921, box 1, Fall-LC. For Pelaez's charges against the oilmen and Doheny's response, see *NYT*, July 16, 17, 1921.

27. Linder, "Every Region for Itself," 171. For the most relevant items from Fall's files, see Papers of Albert B. Fall, Senate Office Files—Mexican Affairs, microfilm edition, reel 30, docs. 1250 (Pelaez letter to Buckley), 1953, 1956, 2499, 2500, 2515, 2528, Fall-Alb. As a reflection of the tenor of the material, Obregón had Buckley arrested and deported in November 1921 for his political activities on behalf of the American Association of Oil Producers in Mexico. A recent work that continues the tradition of uncritically perpetuating every accusation against Doheny and Fall is Linda B. Hall, *Oil, Banks, and Politics: The United States and Postrevolutionary Mexico, 1917–1924* (Austin: University of Texas Press, 1995).

28. Consul, Claude Dawson, "July Happenings in the Tampico Oil Fields," Aug. 6, 1921, RDS, 812.6363/922; Vice-Consul, Jack Hickerson, "Petroleum Shipments from Tampico District for July, 1921," RDS 812.6363/944. Export figures are from the monthly reports of *OTJ*, and Mexican tax figures are from Mar. 1922, p. 14. Taxes collected in 1921 totaled $72,885,882 pesos, of which $62,734,833 came from production and export taxes on oil. Tax receipts of the Mexican treasury for 1921 and 1922 are given in *WSJ*, Mar. 20, 1923.

29. H. Walker to Charles V. Safford, Aug. 25, 1921, box 106, Albert B. Fall Papers, Huntington Library, San Marino, Calif. (hereafter cited as Fall-Hunt).

30. Letter from the Petroleum Committee to Adolfo de la Huerta, Secretary of Finance and Public Credit, Aug. 29, 1921, RDS 812.6363/1231. Subsequent quotations are also from this source.

31. See "Mexican Producers in Race against Salt Water," *MWS*, Oct. 15, 1921.

32. "Committee Memorandum Giving Survey of Petroleum Industry of Mexico," Apr. 24, 1922, exhibit F, RDS 812.6363/1135.

33. "Committee Plan Petroleum Development Company," Apr. 26, 1922, exhibit G, RDS 812.6363/1135.

34. "Secretary de la Huerta's counter proposal," Apr. 26, 1922, exhibit H, RDS 812.6363/1135. Quotation is from "Committee Reply to First Three Drafts of Sec. De la Huerta's Counter Proposal," May 1, 1922, exhibit N, RDS 812.6363/1135.

35. Editorial, *El Democrata,* Aug. 15, 1922, copy in RDS 812.6363/1179.

36. RDS 812.6363/1228.

37. *WSJ,* Oct. 25, 31, 1922; "Memo on conversations with H. N. Branch," Sept. 26, 1923, RDS 812.6363/1447½.

38. Smith, *The United States and Revolutionary Nationalism in Mexico,* 211–28; Hall, *Oil, Banks, and Politics,* chap. 7.

CHAPTER 11

1. *OTJ,* May 1923, p. 24.

2. Ibid., Feb. 1923, p. 17.

3. *NYT,* Mar. 17, 1923.

4. Ibid., Aug. 21, 1920. *MWS,* Oct. 30, 1920, pp. 936–37; Dec. 11, 1920, pp. 149–50; Dec. 24, 1921, p. 266. *LAT,* Mar. 30, 1921; RDS 812.6363/645.

5. *NYT,* Apr. 5, 1923; *LAT,* Aug. 8, 1923.

6. *LAT,* Feb. 5, Mar. 26, Apr. 20, 1923; *NYT,* Jan. 4, 1923; *WSJ,* Mar. 24, 1923.

7. *Summary of Operations, California Oil Fields* (San Francisco: California State Mining Bureau,), vol. 9 (Aug. 1923), 10–12; *LAT,* July 17, Dec. 1, 1923. Apparently, the dock was not supposed to be sold to a commercial enterprise, especially not to one that posed a potential fire hazard, and Doheny, along with the Harbor Commission, came under attack from several public organizations. See *LAT,* Aug. 29, 31, Sept. 1, 1923; *OA,* Aug. 1924, p. 24.

8. Oil from the southern fields, at 19 degrees Baume, yielded about 84% fuel oil, 11% gasoline, and 4% kerosene, with a 1% loss. Heavy crude, used for asphalt and gas oil, gave less than 3% gasoline. See W. M. Fraser, "Refining Light and Heavy Mexican Crude," *OTJ,* Sept. 1922, pp. 48–54.

9. *WSJ,* Dec. 30, 1922; Jan. 5, 1923.

10. Financial information from *Moody's Analysis of Investments* (1924) and the *CFC.*

11. *CFC,* Dec. 1, 1923, p. 2442; *OTJ,* Jan. 1923, p. 48.

12. Albert B. Fall, "How the Government Creates Investment Opportunities," *MWS,* June 24, 1922, pp. 249–50.

13. Albert B. Fall to H. Foster Bains, Oct. 30, 1922, box 1, Fall-Alb.

14. Doheny's comment is in *CFC,* Jan. 6, 1923, p. 84. Terms are explained in *United States v Pan American Petroleum Co. et al.,* 6 F2d 43, 48–49, May 28, 1925. A brief discussion of the contract in relation to all other agreements pertaining to

the petroleum reserves is found in Reginald W. Ragland, *A History of the Naval Petroleum Reserves and of the Development of the National Policy Respecting Them* (Los Angeles: n. p., 1944), 135–46.

15. *OTJ*, Jan. 1923, p. 48; *WSJ*, Dec. 15, 16, 1922; *OA*, Jan. 3, 1923.

16. J. O. Swartz, "In Quest of New Production," *MWS*, Mar. 3, 1923, p. 854.

17. Edmund Burke to Admiral J. K. Robison, Jan. 23, 1923, box 200, Papers of Thomas J. Walsh, Manuscript Division, Library of Congress.

18. *LAT*, Nov. 28, Dec. 1, 1923; *CFC*, Dec. 1, 1923, pp. 2442–43; Dec. 22, p. 2780. Ward K. Halbert, "New Orleans Refiner Widens Market By Barging Oil to Memphis," *NPN*, Feb. 6, 1924, pp. 17–18.

19. V. B. Guthrie, "Four Leaf Clovers Appear in New Orleans; May Bloom Elsewhere This Year," *NPN*, Feb. 27, 1924, pp. 62–70; F. McGregor McGinnis, "Endless Chain of Service," *OA*, Oct. 1924, p. 54. For a short description of the ads, see "Homely Facts Drive Home Selling Facts in Advertising Series," *NPN*, Nov. 26, 1924, pp. 139–44. The whole series of quarter-page features is in the *Atlanta Constitution*, Oct. 6, 9, 16, 23, 30, Nov. 20, 1924.

20. *LAT*, Dec. 1, 1923. For the Mexico City station, see *NPN*, July 30, 1924, p. 55; Nov. 12, p. 69.

21. *NPN*, Aug. 27, 1924, p. 75. Production figures are from *Moody's Industrials*, 1931, 2695. California production is from a company prospectus included in *United States v Pan American Petroleum Company*, W 102-J, box 897, folder 59, RG 21, Records of the District Courts of the United States, National Archives, Pacific Southwest Region, Laguna Niguel, Calif. *NYT*, Apr. 21, 1923.

22. H. S. Reavis, "Faulty Leadership Menaces Oil Industry," *OTJ*, Sept. 1923, pp. 21–22; *LAT*, Sept. 16, 1923. For the La Follette investigation, see Senate Committee on Manufactures, *High Cost of Gasoline and Other Petroleum Products: Hearings before a Subcommittee of the Committee on Manufactures*, 67th Congress, 4th sess. (Washington, D.C.: GPO, 1923), published in 5 parts. In Feb. 1923, Herbert Wylie, president of Mexican Petroleum, and J. J. Cotter, vice-president of Pan American Petroleum, testified before La Follette about the sales and operations of the Doheny companies, including a discussion of the Elk Hills lease (see pt. 5, 1179–1222).

23. The hearings were published in three volumes as *Leases Upon Naval Oil Reserves*. For Walsh's comments, see Theodore M. Knappen, "What I Think of the Oil Scandal, An Exclusive Interview with Senator Walsh," *MWS*, Mar. 15, 1924, p. 841; Thomas J. Walsh, "What the Oil Inquiry Developed," *The Outlook* (May 21, 1924): 96–98. For a thorough discussion of the scandal, see Burl Noggle, *Teapot Dome: Oil and Politics in the 1920s* (New York: W. W. Norton, 1962). A popular, but exaggerated, account is Morris Robert Werner and John Starr, *Teapot Dome* (New York: Viking Press, 1959).

24. Knappen, "What I Think of the Oil Scandal," pp. 841–43, 892–93.

25. *Leases Upon Naval Oil Reserves*, 1771–72. Fall's role is best described in

David H. Stratton, "Albert B. Fall and the Teapot Dome Affair" (Ph.D. diss., University of Colorado, 1955).

26. A. B. Fall to Emma Fall, May 12, 1920, box 7, Fall-Hunt.

27. Ibid., July 23, 1921.

28. Ibid., Aug. 8, 1922.

29. *Leases Upon Naval Oil Reserves*, 1936–41.

30. Ibid., 1780–84. For a historical comparison of Fall's conduct with that of other officials similarly charged, see John T. Noonan Jr., *Bribes: The Intellectual History of a Moral Idea* (Berkeley and Los Angeles: University of California Press, 1984), 564–69.

31. See Albert B. Fall to Henry A. Wise, July 1, 1925, box 1, Fall-Alb. Quotations from Lucille Miller regarding Edward and Estelle Doheny, interview by Rita Faulders, Dec. 1984, AALA.

32. *Leases upon Naval Oil Reserves*, 973–88, 1006, 1014.

33. Ibid., 990–1013.

34. For interpretations on the damage to the campaign, see Herbert A. Gelbart, "The Anti-McAdoo Movement of 1924" (Ph.D. diss., New York University, 1978), 114–44 passim; Burner, *The Politics of Provincialism*, 107–9.

35. Theodore M. Knappen, "Who Will Win the Democratic Nomination?" *MWS*, June 21, 1924, pp. 249–50; *WSJ*, "A Talent for Suicide," Feb. 4, 1924; "A Voice From the Tomb," Feb. 11, 1924.

36. W. G. McAdoo to F. H. McAdoo, Jan. 28, 1924, General Correspondence, box 294; Tumulty to McAdoo, Nov. 20, 1919, box 536; McAdoo to Tumulty, Nov. 21, 1919, box 526; W. G. McAdoo to Thomas J. Walsh, June 13, 1925, box 212, McAdoo Papers, Library of Congress.

37. C. W. Barron, "Edward L. Doheny the Oil Pioneer," *WSJ*, Feb. 21, 1924.

38. Warren C. Platt, "Shall Politicians Lynch Oil?" *NPN*, Feb. 27, 1924, pp. 17–22; Thomas A. O'Donnell, "Only Three Per Cent of the Industry Involved in Controversy," *NPN*, Mar. 12, 1924, p. 28; *OTJ*, February 1924, p. 23.

39. "Navy Drafting Plans for Lease Control," *OGJ*, Mar. 27, 1924, p. 36.

40. *CFC*, Mar. 22, 1924, p. 1402.

41. A. B. Fall to E. L. Doheny, July 31, 1925, box 1, folder 1, Fall-LC; *WSJ*, Feb. 8, 16, 18, 1924; *CFC*, Feb. 9, Mar. 22, 1924; Pan American Petroleum & Transport Company, *Annual Report*, 1923, pp. 10–11.

42. Fuel oil quotation in "Bright Outlook for Pan-American," *MWS*, Mar. 14, 1925, p. 854. Genius quotation from "Has Pan American Discounted All Unfavorable Factors?" *MWS*, Dec. 20, 1924, p. 303.

43. *LAT*, July 26, 1924.

44. Stewart quoted in *OTJ*, Feb. 1923, p. 102; Paul H. Giddens, *Standard Oil Company (Indiana): Oil Pioneer of the Middle West* (New York: Appleton-Century-Crofts, 1955), 239–40.

45. *NPN*, Feb. 10, 1926, pp. 47, 51; Mar. 17, 1926, pp. 25–26. After this spate

of oil mergers, Walker went on in 1929 to become president of Bancamerica-Blair Corporation, and he served as chairman of Transamerica Corp. in the early thirties and ended his career at Kuhn, Loeb & Co. Obviously, Walker was a talented financial player, but his relationship to Doheny—as ally or opponent—is unknown. See *National Cyclopedia of American Biography,* 126.

46. See Special Report on Pan American Petroleum & Transport Company, RG 122, Records of the Federal Trade Commission, Economic Division, Economic Investigation Files, 1915–1938, Oil Senate Commission, box 3378, National Archives, Washington, D.C.

47. *WSJ,* Mar. 12, 20, 27, Apr. 2, 1925; *LAT,* Mar. 12, 1925. Despite the *Journal*'s circumspection, V. B. Guthrie of the *NPN* had already reported that Blair & Co. held an option on the Class A voting stock of Pan American Petroleum and was negotiating between Stewart and Doheny. See "Standard of Indiana in New Deal to Assure Itself Production," *NPN,* Mar. 18, 1925, pp. 33–35.

48. *NPN,* Mar. 18, p. 34; Apr. 1, 1925, p. 33. For a survey of press comments on the merger, see "Another Big Oil Combine," *Literary Digest,* Apr. 25, 1925, pp. 13–14.

49. Sadly, Edward Jr. would end up being killed in 1929, the victim of a murder/suicide at the hands of his valet and close associate. Given his son's condition and wanting no more scandal, Doheny persuaded the Los Angeles police to wrap up their investigation almost immediately with an official conclusion that the perpetrator had been insane. For some comment on the loose ends of the case, see Leslie T. White, *Me Detective* (New York: Harcourt, Brace and Co., 1936), 106–14.

50. Doheny to Fall, July 2, 1925, box 1, folder 1, Fall-LC.

51. *United States v Pan American Petroleum Co.,* 6 F2d 43, 53, 55, 89, 1925.

52. See *NPN,* May 27, 1925, p. 126; Aug. 19, 1925, p. 35; Sept. 30, 1925, p. 156.

53. *Pan American Petroleum Co. v United States,* 9 F2d 761, 773, Jan. 4, 1926; *Pan American Co. v United States,* 273 US 503–10, October 1926.

54. See Gary Libecap, "What Really Happened at Teapot Dome?" in Donald N. McCloskey, *Second Thoughts: Myths and Morals of U.S. Economic History* (New York: Oxford University Press, 1993), 157–62.

55. For a positive report on these themes and Doheny's testimony, see the coverage from the *WP,* Dec. 2–17, 1926. A survey of opinion about the verdict, from papers around the nation, is in *NYT,* Dec. 17, 1926.

56. *NYT,* March 23, 1930.

57. *LAT,* Feb. 2, 4, 5, 1926.

58. *Petroleum World* (Aug. 1932): 27–30; Charles S. Jones, *From the Rio Grande to the Arctic: The Story of the Richfield Oil Corporation* (Norman: University of Oklahoma Press, 1972), 133–45.

59. See Atlee Pomerene, Special Assistant to the Attorney General, to Harry W. Blair, Department of Justice, Feb. 26, 1934, box 34; H. A. Stewart to Frank Harrison, Feb. 19, 1937, box 48, RG 60, file 412, "*United States v Pan American Petroleum Co.,* 1927–35," National Archives, Washington, D.C.

CONCLUSION

1. Israel M. Kirzner, *Discovery and the Capitalist Process* (Chicago: University of Chicago Press, 1985), 7–13, 54–67.

2. Leonard Fanning, *Foreign Oil and the Free World* (New York: McGraw-Hill Book Company, Inc., 1954), 26.

3. *The Texaco Star* 15 (June 1928): 5–12.

4. The details of Lucille Miller's role in this incident were related to the author during conversations with Monsignor Francis J. Weber, archivist of the Doheny collection, AALA.

5. Ellen Shaffer, "Reminiscences of a California Collector," *The Book Collector* 14 (Spring 1965): 49–59; Lucille V. Miller, "Edward and Estelle Doheny," *Ventura Country Historical Society* 6 (Nov. 1960): 15–20; Rita Reif, "Books Tell Tales of Art and Money," *NYT*, July 2, 1989.

6. *Town & Country*, Dec. 1991.

INDEX

Historical Perspectives on Business Enterprise Series
Mansel G. Blackford and K. Austin Kerr, Editors

The scope of the series includes scholarly interest in the history of the firm, the history of government-business relations, and the relationships between business and culture, both in the United States and abroad, as well as in comparative perspective.